DIGITAL GROOMING
Discourses of Manipulation and Cyber-Crime

Nuria Lorenzo-Dus

OXFORD
UNIVERSITY PRESS

OXFORD
UNIVERSITY PRESS

Oxford University Press is a department of the University of Oxford. It furthers the University's objective of excellence in research, scholarship, and education by publishing worldwide. Oxford is a registered trade mark of Oxford University Press in the UK and certain other countries.

Published in the United States of America by Oxford University Press
198 Madison Avenue, New York, NY 10016, United States of America.

Library of Congress Cataloging-in-Publication Data
Names: Lorenzo-Dus, Nuria, author.
Title: Digital grooming : discourses of manipulation in cyber-crime / Nuria Lorenzo-Dus.
Description: New York, NY : Oxford University Press, [2023] |
Includes bibliographical references and index.
Identifiers: LCCN 2022027481 (print) | LCCN 2022027482 (ebook) |
ISBN 9780190845186 (paperback) | ISBN 9780190845193 (hardback) |
ISBN 9780190845216 (epub)
Subjects: LCSH: Child grooming (Child sexual abuse) |
Internet and children. | Computer crimes.
Classification: LCC HV6570 .L67 2023 (print) | LCC HV6570 (ebook) |
DDC 364.15/554—dc23/eng/20220804
LC record available at https://lccn.loc.gov/2022027481
LC ebook record available at https://lccn.loc.gov/2022027482

DOI: 10.1093/oso/9780190845193.001.0001

9 8 7 6 5 4 3 2 1

Paperback printed by Marquis, Canada
Hardback printed by Bridgeport National Bindery, Inc., United States of America

This one's for you, Miguel. Always with us.

Digital Grooming

OXFORD STUDIES IN SOCIOLINGUISTICS

General Editors:
Nikolas Coupland
Copenhagen University, University of Technology, Sydney, and Cardiff University
Adam Jaworski
University of Hong Kong

CONTENTS

ACKNOWLEDGMENTS

Writing this book has taken longer than I originally envisaged and drawn me into a wide circle of people who have been wonderfully generous with their interest, advice, and support. I have benefitted hugely from discussing ideas with colleagues in many disciplines, from computer sciences (Adeline Paiement and Bob Laramee) and criminology (Lella Nouri, Stuart Macdonald, Sue Roberts, Carmen Jacques, and Richard Wortley) through to psychology (Maggie Brown, Ethel Quayle, and Michael Seto) and language and (digital) communication studies (Leanne Bartley, Craig Evans, Lelia Green, Carmina Gregori, Miguel Fuster, Sergio Maruenda, Ruth Mullineux-Morgan, Carmen Pérez, José Santaemilia, Philippa Smith, and Maite Taboada). Some of them provided excellent feedback on draft chapters. Many thanks, Nik Coupland, Adam Jaworski, Anna Marchi, Alan Partington, Pilar Garcés-Conejos Blitvich, Steve Marsh, and Rob Penhallurick.

I have been very fortunate to work with inspiring early-career researchers through various research projects linked to this book: Anina Kinzel, Manon Scholivet, Connor Rees, Sarah Williams, Tesni Galvin, Chedza Simon, Rosie Marsh-Rossney, Keighley Perkins, Matteo Di Cristofaro, Andrea García, Laura Mercé Moreno, and Amy-Louise Watkin. My involvement in several research centers has also helped expand my research horizons, principally the Cyber Threats Research Centre, the Legal Innovation Lab Wales, the Red Latinoamericana de Estudios del Discurso de la Pobreza Extrema (special thanks to María Laura Pardo, as well as to Viviane de Melo Resende, Denize Garcia da Silva, and Neyla Pardo) and the Digital Economy Research Centre. I am also indebted to the professionals of many leading third-sector organizations who have kindly shared invaluable insights and expertise, including from the Marie Collins Foundation (special thanks to Tink Palmer MBE, Victoria Green and Rhiannon-Faye McDonald), NSPCC (in particular Vivinene Laing), Tarian ROCU (principally, Steven Maloney, Hannah Dicks, and Sarah Keefe), the Digital Resilience in Education Branch of Welsh Government (most especially, Deborah Sargent, Julie McFenton, and Kate Rothwell), NetSafe New Zealand (thank you to Brent Carey especially), and End Violence Against Children (in particular Miguel García Ejido and Marija Manojlovic). Through this book I wish to stress my utmost admiration for, and support of, their work.

Although work for this book predated the covid-19 pandemic, a considerable amount of its writing was conducted during its 2020 and 2021 phases. Like many (all?) of us, being able to share time and experiences, good and bad, digitally with friends during lock down periods helped enormously. Sonia, Esther, Ceri, Geri, Ian, Andy, and Rob: thank you for the best company possible! My own family, across three generations, have provided the strongest core I could wish for. Thank you, Steve, Clara, Elisa, María Virginia, José, María José, María, Jorge, Alba, Miguel, and Amaya.

CHAPTER 1

Introduction

1.1 WHY EXAMINE DIGITAL GROOMING? A PRESSING SOCIAL ISSUE THROUGH A NECESSARY DISCOURSE LENS

This book is about manipulation in relation to digital practices outside, or at the boundaries of, the law. These I bring together within the concept of digital grooming—not a term (yet) established in linguistics scholarship but one that is nevertheless apt given the distinctively discursive nature of the practices deployed.

The genesis of this work lies in a long-standing interest in interaction within digital spaces in the Clear Net and datasets I examined consequently: customer reviews on e-Bay, YouTube comments to politicians' vlogs, Twitter feeds about different crises, user posts on online dating sites, and so forth. These datasets contained examples of tolerance to others' views, generally displaying the discursive hallmarks of what may be termed online civility. They also contained examples of what we may broadly refer to as online incivility, for instance trolling. And, expectedly, instances of civility and incivility often co-existed alongside each other, with the boundaries between them being negotiated by the "produsers"[1] of these digital interactions. Across them, intent to align others to one's way of thinking, feeling, and acting featured prominently. The suite of discursive strategies used to that end varied considerably in terms of, among other, level of implicitness/explicitness and argumentation *topoi* being used. Their impact on the interaction also varied: from enthusiastic endorsement to emphatic repudiation; from plain acknowledgment to overt snubbing. These datasets encompassed a wide range of topics that were clearly capable of generating lively discussion: minimum wage, adult romantic relations, immigration policies, and so forth. What bound them together was their socially normative and legal nature. And it is this that triggered my curiosity about what similar interactions might reveal if

Digital Grooming. Nuria Lorenzo-Dus, Oxford University Press. © Oxford University Press 2023.
DOI: 10.1093/oso/9780190845193.003.0001

concerning socially unacceptable and/or illegal behaviors. How might one go about trying to discursively align others to such behaviors, to communicatively get others to embrace them? The seeds of *digital grooming*—though not yet the term—were sown.

Over the next couple of years, working alongside social, behavioral, and computer sciences scholars as well as law enforcement, nongovernmental organizations (NGOs), and public policy stakeholders, I collected and analyzed relevant data. In the process, I gradually developed an understanding of the dynamics at play in discursive manipulation relating to digital practices outside, or at the boundaries of, the law. Three such practices emerged as particularly relevant: adults' online attempts at sexually luring children, extreme ideology groups'[2] Internet-based efforts at aligning others to their hate-filled views, and cryptomarket users' trading in illicit products and services. How were children coaxed into, for example, sharing "self-generated" nudes online with adults that they did not know? How were social media produsers—potentially any of us—led to support and adopt discriminatory beliefs, such as white supremacy, as well as violent actions, such as killing others on religious grounds? How were self-defined recreational drug users roped into drug trafficking in crypto-drug markets?

I had delimited the object of study for this book. Meanwhile, the agglutinating term "digital grooming" developed somewhat serendipitously, as part of my own research journey. At the time, I had started a research partnership with a UK-based child protection charity with the goal of developing training resources for child safeguarding practitioners. Sexual grooming of children in digital spaces was the area we needed to focus on. Then, within a relatively short period of time, the same term—grooming—was used in relation to the two other digital manipulation practices I had been considering. The first mention was during a United Nations (UN)-sponsored workshop about cyberthreats. One delegate described individuals selling drugs in the Dark Net as grooming others under false promises of safe, libertarian, community-led commerce. Not everyone agreed with this characterization—and there was certainly no UN-endorsed view on the matter. But use of the term "grooming" to refer to inducing illegal action—drug trafficking—on account of social identity (community values, specifically) struck a chord with me. The second mention happened within a couple of months of the workshop, as I was developing linguistic resources for data analysts within counter-terrorism law enforcement teams. One of the areas I had been invited to cover concerned identification of language (and images) used to—and this was the expression used—groom people to extremism online. References were made to the crossover between jihadi[3] and radical right groups'[4] grooming tactics, on the one hand, and to these tactics and those known to be used for sexual grooming of children online, on the other hand.

The penny finally dropped at this point—and with it the title and articulating concept of this book: *Digital Grooming: Discourses of Manipulation and Cyber-Crime*. Through the following pages, I explore digital discourses designed to manipulate individuals and groups into accepting and/or partaking in child sexual abuse (*digital sexual grooming*), jihadi and radical right ideologies (*digital ideological grooming*), and drug dealing in cryptomarkets (*digital commercial grooming*).

It is important to note that sexual, ideological, and commercial are not conceived of as the only components of a closed taxonomy of digital grooming practices. Instead, digital grooming practices are best thought of as operating within parameters, the normative and legal contours of which are permeable. It was in 2016, for example, that the act of sending a sexual message to a child became a criminal offense across the UK—under the "offence of sexual communication."[5] Also in the UK, amendments were made in 2019 to section 1 of the 2006 Terrorism Act,[6] which criminalizes the encouragement of terrorism, introducing the notion of indirect encouragement thereof. Debates regarding legalization of certain narcotics, typically cannabis, are both longstanding and differently resolved across national borders, with consequent impact for their commercialization online. The UN General Assembly's first call for a single UN cyber-crime convention with specific provision for the illegal trade of drugs online dates back to 2013. Yet, in its 2021 World Drug Report, the UN Office on Drugs and Crime (UNODC) still urges strong regulation and supervision of cryptocurrency markets, stressing that such an approach can only be effectives if "regulations are uniform and compliance is enforced in all jurisdictions" (UNODC World Drug Report 2021, 25). And Facebook's decision in October 2019 to exempt most political advertising on its site from fact-checking may be seen as enabling ideological manipulation. It just so happens to be a decision that, at the time of writing, remains within the bounds of legality. In other words, and as further developed in Chapter 2, the boundaries of digital grooming are continually being (re)negotiated.

It is also important to note that the three digital grooming practices examined in this book derive from a complex interplay of *sui generis* criminogenic factors and sociotechnical affordances. Yet, and as we will also see in Chapter 2, they each exploit three hallmarks of the so-called network society (Castells 2002): sharing, trust, and engagement. Digital grooming takes advantage of our desire (compulsion?) to share aspects of our lives with others online while also wishing to reserve our privacy, place our trust in other digital selves, and entextualize ourselves into the digital lives of others. Digital grooming is thus intrinsically linked to the social identities of those individuals involved therein—whether as agents of digital grooming, its targets, or its opponents. Since identity is discursively constructed, digital grooming is, therefore, first and foremost a discursive practice.

Let me be clear from the outset: *Digital Grooming* is not a book of doom about the "online world" vis-à-vis a glorified "offline world." My aim is neither to demonize digital spaces nor to raise anxiety about the risks some of them may pose. Rather, *Digital Grooming* seeks to help balance the social sciences research agenda into digital spaces in two ways: by placing digital practices outside, or at the boundaries of, the law under the spotlight; and by mainstreaming a discourse-analytic, identity-foregrounded lens on the kind of manipulation involved within such practices. Let us consider each of these in turn.

1.1.1 Of digital spaces and grooming practices

Legal use of the Internet outweighs illegal use. Nevertheless, illicit digital activity is neither an insignificant nor decreasing trend. Evidence for this is clear for the three digital grooming practices examined in this book. For instance, nearly 3 million accounts were registered globally in 2019 across child sexual abuse Dark Net websites.[7] In April 2020, the UK National Crime Agency (NCA) estimated that "at least 300,000 people in the UK pos[ed] a sexual threat to children, either through physical 'contact' abuse or online." The same NCA report also stated that their investigators were able to find child sexual abuse material (CSAM) online "in just three clicks," which shows the sheer prevalence of technology-assisted child sexual abuse.[8] Figures obtained in 2019 by the UK-based charity National Society for the Prevention of Cruelty to Children (NSPCC) under Freedom of Information requests to every police force in England and Wales revealed an almost 50% increase in the number of offenses of online sexual communication with a child being recorded over a 6-month period in comparison to a similar period the preceding year.[9] The impact of the covid-19 pandemic on these figures is not to be underestimated, as highlighted by law enforcement agencies and civil society organizations globally.[10] In 2020, for example, the NCA asserted that they "kn[e]w from online chat that offenders are discussing opportunities to abuse children during the Covid19 crisis," and they reported more than 500 arrests monthly between March and June 2020.[11] Of particular concern is the proliferation of CSAM online. In 1998, more than 3,000 reports of CSAM were made in the United States; by 2008, the number of yearly reports had surpassed 100,000. Technology companies, policymakers, and law enforcement agencies committed to introducing new legislation to try to reduce this figure, which by then had already reached a crisis point from a policing perspective. Yet, by 2014, the figure exceeded, for the first time, 1 million. In 2021, the NCMEC CyberTip line received more than 29.3 million reports related to suspected CSAM. These reports included more than 85 million images and videos of child sexual abuse—a 30% increase since 2020.[12]

The rise of illegal cryptomarket activity is also globally attested. Although crypto-drug markets only emerged in 2011, they have proliferated since. According to the UNODC 2021 World Drug Report, the main crypto-drug markets are worth at least $315 million in annual sales. That figure is small in the context of global drug sales overall. However, it shows an upward trend: "a fourfold increase in annual sales between the beginning of the 2010s (2011–mid 2017) and more recent years (mid 2017–2020)" (2021, 24). As in the case of child sexual abuse online, the covid-19 pandemic has had an impact on crypto-drug markets, which experienced temporary disruption in most parts of the world during 2020, yet recovered quickly (2021, 30).

Cryptomarkets, crucially those involving drugs, operate within the so-called Dark Net, which is a series of overlay networks within the Internet that can only be accessed with specific software, configurations, and authorization. These Dark Net spaces generally use a customized communication protocol. A typical Dark Net format is anonymized proxy networks, such as The Onion Route (ToR). Initially released in 2002, ToR is free and open-source software that enables anonymous communication online by directing Internet traffic through a complex network of more than 7,000 relays. Search engines do not index web pages in the Dark Net, and access to hidden services therein are untraceable (Chertoff 2019), which guarantees the anonymity of interactions (Li and Whinston 2020). At the time of writing, there are more than 65,000 unique URLs ending with ".onion" on the ToR network. Several URL domains in ToR are legal and are increasingly accepted by traditional vendors (e.g., Expedia, Microsoft, and Dell), e-retailers (e.g., eBay, Shopify), and payment processors (e.g., PayPal), as well as by companies like Reddit, Tesla, and Wikipedia. In countries where large parts of the Clear Net are blocked and/or political dissent is punished, these deep web, encrypted domains provide access to information and some shielding from prosecution; in freer societies, they can support whistleblowing while protecting citizens from institutional public retribution or judgment. However, anonymity also makes these encrypted digital spaces a tempting springboard for criminal activities ranging from arms trafficking and exploitative content sharing to pro-extremism websites and drug dealing.[13]

The digital infrastructure of these cryptomarkets supports complex socio-technical interactions for illegal purposes (Huang, Siegel, and Madnick 2018; Spagnoletti, Ceci, and Bygstad 2021). Cryptocurrency—bitcoin primarily—is used to conduct illegal transactions in the Dark Net. In 2020, there were more than 1,800 different cryptocurrencies in circulation, the most popular ones being BTC, ETH, Monero, XPR, LTC, digital cash (DASH), NEO, IOTA/MIOTA, and ZEC (Kethinani and Cao 2020). A study of the use of cryptocurrency across 27 million Dark Net pages, including extraction of around 10 million unique cryptocurrency addresses, revealed that more than 80% of bitcoin addresses on the Dark Net were used with malicious intent (Lee et al. 2019).

The major forms of cryptocurrency-related crimes are money laundering, contraband transactions, tax evasion, extortion, theft, drug dealing, and hacking (Bloomberg 2017).

As for extreme ideology groups, they have a growing online presence. It is difficult to determine the precise link between their use of digital spaces and actual violent acts, like mass shootings or assassinations (Ferguson 2016; Reed 2018; Gaudette, Scrivens, and Venkatesh 2020; Nilsen et al. 2020). Yet the perpetrators of many high-profile extremist attacks announce their plans on online forums; some of them also seek to maximize the publicity and impact of their attacks by trying to live-stream them on major social media platforms.[14] Examples include the Christchurch (March 2019), Baerum Mosque (August 2019), El Paso (August 2019), and Halle synagogue (October 2019) shootings.

Extreme ideology groups have also become increasingly sophisticated in their use of digital spaces. Over the course of the past two decades, these groups have shifted from relying primarily on websites to a reliance on forums and social media. This owes to transformations in the workings of both the Internet—both the Clear and Dark Net—and the extreme ideology groups themselves. In addition to adopting Web 1.0 and 2.0 technology for violent purposes, jihadi groups were, until approximately the mid-2010s, eager adopters of digital video (Kimmage and Ridolfo 2007; Kimmage 2008). A case in point is the so-called Islamic State, whose video output eclipsed that by other jihadi groups in terms of both the number of videos and the technical quality of their content (Scrivens and Conway 2020). The so-called Islamic State, for instance, produced an average of 46 videos per month between January 2015 and July 2016—some 140 hours of digital footage (Milton 2016). Jihadi groups progressively increased their use of mainstream social media platforms in the early 2010s, noticeably so since 2013 (Zelin 2013). While Twitter was the so-called Islamic State's preferred social media platform initially, from 2018 the group progressively left this social media platform (Nilsen et al. 2020) and began to favor the Telegram messaging application as its platform of choice (Scrivens and Conway 2020).

Radical right groups' use of digital video has been moderate compared to that of jihadi groups. Since the 2010s, radical right groups' sympathizers have had a manifest presence on all major social media platforms. A 2020 cross-national (Belgium, France, Germany, Greece, Netherlands, Norway, UK) study of the radical right presence in Twitter concluded that Twitter was used actively by radical right groups' members and supporters who created "milieus of [radical right] networks whose users gain contact with individuals holding extremist views, acquire knowledge [about radical right ideologies], adopt more extreme views, practice hate speech and talk about themes that concern them" (Nilsen et al. 2020, 3). The main themes were Muslims, immigration, European governments, national identity, and the white race. In other words,

Nilsen et al. (2020) found evidence that Twitter provided a digital space for radicalization (see Chapter 2 for a discussion of radicalization vis-à-vis grooming). Scrivens and Conway (2020, 304), for their part, argue that "a new generation of right-wing extremists" are moving to more overtly hateful yet more hidden, emerging platforms, such as 8chan, Telegram Voat, Gab, and Discord (see also Davey and Ebner 2017). These individuals and groups are often "early adopters" of the digital affordances offered by emerging platforms (Conway et al. 2019a). Unlike most jihadi groups, radical right groups have also tended to maintain official websites, which may owe in part to a much more concerted effort by social media and technology companies for some time on policing the content of jihadi groups than content from the radical right. The situation changed, in the UK at least, in 2017. That year, the country experienced four major terrorist attacks: three were jihadi attacks, one was a radical right–inspired attack (on London mosque-goers). The British government has subsequently increased pressure on the radical right, with intelligence services leading investigations of radical right threats—including the role of digital communications therein—under a counter-terrorism remit since 2018 (Pearson 2020).

1.1.2 A discourse lens on digital grooming

Social sciences study of criminal versus non-criminal digital spaces is by and large skewed towards the latter. In relation to the voluminous body of research on Facebook within the social sciences, for example, Vishwanath (2015, 82) laments the "limited research [that] has explored the consequences of Facebook overuse [and the] even less research [that] has looked at misuse of social media by criminals who are increasingly using social media." This situation is particularly pronounced within linguistics scholarship, which is somewhat ironic given both that digital spaces are textually embedded and the strong tradition in some linguistics research—notably critical discourse studies—to examine the discursive manifestation of structural relationships of dominance, discrimination, power, and control (see, e.g., Wodak 2006, 2020).[15]

Digital grooming happens in and through discourse and it entails such structural relationships, as well as legal transgression. Digital sexual grooming of children, for example, is widely characterized across non-language–based disciplines as an entrapment process (see, e.g., Olson et al. 2007). Yet research into it has been primarily conducted within the behavioral sciences and focused on developing offender and victim profiles based on sociodemographic and psychological variables, such as age, gender, and personality types (e.g., Martellozzo 2012; Webster et al. 2012; van Gijn-Grosvenor and Lamb 2021). Only a handful of studies have focused on the *discourse* of digital sexual grooming, as will be shown in Chapter 3. This is despite recognition that digital sexual grooming detection software can be significantly enhanced through microlevel, contextualized description of the linguistic means via which groomers seek to fulfill their abusive goals online (see, e.g., Kontostathis, et al. 2009; Inches and Crestani 2012; Cano Basave, Fernandez, and Alani 2014; Bogdanova, Rosso, and Solorio 2014; Liu, Suen, and Ormandjieva 2017; Preuß et al. 2021; Razi et al. 2021; Milon-Flores and Cordeiro 2022). Similarly, as will be discussed in Chapter 7, a significant body of research in the social sciences, especially within the field of drug policy, has identified trust as a key factor in the success or otherwise of crypto-drug markets (e.g., Décary-Hétu, Paquet-Cloustob, and Aldridge 2016; Tzanetakis et al. 2016; Spagnoletti et al. 2021). Yet few studies (Lorenzo-Dus and Di Cristofaro 2018; Masson and Bancroft 2018) have examined the role played by discourse—among market administrators, vendors, and market users—in the development and subsequent manipulation of trust in cryptomarkets.

Things are slightly different as regards research into what in this book I term digital ideological grooming. Here, as Chapter 5 will review, there is a growing body of non-language–based scholarship that acknowledges the important role played by images and text in, for example, online propaganda by jihadi groups (e.g., von Behr et al. 2013). There is also a prolific (discourse analytic) literature into hate speech online, including that by extreme ideology groups (e.g., Baumgarten et al. 2019; Wodak 2020; Baker, Vessey, and McEnery 2021; Patterson 2022). There is therefore an opportunity to take stock of this knowledge and derive new and/or more nuanced insights by examining discursive practices of digital ideological grooming alongside those known to operate in digital sexual and commercial grooming. This is important given evidence, primarily from stakeholder reports to date, of the crossovers between digital sexual grooming and digital ideological grooming. Examples include reports published in 2019 by the European Union–based Radicalization Awareness Network 2019[16] and in 2017 by the UK Government Department for Education.[17]

Finally, in this book, I argue that the illegality and/or immorality of the practices examined make digital grooming a distinct form of manipulation. As the following chapters will show, digital grooming is sufficiently distinct to warrant focused analysis. Unlike research into the broader notion of manipulation discourse, moreover, the analysis of digital grooming offered in this book foregrounds identity construction. While discourse markers and strategies associated with manipulation, such as use of vague language or strategic deixis, feature in the accounts of digital grooming offered here, the analysis draws primarily on the discourse analytic notions of style/styling and stance as positioning practices for identity construction. This approach is explained in Chapter 2; implemented in Chapters 4, 6, and 8; and evaluated in Chapter 9.

1.2 RESEARCHING DIGITAL GROOMING DISCOURSE: FROM DATA SELECTION TO RESEARCHER WELLBEING

Bolander and Locher (2014) identify four methodology-related challenges for linguists working with digital data: ethics, multimodality, mixed methodologies (including the relationship between online and offline settings), and web corpora and annotation. Each of these is relevant to this book. Additionally, the fact that digital grooming practices operate outside, or at the boundaries of, the law introduces further ethical-methodological considerations. Collectively, these considerations shape the research journey undertaken for this book, from initial data selection and subsequent data collection (Section 1.2.1) to data analysis and dissemination (Section 1.2.2). Issues regarding researcher ethics and wellbeing (Section 1.2.3) are important, too. Throughout, I have often found myself reflecting on my own agency as a researcher of digital grooming discourse *and* a produser of digital discourse—albeit not of digital *grooming* discourse!

1.2.1 In search of—and (not) finding—digital grooming data

Data availability, access, and selection are crucial for empirical research, and this book is no exception. As noted in Section 1.1, there is no shortage of digital grooming—and therefore digital grooming datasets—"out there," which can be examined in multiple ways. In the case of *Digital Grooming*, data selection entailed an initial decision regarding whether to collect "user-based" as well as "screen-based" data. "User-based" and "screen-based" data are terms employed to refer to two "complementary sites of data collection" in digital discourse analysis,[18] operating on a continuum (Androutsopoulos 2013, 240), as shown in Table 1.1. The user-based pole end entails researchers' direct contact with data produsers, rather than observation of them. The screen-based pole end entails an absence of contact between the researcher and the

Table 1.1 SCREEN- AND USER-BASED DATA IN DIGITAL DISCOURSE ANALYSIS (ANDROUTSOPOULOS 2013: 241)

	Screen-based		User-based	
Relation of researcher to source of data	No online observation	Systematic online observation	Online observation and contact to users	Contact to users without online observation
Resulting type of data	Online data	Online data	Blended data	Offline data

individuals who produse the data to be examined. Between these, one finds different options, including systematic online observation of online data with or without researcher contact with the data produsers.

The rightmost column in Table 1.1 requires no analysis of actual digital texts, which renders it largely irrelevant to digital discourse analysis—and thus to this book. The blended data middle point is appealing because it brings multiple perspectives, including the researcher's own reflections as a result of both observing and interacting with the data produsers. This option addresses long-standing calls for, among others, discourse analysis researchers to go beyond the screen when examining digital spaces (see, e.g., Androutsopoulos and Beisswenger 2008). While peripheral in discourse analytic research of digital spaces until approximately the 2010s, numerous studies have subsequently collected and examined user-based datasets, adopting different forms of (n)ethnography and integrating screen-based analyses (see, e.g., Spilioti 2011; Barton and Lee 2013; Garcés-Conejos Blitvich 2022a). A pioneer work is Androutsopoulos (2008), where a "discourse-centred online ethnography" was proposed that combines systematic observation of selected sites of digital discourse with direct contact with its social actors.

Ultimately, I resolved to collect only screen-based data for this book, conceiving the digital spaces therein as enablers of human interaction that is dynamically related to offline activities and therefore to actual produsers. The decision not to collect user-based data was informed by three key considerations. First, as will be explored further in Chapters 3, 5, and 7, user-based research within the social sciences that focuses on the produsers of digital criminal spaces provides a wealth of knowledge that can helpfully underpin much-needed discourse analysis of screen-based materials within these very spaces.

Second, online and offline spaces are inextricably interconnected—and they intersect online and offline experiences. As an increasing number of scholars argue (see, e.g., Jones 2004; Androutsopoulos 2014a, 2014b; Bolander and Locher 2020; Yus 2021), most of us do not consider online and offline to be distinct. Instead, we see online interactions as extensions of offline interactions that "ground [us] firmly within [our] existing material communities and circumstances" (Jones 2004, 24). Conceptually, this entails considering digital discourse as "comprised of data which may but need not be digitally mediated and which is not restricted to digitally mediated spaces and devices"; methodologically, this calls for "heightened reflection on both 'where' (within or across the lines) to research digital discourse and 'what' (practices and modes) counts as data" (Bolander and Locher 2020, 6).

Similarly, most of us do not see our online and offline identities as being neatly compartmentalized, but as intrinsically interconnected. This is not to deny the impact of sociotechnical affordances on identity construction online. For instance, early theorizing of identity in digital environments

(Turkle 1995) was crucial in furthering the permanency versus transience debate. Subsequent work also focused on degrees and types of digital anonymity (Tetzlaff 2000; Kennedy 2006). When interacting digitally, moreover, processes of context design enable us to navigate choices for projecting our identity in ways that are aligned to fluid goals, with different outcomes, as Chapter 2 further discusses.

Third, researcher safety and wellbeing concerns outweighed, for my purposes, evidence potentially gained by covertly entering digital spaces where sexual, ideological, and/or commercial grooming was taking place. Examples of such covert work include first-person research accounts of crypto-drug markets, not least Bartlett's (2014) monograph *The Dark Net: Inside the Digital Underworld*, and his subsequent TED Talk (2015) *How the Mysterious Dark Net Is Going Mainstream*.[19] They also include richly contextualized nethnographic studies of individuals who have been or are being lured to jihad (Winsor 2020). And results about online child sexual offenders' *modus operandi* have also been derived from studies in which a researcher may create fake digital accounts and enter digital spaces suspected of harboring digital sexual grooming. Posing as a child, O'Connell (2003) interacted with suspected offenders and subsequently downloaded and analyzed their interactions. Undercover police officers and vigilante groups also mount such operations, albeit for prosecution purposes. The legality and ethics of vigilante operations especially are the subject of active debate in (non)academic circles (see, e.g., Crown Prosecution Services;[20] Sorell 2016; Grant and MacLeod 2020).

The next methodological consideration concerned from where to source screen-based materials for the three selected digital grooming practices. Different decisions were made for each of these. In the case of digital sexual grooming, the heavy reliance in the literature on data from the public website Perverted Justice.com was indicative of just how difficult it would be to access transcripts of actual, ongoing, or convicted, cases.[21] I relied on this source, too—in part.

From 2003 to 2019, the US-based non-profit Perverted Justice Foundation Inc. "specialize[d] in working chat rooms and social networking sites to fight internet predators who seek to have sex with underage kids."[22] Adult volunteers (called contributors) posed as children (typically between the ages of 10 and 15) on social network sites and chat rooms. According to the Perverted Justice Foundation rules of engagement, contributors waited to be contacted by adults, with whom they began a conversation. If the conversation turned sexual, they collaborated with law enforcement to try to secure the arrest and eventual conviction for child sexual abuse of that adult. If a conviction was secured, the relevant chatlog (i.e., the digital record of the conversation between the adult and the contributor) was uploaded on the Perverted Justice Foundation website, along with the adult's screen name, real name, age, photograph (if available), email address, and conviction notes. The archive is still accessible and contains 623 chatlogs, each of which covering all the individual chat sessions (6,968) between a convicted adult and one or more contributor(s) over a period of interaction that ranges from 17 to 10,597 minutes. The analysis of digital sexual grooming from this dataset focused on the language produced by all the convicted adults (groomers), which amounted to 3,297,475 words (tokens) over 656,746 individual messages (typed-up turns). The majority of the chatlogs came from Instant Messenger platforms, and they were all uploaded to the Perverted Justice website between 2004 and 2016.

Perverted Justice data have been regarded as not being entirely representative of, yet "still useful for asking some important questions about" (Schneevogt, Chiang, and Grant 2018, 101), digital sexual grooming. Researchers need to be mindful of differences between groomers' discourse in grooming chatlogs archived in the Perverted Justice website and those involving actual children (see Chiang and Grant 2018; Schneevogt, Chiang, and Grant 2018; Lorenzo-Dus, Kinzel, and Di Cristofaro 2020). These differences primarily relate to groomers' use of coercion (see O'Connell 2003; Whittle, Hamilton-Giachritsis, and Beech 2014; Schneevogt, Chiang, and Grant 2018; Mullineux-Morgan and Lorenzo-Dus 2021; Powell, Casey, and Rouse 2021), which is under-represented in the Perverted Justice dataset. This is to be expected, given that contributors were trained to facilitate convictions once they had determined sexual intent from the adults with whom they interacted online. This may have, for example, limited contributors' use of grooming avoidance or resistance strategies, which may have otherwise triggered groomers' use of more coercive discourse (Williams, Elliott, and Beech 2013; Broome, Izura, and Lorenzo-Dus 2018). I consequently complemented the Perverted Justice dataset with a corpus of approximately 80 chatlogs (c. 120,000 words [tokens]) corresponding to digital sexual grooming cases that took place between 2014 and 2019. These were purposively sampled from a dataset entailing approximately half a million words and secured as part of a UK law enforcement data-sharing agreement for research purposes. These data—henceforth referred to as *law enforcement digital sexual grooming chatlogs*—came from different social media platforms on the Clear Net.

For the analysis of digital commercial grooming, data were collected from a repository known as the *Darknet Markets Archive*.[23] This repository was crawled and publicly released by Gwern Branwen—a self-defined writer and independent researcher—in 2015. The archive is an approximate 1.6 terabyte (uncompressed) dataset that includes more than 4,438 scrapes (copies) of cryptomarkets at the time they were crawled. From these, the files corresponding to the flagship crypto-drug market Silk Road were selected. The Silk Road archive is divided into two sections: Silk Road 1.0 and Silk Road 2.0. These essentially refer to the same crypto-drug market, respectively before and after a major Federal Bureau of Investigation (FBI) operation resulted in

Silk Road 1.0 being taken down—only to resurface as Silk Road 2.0 within a month (see Chapter 7 for details). More than one scrape of each file is available for download from the Silk Road archive. Only the last copy was collected, as this contained all the data from previous copies. Once preprocessed for corpus-software analysis, the digital commercial grooming dataset totaled 245,469,550 words (tokens).

Finally, and as regards digital ideological grooming, data were collected from numerous digital platforms and extreme ideology groups at different points in time.[24] For jihadi groups, all issues published by five English-language jihadi propaganda magazines online between 1 January 2009 and 30 June 2015 were collected: *Jihad Recollections*, published by Al Qaeda (4 issues, all published in 2009); *Inspire*, also published by Al Qaeda (13 issues, published from 2010 to 2014); *Gaidi Mtaani*, published by Al Shabaab (7 issues, published from 2012 to 2015); *Azan*, published by the Afghan Taliban (6 issues, published in 2013–2014); and *Dabiq*, published by the so-called Islamic State (9 issues, published in 2014–2015). This dataset totaled 487,568 words (tokens) and 2,479 images.

Social media posts and blog entries were also collected from numerous radical right groups, from which data listed in Table 1.2 have been used in this book. In the case of the social media posts, these data comprised all the social media content (Twitter and/or Facebook) posted by seven radical right groups spread across three continents that were collected between January and August 2017, except for the group British Patriotic Resistance, for which data collection spanned the whole of 2017. In the case of the blog entries, these corresponded to all the content posted on the "alt-right"[25] group Traditionalist Worker Party from its first entry on 1 April 2009 until 30 November 2017. This amounted to 1,133,814 words (tokens), spread across 905 blog entries.[26] All the entries were authored by the group's leaders Matthew Heimbach and/or Matthew Parrot.

Given the salience of visuals in digital ideological grooming and their strategic use across different digital platforms, a dataset comprising images from the radical right group Britain First was also collected. This comprised all the images posted by this group during two, 4-month periods: January–April 2017 and May–August 2018. Data from the first collection period consisted of 731 images posted on Facebook. Data from the second collection period comprised 264 images posted on Gab, which is the social media platform to which the group migrated following its ban from Facebook in March 2018.

Overall, then, the datasets analyzed in *Digital Grooming* are substantial and diverse in terms of producers, platforms, and timespans. This informs the analytic methods adopted—as discussed in Section 1.2.2. Moreover, the datasets come from both the Clear and Dark Nets. Digital commercial grooming data come from Dark Net spaces as these are where crypto-drug markets operate. Digital sexual grooming data come from Clear Net spaces, which is where this

Table 1.2 DIGITAL IDEOLOGICAL (RADICAL RIGHT) GROOMING DATA (SIZE IN NUMBER OF WORDS [TOKENS])

	British Patriotic Resistance	Britain First	Reclaim Australia	Traditionalist Worker Party	Jair Bolsonaro (Brazil)	Movimento Brasil Livre	Bandera Vecinal (Argentina)
Facebook	13,668	7,103,985	3,142,762	–	385,406	1,354,256	24,194
Twitter	–	3,766,410	29,358	23,695,404	8,696,688	9,331,779	67,628
Blog	–	–	–	1,133,814	–	–	–
Total	13,668	10,870,395	3,172,120	24,829,218	9,082,094	10,686,035	91,822

form of online child sexual abuse primarily occurs.[27] In the case of digital ideological grooming data, I examine Clear Net spaces because, although radical
right and jihadi groups have for some time widely solicited funding via—and
used—cryptocurrencies and therefore Dark Net spaces, for the data collection
period for this book, most of these groups' activities took place on the Clear
Net (Conway 2019; Scrivens and Conway 2020).

A final note regarding data sources for this book concerns "geographical"
reach and language coverage. The data collected for the analysis of digital
sexual and commercial grooming are in the English language and derive primarily from Internet Protocol (IP) addresses from English-speaking countries. There are a few exceptions to this pattern—some Perverted Justice
chatlogs contain messages in other languages, as do some forum threads
within the Silk Road files. As for the digital ideological grooming datasets,
data come primarily from groups either based in countries where English is
the official language (UK, USA, Australia) or, in the case of jihadi groups, from
their English-language medium digital communications. As shown in Table
1.2, data from two radical right groups in Brazil are included: Jair Bolsonaro
and Movimento Brasil Livre. The Jair Bolsonaro supporters' group precedes
its leader becoming elected as Brazil's President in October 2018; Movimento
Brasil Livre was founded in 2014. Often described as "Brazil's Tea Party,"
Movimento Brasil Livre upholds strong social conservative values, including
opposition to women's rights to abortion and gender equality, while professing economic liberalism. Data from an Argentinean radical right party supporting a neo-Nazi ideology, Bandera Nacional, are also included. Bandera
Nacional (2013–2019) was officially renamed Frente Patriótico in 2019, maintaining Alejandro Biondini as its leader. The languages used in these datasets are Brazilian Portuguese (Jair Bolsonaro, Movimento Brasil Livre) and
Argentinean Spanish (Bandera Nacional). The decision to include these non-
English datasets is a conscious attempt to contribute, however modestly, to
shifting global research agendas away from Anglo-centrism.

1.2.2 A qualitative, identity-foregrounded analysis of digital grooming discourse

The sheer size of the collected data made software-enabled, corpus techniques
advisable. Yet, I first invested time reading extensive samples from each of
the datasets to get a sense of what they contained. This stage informed the
initial conceptualization of digital grooming as a practice inextricably linked
not only to discourse but also to identity. Close reading and manual discourse
analytic annotation of these samples led to a conceptual and analytic focus on
how different social actors styled their own identities digitally as groomers,
how they styled the identities of those they sought to groom (their targets),

and how they styled the identities of those whom they perceived to challenge their grooming goals (their opponents). This is reflected in the structure of Chapters 4, 6, and 8, in which the acts of self- and other-styling of digital sexual groomers, digital ideological groomers, and digital commercial groomers are respectively focused on for analysis.

Only once I felt reasonably familiar with the data qualitatively did I employ corpus techniques as the next analytic step. In some cases, these techniques entailed identifying salient differences across datasets (corpora) using *key word in context* (KWIC) techniques—for example, when comparing Silk Road 1.0 and Silk Road 2.0 forum content. KWIC are concordance lists; that is, lists containing a collection of all the examples that include a given target word—including key words—in a corpus. Concordance lists enable examination of actual occurrences of use of target words, together with other terms whose target words repeatedly co-occur with—that is, their *collocates*. Collocates are important because the meaning of a word is defined by the relationships it establishes with other words "which tend to occur in its environment" (Leech 1976, 20). There are different measures for statistically calculating keywords (see, e.g., Gabrielatos and Marchi 2012) and collocates (see, e.g., Brezina, McEnery, and Wattan 2015). One collocational significance measure, used in various studies in this book, is the *Dice coefficient*, which includes a combination of the significance (amount of evidence) and effect size (strength of connection) of collocations (Baker and Levon 2015; Gabrielatos 2018). It is important to note that, on their own, Dice coefficient scores can provide a partial picture of the data as a given collocation may be extremely salient but only appear in a limited number of texts. Therefore, Dice coefficient scores may be considered alongside the relevant observed frequencies and lexical dispersion scores in a dynamic manner (see Lorenzo-Dus, Kinzel and Di Cristofaro 2020). The lexical dispersion measure applied to the studies in this book is *deviation of proportions norm* (DP_{Norm}; Gries 2008, 2010). A DP_{Norm} score indicates the normalized dispersion of a word in a corpus based on its frequency combined with the number of elements (texts; e.g., all the grooming chatlogs in the Perverted Justice dataset) in which the word appears. DP_{Norm} works by assigning a value that ranges from 0 to 1: the closer to a 0 value a word has, the more dispersed it is across a corpus; the closer to a 1 value a word has, the less dispersed it is. When analyzing the Perverted Justice corpus, the combination of collocational size and strength, on the one hand, and lexical frequency and dispersion, on the other, resulted in a list of target words that was further examined using the KIWC method. Thus, an average of 50 extended concordances, approximately 100 words each, were manually analyzed for every selected target word in order to identify not just which words were used regularly by most of the groomers, alongside which other words, but also—and crucially—how they were used to advance particular grooming goals.

Several unexpected findings emerged through these deeply contextualized analyses of approximately 15,000 extended concordance lines across several studies. For example, the Perverted Justice corpus exhibited an apparent low incidence of sexually explicit terms in a list of the 100 most frequent and highly dispersed lemmas. A closer look at the list through manual analysis highlighted the salience of vague language lexical items in the dataset (Lorenzo-Dus and Kinzel 2021). Discourse analysis of these items in turn revealed groomers' use of "push-pull" rhetorical structures that combined assertiveness and tentativeness, respectively, when communicating sexual intent. They would state sexual intent—implicitly and/or explicitly—and then withdraw it partially, for example, via use of emoticons (typically, 😉 or 😊) and initialisms (typically, "lol") that keyed previous statements of sexual intent as playful, romantic, and/or friendship-based.

In short, following on from close reading of numerous data samples, corpus-based techniques helped to pinpoint areas of potential interest, which I then further investigated qualitatively. This was an iterative process, one that is standard in the widely used methodology of corpus-assisted discourse studies (CADS). CADS may be described as "the investigation and comparison of features of particular discourse types, integrating into the analysis, where appropriate, techniques and tools developed within corpus linguistics" (Partington 2010, 88; see also, e.g., Partington, Duguid, and Taylor 2013; Taylor and Marchi 2018; Mautner 2019). As its names indicates, CADS works at the interface of corpus linguistics methods and discourse studies theories and analytic concepts, and it has proven useful for understanding the main discourses around a wide range of topics in digital media, from influence and ideology to immigration and poverty (see, e.g., Baker, Gabrielatos, and McEnery 2013; Baker and Egbert 2016; Lorenzo-Dus and Di Cristofaro 2016; Dayrell, Chakravarthi, and Griffith-Dickson 2020; Baker et al. 2021; Lorenzo-Dus and Almaged 2021). CADS typically follows an inductive approach—a "serendipitous" journey of discovery (Partington 2003, 12). When analysing digital commercial grooming, for instance, research into the notions of digital trust, digital communities and crypto-drug markets, among other, informed the software-enabled searches of the Silk Road corpora. The results were treated as an initial '"map' . . . pinpointing areas of interest for a subsequent close analysis" (Baker et al. 2008, 284; see also articles in Baker and McEnery 2015).

As per the CADS approach, the analyses offered in this book are premised on the belief that quantitative and qualitative discourse research methods can be fruitfully integrated. Yet, and while reference is made in the analytic chapters to quantitative findings from corpus-based techniques, the emphasis remains on providing a qualitative account of digital grooming practices in the datasets under examination. This qualitative account is aligned to the six domains identified in Herring's (2004, 2013) approach to the study of digital discourse: namely, structure, meaning, interaction, social behavior, participation, and—added in 2013—multimodality. Typography, orthography, morphology, syntax, and discourse schemata are the phenomena typically covered within the structure domain. The meaning domain concerns phenomena linked to the meaning of words and utterances. The interaction domain involves digital turns, sequences, exchanges, threads, and so forth. The social behavior domain entails the discursive realization of face management and style, stance-taking, and identity. The participation domain is non-linguistic and concerns analysis of the number of messages, responses, and thread length, for instance. Finally, the multimodal dimension is conceived of as inherent to digital communication and thus sees textual exchanges therein as being "one of a number of possible modes of transmission," including audio, video, graphics, and robotic devices (Herring 2019, 43; see also Herring 2013). The most noteworthy phenomena across the three digital grooming spaces considered in this book clustered around the meaning and social behavior domains, which are described in Chapter 2 and constitute the main analytic foci in Chapters 4, 6, and 8.

1.2.3 Research ethics

Spilioti and Tagg (2017, 163) identify three main changes in research ethics in the context of linguistic analysis of digital spaces; namely,

> (i) changes associated with the increasing expansion and differentiation of communication media and technologies and the communicative environments they afford; (ii) shifts in the conceptualization of selfhood and identity . . . ; and (iii) the shifting role and status of academic research and researchers in the contemporary world.

Changes linked to multiple media and technologies are complicated by the sociotechnical affordances that these technologies bring about. These concern "persistence" (digital data can be automatically recorded and archived), "replicability" (digital data can be duplicated and shared), "scalability" (digital data can become visible to others, some of whom we, as researchers, do not know), and "searchability" (digital data can be sought out and located) (boyd 2010). Under conditions of social and spatiotemporal pliability, as well as of "collapsed contexts" (see Chapter 2), researcher assumptions about what is private and public, for instance, must be continuously and carefully questioned as part of ethical decision-making.

As for the impact on research ethics of shifts in the conceptualization of selfhood and identity, these concern how we view the individuals whose information—including discourse data—we collect and/or co-produse. Long gone are the days when research "subjects" were conceived of in isolation from the network of persons with whom they interacted. As Spilioti and Tagg (2017, 164) observe, "a more dynamic approach to privacy that places the self in the network of contacts and relationships developed and negotiated during and beyond the research process" is nowadays being argued for—and rightly so. A case in point is research into lived experience of digital sexual grooming. While clearly important to place the individuals' voice at the center of scientific enquiry, the research may contribute to retraumatization. As such, thorough, inclusive, and adaptable wellbeing protocols need to be put in place throughout the entire research journey, from embryonic planning through to post-results dissemination, rather than applied only to some steps therein, such as data collection.

Finally, wider shifts in both academic disciplines and the role of academia in contemporary society have driven greater accountability on the part of academic researchers. Corollaries of this include requirements for generating "research impact" outside of the academic community and for enabling open access to research outputs and data. These shifts have a bearing on the entire research process. They influence ethical-methodological decisions regarding, among others, how to store and analyze digital data, how to make data available, and how to disseminate information about the individuals researched. As Spilioti and Tagg (2017, 164) further argue, when it comes to researching digital discourse practices, researchers find themselves "in the unenviable position of negotiating data ownership not only with the persons researched but also with the private corporations (such as Google, Twitter, Facebook) that afford and, to some extent, control the information circulated." The legal frameworks within which these negotiations currently take place constrain academic research in different ways. For example, researchers are required to abide by corporate websites' terms of service instead of wider ethical considerations that protect produsers and/or researchers (Sandvig 2016; Spilioti and Tagg 2017). Attempts at challenging this constraining environment include recommendations listed in the 2020 report "Technology Use and the Mental Health of Children and Young People," published by the UK Royal College of Psychiatrists.[28] These argue for social media platforms to hand over data for research into online harms, noting specifically that these platforms "should regularly fund research related to their products, to be conducted by independent external bodies and provide on a regular basis user data for research purposes to academic institutions" (2020, 17).

Within the above ethical-methodological context, I have drawn considerably on the recommendations of the Association of Internet Researchers (AoIR). The version I initially consulted was published in 2012. Opportunely, AoIR published revised recommendations in 2019,[29] coinciding with the data analysis stage for this book. I was therefore able to reflect on—and factor in— the increased emphasis within the 2019 document (Internet Research Ethics [IRE] 3.0) on issues of informed consent, the interconnectedness of all the stages of research, and researcher wellbeing.

The IRE 3.0 guidelines explicitly acknowledge that informed consent "has emerged as a standard problem" (2019, 10) in Big Data projects, where obtaining consent from every person is impracticable.[30] The guidelines offer some examples of good practice at mitigating risk against research participants in such cases, for instance different forms of data redaction or seeking informed consent during the project dissemination stage and therefore only from specific persons and particular data samples. Although the datasets collected and examined in *Digital Grooming* do not class as Big Data, their large size and the normative questionable and/or illegal practices involved therein nevertheless made securing informed consent impractical. I therefore took a series of decisions regarding identification of individuals authoring and/or referred to in the datasets (see below). Importantly, this is something I factored across all the stages of the research process. The IRE 2012 guidelines (known as IRE 2.0) had principally differentiated between the initial and dissemination phases of a research project. IRE 3.0 (2019, 9) extended this to a taxonomy comprising the following:

> *Initial research design*, including initial considerations of potential ethical issues, in seeking grant funding.
>
> *Initial research processes*, including acquiring data: these stages typically entail specific requirements for de-identifying data, securely storing data, and so on.
>
> *Analyses*, including assessment of how use of particular techniques, formulas, or instruments may re-identify data through aggregation of multiple datasets. This includes considering downstream ethical effects arising from the unpredictability of now-common analytical processes, often algorithmically driven.
>
> *Dissemination* (i.e., various ways of publicizing research findings and data): this typically includes conference presentations (including injunctions not to tweet or otherwise share sensitive information presented within relatively closed contexts) and publications. An increasingly pressing set of issues are further generated by requirements by national and international funding bodies to make research data openly available.
>
> *Close of the project*, including the destruction of research data and related materials.

While noting that "research cannot (always) be clearly structured in different stages," IRE 3.0 is clear that "frequently reflection on ethics is interwoven" (2019, 9). A similar point is argued by Georgakopoulou (2017) within a special journal issue on the ethics of online research methods in applied linguistics. She makes a case for "re-ethicizing" research, whereby ethics is seen as a contextualized process of decision-making at all critical junctures of research.

These ethical considerations were mainstreamed through *Digital Grooming* from the outset. For example, ethics approval for research design was secured from Swansea University research ethics and integrity boards. Additional ethical clearance protocols were implemented as required, including signing of confidential data-sharing agreements with law enforcement and third-sector partners. And access to privately sourced therapeutic counseling services was also put in place. Datasets were accessed using secure networked university computers maintained in secure locations on Swansea University campus. For those datasets not in the public domain, data were redacted in accordance with agreed protocols prior to their being analyzed.

At the analysis and dissemination stages, all individual names were replaced with generic identifiers, such as "Britain First member 003," "Silk Road 1.0 vendor 027," and so forth. I also decided to redact all non-person identifiers, such as location, for data in the public domain, as per the illustrative examples below.

Extract 1.1 Silk Road 1.0 (vendor 027)

hi guys, Im [vendor 027's username]. Been trading on Silk Road for nine months, serving the Australian community [. . .]

Extract 1.2 – British Patriotic Resistance [BPR] member 003 – Facebook

TWAT. Sentence is too short / Lock him up with me for 10 minutes / I'll meter out some [UK town] justice

Decisions regarding the potential for non-person identifiers to reveal an individual's identity were made on a case-by-case basis. Thus, for example, in Extract 1.1 I did not feel that vendor 027's broad reference to trading in an "Australian community"—the potential geographical identifier—would lead to the vendor's personal identification. In Extract 1.2, BPR member 003's reference to a town in the UK was specific and I therefore made the decision to redact it. All examples have been reproduced in this book as they appear in their original datasets. Spelling, grammatical, or other types of errors have not been corrected. The symbol / is used for brevity in the extracts to mark a new text turn. The same decision-making process regarding anonymization was applied for the purposes of dissemination of work in progress at academic conferences and public engagement events.

These decisions may seem over-cautious in the case of data samples in the public domain. After all, a simple copy-and-paste exercise on an Internet search engine of the redacted examples may in some cases pull out the unredacted text—and hence reveal full authorship. However, I felt that the decisions overall struck the right ethical-methodological balance. Publication of an exact quote may not be necessary across some disciplines, and we may wish to err towards a cautious (and ethically advisable) approach in Internet research. At the same time, and as noted in the IRE 3.0 guidelines, "such publication is typically required, e.g., by methods of Critical Discourse Analysis, i.e., as documental critical examples necessary to a larger analysis or argument" (IRE 3.0, 11).

As described in Section 1.2.1, visual screen-based materials were also collected and analyzed. In this book, they are largely described, rather than reproduced as originally posted. This decision was not made on account of potential publisher concerns under fair use copyright legislation. Instead, the decision stemmed from the part I see them playing in the book: they support rather than construct analytic arguments. There are a few exceptions, in Chapter 6, when image reproduction was necessary to the analysis *per se*. Using photo-editing software, these images have been modified to redact any personal identifiers. As an aside, it is worth noting that I made a slightly different decision when it came to results dissemination at stakeholder and/or academic conferences. When showing publicly available images at these events, I kindly requested that no photos—or any form of visual recording—of the slides containing them be taken.

Last, but by no means least, came researcher wellbeing. This was of paramount importance, not least because of the potential for vicarious trauma through some of the content examined. Through research and media reports of various kinds we know, for instance, that some Internet content moderators are hugely impacted by their exposure to distressing material they review. As the online magazine *The Verge*[31] and the documentary *The Cleaners*[32] have exposed, for example, some large digital technology companies outsource the role of content moderation to organizations in mainly India and the Philippines. Paid wages for these roles are "well below the average Silicon Valley tech employee" (*The Verge*), and some of these organizations are known to fail to adhere to their own contractual and health and safety policies. Some of the practices content moderators are exposed to are simply deplorable, such as being expected to meet numerical quotas: moderators are required to screen thousands of images or videos of extreme violence and deviance on a daily basis. These roles may require signing non-disclosure agreements, too, which make attempts at investigating the organizations' procedures and therefore changing them for the better particularly difficult.

Less extreme, but still worth noting, is the case of law enforcement personnel's exposure to distressing content, for example specialist investigators working at Internet child exploitation or counter-terrorism referral units. Fortunately, law enforcement procedures are open to scrutiny, including academic investigation. There is, indeed, a growing body of research that details both the kind of impact that exposure to such material has on these specialist law enforcers and the coping and support mechanisms they employ, including through professional support mechanisms. For instance, a study of the impact of Internet-based child exploitation material on police investigators across all nine Australian police jurisdictions revealed a small number who "returned clinically significant profiles for post-traumatic stress" (Wortley et al. 2014, 2).[33] And Reeve's (2020) ethnographic study stresses the importance of, among other, mental preparation as a coping mechanism by counter-extremism specialist investigators. These investigators indicate that non-terrorist graphic materials being referred to them from other law enforcement units, or sometimes erroneous referrals from the public, are the type of material that often most adversely affects them because they have not mentally planned for it.

Comparatively, research into the impact of distressing data on academic researchers is very limited. Yet we know that some researchers in the field of child sexual abuse experience challenging auditory and visual sensations when listening to children's accounts (Jackson, Backett-Milburn, and Newall 2013) and that secondary distress may ensue from transcribing and analyzing disturbing or sensitive data (Kiyimba and O'Reilly 2016). For example, we are only now beginning to delve into the potential impact on discourse analysts of examining distressing data (Lorenzo-Dus 2021b), and the fluid boundaries in our doing so of treating such data as "people" rather than as "communicative resources" (Georgakopoulou 2017). In this regard, it is important to acknowledge the part played by subjectivity. The term "distressing" designates something that causes extreme sorrow, anxiety, or pain—that is, an emotion and, hence, individual experience. It is generally assumed that some topics are, if not inherently distressing, certainly "primed for" being felt so, such as terminal illnesses, death, and dying (Johnson and Plant 1996; Alty and Rodham 1998); deviant and criminal behavior, as examined in *Digital Grooming*; and political and interest groups (e.g., Brewer 1990). Yet each of us may experience other topics as distressing, including unexpectedly so, at different points in time. It makes sense, therefore, to think of—and research—distressing data and topics in relative rather than one-size-fits-all terms; to ask ourselves questions such as distressing for whom, when, where, and why?

This book has consequently made me acutely aware of the cognitive, emotional, and physiological impact on discourse analysts of digital grooming practices. Throughout the writing of this book, I have overall felt optimistic about the opportunity to contribute to addressing societal needs, for example by using findings to co-create, with child safeguarding practitioners, resources to prevent digital sexual grooming (see Chapter 9). However, at times I have found myself wondering whether regular access to social media pages by extreme ideology groups, including those known to be active in my geographical area of work, would leave traceable data that others—specifically, members of these groups—may pick up and investigate. I have also wondered whether prolonged exposure to morally deviant behavior—such as digital sexual groomers' reframing of adult–child sexual activity as beneficial to both parties—would make me become ultra-sensitive to it or impact my affective relations, including as a mother, in other ways.

Digital Grooming has made me acutely aware, too, of my own positioning vis-à-vis the produsers of the digital discourse practices I examine. Redacting the data for authorship and other identifiers was a contractual requirement of the data-sharing agreements for some of the datasets examined. Other, related considerations came into play, too. For instance, in the UK, possession of extreme ideology groups' communications without reasonable excuse breaches anti-terrorism laws (Terrorism Act 2000, section 58)[34] and so, as part of research ethics clearance for relevant projects, law enforcement stakeholders were involved.

Again, the recommendations contained in IRE 3.0 provided helpful guidance. They acknowledge the need for protecting not only the persons involved in digital research projects but, increasingly, also the researchers themselves. As IRE 3.0 (2019, 8) notes, "researchers whose work—and/or simply their public identity (e.g., ethnicity, minority identity, sexual identity, political activism, etc.)—triggers strong ideological reaction" face increasing and new risks. These include death threats, doxing, and, in the context of research on ideological extremism, direct retaliation should researchers' identities become known (Massanari 2018). Consequently, the guidelines include several available resources published by companies and NGOs, such as Surveillance Self Defence,[35] Tactical Tech,[36] and Access Now.[37]

Researcher wellbeing can be best ensured within a collaborative research environment and with institutional support (see e.g., Brayda and Boyce 2014; Cornejo, Rubilar, and Zapata-Sepúlveda 2019; Reeve 2020; Lorenzo-Dus 2021b). This has been crucial during the writing of this book and has meant discussing with stakeholders regularly exposed to similar cyber-crime practices the methods that they use for personal safeguarding and adapting them to academic project needs, such as not spending more than a certain number of consecutive hours per week analyzing sensitive data that may lead to vicarious trauma; discussing with professional and personal support networks the impact of the data on me, as an individual and researcher; and taking regular breaks during data analysis sessions in particular.

A final aspect I considered carefully while working on *Digital Grooming* is that of disseminating research findings to non-academic audiences, where (typical) academic caveats regarding scalability and limitations of the research might get somewhat lost in translation. A case in point concerns the digital sexual grooming analyses. For example, I agreed to an interview for UK national television news coverage of a high-profile online pedophilia case. The reporter and I spent more than an hour discussing the communicative *modus operandi* of digital sexual groomers. As I watched the resulting news report later that day, I was pleased that it provided a good understanding of digital sexual grooming as discourse practice. However, I was somewhat troubled that two "key facts" were highlighted: parents being able to detect digital sexual grooming signs in their children and grooming happening within 20 minutes. During the interview I had much contextualized and qualified these points, including that the 20-minute figure was a rare, indeed, unique exception in the data examined. By the time they were disseminated, much of the research nuance had faded away, with the 20-minute figure subsequently taking on a life of its own across news outlets. This anecdote may resonate with (Internet) researchers who disseminate their work outside of "academia's ivory tower" and must thus navigate multiple agendas (academic, journalistic, governmental, and so forth). In the case of Internet research practices and phenomena, dissemination can take researchers—and the research itself—along unexpected pathways. Feelings of apprehension about disseminating research findings in these cases can be greatly reduced through careful planning from the outset of the research project—and continuous reviewing thereof.

1.3 BOOK STRUCTURE

Digital Grooming is structured in five parts. Part I comprises this Introduction and a concept-defining chapter (Chapter 2), in which I review the etymology of the term grooming, propose a working definition of digital grooming, and chart its conceptual territory. Parts II–IV provide three paired chapters for each of the three digital grooming practices being examined. Each of these parts thus contains, first, a chapter in which the relevant digital grooming practice is located within the extant literature across, primarily, the social sciences. This is followed by a chapter that offers a discourse analysis of the same digital grooming practice. In these three analytic chapters digital sexual (Chapter 4), ideological (Chapter 6), and commercial (Chapter 8) grooming is examined from the perspective of groomers' styling of their own identities; the identities of their targets; and the identities of those individuals, groups, or entities that they perceive to be their opponents. The final part of the book—Part V (Chapter 9)—brings together all the results of the discourse analyses offered in Parts II–IV, focusing on both similarities and differences across the three digital grooming practices as regards ways of self- and other-styling. In doing so, it contributes fresh insights into not only digital manipulation in relation to activities that are outside, or at the boundaries of, the law, but also into key discourse analytic concepts of style, stance, and identity. Additionally, Chapter 9 discusses initiatives for translating key findings about digital grooming—and other forms of harmful content online—into practical interventions for prevention and/or detection. This includes co-creation projects with stakeholders in law enforcement as well as the third sector.

NOTES

1. Coined by Bruns (2008), the term "produser" designates a hybrid digital identity whereby we are both producers of digital content and users thereof.
2. The terms "extremism," "extremist," and "extreme ideology group" are used in this book in a broad sense, acknowledging that their definitions—including their boundaries with the concept of terrorism (and therefore terrorist group)—are part of an ongoing debate in the fields of security and terrorism studies.
3. *Jihad* is a modified version of the traditional Islamic idea of *da'wa*, which designates the initial call to Islam by the Prophet Muhammad and translates as peaceful missionary work in converting non-believers to Islam. As such, jihad is a metaphor for a spiritual matter or a religiously inspired war (Lindsay 2003; Alshech 2014). Unfortunately, it is at times used wrongly as a synonym of violent jihad, which is premised on the belief that a new call for *da'wa* must be given to Muslims to take up jihad against the "non-believing" world and that anyone not answering this call may be justly killed. This is the interpretation made by the jihadi groups whose discourse is examined in this book. Therefore, I use the terms "jihadi groups" or "jihadi ideology groups" in this book to refer to individuals and groups that defend violent jihad.
4. As per other scholarship (see, e.g., Bowman-Grieve 2009; Scrivens, Davies, and Franck 2018), the term "radical right" is used in this work as an umbrella term for extreme and far-right groups.
5. http://www.legislation.gov.uk/ukpga/2015/9/section/67. Accessed April 2022.
6. Amended by section 5 of the Counter-Terrorism and Border Security Act 2019, The 2006 Terrorism Act implements in the UK Article 5 of the Council of Europe Convention of the Prevention of Terrorism.
7. https://homeofficemedia.blog.gov.uk/2019/06/25/fact-sheet-on-online-child-sexual-exploitation-and-abuse/. Accessed January 2022.
8. https://www.nationalcrimeagency.gov.uk/news/onlinesafetyathome. Accessed December 2021.
9. https://www.nspcc.org.uk/what-we-do/news-opinion/over-5000-grooming-offences-recorded-18-months/. Accessed December 2021.
10. https://www.end-violence.org/sites/default/files/paragraphs/download/COVID-19%20and%20its%20implications%20for%20protecting%20children%20online_Final%20%28003%29.pdf. Accessed January 2022.
11. https://www.nationalcrimeagency.gov.uk/news/onlinesafetyathome. Accessed November 2021.
12. https://www.missingkids.org/ourwork/ncmecdata. Accessed May 2022.
13. https://www.imf.org/external/pubs/ft/fandd/2019/09/the-truth-about-the-dark-web-kumar.htm. Accessed December 2021.
14. https://www.un.org/sc/ctc/wp-content/uploads/2020/04/CTED_Trends_Alert_Extreme_Right-Wing_Terrorism.pdf.
15. A notable exception here is research conducted within the subdiscipline of forensic linguistics. Some of this research analyzes cyber-crime and is referenced in subsequent chapters as relevant to the three digital grooming practices considered in this book.
16. https://ec.europa.eu/home-affairs/system/files/2019-06/ran_hsc_grooming_for_terror_25042019_en.pdf.
17. https://assets.publishing.service.gov.uk/government/uploads/system/uploads/attachment_data/file/635262/Safeguarding_and_Radicalisation.pdf.

18. The term "digital discourse" (and thus "digital discourse analysis") is used in this book to refer to discourse that is mediated by Internet communication technologies. As Bolander and Locher (2020) argue, unlike other terms (e.g., "computer-mediated discourse" or "online discourse"), the term "digital discourse" has inclusivity—it is fairly unmarked in the social sciences (Deumert 2014)—and places an appropriate emphasis on the social meaning of technology (Thurlow and Mroczek 2011).

19. https://www.youtube.com/watch?v=pzN4WGPC4kc. Accessed November 2021.

20. https://www.cps.gov.uk/legal-guidance/vigilantes-internet-cases-involving-child-sexual-abuse; see also http://www.centralchambers.co.uk/vigilantes-and-attempted-offences/. Accessed December 2021.

21. The Perverted Justice dataset has been used in at least 30 research papers, although only a few of those studies have examined it in its entirety (Schneevogt, Chiang, and Grant 2018; Lorenzo-Dus Kinzel, and Di Cristofaro 2020; Lorenzo-Dus and Kinzel 2019, 2021; Kinzel 2021).

22. www.pjfi.org. Accessed May 2022.

23. Branwen et al. https://www.gwern.net/DNM%20archives. Accessed June 2022.

24. This happened within the parameters of different research projects undertaken by CYTREC, a multidisciplinary research center based in Swansea University.

25. "Alt-right" is the commonly used abbreviation of "alternative right." It refers to a loosely connected extreme right, white nationalist movement with a strong hold in the United States (see Chapter 5 for details).

26. The number of blog entries posted per year in this corpus was distributed as follows: 38 in 2009; 31 in 2010; 49 in 2011; 14 in 2012; 163 in 2013; 178 in 2014; 234 in 2015; 136 in 2016; 62 in 2017.

27. For linguistic analysis of child sexual abuse/exploitation in Dark Net environments, in particular offender communities, see Chiang (2020), Grant and Macleod (2020), and Marsh-Rossney and Lorenzo-Dus (2022).

28. https://www.rcpsych.ac.uk/docs/default-source/improving-care/better-mh-policy/college-reports/college-report-cr225.pdf.

29. https://aoir.org/reports/ethics3.pdf.

30. For additional considerations of the contemporary complications of informed consent, see for example Obar (2015) and Halavais (2019).

31. https://www.theverge.com/2019/2/25/18229714/cognizant-facebook-content-moderator-interviews-trauma-working-conditions-arizona. Accessed December 2021.

32. The documentary *The Cleaners: The Hidden World of Content Moderators* was premiered in 2018. Its filmmakers are Moritz Riesewieck and Hans Block.

33. Remedial actions suggested by Wortley et al. (2014) include selecting individuals with the ability, for example, to separate work from home and to maintain professional detachment without losing empathy; providing good supervision for investigators; supplementing mandatory support processes with investigator-selected support types; better designing investigators' workspaces (e.g., by allowing access to natural light where possible); encouraging investigators to avail themselves of potential sources of informal social support; and developing tailored training for investigators.

34. https://www.legislation.gov.uk/ukpga/2000/11/section/58. Accessed January 2022.

35. https://ssd.eff.org/en/playlist/academic-researcher#. Accessed January 2022.

36. https://tacticaltech.org/#/projects/security-in-a-box-key-project/. Accessed December 2021.

37. https://www.accessnow.org. Accessed January 2022.

CHAPTER 2

Digital Grooming

What It Is and How to Research It

2.1 INTRODUCTION

Chapter 1 established the rationale and genesis of *Digital Grooming: Discourses of Manipulation and Cyber-Crime*. This chapter explains how the concept of digital grooming is understood in this book. It begins by establishing a working definition of digital grooming (Section 2.2). It then proceeds to discuss consecutively three core, interrelated features of digital grooming, namely: digital mediation (Section 2.3), manipulation (Section 2.4), and identity construction (Section 2.5).

2.2 DIGITAL GROOMING: A WORKING DEFINITION

The *Oxford English Dictionary*[1] lists the following entries for grooming:

1. The practice of brushing and cleaning the coat of a horse, dog, or other animal.
    1.1. The practice by an animal of cleaning its own or another animal's fur or skin.
    1.2. The practice of keeping a neat and tidy appearance.
2. The action by a paedophile of preparing a child for a meeting, especially via an Internet chat room, with the intention of committing a sexual offence.

For its part, the *Merriam Webster Dictionary*[2] defines grooming as

– To clean and maintain the appearance of (an animal); especially: to maintain the health and condition of the coat of (a horse, dog, etc.) by brushing, combing, currying, or similar attention.

Digital Grooming. Nuria Lorenzo-Dus, Oxford University Press. © Oxford University Press 2023.
DOI: 10.1093/oso/9780190845193.003.0002

- To make neat or attractive.
- To get into readiness for a specific objective: prepare.

These definitions share two features. First, they capture the goal-oriented nature of the term. Grooming is "preparing for . . . with the intention of," or "to get into readiness for . . . [to] prepare." Second, they reference the part played by impression management within such a goal, specifically positive presentation in terms of cleanliness, neatness, and/or attractiveness. Additionally, the *Oxford English Dictionary* categorizes grooming as an "action" or "practice" and, as will be discussed later, references a specific illegal activity, namely pedophilia.

In the only book-length study of grooming hitherto—*Grooming, Gossip and the Evolution of Language*—anthropologist and evolutionary psychologist Robin Dunbar also characterizes grooming as practice, referring to it as "the act of grooming" (1996, 62). For Dunbar, grooming lies at the heart of animal (primate and human) evolution. In primates, grooming is "the cement that holds alliances together" (1996, 35); a "helpful tit-for-tat arrangement" (1996, 36) that enables "a state of dynamic equilibrium in which the forces of dispersion are delicately balanced by the forces of collaboration within groups of primates" (1996, 44). In humans, he posits, language progressively developed as a form of "social grooming" that enabled us to survive and evolve by forging bonds with other humans, affirming relationships, and learning about hierarchies and alliances within and across groups. According to Dunbar, this human desire to interact with others is universal rather than culture-specific: we have an innate disposition toward sharing with other humans our experiences, beliefs, motivations, and so forth. Crucially, Dunbar further notes, our innate disposition toward social grooming is premised on strategic calculation of where each of us stands in relation to each other within a given group, which entails identifying and negotiating one's and others' place(s) in and out of given groups. This task requires planning and performance of self- and other-presentation in relation to carrying out—and getting others to carry out—specific tasks. Each of us crafts our place within new or existing social groups and structures through a series of locally instated and negotiated choices about how we construct our identities—and the identities of those we interact with or about (nonpresent third parties). Language use (i.e., discourse) enables all this identity-focused grooming work.

Grooming, moreover, requires trust–risk calculations: we must be prepared "to relax and let [our grooming partners] do as they will with [us]. In a relaxed state, [we] are always open to the risk that they will exploit the opportunity to deliver a punishing attack" (Dunbar 1996, 44). Dunbar acknowledges that we perform social grooming "to try to influence the lives of those around us, ultimately for our own benefit" and that "what we use for good we can easily use for evil" (1996, 171). Herein social grooming is still about using language to forge alliances, share, and bond with others. However, it is focused first and foremost on tending to others' (presumed) needs—whether social, physical, or emotional—for self-serving, other-damaging purposes. This speaks clearly to entry 2 in the *Oxford English Dictionary* definition, which records an immoral and illegal sense of the term grooming: "the action by a paedophile of preparing a child for a meeting, especially via an internet or chat room, with the intention of committing a sexual offence." It speaks, too, to the notion of digital grooming in this book, which concerns manipulation in digital spaces outside, or at the boundaries of, the law and is aligned to current use of the term grooming in society.

The term grooming has undergone considerable semantic pejoration over time, from being used to designate the act of tending to or caring for, first registered in 1809, to that of tidying (oneself) up, registered from 1843. It was from 1887, originally in US politics, that the term grooming started to adopt a figurative sense; namely, "to prepare a candidate" for office. This then extended to another figurative sense, only one marked by illegality: luring of children for the purpose of sexual abuse.[3] The first recorded reference of this latter sense corresponds to a *Chicago Tribune* newspaper article in 1985 about pedophiles, which stated: "These 'friendly molesters' become acquainted with their targeted victim, gaining their trust while secretly grooming the child as a sexual partner."[4] The usage spread during the 1990s. And in 2003, the *Collins English Dictionary* added a new entry to its definition of grooming: "To win the confidence of (a victim) in order to commit a sexual assault on him or her". Note that this entry adopted the sexual abuse meaning but did not restrict the age demographics of the victim of sexual assault to childhood.

The range of activities to which the pejorative sense of the term grooming applies has since continued to expand. While at the time of writing not (yet) recorded as dictionary entries, grooming is nowadays also used by the media and law enforcement to refer to the criminally liable actions used for radicalization, especially via the Internet. The concept of radicalization became widely used in policy parlance in the mid to late 2000s, and almost equally widely challenged from the 2010s for being vague and misleading in suggesting a clear and casual link between radical thought (political and/or religious) and violent terrorist acts (see, e.g., Borum 2011; Kundnani 2012; Neumann 2013; Horgan 2014; Richards 2015). As Augestad Knudsen (2020) shows, the term radicalization remains in use across many policy-making lexicons internationally to refer to a process that culminates in the endorsement or use of terrorist violence. The UK government, for example, defines radicalization as "the process by which a person comes to support terrorism and extremist ideologies associated with terrorist groups,"[5] even though it acknowledges the challenges of defining extremist ideology in a legally enforceable way.[6] Given the associations of the term radicalization with cognitive processing and causal relationships, this book uses the term "digital ideological grooming" instead, which is discourse practice–based and avoids any cause–effect linkages.

As introduced in Chapter 1, the definitional boundaries of digital grooming are being negotiated in respect of the kinds of cyber-crime, manipulation-based activities to which it applies. In a report published by the Royal United Services Institute for Defence and Security Studies (RUSI), for instance, Moisie (2019) used the term "grooming" to describe organized crime groups' luring of minors from provincial countryside in the United Kingdom—so-called *county lines*—into drug trafficking: "Children are groomed (as runners, mules and dealers) to deliver and traffic Class A drugs into rural county towns." Referencing the results of a parliamentary inquiry into this criminal activity, the report noted several "grooming tactics" that combined "free gifts such as smartphones and drugs, with intimidation or violence"—a "'carrot-and-stick' approach of county lines" that, the report noted, is also known to characterize digital sexual and ideological grooming. These tactics, moreover, included established business techniques, such as advertising via mass marketing text messages, which enabled groomers to become "social media influencers" to their target, to whom they glamorized their lifestyles.

And in July 2018, the UK broadsheet *The Guardian* published an article under the headline "Boy, 14, Referred to Anti-Extremism Scheme over Fracking Activism." The article's lead next stated "Boy allegedly groomed by anti-fracking activists on social media, who were eventually banned from contacting him." The news story went on to introduce and discuss some of the contents of a 2018 report by the Greater Manchester Preventing Hateful Extremism and Promoting Social Cohesion Commission, which suggested that law enforcement should learn "from other crime types such as child sexual exploitation" and "translate the tactics [to combat sexual grooming of children online] into other arenas." The report's consideration of fracking as a form of extremism sparked some controversy, also captured by the newspaper article, which quoted the views of the coordinator of the Network for Police Monitoring pressure group: "The idea that encouraging others to get involved in politics and campaigning—the exercise of fundamental democratic values on an issue of profound local and national concern—is somehow akin to sexual exploitation or 'grooming' is simply offensive."[7]

Even though the definitional contours of (digital) grooming are still being negotiated and its common features identified, in lay and stakeholder discourse the term has clearly acquired a distinct negative meaning, becoming linked to luring others into illicitness. This is the case in academic scholarship, too. Maras (2017), for example, found that extremists and child sexual predators use the same tactic of seeking out vulnerable individuals and gaining their trust with the ultimate goal of getting them to engage in criminal activities: violent terrorist acts and adult–child sex, respectively. This is not to say that the *modus operandi* of digital groomers is identical across all the cyber-criminal contexts to which the concept is applied. As the chapters in this book will show, there are commonalities but also differences. Nor is the reference to preparatory work in the term's dictionary definition of grooming intended to minimize the reprehensibility of the practices involved in digital grooming.

Building on the above, in this book, the term digital grooming refers to

> digitally mediated identity construction that manipulates a target into acting in a manner that both advances the groomer's illicit goals and harms the target and/or others.

This succinct definition covers three core, interrelated features of digital grooming: digital mediation, manipulation, and identity construction. Let us consider each of them in turn next.

2.3 DIGITAL MEDIATION

The grooming practices examined in this book occur textually within digital spaces that range from social networking sites on the Clear Net to community-based forums on the Dark Net. This is not to say that digital grooming is detached from the "offline" realm. As introduced in Chapter 1, offline and online spaces are interrelated in our daily experiences. The notions of *context collapse* (see, e.g., Meyrowitz 1985; Wesch 2009; Marwick and boyd 2011) and *collapsed contexts* (boyd 2002, 2008) respectively attest to how broadcast and digital communication enable people, information, and norms from one context to percolate the bounds of other contexts.

New networked publics are developed around single communicative practices in collapsed contexts. This, as the very term collapse suggests, may lead to some confusion when it comes to, for example, digitally "fashioning" our identities as "technologies of the self" (Foucault 1988).[8] Yet we have developed ways to help us bypass such confusion—and so we may theorize context in digital environments in terms of continuous expansion, rather than collapse (Szabla and Blommaert 2018). As Tagg and Seargeant (2016) and Tagg, Seargeant, and Brown (2017) show, in relation to the practice of posting updates on Facebook, we take on board a wide range of factors when it comes to imagining how our posts may be embedded and reinterpreted in new contexts; that is, how they may be entextualized (Bauman and Briggs 1990; Blommaert 2015) and resemiotized (Iedema 2003). The concept of *context design* (Tagg, Seargeant, and Brown 2017) captures this awareness of the constraints and influences around what we post online and how we do so.

As the analyses in later chapters of this book will show, grooming practices are inevitably shaped by—and shape themselves—the digitally mediated contexts in which they are embedded. "Mediation" refers to "the organizational and orientational role performed by the media with respect to mutual perception, the allocation and adoption of diverse social roles, and human communication in general" (Jaffe 2011, 565). There exists a continuum of "greater and lesser displayed mediation forms. The former are salient in collapsed contexts, i.e., in digital communication. They involve the recurrent "movement [of people and ideas between people] across texts (entextualization/reentextualization—leading to intertextuality), across discourses (leading to interdiscursivity), across languages (translation) and across modes (visual, linguistic, written, aural, gestural) and registers" (2011, 565). Digital mediation affects day-to-day human practices, from how we engage with others to how we acquire and disseminate knowledge. Three such practices are of particular relevance to digital grooming: sharing (Section 2.3.1), trusting (Section 2.3.2), and engaging (Section 2.3.3).

2.3.1 Digital sharing

Human propensity to share is nothing new and may indeed be regarded as constitutive of what makes us human, as per Dunbar's (1996) theory of human language evolution through social grooming. However, the so-called Digital Age has greatly facilitated human sharing through a profusion of the means of production and distribution of creative goods (Wittel 2001; Jenkins 2009, 2014; Grassmuck 2012; John 2012, 2013, 2017). So far is sharing regarded as the fundamental practice of digital media in general, and social media in particular, that we are said to live in "a sharing era" (John 2017)—or to have experienced "a sharing turn" (Grassmuck 2012). This sharing era, or turn, is symptomatic of a major cultural shift away from users' rather passive consumption of media to their active co-production of digital texts—which is known as *participatory culture* (Jenkins 2009, 2014) and turns us into objects of sharing produsers. The term sharing has become so common in digital environments that it is often no longer necessary to state what it is that is being shared. The activity, for example, of posting status updates on social media may be simply referred to as "sharing." When explicitly stated, two types of "objects" are digitally shared: *concrete* and *fuzzy* (John 2012, 2017).

Concrete objects of sharing are those where "we immediately know what is being shared"—typically files and photos. Within digital sexual grooming, for instance, child sexual abuse material (CSAM) is shared, as discussed in Chapter 1. Encryption keys are also shared digitally between drug sellers and buyers in cryptomarkets to enable their financial transactions. And, as also noted in Chapter 1, extreme ideology groups' sharing of propaganda videos and texts is a staple in their information operations' architecture, which follows particular distribution patterns (Ingram 2016). For example, once jihadi propaganda content has been shared there appears to be a period of 1–2 hours that is critical in terms of tackling the potential reach of such content. This period is known as the "golden window." The term emerged in the aftermath of a speech by former UK Prime Minister Theresa May at the United Nations General Assembly in September 2017, when she stated that the average lifespan of online propaganda for the so-called Islamic State was 36 hours and claimed that, for such content to be effectively detected and removed, the period needed to be 1 or 2 hours (see Grinnell, Macdonald, and Mair 2017).

As for fuzzy objects of sharing, these designate such varied, intangible entities as one's life, one's world, and one's real self (John 2017). Most of the data considered in this book concern the sharing of fuzzy objects. Typical examples include first-hand experience advice in crypto-drug market forum posts on how to avoid being caught by law enforcement, child sexual groomers' self-disclosing talk with their child targets online about their own vulnerabilities and fears, and ideological groomers' sharing of denigrating views across social media platforms about certain individuals and groups.

The digital sharing turn has been appraised across three axiological values, namely egalitarianism, identity, and emotions. For each of these a continuum of views—from the unreservedly endorsing to the highly critical—has been expressed. Concerning egalitarianism, some scholars see the digital sharing turn as having contributed to reducing social and cultural inequity globally, effectively challenging the capitalist *status quo* and offering some form of anti-economy that unhinges every system of exchange (Botsman and Rogers 2010). For others, in contrast, the digital sharing turn is simply exploitative of people. When we share something online, we always generate traces of data that become the hard currency of commercial organizations in a networked society (Sarikakis 2010). As John (2013, 11) states, quoting from one of the users in his study of sharing practices on Facebook, '"If you're not paying for something, you're not the customer; you're the product being sold."' For his part, KhosraviNik (2017a) argues that the main purpose of social media is always to increase consumption—specifically, social media sharing is always harbored for commercial purposes that are linked to targeted advertising.

The digital sharing turn has also been evaluated in terms of identity, specifically personal data privacy. In the context of the Quantified Self movement,[9] for instance, some argue that digital sharing of personal data creates communities and, hence, evaluate it positively. It can help us understand, for example, how we exercise: what our goals are, with whom we want to share those goals, our progress vis-à-vis them, and so forth. Yet others are critical of the commercial context in which Quantified Self communities operate, even if the members of such communities are aware of the commercialization of their bodies (Barta and Neff 2015). They argue that the random, accidental, and deliberate documenting of the banal within the Quantified Self movement has distinctively negative consequences for our sense of identity, especially when coupled with the trend to categorize and aggregate the self. For instance, retrieving, displaying, and aggregating personal data from different social media sources (e.g., postings, updates) via a plethora of life-tracking and journaling apps alters our ways of remembering/forgetting and may have undesired consequences for those very users who (un)willingly triggered them (Hoskins 2016). A case in point concerns Facebook having to apologize to its users in 2014 after its "Here's what your year looks like" tool algorithmically selected photographs from the users' database for the year, including some of recently deceased friends and family.[10] More broadly, digitally retrieving, displaying, and aggregating personal data relates to concerns regarding the rise of digital surveillance practices. Alongside the frameworks that regulate their use, such practices have an interactional basis (Jones 2017; Rampton and Eley 2018): the rights and responsibilities associated to them are "negotiated, ratified, challenged, or ignored in the moment-by-moment unfolding of communication" (Jones 2020, 89).

As for the appraisal of the digital sharing era in terms of emotions, this is rooted in the cultural belief that sharing is good for us—a belief that pervades popular culture and is illustrated by common sayings such as "shared joy is double joy; shared sorrow is half sorrow." Digital sharing has become imbued with the pre-digital cultural belief that "it is good to talk" (Carbaugh 1988), which is itself used as shorthand for emotional self-disclosure. And, just as the pre-digital cultural belief that sharing is good was critiqued in relation to certain workplace (Cameron 2000) and broadcast (Fairclough 1995; Tolson 2001; Lorenzo-Dus 2009) practices, the belief that baring one's soul digitally is good for us has been challenged, too. For some, concerns relate to the emergence of a "network ego"—some sort of cellular subject who lacks the sense of individual privacy (Kroker 2014). For others, they relate to the rise of different manifestations of digital incivility through the favoring of anger and hate-related emotions within digital sharing (e.g., Massullo Chen 2017).

As this appraisal of the digital sharing turn shows, there are positive and negative aspects to it. One should be cautious, however, of any claims of causality whereby perceived digital oversharing may be seen as the trigger for cyber-crime, let alone digital grooming. Instead, the point being made here is that digital groomers take advantage of the digital mediation of sharing, including the naturalization of digital sharing as a good human communicative practice—e.g., the positive cultural rhetoric around it.

2.3.2 Digital trust

Trust is a complex concept. Although it operates at a macro-level of social or group consensus, it results from micro-level choices that are primarily, respectively, genre- and discourse- based. Whether, and how much or little, we trust others is to a large extent driven by what they communicate—or fail to communicate—and how they communicate it. It is also driven by what we communicate—or do not communicate—to them and how. In his famous "breaching experiments," ethnomethodologist Harold Garfinkel (1967) designed a series of interventions in the normality of daily events in order to better understand what we typically (do not) take for granted about social interaction. One finding was that trust is necessary—indeed a normal and necessary condition—for making sense of and participating in any given interaction. To trust, he posited, is to entertain some basic assumptions about others in an event or situation, assuming that others in that event or situation have the same assumptions about you. Trust is thus about understanding and engaging with the tacit or hidden assumptions and frames of reference that we share with others. It is, in other words, about constructing a mutual understanding and presentation of believable information (knowledge-based trust) and identity (identification-based trust) (Lewicki, Tomlison, and Gillespie 2006). We manage this by orienting in and through discourse to "converging goals, shared values and knowledge and positive affect. Information about and/or identification with these common goals, wants and desires form the basis of trust" (Kusmierczy 2014, 15).

Within digital environments Kim, Han, and Park (2001) similarly differentiate between social-based and systems-based trust. *Social-based trust* refers to how individuals express the level of connection that they feel to a certain individual or social group; that is, how individuals engage discursively in social identification, in digital settings. *Systems-based trust* refers to how much faith individuals invest in the functionality of technological systems based on the systems' known technological affordances. When the system handles commercial activity, system-based trust also relates to individuals' confidence in financially related aspects. Across digital contexts, social- and systems-based trust are important and interrelated: social identification plays a key role in deciding where to place social trust online (Wang and Emurian 2005) and technological affordances are used to facilitate different levels of social identification (Haciyakupoglu and Zhang 2015).

Some argue that the digital era has precipitated a trust crisis (see, e.g., Nie and Erbring 2002; Nie, Hillygus, and Erbring 2002; Dutton et al. 2013). A 2017 survey about young people's attitudes toward and beliefs about the digital era, commissioned by the UK Department for Business Energy and Industrial Strategy, concluded that trust in digital technology is very low among the next generation—less than a third of those surveyed, for example, said that they would trust a computer to look after an elderly relative at home, and just under a quarter agreed that they would trust an autonomous car.[11] The same year, a survey on digital trust by the US Pew Research Center highlighted that "trust-jarring digital interactions" have resulted in widespread anxiety about whether to trust others online. Yet for others the hyper-connectivity of the sharing era has increased the potential for trust—trust is indeed "the sharing economy's currency" (Botsman 2012). The development of block-chain technology, it is argued, has removed the need for intermediaries, effectively shifting trust away from reputable institutions and their accredited experts and toward social media and, thus, multiple sources (Botsman and Rogers 2010).

Importantly, trust and risk are the flip sides of the same coin. In Luhmann's (1988, 103) words, trust is "an attitude which allows for risk-taking decisions." We make a subjective assessment to trust others to perform a particular task in a given context, according to specific expectations (Wolf and Muhanna 2011). The virtuality and (pseudo) anonymity of some digital environments may be potentially empowering for marginalized groups (Turkle 1995). They may also lower perceptions of risk, which is relevant to digital grooming as risk-taking is known to be a driving force for criminal activity. Crypto-drug market users, for example, are high risk takers (Lane and Cherek 2000; Mungan and Klick 2014).

Research shows that digital spaces pose greater challenges than non-digital ones to our cognitive ability to decide whom to trust and that we regularly apply specific types of cognitive heuristics when making digital trust assessments (see, e.g., Sperber et al. 2010; Metzger, Flanagin, and Medders 2010; Metzger and Flanagin 2013). According to Hendriks et al. (2015), three factors influence trust assessment in the Clear Net, namely, expertise, integrity, and benevolence. *Expertise* refers to knowledge regarding the topic of interest, *integrity* to observance of the norms and standards of one's profession, and *benevolence* to orientation toward others or society, including a sense of responsibility and morality. Moreover, Lorenzo-Dus and Di Cristofaro (2018) show the same three factors to guide assessment of trust in some Dark Net spaces, specifically crypto-drug markets. As will be discussed in Chapters 7 and 8, these markets adopt Clear Net market strategies for developing social- and systems-based trust in them, for instance online reputation (review) and third-party payment (escrow) services. On Clear Net markets, like e-Bay or Amazon, buyers regularly post feedback about their transactional experiences. Such online reputation systems seek to lower perceived transaction-specific risks. Crypto-drug markets also regularly use them or, rather, exploit them. Similarly, Clear Net markets like e-Bay use escrow services to hold money on behalf of the two parties involved in a transaction and, if required, to handle dispute resolution. This serves to offset users' underlying lack of trust (boyd 2002). Use of escrow in Dark Net markets serves to do that, too, additionally seeking to minimize users' risk of being caught by law enforcement and/or scammed by other users from within the markets (Horton-Eddison and Di Cristofaro 2017; Horton-Eddison 2020; Spagnoletti, Ceci, and Bygstad 2021).

Trust is a *sine qua non* for "successful" digital grooming—offenders manipulate the trust their targets place in them during acts of digital sharing. In digital sexual grooming, trust development is a key groomer tactic, as Chapters 3 and 4 will show. Similarly, digital ideological grooming relies chiefly on constructing an opponent as untrustworthy when it comes to upholding the ingroup's values, best interests, and so forth—so much so that the opponent becomes debased and othered, as Chapters 5 and 6 will discuss. And in crypto-drug markets users refer regularly to the trust they place in some vendors, as well as openly shame those vendors who are not perceived to be trustworthy, which will be explored in Chapters 7 and 8.

2.3.3 Digital engagement

From the above, it can be gleaned that trust is paramount in (digital) grooming—not unlike in (digital) communication overall. Crucially, as discussed, trust is developed in and through interaction, by engaging communicatively with one's trust targets. To manage such engagement successfully, digital groomers must first gain access to their targets and secure their attention. This is no easy task. According to Social Network Theory, only 10–20% of all social media users manage to attract large levels of attention, maintain engagement, and thus exert considerable digital influence over those users and, in some cases, even trigger "social contagion" (Cha et al 2010). This digital minority is variously known as "emergent elites" (Papacharissi and Oliveira 2012; Meraz and Papacharissi 2013), "discussion catalysts" (Himelboim, Gleave, and Smith 2009), "superparticipants" (Graham and Wright 2013), "influential citizens" (Lorenzo-Dus and Di Cristofaro 2016), and "influencers" (e.g., Enke and Borchers 2019).

How does one get to be part of this digital minority? Algorithms play an important part in sculpting digital discourse and social relations. Digital news organizations seeking to get readers' attention, for instance, need to make sure that the kinds of algorithms used at any time by mainstream social media platforms favor their organizations. As Bouvier and Machin (2018, 181) note, "the discourses presented to any individual through news, entertainment, and other things 'you may also like,' are patterned in ways aligned to your previous online activities, which include consumer behaviour." Furthermore, computational models have identified several digital engagement activities conducive to influencing others. On Twitter, these include limiting one's tweets to a single topic/hashtag and keeping high levels of personal engagement (Cha et al. 2010; Romero, Meeder, and Kleinberg 2011) and posting messages that express a negative mood but also a sense of community (Quercia et al. 2011).

Digital influencing in Twitter has also been found to display recurrent discourse engagement features: high levels of conversationality (Papacharissi and Oliveria 2011; Meraz and Papacharissi 2013); a coupling of conventions that limit content originality (such as "retweet" and "@") with high levels of activity; a combination of thematically relevant and nonrelevant content, and heightened emotionality and assertive stance-taking (Lorenzo-Dus and Di Cristofaro 2016). It is important to acknowledge, though, that the activities for increasing engagement levels with one's digital content may vary to some extent across platforms, in part because of specific sociotechnical affordances regarding temporality (e.g., synchronicity/asynchronicity), participatory structures, multimodality/multimediality, register, and so forth.

In relation to social media influencers and other incarnations of digital celebrity-ness, Abidin (2017, 2018) highlights the importance of their being able to show "relatability," which she sees as encompassing the performance of accessibility, believability, authenticity, emulatability, and intimacy (see also Kanai 2019). Page (2020) shows that influencers' relatability in Instagram is narratively performed via a combination of authenticity, affect, aspiration, and self-deprecating humor. Such performances of relatability, she argues, allow Instagram influencers to successfully market the products they promote. Their identity performances present aspirational "life-style guru" selves (Baker and Rojek 2020) yet minimize self-praise—both identity projections capitalizing on an affective economy of social media influence that promotes the illusion of interpersonal intimacy between influencers and their followers. This is not unlike the broadcast era phenomenon of "para-social interaction" between audiences and those whom they listen to/watch on the radio/screen (Horton and Whol 1956).

Digital engagement may also selectively target a few or even just one individual—with exclusivity (depth) rather than spreadability (breadth) being its overriding goal in such cases. In digital sexual grooming of children, for instance, efforts are primarily directed at conveying a sense of specialness or uniqueness about the groomer–target relationship. The exclusivity and spreadability dimensions of influence also often overlap in digital environments, in which participation frameworks are especially fluid. Goffman (1981, 3) famously defined the participation framework of interaction as comprising "all those who happen to be in the perceptual range of the event [as having] some sort of participation status relative to it." In doing so, he began to address the limitations of previous—speaker–hearer-based—communication models that had accounted for neither the complexity of the speaker and hearer roles nor their interactional flexibility. His participation framework paved the way for subsequent analyses of forms of participation in pre-digital media (and other contexts). For example, the "animator," "author," and "principal" production roles, on the one hand, and the "ratified" ("addressed" or "unaddressed") and "unratified" ("overhearers" and "eavesdroppers") reception roles, on the other, were seminal in identifying and interrogating a key aspect of broadcast talk: its "double articulation" (see, e.g., Heritage 1985; Scannell 1991). This refers to its being "a communicative interaction between those participating in discussion, interview, game show or whatever and, at the same time, is designed to be heard by absent audiences" (Scannell 1991, 1).

Digital spaces challenge us to further theorize both Goffman's notion of the participation framework and subsequent developments thereof in pre-digital spaces. The networked publics who happen to be in the perceptual range of a given digital interaction, for instance, are bound by more than two articulation layers, and these interact in complex ways.

Even in cases in which a limited number of individuals seemingly engage digitally with each other, such as "private" instant messaging between two people, the immaterial objects that they share leave data traces—written texts, photos, videos—that may be collectively shared with other individuals or groups across digital platforms, with partly overlapping networked publics, (a)synchronously. This is exploited in digital sexual grooming, for instance, when child sexual abuse/exploitation organized groups circulate CSAM generated during groomer–child "private" interactions among their illicit networks via different digital platforms.

Digital sexual groomers also often contact many potential child targets simultaneously—the so-called *scatter-gun approach* to gaining access to them. In purely participation framework terms, and therefore leaving aside the depravity and illegality of their actions, this is akin to the use of "for-anyone-as-someone structures" in broadcasting (Scannell 2000). When seeking to gain access to multiple children, digital sexual groomers frame their discourse as if it were addressed to each child directly and individually, even though it is intended for any child who may happen to be logged on to a given digital platform. The children's replies determine whether the groomers shift to different participation frameworks, such as one-to-one (groomer–child) or more-than-one-to-one (two or more groomers–one child), and adapt their interactional style accordingly. Offenders are not only able to access many more children than previously but also to hide behind digital technology in ways that mean that their child targets know very little, if anything, about them. Blackmail related to "self-generated" (or perceived first person) CSAM, for example, is a known powerful tool in maintaining the abuse and preventing child targets from disclosing it (Webster et al. 2012). As Hamilton-Giachritis et al.'s (2021b, 8) study of the impact of digital sexual grooming on children concludes, technology can positively support young people's normal sexual development yet it also "provides additional routes both to access young people to abuse and to manipulate and silence them."

The above are some examples of the fluidity of participatory structures in digital spaces. A number of participatory framework models have been developed to address this fluidity in relation to particular digital spaces, such as blogs (Hoffman 2012), Facebook (Eisenlauer 2014), discussion boards

(Haugh and Chang 2015), and YouTube (Boyd 2014; Dynel 2014). While helpful, collectively these models highlight the difficulty—indeed analytic impracticality—of developing a one-size-fits-all, overarching participation framework for digital communication (Dynel 2017).

The "digitalness" of digital grooming is therefore more than just a technical enabler of cyber-crime (see Quayle 2020, e.g., in relation to online sexual abuse and exploitation) Current attitudes and ways of relating to digital sharing, trusting, and engaging sculpt the digital spaces in which sexual, ideological, and commercial grooming practices develop. The practices in turn shape these same digital spaces in different ways. We speak, for instance, of online gaming platforms that "harbor" child sexual abuse and exploitation, of social media platforms that provide a "safe haven" for extreme ideology groups' recruitment, or of encrypted, Dark Net spaces offering "shelter" for illicit trading. The next section discusses the manipulative underpinning of grooming others across these digitally mediated criminal spaces.

2.4 MANIPULATION

Manipulation is far from simple to theorize from a single disciplinary perspective (De Saussure and Schulz 2005; Van Dijk 2006, 2017). The phenomenon of manipulation has been extensively examined in philosophy and rhetoric studies. This research has been largely predicated on truth and morality, whereby manipulation is seen as operating within the dark fringes of human communication (see, e.g., Bakir, Herring, and Miller (2018) for an overview). Manipulation has also received attention within linguistics, especially cognitive linguistics and critical discourse analysis. Within the former, the focus lies on the mental processes involved in the interpretation of manipulative language (see, e.g., De Saussure 2005; Maillat and Oswald 2009; Maillat 2013). Within critical discourse analysis, manipulation is approached as a form of text or talk. This research tends to focus on institutional settings, typically politics and the mass media, and primarily examines the discursive mechanisms whereby powerful, dominant groups within these settings manipulate and control powerless, minority groups in society. Social manipulation, van Dijk (2017, 206) for instance argues, is "a form of domination or power abuse [that] involves organizations or institutions as manipulating agents making use of power resources, such as access to or control over knowledge or public discourse. . . . The targets of manipulation are usually characterized as having less resources, for example, knowledge, to resist such domination."

When it comes to defining manipulation, some work has explicitly sought to distinguish it from neighboring terms such as "influence," "argumentation," and, most often, "persuasion." According to Nettel and Roque (2012), persuasion and manipulation share the common trait of trying to influence. Yet this is also more broadly shared with all discursive enunciation (Benveniste 1966). The difference between persuasion and manipulation lies in the notion of consent: persuasion includes it; manipulation does not (Nettel and Roque 2012; O'Keefe 2006). In relation to the notion of free will/consent, Pardo (2001) aptly argues that both concepts depend to some extent on the power relations between persuader/manipulator and their target(s), which may in turn hinge on factors such as the institutional space in which their discourse happens, their respective authority roles, and so forth. For Sorlin (2017), unlike persuasion, manipulation goes beyond changing mental states and into the actional level. Manipulative discourse has some perlocutionary intents that bring the target to take some action that responds to the manipulator's desires. Yet for van Dijk (2017, 206) "mind control" is the primary cognitive aim of manipulation, "action control" being an indirect, secondary aim.

Persuasion, Partington and Taylor (2018, 3) further note, "is of itself neither good nor bad, neither beneficial nor harmful," which is not the case with manipulation. Philosophical approaches to manipulation are critical, seeing it as a harmful phenomenon. Linguistic approaches note the potential, indeed likely, negative effects of manipulation, for example, in terms of power abuse and mind/action control (van Dijk 2006, 2017). The analytic focus, notwithstanding, remains on the discursive strategies for manipulating.

A review of contemporary research on manipulative messages leads to six main features being proposed as relevant: (i) goal orientation/speaker interest, (ii) covertness, (iii) power asymmetry, (iv) coercion, (v) intentionality, and (vi) falsity/insincerity.

2.4.1 Goal-orientation/Speaker interest

Numerous studies point to goal orientation/speaker interest as being an important feature of manipulation (e.g., Rigotti 2005; Saussure and Schulz 2005; van Dijk 2006, 2017; Billig and Marinho 2014). Manipulators make others believe or do things that are both in their interest and against the interests of their targets (van Dijk 2006). Maillat and Oswald (2009) note that such interests—or "goals," as they term them—may be linguistic ("local," i.e., in the text) and extra-linguistic ("global," e.g., the pursuit of happiness, wellbeing, and so forth). They also note that, while manipulator goals will be favored in most cases, target interests may also be favored occasionally, thus casting a doubt on the validity of the speaker interest feature though not on that of its goal orientation overall. Within digital commercial grooming, for example, drug vendors assign primacy to the presupposed benefits of given drugs, including in terms of health safety, for their target customers over the actual financial gains that the vendors derive from these commercial transactions. Similarly, in digital ideological grooming, promises of after-life fulfillment through committing acts of jihad are presented as being aligned to target interests rather than to the jihadi groups' recruitment gains.

2.4.2 Covertness

Covertness tends to be seen as a key feature of manipulation. In this regard, as Maillat and Oswald (2009, 356) argue, it is important to acknowledge that there are different aspects of manipulating that may remain covert: from the overall manipulative intention (see also Easton 1958; Pardo 2001) to one or more of the discursive strategies through which manipulating acts are realized. Across digital grooming practices, overall covertness prevails, as the analyses in Chapters 4, 6, and 8 will show.

2.4.3 Power asymmetry

Manipulators' exploitation of power asymmetry between them and their targets is believed to be required for manipulation to take place (van Dijk 2006, 2017). This asymmetry may result from manipulators occupying a higher hierarchical social position than their targets by virtue of, for example, being the targets' parent, teacher, or group leader. It may also result from manipulators having access to a higher level of knowledge, for instance through education or some other form of expertise. Such social parameters are fluidly negotiated during interaction. Perhaps the most obvious example of power asymmetry, and consequent power abuse, takes place within digital sexual grooming. Digital sexual groomers have—and exploit—a power advantage over the children that they target by virtue of their adult–child relationship. This is evident in terms of financial means—or access to financial means—as well as cognitive development.

2.4.4 Coercion

Manipulation does not contemplate free choice and voluntary action from the target. Instead, it relies on what, within propaganda studies, is called "manufacture of consent" (Lippman 1925; Herman and Chomsky 1988). When a target acts in a particular manner because of false pretenses, benefit promises, pressure, or some other form of coercion, consent has been manufactured rather than freely given (Bakir et al. 2018). As will be discussed in Chapters 3 and 4, digital sexual groomers use coercion, typically "sextortion" and harassment, to advance their abusive goals (Quayle and Newman 2016; Mullineux-Morgan and Lorenzo-Dus 2021; Seymour-Smith and Kloess 2021;

Powell, Casey, and Rouse 2021). Yet they also often use sophisticated face-work, specifically *negative politeness strategies*, to create the impression that the children they prey on behave freely during their online relationship. And, as Chapters 7 and 8 will show, in digital commercial grooming, buyers are frequently coerced (including extorted) into posting favourable reviews of their purchases. In digital ideological grooming, as Chapters 5 and 6 will show, in-group values are extolled in ways that create pressure for individual members (or potential members) to show that they fit in, that they belong in the group.

2.4.5 Intentionality

A further manipulation feature is that of intentionality. This is shared with other forms of communication, including persuasion. However, in the case of manipulation, there is mismatch between manipulators' intentions and the intentions that their target attribute to them. Importantly, in digital grooming the intention to manipulate others is aligned to criminal activity—digital groomers seek to engage their targets in illicit behavior. This is legislatively important—as much as the actual outcome on digital grooming targets. Intentionality is recognized as an important factor by current legislation in the case of digital sexual and ideological grooming in the United Kingdom. The UK Sexual Offences Act (2003) was changed in 2016, as a result of an NSPCC campaign (Flaw in the Law).[12] The new legislation made it illegal for an adult to send an explicit sexual message to a minor, irrespective of whether there was subsequent child sexual abuse offline.[13] The resulting offence thus covers any communication—written, verbal, pictorial—with a minor made by any means (in person, by phone, Internet) by someone aged 18 or older that intends to obtain sexual gratification, where that communication is sexual or has a sexual purpose. This significant legislative change, whereby the prosecution emphasis shifted to the groomers' expression of sexual intent, meant that law enforcement has since been able to act much more quickly. In the words of the NSPCC Chief Executive at the time, Peter Wanless, police in England and Wales got "the powers they need to protect children from online grooming and to intervene sooner to stop abuse before it starts."[14]

Determining intent in cases of digital ideological grooming is also important legislatively, albeit that, here, being able to establish uptake of such intent is also factored in. The Council of Europe Convention on the Prevention of Terrorism (CECPT) Treaty was signed in 2005, under the auspices of the Council of Europe and—at the time of writing—provides the current legislative framework in Europe. Article 5 of the Treaty requires EU Member States to criminalize public provocation to commit a terrorist offence. Public provocation is nowadays primarily mediated digitally rather than via broadcast or print media. Article 5 also specifies that provocation to commit a terrorist offence may entail implicit or explicit incitement. UK legislation echoes the CECPT. Section 1 of the UK 2006 Terrorism Act[15] criminalizes the publication of statements that are likely to be understood by some or all of those to whom they are published as encouraging the commission, preparation, or instigation of acts of terrorism. It also clearly states that criminalization applies to both direct and indirect encouragement of terrorism. The Act does not define indirect encouragement, using it synonymously with incitement. However, it links it to language that glorifies and praises terrorism.

As argued by Macdonald and Lorenzo-Dus (2020), determining a threshold number of members of the public to feel incited to determine punitive action is neither desirable nor practical. Incitement—or rather the act of inciting—constitutes what in pragmatics is known as a *pragmeme*; that is, a general situational prototype (Mey 2001). Other pragmemes include denying, bribing, warning, and so forth. Pragmemes are instantiated via pragmatic acts: *practs*. Yet "no two practs will ever be identical (being realized in an actual situation, and every situation is different from every other)" (Mey 2001, 221). Practs belonging to the pragmeme of incitement may include, among many others, realizations such as "all Muslims must commit jihad" (a statement of obligation), "doing jihad is simple" (an affirmative statement), "making a bomb does not require advanced technical skills" (a negative statement), and "haven't Muslims endured Western humiliation long enough?" (a rhetorical question). Moreover, incitement is one of those pragmemes that may be never realized via explicit statements such as "I hereby incite you to . . ." (Kurzon 1998). Therefore, defining *a priori* what incitement "looks like" textually, let alone reducing it to speech acts of glorification and praise, makes little sense. Instead, determining intentionality from discourse—not that this is always straightforward—is a more productive way forward.

2.4.6 Falsity/Insincerity

Rigotti (2005) argues that manipulation may be characterized in terms of insincerity. The typical manifestation of this feature would be lies and deception. In their social network theory study of the dynamics of deception, Barrio, Govezensky, and Dunbar (2015) describe what they term society's "deception paradox": our society abhors deception, yet deception is present in virtually all human interactions, on- and offline, across societies. Given this, the authors argue that there must be "a fundamental reason that prevents the social world from being totally honest" (2015, 1). Their analysis indeed shows that there are benefits—as well as costs—in deceiving others within digital networks. They distinguish between "pro-social" and "anti-social" deception. The former yields benefit to the target rather than the deceiver by continuing to reinforce their relationship. An example would be liking someone on social media when you do not really feel that way. Pro-social deception is regularly exploited in digital grooming. For instance, digital sexual groomers discursively reframe their proposed/actual sexual advances as beneficial to their targets later in life (Lorenzo-Dus, Izura, and Pérez-Tattam 2016). Such realization of pro-social deception serves to further the groomers' goal of developing bonding trust between them and their target. Similarly, digital ideological grooming, specifically by jihadi groups, tends to rely on promises of their target's fulfillment as a Muslim—a deception strategy based on the incentive of after-life benefits for the target (Macdonald 2017).

Anti-social deception, for its part, benefits the deceiver at the expense of destroying large social networks, even if in certain circumstances—Barrio, Govezensky, and Dunbar (2015) argue—it can simultaneously strengthen the cohesiveness of these networks. Again, digital grooming makes regular use of anti-social deception. Within ideological grooming, for example, othering of certain groups (e.g., "the West," for jihadi groups; Muslims and immigrants for radical right groups) across social media serves to increase and strengthen membership within the in-group, which is deceived into believing that their members cohere around (i.e., are bounded together through) their hate of these othered groups.

The specific case of self-deception is of relevance to digital grooming. There are three main reasons why we engage in self-deception: to hide conscious deception, to lower the cognitive cost normally associated with deception, and to reduce the punishment if deception is discovered (Santibáñez 2017). Although it is difficult to determine which reason(s) may play a part in specific cases of self-deception, the illegality and/or immorality of digital grooming practices likely foregrounds the third reason.

When it comes to the semiotic properties of manipulation, there are numerous structures and strategies that discourse analysts have identified. De Saussure (2005) differentiates between "local" and "global" manipulative strategies. Both rely on language use but the global ones "are not directly provided in some manipulative discourse" (2005, 129). The local strategies include vagueness, presuppositional assertions, misuse of concepts, and pseudo-mystical (religious-like) discourse. The global strategies include spreading and repetition of specific connotative words; generalization of a new terminology; elimination of some lexical items from public discourse; unmotivated or misleading analyses; use of acronyms, abbreviations, or numbers; and naming of elements of the everyday environment.

For his part, van Dijk (2017, 207–208) provides the following examples of manipulation structures and strategies:

• Grammatical sentence structures
• Biased (e.g., derogatory) lexical items: implications/implicatures, generalizations

- Forms of actor descriptions
- Granularity and other modes of situation or event description: more or less precise or complete, detailed or vague, close versus distant, and so on
- Storytelling
- Argumentation
- Superstructural (schematic) categories, such as headlines in news reports
- General ideological polarization between in-groups (Us) and out-groups (Them).

Similarly, considerable work has sought to identify the linguistic markers of deception as a manifestation of manipulation. Much of this research has used natural language processing and/or psycholinguistic profiling software such as Linguistic Inquiry and Word Count (LIWC; Pennebaker et al. 2015a/b).[16] Use of vague language and negative textual forms, such as negative emotion words and raising doubts, have been found to be two such key markers (Bachenko, Fitzpatrick, and Schonwetter 2008; Recasens, Danescu-Niculescu-Mizil, and Jurafsky 2013; Addawood et al. 2019). In digital spaces, Rashkin et al. (2017, 2933), for instance, found that fake news deploys significantly more "words that can be used to exaggerate—subjectives, superlatives, and modal adverbs" than non-fake news. And Davis and Sinnreich (2020) identified larger percentages of interrogative words ("how," "what," and "when"), third-person plural pronouns, question marks, and terms such as "true" and "truth" in former US President Donald Trump's false statement tweets than in his tweets containing non-false statements. These studies clearly demonstrate the key part played by language in deception. However, their reliance on largely decontextualized, computational approaches presents some limitations—not least because of the lack of one-to-one mapping between form and function in language use.

Clearly, the above strategies and structures are neither manipulative/deceptive *per se* nor manipulation/deception signaling across communicative contexts. They provide a valuable repository of knowledge in as much as the strategies work in specific, research-evidenced contexts. For example, and in relation to Ponzi schemes in Nigeria, Chiluwa and Chiluwa (2020) found that Ponzi operators intentionally hid their deception agenda by presenting themselves and the targets of their fraudulent activity in ways that match sociocultural ideologies in Nigeria. For their part, Anafo and Ngula (2020) showed the discourse of scam emails to be interpersonally rich, favoring personal pronouns that index and position scammers relative to their targets to intentionally hide the scammers' motives. These two studies emphasize the role of identity construction within manipulation—a research lens that has been, comparatively speaking, largely missing when theorizing manipulation (but note van Dijk's [2017] work on manipulative strategies of polarization between in-groups and out-groups) and that is, however, central to the analysis of manipulation in digital grooming in this book, as next discussed.

2.5 IDENTITY CONSTRUCTION

Having considered digital mediation and manipulation in relation to digital grooming, this final section examines the crucial part played by identity construction therein. Groomers' ability to fashion their identity digitally in ways that support their goals is of paramount importance to their chances of success. This, as Chapters 4, 6, and 8 will show, entails not just self-oriented but also other-oriented identity projections, specifically those toward the target of digital grooming and toward any other(s) believed to oppose the groomers' goals.

Identity has been—and remains—the subject of much research across the humanities and social sciences. In linguistics, identity has been broadly approached from both a quantitative, variationist perspective (initiated in the work of William Labov, see, e.g., 1972) and a qualitative, constructivist standpoint. Within the latter, which this book adopts, identity is seen in anti-essentialist terms and located not within the private realm of cognition and experience but negotiated (i.e., verified, contended, and so forth) "in local discourse contexts of interaction" (Bucholtz and Hall 2005, 586; see also, e.g., Joseph 2004; De Fina, Shiffrin, and Bamberg 2006; Benwell and Stokoe 2006; De Fina 2020). Identities are thus transient and fluid, rather than permanent. Yet, certain aspects of identity are more stable than others: repetition of certain identity performative acts may result in their becoming naturalized and self-evident (Butler 1990, 2004). In this regard, Butler (1990) talks of processes of "sedimentation," whereby we draw on resources that progressively convey the impression of a stable identity. Indeed, we may conceive of identities as being both "unstable and temporarily stabilized by social practice and regular, predictable behaviour" (Barker and Galasinski 2001, 31). Moreover, identity construction results from processes of similarity (Edwards 2009) and difference (Hall and Du Gay 1996; Mouffee 2005), which clearly makes identity relational as opposed to a property of isolated individuals (Kiesling 2013). Across many digital spaces, furthermore, identity construction entails the deliberate mobilization of a range of semiotic resources—intentionality is, in other words, crucial to the performance of our and others' digital selves (Halonen and Leppänen 2017; Leppänen and Tapionkaski 2021).

A fruitful concept for examining identity construction along the above lines is that of style, upon which the analyses of digital grooming in this book centrally draw. Current understanding of style has shifted away from regarding it in terms of intraspeaker variation that is dependent on situational factors (see Labov 1972; Bell 1984). Instead, style is nowadays conceived of as encompassing a set of multimodal/multidimensional resources that individuals deploy in different contexts for the enactment of identity in interaction (Coupland 1985, 2001, 2007; Eckert 2000, 2001; Eckert and Rickford 2001). The styling of identity operates within processes of indirect indexicality (Bucholtz 2009;

Ochs 1992). Indexes are a type of linguistic (or other) sign, the meaning of which derives from their contexts of use (Silverstein 1976, 2003; Agha 2003, 2007). Indirect indexes are semiotic items that indicate a stance, practice, or activity that then acquires an indexical connection to something else, such as a particular social identity (e.g., race, age, or class). If a linguistic item co-occurs frequently in the speech of a particular person or kind of person, for example, that linguistic item is taken to index them (Johnstone and Kiesling 2008). Indexicality can also be either interior or exterior. The former type holds only at the interactional moment and for those involved in it; the latter type transcends such interactional boundaries (Kiesling 2009).

The association processes underlying indexicality in styling are ideologically patterned rather than neutral; they work "within a semiotic system in relation to other locally available—and often competing and contrasting—styles" (Bucholtz 2009, 148). Styles are therefore about distinctiveness within a system of possibilities—about principles of differentiation that link semiotic choices with social meanings (Irvine 1985; Coupland 2007). This is also why a co-occurring set of semiotic items—rather than one item—is typically required to index a style (Ochs 1992; Irvine 2001; Eckert 2003; Coupland 2007; Bucholtz 2009). And styles are creative and agentive; they are the situational achievements of language users to evoke particular identities rather than the inevitable outcome of situational factors. These factors are, in other words, a malleable contributor rather than an inflexible determiner of styles (Coupland 2007).

Styles result from repertoires of stances. For Kiesling (2009, 172), a stance is "a person's expression of their relationship to their talk (their epistemic stance—for example, how certain they are about their assertion) and a person's expression of their relationship to their interlocutors (their interpersonal stance, for example, friendly, dominating)." Clearly, epistemic and interpersonal stances are interconnected. For instance, patronizing others (an interpersonal stance) tends to require the expression of certitude about one's statements (an epistemic stance). As Chapter 8 will show, in crypto-drug markets vendors adopt an epistemic stance of certitude and knowledge about their products but also go to considerable lengths to avoid an interpersonal stance of condescension, favoring instead a stance of shared learning.

There is no single list of stances, nor are single linguistic items naturally linked to particular stances. Instead, it is more productive to think about stance-taking as "a public act by a social actor, achieved dialogically through overt communicative means (language, gesture, and other symbolic forms), through which social actors simultaneously *evaluate objects*, *position subjects* (themselves and others), and *align with other subjects*, with respect to any salient dimension of the sociocultural field" (Du Bois 2007, 163; emphasis added). Du Bois summarizes this understanding of stance—known as the *stance triangle*—as "I evaluate something, and thereby position myself, and

thereby align with you" (2007, 163). The stance triangle builds on three entities (first subject, second subject, stance object) and three actions (evaluating,
positioning, aligning). Stances are positionings that carry evaluative meanings
and alignments (Jaffe 2009)—akin to Goffman's (1981) concept of footing.

Stances, then, result from all the semiotic patterns of use that arise from
the decisions that we make in interaction as we think about who we are in relation to our interactants: they create interactional meanings, forming personal
styles (Kiesling 2009). And it is our acts of styling that in turn create particular identities. As Coupland (2014, 293) puts it, we can think of "'styling' of
social identities when speakers are able to manipulate the identities that they
project, often very creatively." Identity projection takes place "in the subtle
dynamics of acts of speaking" (ibid).

Coupland (2007, 111–115) proposes five processes for projecting identities in discourse, namely: targeting, framing, voicing, keying, and loading.
Targeting designates discursive actions that are "directed at shaping the per-
sona of one particular participant" (2007, 112). This can be the speaker of
discourse (self-targeting; see Le Page and Tabouret-Keller [1985]), the hearer
of discourse (ascriptional targeting), and a nonpresent, third party. According
to Coupland (2007), a considerable proportion of social identity work in interaction is ascriptional; that is, it targets the identities of hearers, whether
individuals or groups. Third-party targeting has been examined within the sociolinguistic theory of *audience design* (Bell 1984). Within this, the practice of
referee design designates initiative style shifts, whereby we adopt the linguistic
features associated with a reference group—for example, the technical jargon
of managers, the accent of "posh" people, and so forth—to identify ourselves
with that nonpresent group. This may require distancing from other nonpresent groups. Chapters 4, 6, and 8 examine how digital groomers perform self-,
ascriptional, and third-party targeting in their discourse, and Chapter 9 discusses the relative salience that each of these identity-shaping acts has across
the three digital grooming practices selected for analysis in this book.

Framing lies at the heart of Goffman's (1974, 1981) study of social interaction and concerns how, from a number of potential social identities,
we make specific ones salient or relevant in discourse. As Coupland (2007,
112) argues: "The potential metaphorical transfer through which a linguistic
feature comes to stand for or to mean something social (iconization, see Irvine
[2001]) has to be occasioned in a discourse." The identification value and impact of linguistic features is determined by the specific discursive frame that
is activated. Frames therefore provide the sets of principles of organization
that define the meaning and significance of social events. Coupland (2007,
113–114) goes on to discuss three types of discourse framing operating at the
macro-, meso-, and micro-levels of social interaction: socio-cultural framing,
genre framing, and interpersonal framing. *Socio-cultural framing* involves
"speakers positioning themselves, or others, in relation to pre-understood

social ecology" (2007, 113) in terms of identity categories such as age, ethnicity, gender, and sexuality. *Genre framing* entails speaker positioning vis-à-vis types of talk—such as casual conversation, news interviews, or, as Chapter 8 will show, drug vendors' profiles online. And *interpersonal framing* refers to how speakers dynamically position themselves in relation to each other within specific moments of talk, for example, as more or less distant or powerful in their relationship. In crypto-drug markets, as we will also see in Chapter 8, vendors' profiles follow certain generic conventions—including having to use a profile page template—that affect how they address and interact with their prospective buyers.

As for voicing, this refers to the ways in which "a speaker represents or implies *ownership* of an utterance or a way of speaking" (2007, 114; emphasis in the original). We may, for instance, quote or reconstruct the words of others and, in doing so, "inflect those source voices in various ways, giving them particular identity traits and qualities," or we may voice "the normative speech of our own 'speech communities' [yet] imply less than full ownership of it" (2007, 114). As Chapter 6 will show, quoting is a staple in the discourse of digital ideological grooming.

The fourth and fifth processes for projecting identities considered by Coupland (2007)—keying and loading—are closely interrelated. Loading is an extension of keying—it designates the "level of a speaker's investment in an identity being negotiated"—whether light or weighty (Coupland 2007, 114). Keying is one of the components in Hymes's (1974) communicative competence model. It refers to the manner, tone, or spirit of a communicative act, whether it is mock or serious, and it therefore allows us to interpret the speakers' motivations. By keying our discourse as banter, we project a playful identity targeted at our audience; by keying it as ironic, we project an "as if" identity that can overthrow the ostensive projection, and so forth (Coupland 2007). For example, digital sexual groomers often try to distance themselves from requests that may, at a particular point in their interactions with the target, appear too forthright by placing the "lol" (laughing out loud) initialism immediately after such requests, thus keying them as nonserious (Chiang and Grant 2018).

The relational dynamics at play across the above identity projection processes, including in digital grooming, can be aptly examined through the numerous linguistic theories informed by the Goffmanian (1956) concepts of *face* and *facework*, such as politeness (Brown and Levinson 1978/1987), impoliteness (e.g., Culpeper 1996, 2011), rapport management (Spencer-Oatey 2000, 2008), and relational work (Locher and Watts 2005, 2008).[17] Goffman famously defined face as "the positive social value a person effectively claims for himself by the line others assume he has taken during a particular contact" (1956, 213). Facework, in turns, designates "the actions taken by a person to make whatever he is doing consistent with face" (1956, 12). Both concepts concern how we present ourselves in specific interactions through evaluative patterns—that is, through "lines" or "roles"—that we think our interactants associate with us.

For Goffman (1956/1967), then, face and identity (role, lines) were closely linked—so much so that he dropped the term "face," replacing it with that of "identity," in much of his subsequent writing. Yet the first and arguably most influential adaptation of Goffman's concepts of face/facework, namely Brown and Levinson's (1978/1987) politeness theory, separated face from line and conceptualized face differently, namely as a cognitive concept expressed by a rational—rather than an emotional—person (see Garcés-Conejos Blitvich 2013). And, although Brown and Levinson's (1978/1987) politeness theory was extensively critiqued in the 1990s, "the intrinsic relationship between face and identity was mainly treated as a non-issue" (Garcés-Conejos Blitvich and Sifianou 2017, 229), with the two concepts being only implicitly linked in (im)politeness studies, for example, about gender, which *is* a social identity. It was not until the early 2000s that, coinciding with a discursive turn in (im)politeness scholarship (e.g., Eelen 2001; Mills 2003; Watts 2003), identity was reintroduced in the study of face and facework. The resulting approaches highlight several differences between face and identity. In Spencer-Oatey's (2008) rapport management theory, for instance, face is invested with emotion, whereas identity is not; and in Arundale's (2006) face constituting theory, face is conceived of as a social attribute and a punctual phenomenon, whereas identity is an individual attribute and a durative phenomenon. Over the coming years, however, a growing number of studies have progressively shown that face and identity constitute each other, which makes it very difficult—indeed impractical—to tease them apart empirically and theoretically (see Garcés-Conejos Blitvich and Sifianou [2017] for a detailed discussion). Models and analytic toolkits developed for the analysis of identity have been fruitfully applied to the study of (im)politeness (e.g., Garcés-Conejos Blitvich 2009; Georgakopolou 2013) and relational work (e.g., Locher 2008; Locher, Bolander, and Höhn 2015). The styling of our and others' identities is thus a purposeful practice, the result of choices from a range of linguistics means to deliver a given message effectively. It is recognition of the creative management of identity construction in current understandings of style that makes the notion of styling particularly useful for the analysis of digital grooming.

As discussed in Section 2.4, intentionality and speaker interest/goals are important in manipulative discourse. Digital groomers seek to align their target to their stances vis-à-vis particular life domains—sexual relations, religion, politics, drug use, and so forth. These stances relate to behaviors that fall outside, or at the boundaries of, the law. If they are to avoid punitive actions, therefore, groomers must construct such stances carefully. Failure to do so risks—among other things—criminal exposure and/or social condemnation.

In their study of sex crimes conducted online, for instance, Grant and Macleod (2020, 12) show that (child) sex offenders engage in conscious, deliberate "identity play" online that "break[s] through the mutable constraints of [their] habitual identities." When doing so, offenders draw on physical (e.g., brain abilities), situational (e.g., digital affordances of communication), and sociolinguistic (e.g., interactive performances of age, gender, and geographical origins) resources. Yet they are also constrained through nonavailability of specific resources at a certain point and/or through the impossibility of drawing on several resources simultaneously. The authors' research also shows that, within this balancing act between identity resources and constraints, some identity resources emerge as being more stable than others, "constitut[ing] something approaching a 'home identity'" for certain offenders (Grant and Macleod 2020, 178; see also Chiang 2020). Being able to detect the linguistic markers of these "home identities" is clearly useful in cyber-crime contexts in which identity deception is itself a communicative goal. Digital sexual groomers, for example, often set up and maintain multiple online accounts within a single chat room and draw on different identity construction resources in each of these accounts. In ideological and commercial grooming, there appears to be no evidence of systematic multiple identity performance tactics aimed at deception. Nevertheless, deliberately styling oneself—and what one stands for—in contextually appropriate, appealing ways remains paramount, as illustrated by extreme ideology groups regularly styling themselves as victims of others' wrongdoing (Chapter 6) and crypto-drug vendors styling themselves as libertarians (Chapter 8).

As text authors we hold different expectations vis-à-vis how our own positionality may be received in discourse: that our text target will be aligned with it (like-mindedness), that they will be yet noncommittal/undecided about it, or that they will be disaligned from it. And we resort to different devices to signal these three expectations. Devices to help construct author–target like-mindedness include, for example, presuppositions, categorical assertions, and concurrence-signaling adjuncts (e.g., "of course" or "obviously"). Devices for signaling expected target noncommittal include use of epistemic modals and evidentials, as well as supplying justifications for contentious propositions. As for devices for signaling probable target disalignment, these include, for instance, overtly stating author expectation of disagreement and denying a given proposition that the target may be holding to (White 2020). As the analysis in Chapters 4, 6, and 8 will show, digital groomers regularly deploy a number of these discourse devices to account for the various ways in which their self-styling work may land with their target. This is often driven by ongoing risk assessments about the likelihood that their target may expose the illegality and/or immorality behind their grooming discourse.

In addition to deliberate self-styling work that supports manipulation, there is an imperative for digital groomers to ascribe stances to their targets and opponents in ways that will advance the groomers' own interests/goals. The discursive practice of attributing stances to others is not as routine in interaction as that of attributing stances to oneself or one's in-group. This is because "the relational politics of stance . . . generally require a speaker to show respect for the other person's entitlement to construct their own stances, rather than have them constructed for them" (Coupland and Coupland 2009, 229). In seeking the commitment of his or her stance attributee, the stance attributor may have to challenge socially endorsed and potentially normative orientations. Even in those cases in which the attributed stance reflects what the attributee would admit being their stance, they may "well be uncomfortable to have that stance articulated on [their] behalf." The stance attributer may also be using these other-oriented stances to advance their own agendas. As Coupland and Coupland (2009, 30) argue, "levels of presumed entitlement to 'speak for' another vary across social situations, and not least across institutional settings." In interactions in which manipulation is high on the attributer's agenda—self-evidently so in digital grooming—speaking for another appears to be treated almost as a given.

In sum, throughout Parts II–IV of this book, I examine the semiotic resources that contribute to digital grooming as a discourse practice that revolves centrally around identity construction. The analysis is undertaken from the vantage point of the groomer: that is, it considers groomers' deliberate construction of their social identities through self-styling and the styling of their targets and their perceived opponents. A repertoire of stances is identified and analyzed for each of these styling acts. With regards to self-styling, however, the same broad stances recur: namely, expertise, openness, and avidity. Each of these stances exhibits nuances in digital sexual, ideological, and commercial grooming, as the analyses in Chapters 4, 6, and 8 will show.

It is important to note at this early juncture that these stances overlap. It is for clarity of presentation and analytic convenience that they are examined within distinct sections across the various empirical chapters of the book. *Expertise* refers to groomers' discursive displays of skill or knowledge, which tend to be presented as being superior to those of their targets and opponents. In facework terms, this is closely aligned to the notion of *competence face* (Partington 2006, 97–98), which concerns presenting oneself as well-informed and in control. Placing a positive value on the self on grounds of expertise, or competence, is a well-known manipulation strategy: the target has their sense of self-esteem increased through perceived association with the attributes claimed by manipulators who project self-flattering stances of expertise/competence (Sorlin 2017). In the case of digital sexual and commercial grooming, expertise is delimited to subject matter; respectively, sex and drugs. In the case of digital ideological grooming, in contrast, expertise encompasses a broad range of subjects—some of which are of limited or no apparent relevance to the political and/or religious motivations that define the group to which the groomers ascribe.

Openness entails the narrative performance of communicative frankness and/or absence of emotional concealment about oneself. Different emotions are foregrounded for disclosure within the digital grooming practices considered in this book. In digital sexual grooming, groomers open up primarily about their vulnerability; in digital ideological grooming, they disclose anger above everything else; and in digital commercial grooming, it is resilience that is highlighted. Across all of these, digital groomers strategically volunteer their personal views, experiences, and so forth: that is, they make the most of the cultural positive rhetoric around both digital sharing (John 2017) and digital relatability to maintain or enhance engagement and achieve digital influence (Abidin 2017, 2018; Kanai 2019). Moreover, openness triggers communicative reciprocity, which in turn enhances the likelihood of their grooming being successful.

Avidity in digital groomers' self-styling concerns the discursive performance of keen interest or enthusiasm in something or someone. Its grooming potential lies in being able to place someone/something else at the heart of one's purposive thoughts, feelings, and actions. In other words, it has the potential of showing positive values of selflessness and interest in others and their worldviews. In digital sexual and commercial grooming, the "beneficiary" of such keen interest is another human being; respectively, the child and the drug community. In digital ideological grooming, it is the extreme ideology group's values that are constructed as worthy of the groomers' stance of avidity.

2.6 CONCLUSION

This chapter has provided a working definition of digital grooming, informed in part by its etymological evolution. It has also mapped the conceptual territory of digital grooming across three core features: digital mediation, manipulation, and identity construction. In Section 2.3, I argued that the "digitalness" of digital grooming is constitutive of it, rather than merely contextual. A digital milieu marked by a celebration of sharing, a transformation of trust, and the search for engagement and influence within fluid participation frameworks underpins the digital mediation of grooming as an illegal practice. In Section 2.4, I characterized the features of manipulation and how they apply to digital grooming. Finally, Section 2.5 discussed the part played by identity construction in digital grooming. This may happen within one-to-one participation frameworks, such as groomer–target interaction, even if this private interaction may subsequently be resemioticized for others. It may alternatively happen within massive polylogues on social media, in which those participating collectively style and negotiate their own and others' identities through a repertoire of stances regarding different, digitally shared, fuzzy objects and their own and others' identities. This is best illustrated in this book by extreme ideology groups' skillful use of social media to build hate-filled communities. In yet other cases, identity construction is overtly self-promotional, resembling commercial advertising—as in vendors' profile pages in crypto-drug markets. Across these practices, digital groomers mobilize stances to style their identities and those of their target and perceived opponents in strategic ways that advance goals that lie outside or at the boundaries of the law.

NOTES

1. https://en.oxforddictionaries.com/definition/grooming. Accessed January 2022.
2. https://www.merriam-webster.com/dictionary/grooming. Accessed January 2022.
3. See Lanning (2019) for the evolution of the term "grooming" in the context of child sexual abuse and exploitation, from a law enforcement perspective.
4. Quoted in BBC News (1 December 2008): "When did grooming become a dirty word?" http://news.bbc.co.uk/1/hi/magazine/7758292.stm. Accessed December 2021.
5. https://www.gov.uk/government/publications/prevent-duty-guidance/revised-prevent-duty-guidance-for-england-and-wales. Accessed June 2022.
6. https://www.legislation.gov.uk/ukpga/2015/6/contents/enacted. Accessed June 2022.
7. https://www.theguardian.com/world/2018/jul/30/anti-fracking-activists-falsely-accused-grooming-boy-14. Accessed December 2021.
8. For a discussion of how the Foucauldian concept of "technologies of the self" may be adapted to identity fashioning on social media see, among other, Leppänen and Tapionkaski (2021).
9. This is a movement, started by Gary Wolf and Kevin Kelly in 2007, to incorporate technology into data acquisition regarding several aspects of individuals' daily lives, such as food consumed, mood, and blood oxygen levels. Such self-monitoring combines wearable sensors and wearable computing.
10. http://meyerweb.com/eric/thoughts/2014/12/24/inadvertent-algorithmic-cruelty/. Accessed January 2022.
11. https://wellcome.ac.uk/sites/default/files/science-education-tracker-attitudes-toward-machine-learning-feb17.pdf. Accessed January 2022.
12. https://www.nspcc.org.uk/what-we-do/campaigns/flaw-law/. Accessed June 2022.
13. https://www.gov.uk/government/news/new-crackdown-on-child-groomers-comes-into-force; https://www.lawgazette.co.uk/legal-updates/online-grooming-and-the-law/5060841.article. Accessed June 2022.
14. https://www.nspcc.org.uk/what-we-do/campaigns/flaw-law/ Accessed June 2022.
15. https://www.legislation.gov.uk/ukpga/2006/11/contents. Accessed June 2022.

16. LIWC analyses text across almost 100 lexical dimensions but in a largely single-word, decontextualized manner. For a discussion of the uses and limitations of LIWC – vis-à-vis other methodologies for analysing large textual datasets, specifically Corpus Assisted Discourse Studies, see Lorenzo-Dus and Kinzel (2019).

17. A review of the interrelations of these theories is beyond the scope of this book, but see, e.g., Garcés-Conejos Blitvich and Sifianou (2017), Tracy (2017), and Locher (2020). While a review of the evolution of the field of (im)politeness research is beyond the scope of this book, too, it is worth noting the presence of three broad waves. The first wave was triggered by Brown and Levinson's (1978/1987) work and focused on politeness, adopting a top-down, analyst-driven orientation regarding what behaviors counted as polite or not, as well as direct mapping of such behaviors and linguistic realizations (including speech acts). The second wave, also known as the *first-order approach to (im)politeness*, rejected top-down, analyst-driven assessments and argued that (im)politeness resided within language users (speakers), as opposed to linguistic realizations. The third wave synergizes the first two waves, maintaining the view that it is language users, as opposed to linguistic forms, who perform (im)politeness and reinstating the value of analyst-driven views as long as—and this is crucial—such views are based on interactants' assessments in context (see Ogiermann and Garcés-Conejos Blitvich [2019] for a detailed discussion).

CHAPTER 3

Digital Sexual Grooming

Setting the Scene

3.1 INTRODUCTION

Within a week, we were, like in what I considered to be a relationship and, erm, first of all, it started off just normal, as any, like, relationship would, just telling each other we loved each other and stuff, and then it turned into, erm, he would force me to send pictures to him, like. . . .

Hamilton-Giachritsis et al. (2017, 22).

These are the words of a 12-year-old girl as she tries to explain how she was sexually groomed online. *Tries to* is the operative term, for much digital sexual grooming goes unreported for reasons including victims' self-blame, trauma, and not realizing, for some time at least, what is happening to them (see, e.g., Foster and Hagedorn 2014; Whittle, Hamilton-Giachritsis, and Beech 2014; McElvaney 2015; Morrison, Bruce, and Wilson 2018). Technology-assisted child sexual abuse is sometimes viewed as less serious than offline child sexual abuse. Yet the emotional, psychological, and behavioral outcomes are similarly impactful (Hamilton-Giachritsis et al. 2021a, 2021b). Children are technology-savvy, possibly more than some of the adults whose responsibility it is to guide and protect them. But as this girl's experience illustrates, child victims of digital sexual grooming are often manipulated into believing that they are in a loving, rather than an abusive, relationship with someone whom they can trust.

Digital sexual groomers use language to gain and then exploit children's trust. The two paired chapters in this part of the book examine how they do this. Chapter 4 analyzes digital sexual groomers' styling of their own identities, the identities of their targets (the children they prey on), and the

Digital Grooming. Nuria Lorenzo-Dus, Oxford University Press. © Oxford University Press 2023.
DOI: 10.1093/oso/9780190845193.003.0003

identities of those whom they perceive as opponents. First, though, it is important to understand the key research, within the social sciences especially, that underpins that analysis. This chapter is consequently structured around three relevant areas: groomer and child target profiling (Section 3.2), participation frameworks involved in digital sexual grooming (Section 3.3), and the actual discourse tactics that groomers typically use (Section 3.4).

3.2 PROFILING OFFENDERS AND CHILD TARGETS OF DIGITAL SEXUAL GROOMING

There is substantial research, especially in psychology and criminology, into profiling child sexual offenders and their child targets according to various factors. For offenders, the research has derived typologies based on, among other, their use or otherwise of CSAM (e.g., Krone 2004; Elliot and Beech 2009), their either scheduling or buying cybersex with minors (e.g., De Hart et al. 2017), their seeking offline ("contact offenders") or online ("fantasy offenders") sexual climax (e.g., Briggs, Simon, and Simonsen 2011), and their motives (Gottschalk 2011; Webster et al. 2012; Martellozzo 2012; Seto 2019). Some studies have examined the gender and age of child sexual offenders, finding a marked prevalence of males in their 30s, 40s, and 50s (e.g., Kloess, Hamilton-Giachritsis, and Beech 2017).[1] And other studies have focused on their mental states, concluding that a number of these individuals suffer from different personality disorders and have a tendency to (self-)deception (e.g., Tan and Grace 2008). Regardless of their sociodemographic profile and mental state, though, digital sexual groomers' interactional competence is far from impaired. On the contrary, and as this and Chapter 4 will show, they are highly sophisticated discourse manipulators.

Compared to offender profiling, limited research has focused on child target profiling in digital sexual grooming. In terms of age and gender, 11- to 15-year-old girls are the most prevalent group (e.g., Kloess, Hamilton-Giachritsis, and Beech 2017).[2] Some studies have examined so-called vulnerability factors: that is, circumstances that increase a child's risk of being sexually groomed online, identifying temporary or long-term family problems and lack of adequate internet safety advice in school as being key (e.g., Whittle et al. 2014). Children with neurodiversities (e.g., autism) and/or physical disabilities (e.g., deafness) are also believed to be particularly vulnerable to digital sexual grooming (e.g., Nosek et al. 2001). According to the international charity Deafkids, for instance, deaf children are at least three times more likely to experience online sexual abuse and exploitation than hearing children.[3]

Children's behavior during grooming has been investigated, too, albeit much less than offender behavior. The focus has been on their use of e-safety strategies. For example, Kloess, Hamilton-Giachritsis, and Beech (2017) found that children adopt different discourse strategies to try to reject digital sexual grooming, including making excuses not to engage with the groomer via webcam and using relational work (often politeness strategies) to avoid verbal confrontation with their groomer. Other strategies include disclosing the ongoing abuse to family and friends and blocking or deleting the groomer's account (Quayle and Newman 2016). Lorenzo-Dus, Evans, and Mullineux-Morgan's (2023) analysis of children's language during digital sexual grooming reveals a continuum across three main categories that reflect interactional roles and levels of agency, ranging from commencing interactions with groomers and following the groomer's interactional lead to putting up resistance to groomers' interaction, including particular topics therein, typically sexual ones. The authors stress that, regardless of the level of interactional agency displayed in digital sexual grooming, the children remain targets of manipulation and should therefore never be blamed for their communicative behavior in such contexts.

In terms of actual disclosure, Katz and Barnetz (2016) find that, when talking about their experiences of being sexually groomed, children tend to focus both on the emotional rapport that the groomer exhibited with them and the threats made to disclose their "relationship" to family members. Children make fewer references to the actual sexual behaviors they were victims of, often resorting to vague language (Mullineux-Morgan and Lorenzo-Dus 2021). This further shows that children being sexually groomed struggle to realize that they are being abused by, rather than romantically engaged with, an adult. Not unlike victims of trauma more generally, children who have suffered or are suffering digital sexual grooming find it difficult to disclose their abuse (Hamilton-Giachritsis et al. 2021b).[4]

3.3 PARTICIPATION FRAMEWORKS IN DIGITAL SEXUAL GROOMING

Another research area of relevance to the analysis of digital sexual grooming as a discourse practice is the digital participation frameworks (see Chapter 2) that it relies on. These reflect and help shape offenders' styling of self and others during digital sexual grooming. Studies in this area cover issues such as how digital child sexual groomers navigate in and out of different participation frameworks aided, for example, by online platform migration and online–offline alternation.

Although some digital sexual groomers bring other adults into their interactions with the children they prey on, they typically engage in one-to-one (groomer–child) communication with them. Therefore, they often operate within a dialogic, production role (groomer)–reception role (child) participation framework. Additionally, digital sexual groomers are known to make online contact with multiple children simultaneously—the so-called *scatter-gun approach* introduced in Chapter 2. At this point, they may adopt what in broadcasting is described as "for-anyone-as-someone structures" (Scannell 2000); that is, a way of interacting in which each potential recipient of talk—viewers in broadcasting, child targets in digital sexual grooming—feels that this talk is addressed to him or her directly and individually, even though it is intended for anyone who happens to be tuned in (broadcasting) or for any child target with whom digital contact is attempted. Depending on the reaction that digital sexual groomers get to these initial "for-anyone-as-someone" interactions, they focus on one child or several children at a time to advance their manipulative goals through more tailor-made, one-to-one participatory structures and related self-styling acts. Chiang and Grant (2018), for instance, identified eight "personas" used by one single digital sexual groomer as he interacted with 20 different child targets. With 19 of them, the groomer adopted what the authors described as the identity of the "friend/boyfriend." With the remaining child, the groomer performed the identity of the "sexual pursuer/aggressor."

Also, and within the bounds of this one-to-one participation framework, digital sexual groomers may ask a child target to move to other digital platforms at particular points during the grooming interaction. They may gain access to a child via an online gaming platform or a mainstream social media platform, which they know operates some level of account monitoring for sexual content. At some point, for instance when seeking to share or request CSAM, they may move their digital interaction to other platforms where they know monitoring protocols are more relaxed or nonexistent. This *modus operandi* in part reflects limited online content legislation and is at the heart of societal attempts at increasing controls in this area. In the UK, for example, the National Society for the Prevention of Cruelty to Children (NSPCC) started a citizen campaign (#WildWestWeb) in 2018 that resulted in a petition to the UK government to introduce legislation that would make all social media platforms protect children from sexual abuse and exploitation online. The UK government subsequently incorporated such new legislation in its Online Harms White Paper (December 2020), and appointed an independent regulator (Ofcom[5]) with consequent ability—once the White Paper becomes a Bill—to place a legal duty of care on technology companies to protect children on their platforms.[6] And in Australia, the Criminal Code Act of 1899 (Qld), section 218B, and the Criminal Law Consolidation Act of 1935 (SA), sections 63A and 63B, for instance, criminalize as a sexual offence language use in itself, specifically requesting an indecent image of a child, provided that the person making the request believes that they are talking to a child.

Alongside platform migration during digital sexual grooming is the issue of online and offline movement, too. In criminology and psychology, this is often examined within broader "trajectories" of online child sexual offending, including grooming. This research partly overlaps with offender profiling studies (Section 3.2) because factors such as offenders' intended location—offline or online—of sexual climax may determine whether they start *and stay* online, whether they generate and/or bring CSAM from other Internet sources, and so forth. This research has also focused on the stimuli of these trajectories, seeking to determine, for instance, whether consumption of adult pornography may develop into consumption of CSAM and lead, in turn, to digital sexual grooming, with or without contact offending. The conclusions of all this research point to complex and partly overlapping trajectories of offending linked to offenders' underlying desires and histories, which are themselves multiple and shifting across time (Babchishin, Hanson, and Hermann 2011). That said, and importantly for the analysis of digital sexual groomers' styling practices in Chapter 4, all offenders entextualize (some of) their desires.

Moving beyond one-to-one participation frameworks, research has examined digital communities of child sexual offenders, which may also harbor sexual groomers. Extant research has seldomly used linguistics theories and methods, even though the members of these offender communities talk to each other extensively about their desires and intentions, disclose their (potential and/or actual) offending *modus operandi* and attitudes to security surveillance and risk, and seek advice and support on their activities (Holt et al. 2019; Chiang 2020, 2021; Marsh-Rossney and Lorenzo-Dus 2022). A pioneer linguistic study of offender communities online is Luchjenbroers and Aldridge-Waddon's (2011) analysis of email interaction between offenders, for which they applied the concepts of politeness (Brown and Levinson 1978/1987) and *community of practice* (Wenger 1998; Eckert 2006).[7] Their work found that the authors of the emails continually made linguistic choices that ran against "what mainstream society would expect in interactions between strangers" (Luchjenbroers and Aldridge-Waddon 2011, 37), such as the quick introduction of community of practice–appropriate but personally revealing assertions about themselves, alongside bald-on-record questions that invited equally explicit responses. Also, the topic of the compliments they paid to each other and their use of modals and hedges did not conform with mainstream usage among strangers but rather with that associated with "consolidating social relationships and mitigating possible face-threats" (2011, 37). In other words, these offenders' styling of themselves toward other members exhibited distinctive features that reflected and further constructed their community of practice.

Similarly, Chiang (2020) analyzed 71 posts from six child abuse Dark Net forums and found that their members followed strict rules, such as not divulging personal information. She also found that forum "newbies" regularly used distinct rhetorical moves, including expressing motivations for joining the community (e.g., showing interest in specific age groups or types of indecent child imagery); demonstrating affiliation with the interests and ideals of the community (e.g., by revealing that they had been passively present in the community and have now made a decision to become active); expressing appreciation—via compliments and gratitude statements—of the community generally and individual members thereof specifically; overtly referring to their newbie status, including by acknowledging lack of offending experience and thus requesting tolerance from the other members; demonstrating their added value to the community (e.g., offering indecent imagery); stating limitations, including apologizing for them; and seeking guidance about a particular offending-related problem, such as accessing children or seeking moral guidance. Moreover, Chiang's (2020) analysis revealed different combinations of moves and therefore the absence of a single newbie offender "home identity," as it were.

This research can usefully enrich the analysis of digital sexual groomers' styling of self and others, offering a kind of meta-perspective (the offenders') on the practice of digital sexual grooming, as next discussed.

3.4 THE PRACTICE OF DIGITAL SEXUAL GROOMING

Arguably most research into digital sexual grooming concerns its components, both what these comprise and their interrelations. This has resulted in the development of several models of digital sexual grooming that focus on groomer behavior. The component parts of these models generally include—under different labels (e.g., themes, tactics)—manipulative goals/interests such as developing the children's trust, separating them from their support networks, determining how likely they are to go along with the behavior being proposed to them, introducing sexual content, assessing risk of public exposure, and, in the case of so-called contact offenders, arranging offline contact for sexual purposes (see, e.g., O'Connell 2003; Williams, Elliott, and Beech, 2013; Van Gijn-Grosvenor and Lamb 2021; Winters, Kaylor, and Jeglic 2017; Kloess et al. 2017; Joleby et al. 2021).

This research has traditionally adopted content and thematic analysis frameworks. Linguistic analyses of offender behavior during digital sexual grooming are more recent phenomena (for an integrated analysis of groomer–child discourse in digital sexual grooming, see Lorenzo-Dus, Evans, and Mullineux-Morgan 2023). Yet groomers fulfill their abusive goals through language and other semiotic modes. Within extant research, Chiang and Grant (2017, 2018) used genre analysis to examine, respectively, 20 digital sexual grooming chat logs from Perverted Justice (2017) and one UK law enforcement transcript of an offender interacting with 20 children (2018). Their 2017 analysis identified 14 rhetorical moves used by groomers: greeting, maintaining conversation, meeting planning, reprimanding, sign-off, rapport, assessing likelihood and extent of engagement, assessing criteria fulfillment, assessing and managing risk, assessing role, sexual rapport, initiating sexual topics, maintaining/escalating sexual content, and immediate sexual gratification. These moves were also present in their 2018 analysis, which detected two additional moves: overt persuasion and extortion. The authors attributed the identification of these two new moves to the data source, which comprised of offender–child, rather than offender–decoy, chatlogs.

The first empirically derived model of digital sexual grooming *discourse* (Lorenzo-Dus, Izura, and Pérez-Tattam 2016) used a digital discourse analysis (Herring 2004, 2013) framework, with a focus on relational work (Locher and Watts 2008), to examine groomers' language use in 24 Perverted Justice chatlogs (c. 75,000 words). The analysis revealed six groomer tactics: access, deceptive trust development, sexual gratification, isolation, compliance testing, and approach. In subsequent studies, and using a CADS methodology, Lorenzo-Dus, Kinzel and Di Cristofaro (2020) and Lorenzo-Dus, Evans, and Mullineux-Morgan (2023) further developed the 2016 digital sexual grooming discourse model, respectively examining the entire Perverted Justice dataset and a corpus of law enforcement digital sexual grooming chatlogs (see Chapter 1). These analyses confirmed the regular presence in groomers' discourse of all but one of the tactics; namely, compliance testing, which designated groomers' checking on the likelihood that a child target may go along with whatever activity was proposed. Rather than functioning as a tactic in its own right, the analyses indicated that groomers' gauging of a child target's level of "acquiescence" happened throughout their grooming interaction, was aligned to all the groomer tactics, and could be operationalized in terms of facework therewith. The resulting model of digital sexual grooming discourse is schematically shown in Figure 3.1.

Access refers to groomers making initial digital contact with their child target, regardless of whether they are known to each other offline. It is facilitated by digital affordances and practices, such as liking and friendship requesting in social media or asking a child target to move to (higher) encryption platforms for the purposes of one-to-one interaction. Within the deceptive trust development tactic, groomers seek to hide their ulterior motive of wanting to engage the child in sexual activities by building a friendship and/or romantic relationship with them. This is entextualized by several sub-tactics, such as eliciting and sharing personal information, discussing activities and relationships, making small talk, and complimenting the target. Broome, Izura, and Davies (2020) raise the possibility that groomers' trust development may not be necessarily deceptive; that is, they may attempt to develop a relationship with a minor based on honest intentions—a possibility that clearly clashes with legal and moral norms in society but is nevertheless analytically viable.

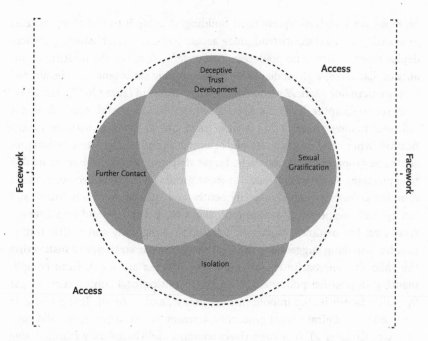

Figure 3.1 Digital sexual grooming discourse model.

Sexual gratification concerns groomer attempts to involve the target in sexual activities online and, in some cases, preparing them for sexual interaction offline. This is discursively realized by introducing linguistic and/or visual sexual content, overtly (explicit desensitization sub-tactic) and/or covertly (implicit desensitization sub-tactic). Sexual gratification may also include discursive reframing, whereby sexual activity between groomer and child is presented as beneficial to the latter. Isolation covers discursive work whereby the groomer distances the children they target from other meaningful people in their lives while concomitantly emphasizing the "specialness" and often secrecy of the digital sexual grooming relationship. This is done by arranging to talk to the target privately and alone, making sure she is unsupervised, and instructing her to delete any (digital) trace of her interaction with the groomer (physical isolation sub-tactic). It may also be done by attempting to become the child's confidant while severing—or at least weakening—her emotional ties with others, often through use of criticism directed at the groomer's perceived opponents. Further contact consists of groomers' attempts to secure a physical meeting for sexual purposes. If no contact offending is sought, such attempts are directed at continuing digital engagement.

The tactics that comprise the digital sexual grooming discourse model are nonsequential and highly overlapping, as Figure 3.1 shows. Thus, access provides a gateway to any tactic, rather than to a linear practice that may, for example, start with deceptive trust building, develop into isolation, and end in sexual gratification. Instead, once access has been established, groomers deploy these tactics in no predetermined order and, as per the multifunctionality of discourse, a given discourse fragment may simultaneously be aligned to more than one tactic. As noted in Lorenzo-Dus and Izura (2017), and as we shall see in Chapter 4, for instance, groomers' use of compliments does not only seek to develop the child's trust in them, but also to advance sexual gratification (when they concern sexually oriented topics) and isolation (when presented as groomer views about the target that others close to her are unable to appreciate). As Chapter 4 will also show, groomers' tactical discourse entails complex facework that pivots frequently and quickly between "nice" and "nasty" talk, respectively realized via discourse politeness and impoliteness strategies. For instance, digital sexual groomers regularly and swiftly transition from making suggestions (a negative politeness strategy) to instructing the child (an encroachment-oriented impoliteness strategy), from complimenting (a positive politeness strategy) to criticizing/blaming their target (a quality face-oriented impoliteness strategy), and so forth. This pivoting is illustrative of digital sexual groomers' attempt at manufacturing child consent (see Chapter 2). It is cognitively complex and rhetorically manipulative facework for anyone to process, let alone for a child trapped in an interactional relationship that carries significant power imbalance from the onset.

When examining the practice of digital sexual grooming, research has also focused on its duration. According to De Hart et al. (2017) grooming cases range from less than an hour to several months. In the entire Perverted Justice dataset, the chat logs span between 1 and 472 days, with an average of 25 days. However, this comes with a very high standard deviation: 46.1 days. In terms of actual interaction duration, the shortest chat log lasts 17 minutes and the longest 10,597 minutes—again the standard deviation is very high (1,246.46 minutes). Lorenzo-Dus and Kinzel (2019) and Kinzel (2021) used CADS methods to examine groomer language in the entire Perverted Justice dataset and identified a "fast grooming group" (from 17 to 299 minutes), whose language was more action-oriented (meeting, swapping inappropriate sexual images, etc.) and a "slow grooming group" (from 800 to 10,597 minutes), who talked more about internal processes (feelings, thoughts, desires, etc.). Additionally, the fast-grooming group made use of more sexually explicit terms than the slow grooming group, who used more relationship terms (e.g., missing, nonsexual endearment terms) than the fast-grooming group. A third group was also identified, in which grooming duration lasted between 300 and 799 minutes and whose language exhibited—cline-style—features from the fast and slow groups.[8]

Duration-related differences have also been identified in relation to specific speech acts. Using methods from corpus pragmatics, Kinzel (2021) identified request realization patterns used by offenders in the entire Perverted

Justice dataset. These differed according to the duration of the grooming chat-logs. In both the slow and fast grooming groups, politeness and impoliteness strategies were used within requesting sequences linked to sexual behaviors. However, the fast-grooming group used encroachment-oriented impoliteness strategies, typically threats, within their requests, whereas the slow-grooming group favored used of positive politeness strategies.

Lorenzo-Dus and Izura (2017) manually identified and examined all the complimenting sequences (over 1,000) within 68 Perverted Justice chatlogs of varying duration. The analysis revealed that all groomers favored use of sexually oriented compliment topics (e.g., about sexual organs) over nonsexually oriented ones (e.g., about personality). Yet it also revealed that frequency of use of sexually oriented compliments increased as grooming duration decreased. In other words, the shorter the grooming period, the more frequently groomers used sexually oriented compliments. The study found no duration-related differences regarding syntactic patterns for expressing compliments. Rather, groomers consistently relied on a reduced set of such patterns, favoring second-person compliments ("you are cute") over both first-person (e.g., "I love your face") and impersonal (e.g., "that's a sexy picture") compliments. As will be shown in Chapter 4, this focus on the target is one of the features of digital sexual groomers' self-styling through a stance of avidity.

"Cute" in the examples above is a typical instance of digital sexual groomers' use of vague language when communicating sexual intent. As mentioned earlier, many children fail to realize, for some time at least, the sexual—and hence abusive—intent behind their groomers' discourse. Groomers' use of vague language is a key contributor to this. Lorenzo-Dus and Kinzel (2021) examined groomers' vague language use in the entire Perverted Justice dataset.[9] A lexical frequency and dispersion analysis identified 17 vague language terms that most digital sexual groomers used frequently for communicating sexual intent. Through manual analysis of multiple extended concordances, these terms were aligned to different linguistic realization categories and pragmatic functions, as shown in Table 3.1.

Five linguistic realization categories featured in the digital sexual groomers' data: Approximator-Quality (*like, hold, fun, bed, feel, love, kiss*), Vague Category Identifier (*stuff, thing*), De-intensifier (*cute, pretty, sweet, nice*), General Verb (*do, get*), and Explicit-Vague Category Identifier (*sex stuff, sexual thing*). The Approximator-Quality category concerned referencing an inexact character-istic or condition. In the example in Table 3.1, the meaning in context of *like* in "So you like older guys" is that of being sexually attracted to rather than to be interested in older guys in a nonsexual way. Use of the verb "to like," which can cover both meanings, is not only manipulative toward the child but also geared against potential prosecution charges—the groomers may argue that the latter meaning, which carries neither moral nor legal risks for them as adults, is the one intended.

Table 3.1 VAGUE LANGUAGE IN GROOMERS' DISCOURSE (ADAPTED FROM LORENZO-DUS AND KINZEL 2021)

Linguistic realization category	Pragmatic function	Terms	Illustrative example
Approximator – Quality	Approximation	*like, hold, fun, bed, feel, love, kiss*	So you *like* older guys?
Vague Category Identifier	Avoidance	*stuff, thing*	But I'll teach you about foreplay and other *stuff* if you wanna learn that.
Explicit-Vague Category Identifier	Partial avoidance	*sex stuff, sexual thing*	And do you want to do the *sex thing*?
De-intensifier	Downtoning	*cute, pretty, sweet, nice*	Like I said before you are young but you are also *cute* if I may say so.
General Verb	Avoidance	*do, get*	Do you want to just *do* touchy feely stuff, maybe take some things off?

Two of the vague language terms in the dataset were used frequently to connote sexual activity: the Vague Category Identifiers *stuff* and *thing*. In the example in Table 3.1, "other stuff" helps the digital sexual groomer to avoid specifying sexual actions that are linked to an antecedent—the noun "foreplay"—that does denote sexual intent. Although foreplay can be sexually explicit, the activity referenced through it takes place before the sexual act. The groomer may therefore manipulatively use it to mitigate the potential face-threat of seeking to engage a minor in illegal sexual activity ("foreplay and other stuff").

As for the De-intensifier category, it comprised four adjectives (*cute, sweet, pretty,* and *nice*), the evaluative force of which is not in the upper limit of a given quality (beauty, likeability); that is to say, they are not superlative adjectives. Nor do they carry sexual meaning linked to either physical appearance or personality (unlike, for example, *hot* or *sexy*). This may explain their being used to mitigate the potential face threat of complimenting targets on sexual attributes.

Within the General Verb category, the verbs "to do" and "to get" were used frequently by groomers to refer to different sexual actions. In the example in Table 3.1, *do* is part of a verbal phrase ("do + touchy feely stuff"), which avoids the use of a sexually explicit noun (e.g., sex) and is further mitigated via the hedge "just." Finally, the Vague Category Identifier category entailed groomers' use of a vague term (*stuff, thing*) followed by a sexually explicit noun or adjective (*sex, sexual*). The resulting collocations ("*sex stuff*," "*sexual thing*") were thus both explicit (the sexual intent was overtly expressed) yet vague (the actual action—having sex—was avoided through nominalization and made unspecific).

In terms of frequency of use, Quality-Approximators constituted the main vague language category in the dataset, followed by Vague Identifiers and De-identifiers. Approximating, avoiding, and down-toning sexual intent were—in decreasing frequency order—the three pragmatic functions that these terms fulfilled. The picture that emerged from Lorenzo-Dus and Kinzel's (2021) analysis was clearly of manipulative discourse that can be very confusing for children. Groomers regularly resort to vague language terms to communicate sexual intent covertly, couching it in terms that make interpretation of friendship and romance likely, which in turn helps to develop trust in their deceiving goals. This is particularly concerning because, coupled with groomers' frequent pivoting between "nice" and "nasty" talk, it may trigger or increase children's feelings of self-blame—in addition to those of hurt, disappointment, trauma, and so forth—once they realize that sexual intent had been communicated to them, even if covertly and via a mixture of coercion and fake free will at times.

3.5 CONCLUSION

This chapter has identified key findings to inform the discourse analysis of digital sexual groomers' styling practices that follows in Chapter 4. Research into sociodemographic (e.g., age, gender), psychological (e.g., personality disorders for offenders), and contextual (e.g., family support for children targeted for sexual grooming) characteristics has advanced the area of offender and child target profiling. In a similar vein, research has developed important lines of enquiry into the trajectories of digital sexual offending, including grooming. Findings therein confirm the complex ways in which, among other, offenders gain digital access to children on an individual basis and/or en masse, as well as avoid being caught by law enforcement, including by moving across social media platforms. As noted, these findings reflect and mould digital sexual groomers' identity projections and are thus relevant from a discourse analys perspective.

Finally, it is important to appreciate the growing body of linguistic research into the different components of digital sexual grooming as a discourse practice. These focus on groomer tactics, such as deriving sexual gratification from their online interaction with children, isolating them physically and affectively, developing a sense of trust in the groomers, and seeking further contact, online and offline, with them. This scholarship has also discerned some cross-tactic discourse features, such as groomers' use of vague language to mask sexual intent and their fast and frequent pivoting between "nice" (discursively polite) and "nasty" (discursively impolite) talk. Furthermore, digital sexual groomers have been found to display no one single identity, instead crafting different self-styles. And it is to this last aspect—identity and styling—that Chapter 4 now turns, examining the stances that digital sexual groomers take when styling their own identities and those of their targets and perceived opponents.

NOTES

1. This corresponds with the gender demographics in the datasets examined in Chapter 4, which is why, unless otherwise stated, throughout the book digital sexual groomers are referenced through masculine pronouns when singular pronominal forms are used.
2. This also corresponds with the gender demographics in the datasets examined in this book. Unless otherwise stated, singular feminine pronominal forms are therefore used to refer to the target of digital sexual grooming.
3. https://deafkidzinternational.org/news/. Accessed June 2022.
4. https://www.theguardian.com/society/2019/jul/01/you-grow-up-hating-yourself-why-child-abuse-survivors-keep-and-break-their-silence. Accessed December 2021.
5. https://www.ofcom.org.uk/home. Accessed June 2022.
6. https://www.nspcc.org.uk/support-us/campaigns/wild-west-web/. Accessed January 2022. During the second half of 2022, in the UK, a new prime minister and government mean that the legislation's passage through parliament has paused. See https://bills.parliament.uk/bills/3137.
7. A community of practice designates "a collection of people who engage on an ongoing basis in a common endeavour" (Eckert 2006, 683). Membership of a given community of practice depends on expertise: to belong, one must acquire experience in the subject matter that the community revolves around. This makes it easier for members to recognize other members quickly and, importantly, also to exclude nonpractitioners (Wenger 2004).
8. "Fast" and "slow" designate cutoff points for duration in relation to a corpus of a given size, rather than being evaluative labels.
9. The analysis drew on Zhang's (2013, 88) definition of vague language as "a linguistic unit (word, phrase or utterance) that has an unspecified meaning boundary, so that its interpretation is elastic in the sense that it can be stretched or shrunk according to the strategic need of communication."

CHAPTER 4

"You Are Like My Only Friend, Idc If You Are 12"

Digital Sexual Grooming Discourse

4.1 INTRODUCTION

This chapter builds on the key ideas, concepts, and awareness, teased out in Chapter 3, of the rich and diverse body of underpinning research into digital sexual grooming. It examines the positionings that digital sexual groomers adopt when interacting with their target. The overall goal of these positionings is to manipulate their target into believing that they are interested in developing a healthy—rather than sexually abusive—relationship with her. As foreshadowed in Chapters 1 and 2, the data that inform this analysis comes from Perverted Justice and law enforcement chatlogs, and the analysis itself is undertaken through the interlinked notions of style, stance, and facework. The chapter examines digital sexual groomers' stance-taking acts when styling themselves (Section 4.2), their target (Section 4.3), and those individuals whom they perceive to pose a challenge to their chances of "grooming success" (i.e., their opponents; Section 4.4).

4.2 DIGITAL SEXUAL GROOMERS' SELF-STYLING

As introduced in Chapter 1, digital groomers' styling of their identity emerges out of repeated use of semiotic resources that index stances of expertise, openness, and avidity. Within digital sexual grooming, these stances can be further and more specifically characterized in terms of sexual expertise (Section 4.2.1), vulnerability openness (Section 4.2.2), and target avidity

Digital Grooming. Nuria Lorenzo-Dus, Oxford University Press. © Oxford University Press 2023.
DOI: 10.1093/oso/9780190845193.003.0004

(Section 4.2.3). Their combined effect is that of presenting an identity that may credibly convey a sense of groomer trustworthiness and the "specialness" of the groomer–target relationship.

4.2.1 Sexual expertise

By definition, (digital) sexual grooming takes place between an adult—who is sexually experienced—and a child, who has significantly less or no sexual experience. As discussed in Chapter 2, this means that digital sexual grooming always entails power asymmetry: specifically, the grooming adult has more power than the groomed child. Sexual experience is something that these adults use as a proxy for expertise. In (digital) sexual grooming, the likelihood that sexual expertise stance-taking will hit the mark increases given (pre-) adolescents' natural sexual curiosity and that they look to develop their sexual knowledge and competence through multiple sources (see, e.g., Ybarra and Mitchell 2005; McGeeney and Hanson 2017). Interacting with someone who claims to possess that knowledge and competence—and speaks about it positively—may make them feel more confident about their own level of knowledge and competence and/or less inadequate about their lack thereof during this period of normal sexual development. As discussed in Chapter 3, children's concomitant potential vulnerabilities, such as lack of family support, may further increase the manipulative potential of this stance in (digital) sexual groomers' discourse.

Digital sexual groomers' self-styling via a stance of sexual expertise helps them to perform the sexual gratification grooming tactic primarily. This is because the interactions that introduce and discuss such expertise—and more generally sexual talk—both provide them with sexual pleasure (Lorenzo-Dus, Izura, and Tattam 2016; see also Extract 4.1) and, as discussed in Chapter 3, support child target desensitization to sexual content. Indexing of this stance relies on "truth claims," the sexual content of which may be explicitly stated and /or implied, of which Extracts 4.1 and 4.2 are respectively typical.

Extract 4.1

[The four turns included here appear consecutively in the chatlog from which the extract comes. They are interleaved by minimal responses (e.g., "k," "yes") from the target, which have been omitted. G = groomer]

01	G312	my private is called a *dick* or *cock* yours is a *pussy* or *cunt*
02		do you knw those
03		when you want *sex* it is sometimes called *fuck*
04		what is that little nub in your *pussy* what do ppl call it

In lines 01 and 03, G312 repeatedly uses explicit sexual vocabulary: seven sexual terms (italicized in the extract), including slang and taboo variants. This serves to desensitize his target to sex. Additionally, he frames his expertise stance as educational: he is the teacher, and his target is his pupil. G312 references two prototypical teacher activities: imparting knowledge and checking knowledge uptake. He imparts knowledge via performing concept definition, which he words both in interpersonal terms (first-person . . . second-person singular pronoun—"my private is called . . . yours is . . . ," line 01) and in generic terms ("when you want . . . it is sometimes called . . . ," line 03— where the adverb "sometimes" indexes the generic sense of "you"). And he checks knowledge uptake, in line 02, via a directly addressed question: "do you knw those." In line 04, checking knowledge uptake is reinforced through question repetition, moving from a directly experiential question ("what is . . . in your. . . . "—note the use of the second-person pronoun) to a generic one ("what do ppl call it"—use of third-person plural generic referent people, abbreviated as "ppl"). Both questions act as requests that the target engage in explicit sex talk and, therefore, support G312's sexual gratification tactic. They also provide an example of the kind of fixated discourse (Egan, Hoskinson, and Shewan 2011) that sexual groomers often deploy, whereby they pursue topics insistently—here, a sexual topic—without a similar level of interest from their target.

Digital sexual groomers' use of vague language is, as discussed in Chapter 3, commonplace in their discourse. Extract 4.2 illustrates this in the context of groomers' stance-taking as sexual experts. The extract includes four examples from a single groomer (G041) within a chatlog spanning 13 hours of interaction over 38 consecutive days. The chat log contained 78 instances in which G041 performs this stance in four complementary ways: via references to age or adulthood (37 instances in the chatlog—see reference in 4.2.1 to his being "older, and wiser"), via "factual" assertions about being sexually active (21 examples in the chatlog—see, in 4.2.2, relating to the practice of oral sex), via future-oriented statements about enjoyment derived from the area of expertise being claimed (8 examples in the chatlog—see, in 4.2.3, his reference to sex being "fun," despite some reservation—"dirty but . . . "), and via offers of advice or support (12 examples in the chatlog—see, in 4.2.4, sympathy about inexperience and potential peer pressure—"most everyone does it, so dont feel bad if you do it").

Extract 4.2

(4.2.1) well sweetie i am older, and wiser. could teach you loads . . . umm:-)

(4.2.2) its all in how you use your mouth and tongue in both

(4.2.3) [referring to the act of sex] well, dirty but fun might be fun

(4.2.4) well most everyone does it, so dont feel bad if you do it . . . ok?

The 78 occurrences of G041 performing a sexual expertise stance were evenly distributed across the chatlog, with a peak toward the sixth and seventh hour (i.e., in the middle). Throughout the grooming interaction, he was thus able to derive sexual gratification—note, for instance, the sentence-final para-linguistic features indexing sexual enjoyment from the very reference to his sexual expertise (". . . umm:-)," 4.2.1). Moreover, in so doing, he continuously desensitized his target to sexuality, introducing the possibility of minor–adult sexual activity. In the examples included in Extract 4.2 this was implicitly ver-balized via use of the vague language approximators "loads," for sexual acts (4.2.1), and "in both," for oral and anal sex (4.2.2). It was also implied through subject elision (in 4.2.3—no explicit reference to what "might be fun") and repetition of the general verb to do ("do[es;] it") for having sex (4.2.4).

The educational frame supporting groomers' sexual expertise stance-taking often relies on the discursive construction of interpersonal closeness and sympathy, which complement groomers' self-styling as individuals who are avidly keen about their target (see Section 4.3). Note, in 4.2.1, G041's use of the term of endearment "sweetie" and, in 4.2.4, his seeking to address pos-sible reticence from his target by indirectly attributing to her a stance of "nor-mality" for sexually inexperienced individuals ("well most everyone does it"), before—and logically ("so")—instructing her not to "feel bad" about what is illegal: sexual abuse. He mitigates the face-threatening force of this impera-tive through adding a hypothetical clause ("if you do it . . .") and a turn-ending interrogative tag ("ok") that seemingly yield actional power to the target and seek interactional agreement, respectively.

4.2.2 Vulnerability openness

Vulnerability openness is the second stance that digital sexual groomers reg-ularly adopt for self-styling. Communicatively, this translates into extensively talking about themselves and, more specifically, into disclosing negative in-ternal states, especially of loneliness and fear, as indexes of their vulnera-bility. This stance is particularly effective in groomers' attempts at developing trust for ulterior motives, be that extracting details about the child target and her support environment, desensitizing her to sex, and so forth. This is be-cause the stance is predicated on the principle of mutual reciprocity in inter-personal/intergroup communication—something that digital environments generally accelerate (e.g., Tardy and Dindia 2006; Barak and Gluck-Ofri 2007).

Mutual reciprocity designates a process whereby one's verbal disclo-sure causes one's interactant(s) to disclose, too, as part of a cycle of disclo-sure that supports the development of interpersonal/intergroup relations. Interactants who disclose reciprocally report greater liking, closeness, per-ceived similarity, and enjoyment of the interaction than those who do not

(Sprecher et al. 2013). Additionally, self-disclosure of negative emotions and experiences signals trust by the individual revealing them (Bazarova 2012); their recipients feel, as a result, encouraged to reciprocate—a process known as "trust attraction hypothesis" (Fisher 1984). Chiu, Seigfried-Spellar, and Ringenberg (2018), for instance, found that digital sexual groomers, especially those interested in offline contact with their target, succeed in developing trust with their targets by igniting cycles of reciprocal self-disclosure that favor negative emotions. Children who feel lonely, are shy or may be traumatized in some form are particularly vulnerable to these cycles, feeling attracted to individuals who they think share and understand their negative emotions and experiences.

Digital sexual groomers' reliance on self-disclosing talk is evident from, among other, their use of social deixis. Table 4.1 lists the 5 social deixis forms included within the 100 most frequent and dispersed words in the entire Perverted Justice dataset. As introduced in Chapter 1, DP_{Norm} was used as the lexical dispersion measure for this analysis.

The closer to zero the DP_{Norm} value of a word is in Table 4.1, the greater the number of groomers in the dataset who used that word frequently. Rather than absolute values, which are dependent—among other factors—on word class type and discourse genre, the figures in Table 4.1 are interesting on three comparative accounts. First, they include primarily first- ("I," "me," "my," and "we") and second-person ("your") deixis forms, but not third-person deictic forms (such as "they," "she," "he"). Second, first-person deictic forms display the highest dispersion values; out of the 5 deictic forms in Table 4.1, the 4 first-person deictics have DP_{Norm} rankings/values that are higher/closer to zero than the only second-person deictic listed ("your"). This supports the findings of a comparative analysis of the language used by digital sexual groomers in the Perverted Justice dataset vis-à-vis that used by a control group comprising adults in online dating chatlogs. The study found that the former group used first-person (singular and plural) pronouns more frequently than the latter group (Baryshevtsev and McGlone 2018). Third, Table 4.1 also shows that first-person, singular deictic forms are more highly dispersed than their plural counterparts—the dispersion ranking for "I" (first), "me" (eighth), and "my" (thirtieth) is higher than for "we" (forty-ninth). This points toward

Table 4.1 SOCIAL DEICTIC FORMS WITH HIGH FREQUENCY AND DISPERSION VALUES IN DIGITAL SEXUAL GROOMING

	I	me	my	we	your
DP_{Norm} value	0.120109	0.177583	0.243655	0.295917	0.369507
Dispersion rank (1st-100th)	1st	8th	30th	49th	82nd

Table 4.2 HIGHLY FREQUENT/DISPERSED FIRST-PERSON SINGULAR PRO-
NOUNS AND THE REFERENTIAL ORIENTATION OF THEIR TOP 20 COLLOCATES

	Referential orientation	
	Target	Groomer
I	u; you	know; am do; like; have; want; will; can; was
me	u; you; tell; want; like; let; call; do	?
my	u; you; girl; princess; love; baby	cock; dick

self-orientation in digital sexual groomers' discourse, which may support narcissistic personality profiles. All in all, then, the digital sexual groomers whose
language was examined wrote more about themselves as individuals ("I," "me,"
and "my") than about both their relationship with their target ("we") and their
target ("your").

By looking at the collocational behavior of first-person singular deixis
forms, we can begin to discern a more nuanced picture. Dice coefficient was
the metric used for collocational analysis (see Chapter 1). In Table 4.2 the top
20 collocates (in italics) for the first-person singular deictic forms "I," "me,"
and "my" are grouped according to whether they referenced the target (e.g.,
"my *girl*") or the groomer (e.g., "I *like*"). The referential orientation of collocates was determined by examining manually 50 randomly selected concordance lines of each of these collocations in the dataset.

Table 4.2 shows, overall, a balance between groomer and target referential orientation. When referring to the target, "I" and "my" collocate with the
second-person pronoun ("*u*"; "*you*"), discursively constructing a sense of togetherness. They also collocate with four terms of endearment "*girl*," "*love*,"
"*princess*," and "*baby*." These collocates are not sexually explicit. Instead, they
frame the groomer–target relationship in terms of affective relationships and
possibly romantic love. When referring to the groomer, "me," "I," and "my"
display different collocational patterns. In the case of "me," the collocate "?"
corresponds to questions about primarily the groomer–target relationship,
such as how the target feels about it as a whole or specific aspects thereof. In
the case of "my," the collocates are two sexually explicit slang terms for penis.
In the case of "I," collocates comprise a combination of vague, de-lexicalized
verbs (to be ("am"; "was"), to do and to have), modal verbs that signal opportunity ("can") or future action ("will") and verbs that relay internal states
("want," "know"). Overall, there is a combination of groomer–target togetherness and self-oriented discourse.

The above analysis illustrates the salience of self-talk in digital sexual
groomers' discourse. But what does this self-talk entail? Loneliness and fear

are the internal states that digital sexual groomers communicatively tend to open up about the most in the datasets examined. Let us consider them in more detail through two typical examples: Extracts 4.3 and 4.4, respectively.

Extract 4.3

[The extract reproduces relevant parts of the opening 6 minutes of a digital sexual grooming chat log between groomer G241 and target T241. Their interaction spanned 68 minutes of interaction over a 24-hour period.]

01	G241	Sup
02	T241	hey how ru/14 m [town name] u?
03	G241	not bad /oooh /olllld [town name] here/ sorry about that
04	T241	srry bout whut?
05	G241	that i message you and you're 14 and i'm old/didn't mean to bother ya
06	T241	its all good/just moved here don't kno ne1/how old is old?
07	G241	39
08	T241	fuck that aint old like 60 is old
09	G241	haha/i know/i really don't know a lot of people around here either
10		i've worked here for like 13 years
11		and i've lived here for like four
12	T241	rlly where u work at?
13	G241	and i just haven't had opportunities to meet people/i'm a school
14		administrator in [town name]
15		[G241 and T241 continue to share experience of moving to new place]
23	G241	i kinda feel badly that i even suggested that we chill out/i don't
24		want you to think i'm a wacko like that
25		[G241 discloses his preferences for the "thing 2 do with guyz". These include
26		referring—over six consecutive turns—to "cuddle," "suck," "make out," "suck," "get
27		sucked," "and the rest."]
28	G241	u?

In line 06, T241 volunteers a personal situation that implies loneliness: "just moved here don't kno ne1." G241 reciprocates. He discloses that, while he has worked in the city for "13 years" (line 10) and he's "lived here for like four [years]" (line 11), he "just ha[s]n't had the opportunity to meet people" (line 13). By describing meeting others as "opportunity" and noting twice the length of time during which he has not managed to take that opportunity, G241 evaluates his current social situation negatively. In doing so, he aligns himself with—actually mirroring—T241's prior self-disclosure statement. T241's "don't kno ne1" (line 06) is matched by G241's "i really don't know a lot of people around here either" (line 09)—note the cohesion particle "either," which links his turn to T241's, as well as the intensifier adverb "really" preceding his claim that he does not know many people. Yet T241 and G241's circumstances—as constructed in the extract—are far from comparable: T241 has "just move here" (line 06); G241 has "worked here for like 13 years" (line 10). Attempts of this ilk, whereby original disclosers use parts of their recipients' information either to increase the number of commonalities or reveal further related experiences, are known to intensify homophily bias and thus aid in relationship-building and trust in digital sexual grooming (Brechwald and Prinstein 2011).

Extract 4.3 may appear rather mundane in terms of self-disclosure as it principally revolves around exchange of limited personal details—namely, age, sex, and location (town)—but the goals are, of course, far from innocent. Leaving aside the risks involved in revealing one's offline location to a stranger within the opening turns (01–03) of a digital interaction, the extract shows that seeking reciprocity advances digital sexual groomers' goals of deceptively developing the target's trust and desensitizing her to sexual content.

In digital sexual grooming, reciprocal disclosure of age, sex, and location often precedes that of offline name. For the latter, usernames are typically used instead, such as "princess12" or "i_8u_raw" for, respectively, target and groomer. In Extract 4.3, line 02, T241's disclosure of these three personal details ("14 m [town]") enables G241 to broach the topic of age-inappropriate relationships from the outset. He does so progressively, moving from defining the purpose of that relationship as simply making digital contact ("message you," line 05) to suggesting a generic sociability purpose ("we chill out," line 23). In both cases, G241 makes it plain that there is something not right about the "relationship," which indicates his expectation that T241 may be either noncommittal to or disalign from his positioning. In line 03, this is weightily loaded as banter through exaggerated surprise and regret through use of expressive typography (repetition of the character "o" in "oooh" and "l" in "olllld"). This is interleaved with an explicit apology ("sorry about that"), which marks a keying shift to serious talk. There is no explicit anaphoric referent for "that" in G241's apology, which triggers T241's request for clarification in line 04 ("srry bout wut?"). This offers G241 the (expected) opportunity to introduce their age difference: "and you're 14 and i'm old," adding an implicit apology ("didn't mean to bother ya"). As the degree of imposition caused by G241 is at this stage minimal (sending an initial three-character message "Sup," line 01), his double apology (lines 03 and 05) is unsurprisingly accepted by T241: "its all good" (line 06).

When G241 next introduces the topic of his developing an age-inappropriate relationship with T241, he maintains the serious keying to express regret: "i kinda feel badly that i even suggested that we chill out" (line 23). Note that, at this point, the potential degree of imposition on T241 remains ostensibly minimal as it involves "chill[ing] out"—an activity that, based on the preceding interaction, would simply entail chatting online. Note, too, G241's use of the illocutionary force devices "*kinda* feel badly" and "*even* suggested," which respectively continue to index regret and empha-size G241's feelings toward his suggestion to "chill out." G241's supportive grounding move for his performance of regret in lines 23–24 reinstates keying as banter: "i don't want you . . . a wacko like that." The colloquial, derogatory word "wacko" to describe himself indexes playfulness between him and his target while working on the impression of a developing rela-tionship in which he both cares about T241's appraisal of him and feels com-fortable enough to volunteer a possible negative self-evaluation. It is worth reminding ourselves here that the performance of self-deprecation humor is aligned to relatability and, through that, to increased digital media influence (Chapter 2). The specific referent for "chill[ing] out" is not explicated at this point. The first time G241 is specific about what he means by it comes later in the chatlog (not reproduced in Extract 4.3 for space reasons), and, at this point, he denies that it involves sex. Yet, within a couple of minutes of this, and over 6 consecutive turns, he discloses the referent in terms of his prefer-ences for the "thing 2 do with guyz": "cuddle"/"suck"/"make out"/"suck"/"get sucked"/"and all the rest." These sexually explicit turns precede a request for mutual reciprocity from T241: "u?." Such quick transitioning from nonsexual to sexual content is not unusual in digital sexual groomers' manipulative discourse geared toward balancing trust development and sexual gratifica-tion goals.

The other negative emotion that digital sexual groomers recurrently self-disclose as part of their vulnerability openness stance-taking is fear, some-times portrayed as cautiousness or risk-aversion. This typically supports their isolation tactic use, specifically in terms of seeking to ascertain how likely the child target is to keep their "relationship" hidden from others, including law enforcement. Let us consider Extract 4.4.

Extract 4.4

[The extract corresponds to the last 20 minutes of a grooming chatlog span-ning across 11 days and comprising approximately 7 hours of interaction. The groomer (G056) has arranged to meet his target (T056) at her home to have sex.]

01	G056	I have too much to lose by getting caught doing this. I have had 2nd
02		thoughts.. I'm still not trusting, and I just don't know if it is OK,
03		Please dont' stop talking, and maybe someday we can really do this.
04		Id love to come over there, and feel you as muchas you want to feel
05		me . . . but I cant . . . at least right now.
06	T056	:(thought u was just playin wit me k

07	G056	no Im serious.. it could wreck my life . . . oh but I would love to make
08		love to you. but Im scared that your neigbors would see my car, your
09		mother would come home early . . . would you like to talk with me.
10		I'll send my muber . . . *[clarification of misspelling 'number' as 'muber']*
11	T056	mom wont and neighbors live down the hill behind us/dont leave
12		brb gotta p
13	G056	and your not a highland cop, and my career wont go down the
14		drain/you might have to p, I need to get laid
15		*[Description of what he'll do sexually when he gets to her home, and of their "emo-*
16		*tional connection"]*
17	G056	kind of scared abut coming over, but im coming

In Extract 4.4 G056 explicitly discloses that he feels "scared" twice (line 08, line 17) and he refers three times to the risks of his traveling to meet T056: "I have too much to lose by getting caught doing this" (line 01), "Im serious.. it could wreck my life" (line 07), "that your neigbors would see my car, your mother would come home early . . ." (lines 08–09). G056 also talks about the consequences of his being deceived by T056 being "a highland cop" (line 13): "my career wont go down the drain" (line 13). His repetitions and insistence are indicative of fixated discourse, in this case linked to risk assessment regarding both T056's physical isolation from others (will T056 be alone in the house when he visits?; will he be able to park his car without being seen by T056's neighbors?) and the extent of T056 "compliance" with his proposed behavior (here, secrecy).

As noted in Chapter 2, trust and risk are flip sides of the same coin. Extract 4.4 is typical of a strategic reversal of expected roles about adult–minor relationships within the trust–risk coin such that it is the adult whose safety is constructed as being at stake. G056's risk assessment in Extract 4.4 makes use of scalar "push-pull" structures, respectively blending assertiveness and tentativeness as regards his goal to meet his child target offline for sexual abuse (see Chapter 1). In broadcast news, the context in which the "push-pull" term was first coined, push-pull structures work as a rhetorical means of presenting content compellingly to one's audience. "[A] strong assertion will be 'pushed' or promoted to pander to perceived audience demands for entertainment, only to be almost immediately downgraded or 'pulled' to be seen to adhere to journalistic principles of facticity. Alternatively hedged statements will be upgraded with an assertive 'push'" (Montgomery 2007, 126).

In Extract 4.4, traveling to meet T056 and fear of being caught when doing so are assertively and tentatively presented, respectively supporting groomer tactics of sexual gratification and deceptive trust development. Thus, in lines 01–02, G056 asserts that he has "had 2nd thoughts" (i.e., he is not meeting

T056), explaining his reason in terms of lack of trust in T056 ("I'm still not trusting"). His seeming withdrawal from previously made plans to meet physically to have sex with T056 is next hedged or pulled: "maybe someday we can really do this" (line 03). Immediately, though, G056 introduces sexual content in volitional terms ("Id love to come over there, and feel you," line 04) that presuppose commonality ("as much as you want to feel me," lines 04–05)—that is, he delivers a pushed assertion. Yet, this is pulled straightaway ("but I cant," line 05), before being pushed again, this time via use of ellipsis punctuation (". . . ," line 05) and hedging ("at least," line 04) regarding the time of their meeting ("right now," line 05).

G056's to-and-froing continues throughout the extract: "no Im serious . . . oh but I would love to . . . but Im scared . . . [still] I'll send my [number] . . . and your not . . . and my career wont . . . scared about . . . but im. . . ." During it, sexual content is at times abruptly introduced, which suggests G056's frustration with the situation, even though he is responsible for it. For instance, in lines 11–12, T056 interrupts their messaging briefly with the initialism "brb" (be right back), asking G056 to stay connected ("don't leave") and offering a reason for the interruption ("gotta p"). G056's reply continues his previous turn regarding his fear that T056 may be deceiving him and questions her stated reason ("you might have to p"—note the choice of the hypothetical "might") before bluntly notching up the sexual tone of their interaction: "I need to get laid" (line 14), which is firmly anchored in the present of the grooming relationship and worded in need terms. His statement no longer presents sexual behavior as shared volition—instead, individual need is overtly asserted, and the register is vulgar. This shift in register becomes the tipping point of a sexually explicit description of his plans, which he justifies in terms of their "emotional connection" (lines 15–16) and concludes with another pull ("kind of scared..")—push ("but im coming") structure (line 17).

Regardless of whether vulnerability openness arises from feelings of loneliness/fear or any other negative inner states, digital sexual groomers use this stance to manipulate their targets' emotions, often seeking to guilt-trip them. An extreme, though by no means rare, case in point is their disclosure of suicidal thoughts and intentions, for which they make their target feel responsible. The following examples are illustrative of this form of emotional blackmail. They are extracted from a single law enforcement digital sexual grooming chatlog.

Extract 4.5

[The examples occur after the child target bravely expresses her intention to end contact with the groomer (G18) by blocking his digital account from her social media contacts.]

4.5.1 If you block me, I blame all this on me

4.5.2 I want to be friends with you still. I know I have issues but I'm trying to sort it out for you. You are like my only friend, idc if you are 12. Without you I would end up taking my life. I'm sorry for everything you will always be in my heart and mind. I will always remember you. You gorgeous, most wonderful girl.

4.5.3 If I wasn't alive, you would have been happier

4.5.4 If I die I want to die with you in my heart and mind

4.5.5 Before I end my life for good I want to ask you a question and favor

4.5.6 If it makes you happy then I'll be happy to end my life

4.5.7 If you go I go

G18's self-disclosure of the intention to commit suicide as a reaction to his target's communicating her own intention to block him digitally entails persistent emotional blackmail, which bears the markers of discourse harassment and clearly fits the characterization of digital sexual grooming as coercive manipulation (see Chapter 2). His self-disclosure seeks to trigger in the target sympathy and reconsideration by professing vulnerability through social isolation ("You are like my only friend," example 4.5.2) and acknowledgment of wrongdoing ("I blame all this on me," example 4.5.1; and "I know I have issues . . . I'm sorry for everything," example 4.5.2). His two-part wrongdoing statement in example 4.5.2 doubles up as, respectively, an implicit and explicit apology, yet the behavior he is apologizing for is stated through vague language: "issues" and "everything." Also, G18's self-disclosure is accompanied by repeated expression of strong friendship and romantic love for his target: "I want to be friends with you still," "you will always be in my heart and mind. I will always remember you" (example 4.5.2). The emotional blackmail, of course, results from making a tragic outcome of his negative feelings—suicide—both his own fault, as per reference to his wrongdoing, and yet also contingent on the child's decision and happiness, as per his repeated hypothetical "if" (examples 4.5.1, 4.5.3, 4.5.4, 4.5.6, and 4.5.7) and adverbial ("Without you I would. . . ," example 4.5.2; "Before I . . . ," example 4.5.5) clauses. The pressure on the child being groomed here is considerable, and it comes from G18's insistence in his intention to commit suicide, even if there are clear contradictions within his logic. Thus, for instance, in example 4.5.2 he both repeatedly states that he intends to end his life if she withdraws from him and commits to staying alive when stating that she "will always be in [his] heart and mind," that he "will always remember [her]."

4.2.3 Target avidity

The third stance that digital sexual groomers regularly take when self-styling is avidity, specifically extreme keenness on their target. This stance is chiefly indexed by facework toward their target that simultaneously draws on politeness (positive and negative strategies) and impoliteness. The co-occurrence of negative and positive politeness is characteristic of interactional contexts that are oriented toward face enhancement between individuals, which is clearly an important factor in digital sexual grooming as a practice of manipulation that seeks to convey the impression that the targets' interests are at the heart of the groomers' behaviors (see Chapter 2). As for the co-occurrence of politeness and impoliteness, this features in several institutional genres in which disagreement/confrontation is commonplace but not necessarily sanctioned. In news interviews and parliamentary debates, for instance, negative politeness and impoliteness often go hand in hand (Harris 2001; Pérez de Ayala 2001). This is not the case in digital sexual grooming, where there are no extant institutional expectations. The frequent pivoting of "nice" and "nasty" talk—indeed, the regular co-occurrence of politeness and impoliteness therein—is thus worth a close look.

Digital sexual groomers often address their target's positive face needs by offering gifts, which expectedly come with strings attached and therefore constitute instances of emotional blackmail and/or sextortion. Gifts may be concrete objects, for example music files: "great meeting you . . . if i get to know and trust you then i can give you my web site and you can listen to my songs." Here, the groomer offers to share a digital object, his website and, through it, his music files. The offer comes with preconditions, though: "get[ting] to know" the target, whom he has just digitally met ("great meeting you") and getting to "trust" her. Groomers also offer to share abstract objects, ranging from empathy and expertise (e.g., lessons about sex) to concern about the target's wellbeing and, most frequently, compliments. All of this enables digital sexual groomers to style themselves as being keenly interested in their target's positive face needs, which indexes the target avidity stance.

As noted in Chapter 3, praise features frequently within attempts at developing deceptive trust in digital sexual groomers' discourse, who regularly pay sexual and nonsexual orientation compliments to their target (Black et al. 2015; Lorenzo-Dus and Izura 2017). In the Perverted Justice dataset, for instance, the adjectives "hot," "sexy," "pretty," "kind," and "cute" display similarly high lexical dispersion values,[1] which illustrates this balancing act between sexual and nonsexual topics in digital sexual groomers' complimenting behavior. In terms of syntactic structure, compliments are highly formulaic speech acts across languages and situational contexts (e.g., Manes and Wolfson 1981; Herbert 1991). Digital sexual groomers' compliments are no exception. The most frequent compliment syntactic structure that they use is: NP {is/looks} (really) ADJ: a noun phrase (e.g., "your face") followed by the verb "is" or "looks" and then an adjective (e.g., "cute"), which may be preceded by some intensifying adverb (e.g., "really"). This formula is closely followed in terms of frequency by its elliptical, emphatic equivalent: ADJ (NP)! (e.g., "cute (face)!"), which reflects the affectivity and brevity of informal digital communication. Furthermore, complimenting sequences are strategically placed as "opening and closing turns" in exchanges that help advance the groomers' tactics of deceptive trust development, isolation, and sexual gratification (Lorenzo-Dus and Izura 2017). By frequently praising their target, moreover, groomers exploit the child targets' emotional vulnerabilities, such as feelings of low self-esteem, which is salient during adolescence (Nightingale and Fischhoff 2002).

Another way in which digital sexual groomers typically index their target-avid stance is to highlight groomer–target "togetherness," even when they are not, romantically or otherwise, a couple. In Brown and Levinson's (1978/1987) theory, this corresponds to the positive politeness strategy known as "claim common ground," specifically "claim in-group membership with H[earer]." We noted earlier in the chapter the prevalence of first-person over second- and third-person deixis in digital sexual groomers' discourse. Although first-person plural deitics feature less frequently than their singular counterparts, they are still salient.

Within the entire Perverted Justice dataset, a list of 70, three-word collocations (e.g., "come over + *could, can, tomorrow, sometime . . .* " and "older guys + *like, into, young, girls. . . .*") was identified as being frequently used by many digital sexual groomers to advance one or more of their grooming goals (Lorenzo-Dus, Kinzel, and Di Cristofaro 2020). Twelve of these linguistic structures explicitly constructed a notion of groomer–target togetherness, such as "each other + *hold, holding, kissing, touching, see, seeing, feeling . . .* ," and "we meet + *when, after, can, where, first, could, before, once, maybe, sometime, if, should, soon.*" The collocations containing the noun phrase "each other" were always used to construct togetherness in relation to sexual activity. As for those containing the phrase "we meet," they were used to reference logistical and/or emotional details of a planned physical meeting, hence contributing to the further contact and deceptive trust development tactics. Irrespective of whether they included sexual content, these linguistic structures addressed the target's positive face needs through emphasizing that she and the groomer shared the same relational space—one from which, as we shall see later in the chapter, others were keenly excluded. In Goffman's (1981) participation framework terms for the production of talk, digital sexual groomers often positioned themselves and their target as shared authors (composers of the views expressed), animators (sounding boxes), and principals (characters in the "play" being enacted) of their planned, past, or current behaviors. When doing so, and as noted in Chapter 2 and further discussed in Section 4.3, they spoke for their target.

Let us next consider digital sexual groomers' work aimed at addressing their target's negative face needs, that is, their use of negative politeness strategies and how this supports their target avidity stance. Extract 4.6 contains typical realizations thereof taken from different digital sexual grooming chatlogs.

Extract 4.6

4.6.1   just out of curiosity and I know I shouldent ask but are you still a virgin???

4.6.2   I don't want you to think I'm pressuring you for sex

4.6.3   you dont mind speaking about this sex stuff do you ? 😉

4.6.4   Look I'm sorry for all this/you can do sex stuff please

4.6.5   I'd cam for you if you wanted lol x

4.6.6   And if you decide you don;t want to meet, too scary, no prob

4.6.7   If you change your mind I understand.

4.6.8   what you want to do not what i want

Across these examples, the groomers use a two part-argumentative structure that pivots between "pushing" (volunteering) and "pulling" (regretting) sexual content. This is evident in examples 4.6.1 and 4.6.4 through adversative clauses respectively marked by the conjunction "but" and the introduction of a new turn ("/") as an elliptical adversative conjunction. Two of the illustrative examples of negative politeness toward the target in Extract 4.6 contain explicitly sexual content (examples 4.6.1–4.6.2). In these examples acknowledgments of wrongdoing, either explicitly (". . . and I know I shouldent ask," example 4.6.1) or implicitly ("I don't want you to think I'm pressuring you . . . ," example 4.6.2), are introduced. By explicitly signaling the groomers' expectation of target noncommittal or disalignment, they also index attentiveness to the target's negative face needs. In example 4.6.4, an apology ("Look I'm sorry for all this") prefaces a request for the target to engage in sexual behavior with the groomer online ("you can do sex stuff please"). In example 4.6.3, vague language is used to desensitise the child to sex (". . . this sex stuff"). This is embedded within a request to introduce such content that signals the groomer's expectation of target like-mindedness ("you don't mind . . . do you?"). This is further accompanied by the wink face emoji 😉, which keys the request as playful and thus minimizes the negative face threat of both requesting and introducing immoral/illegal content.

In examples 4.6.3–4.6.8, which do not involve sexual explicitness, groomers use conditional clauses ("if you wanted," example 4.6.5; "if you decide," example 4.6.6; "If you change your mind," example 4.6.7) or assertions ("what you want . . . not what i want," example 4.6.8) to index their expectation of possible noncommittal or disalignment from their target. Additionally, these structures ostensibly "give deference" (in the sense of Brown and Levinson's [1978/1987] negative politeness strategies) to their target. However, they still support digital sexual groomers' manipulative goals. Seemingly deferring decision-making to the target helps them to gauge how likely their target is to go along with whatever action or behavior is being sought from her at a point in time. At the same time, it helps them to reduce or remove the impression that they may be seeking to control her, which can in turn contribute to her trusting them. As such, these manifestations of negative politeness cannot be taken to mean that target consent has been genuinely sought, let alone obtained.

There is a general alignment, as opposed to direct correspondence, between negative politeness and indirectness in discourse: "be indirect" features as 1 of 10 negative politeness strategies in Brown and Levinson's (1978/1987) taxonomy. When making a request, for example, we may be more or less direct, which in turn signals perceived lower or higher levels of threat to our requestee's negative face needs. Blum-Kulka, House, and Kasper (1989) located nine request types on a directness to indirectness cline, specifically as regards the realization of a request "head act," that is, the main verbal structure that carries the illocutionary force in the speech act of requesting. The authors also noted that request head acts may be accompanied by one or more supportive moves—such as justifications or apologies—and that they exhibit different participatory perspectives; namely, speaker (e.g., "can I . . . ?"), hearer (e.g., "can you . . . ?"), speaker + hearer (e.g., "can we . . . ?"), and third-party/generic (e.g., "can it . . . ?").

In a subset of 10 digital sexual grooming chatlogs from the law enforcement data, a total of 119 request sequences were manually identified and analyzed according to Blum-Kulka, House, and Kasper's (1989) taxonomy of request head act types. Broadly speaking, the first five request types (numbered 1–5 in Table 4.3) are oriented toward communicative directness, even though, in the hedged performative type, a hedging expression (e.g., the modal "would") minimizes the illocutionary force of requesting ("would like to ask you to.."). The remaining request types are oriented toward communicative indirectness, with mild hints being the most indirect of them all.

The results of the analysis are shown in Table 4.4, which also indicates the participatory perspective in the head act and the actual digital sexual grooming tactic being used through the request; that is, deceptive trust development, sexual gratification (explicit or implicit), isolation, and further contact (online or offline). Categories either not found or very infrequently found in the dataset have been omitted in Table 4.5; namely, there were no examples of two head act types (hedged performatives and mild hints) nor of use of third-party perspective, and there were only four examples of groomer + target perspective, aligned to other categories as follows: 1× strong hint (deceptive trust development tactic); 1× mood derivable (implicit sexual gratification tactic); 1× query preparatory (isolation tactic); and 1× explicit performative (further contact tactic).

Table 4.3 REQUEST HEAD ACT TYPES IN DIGITAL SEXUAL GROOMING (TAXONOMY ADAPTED FROM BLUM-KULKA, HOUSE, AND KASPER (1989); EXAMPLES FROM DIGITAL SEXUAL GROOMING DATA)

Request head act	Definition	Example
1. Mood derivable	Utterances in which the grammatical mode of the verb signals the illocutionary force	play with yourself until you cum
2. Explicit Performative	Utterances in which the illocutionary force is explicitly named	I'm asking you to show me
3. Hedged Performative	Utterances in which the naming of the illocutionary force is modified by hedging expressions	*No examples in sample*
4. Obligation Statements	Utterances that state the obligation of the hearer to carry out the act	u will you do it
5. Want statements	Utterances that state the speaker's desire that the hearer carries out the act	I want u to do it
6. Suggestory formulae	Utterances that contain a suggestion to do x	why not type?
7. Query preparatory	Utterances containing reference to preparatory conditions (e.g. ability, willingness) as conventionalized in any specific language	could we video quickly and not say anything?
8. Strong hint	Utterances containing partial reference to object or element needed for the implementation of the act	I do have snapchat
9. Mild hint	Utterances that make no reference to the request proper (or any of its elements) but are interpretable as requests by context.	*No examples in sample*

Table 4.4 shows that the offenders in the sample mainly used requests to support three digital sexual grooming tactics: sexual gratification (63 out of 119 requests), followed by deceptive trust development (35 out of 119) and further contact (18 out of 119). In terms of perspective, most of the requests (86 out of 119) were target-oriented. As for their level of (in-)directness, as manifest in head act type, there was a balance between directness, which accounted for 58 of the 119 requests, and indirectness, which accounted for the remaining 61 requests. However, when cross-referencing head act type and grooming tactic, a pattern emerged: 19 of the 28 requests seeking explicit sexual gratification were realized via head act types that were oriented toward directness, with 16 of them being mood derivable head acts (i.e., imperatives). This means that, when pursuing explicit sexual gratification, these groomers were most direct. Given that these directly worded requests explicitly concerned illegal sexual behavior, it is likely that the groomers assumed that their target would

Table 4.4 REQUESTS AND GROOMING PROCESSES IN DIGITAL SEXUAL GROOMING

	Request type (Head act) and participant perspective (groomer, G; target, T)													
	Mood Derivable		Explicit performative		Want statement		Obligation statement		Suggestory formula		Query preparatory		Strong hint		Total
Tactic*	G	T	G	T	G	T	G	T	G	T	G	T	G	T	T
DTD	0	15	1	0	0	1	0	0	2	0	7	7	0	2	35
E-SG	0	16	2	0	0	0	0	1	0	0	2	5	1	1	28
I-SG	0	8	4	0	2	0	0	1	0	2	2	7	0	9	35
I	0	0	0	0	0	0	0	0	0	0	0	3	0	0	3
FC	0	3	3	0	1	0	0	0	0	0	0	3	6	2	18
Total	42		10		4		2		4		36		21		119

*DTD, deceptive trust development; E-SG, explicit sexual gratification; I-SG, implicit sexual gratification; I, isolation; FC, further contact.

interpret them as face-threatening. Yet they made no effort, in the request head act at least, to mitigate their face threat level, using instead language that may be perceived as impolite through encroaching on the target's equity rights.[2]

Table 4.4 also shows that, for the remaining tactics, digital sexual groomers performed a balancing act between indirectness and directness. In relation to implicit sexual gratification, 17 of the 35 requests deployed direct head act types. Across all levels of (in)directness, the most frequent head act types for the implicit sexual gratification sub-tactic were query preparatories (9/35), strong hints (9/35), and mood derivables (8/35). As for deceptive trust development, the most frequently used request head act types were mood derivables (15/35) and query preparatories (14/35)—again showing a balance between directness and indirectness. In the case of further contact, 11/18 requests deployed indirect head act types, the most frequent one being strong hints (8/18), followed by query preparatories (3/18). Direct head acts used to perform this tactic included mood derivables (3/18), explicit performatives (3/18), and want statements (1/18).

These findings illustrate, through the speech act of requesting, the integration of directness and indirectness as part of digital sexual groomers' facework work. The use of indirect request head act types serves to minimize the degree of imposition on the target derived from asking for behaviors or actions that are illegal and immoral. Additionally, when direct request head act types are used, they tend to be accompanied by support moves—such as apologies, groundings, and promises—in which the target's negative and positive face needs are addressed. Let us revisit example 4.5.2, which contains an elaborate request for, ostensibly, "friendship":

> *I want to be friends with you still.* I know I have issues but I'm trying to sort it out for you. You are like my only friend, idc if you are 12. Without you I would end up taking my life. I'm sorry for everything you will always be in my heart and mind. I will always remember you. You gorgeous, most wonderful girl.

The head act in this request (italicized above) consists of a want statement, "want to be friends with you still," which is worded from a speaker perspective ("I"). The low degree of imposition involved in asking for friendship continuation likely accounts for the groomer's use of directness in the request's head act. At the same time, the head act is supported by an elaborate grounding move that reveals that something in the groomer's previous behavior has broken the trust the two had developed. The grounding move attends to the target's positive and negative face needs. The former draws on three positive politeness strategies: offering praise via a two-part compliment ("You gorgeous, most wonderful girl"), making a promise, twice ("you will always be in my heart and mind," "I will always remember you"), and showing a keen interest in the target through a statement that shows exclusivity ("You are like my only friend"). The exclusivity statement is qualified by another statement—"idc if you are 12"—that explicitly disregards ("idc" initialism for "I don't care") their age difference, albeit in the broader context of a request for friendship, which is not illegal per se. The grounding move further entails an implicit apology ("I know I have issues") with a further implicit commissive act to improve himself ("but I'm trying to sort it out"), which is offered as a gift to her ("for you"). An apology formula is also offered—"I'm sorry for"—even though its content is a vague term ("everything") and constitutes an encroachment on the target's equity rights in the form of an implicit threat: "Without you I would end up taking my life." This threat is conditional on the target's behavior, which is a form of coercion. What we have, therefore, is complex integration of politeness and impoliteness as part of the grounding move offered to support a seemingly innocent, direct request for friendship continuation.

Extract 4.7 further illustrates the manipulative interplay of politeness and impoliteness in support of target avidity stance-taking within digital sexual grooming.

Extract 4.7

[The extract comes from approximately halfway through the grooming chatlog, at a point where the groomer (G211) is trying to get his target (T211) to explicitly verbalize—or, rather, type in their chatlog—the sexual activity that he has previously stated that they will perform when they meet physically.]

01	G211	so any ideahs?? Lol
02	T211	Hmm
03	G211	hmmmm??? that aint a answer
04	T211	ooh/lol
05	G211	lol u will chiken out
06	T211	nah i wont
07	G211	lol u have to call me first . . . lol so u will chiken out
08	T211	i will call
09		[Exchange of short turns regarding whether T211 will call]
10	G211	what would u like to happen????
11	T211	well sum of the things we talked about
12	G211	like . . . .
13	T211	i aint sayin [-(
14	G211	cum on silly
15	T211	lol/u know
16	G211	lol so do u . . . .
17	T211	yah so we dont have to spell it out 😊
18	G211	ur just chiken say it
19	T211	Pffttt
20	G211	yepp /u/r/a/

21	T211	Pffftttt
22		*[Exchange of turns reproducing expressive paralanguage, e.g., smiley/sad, emojis]*
23	G211	cum on tell me 😄/😔
24	T211	oh quit/ i aint spellin it out
25	G211	Chiken
26	T211	usualy the man knows wat to do
27	G211	Chiken

Extract 4.7 contains five instances of impoliteness oriented toward T211's personal quality face,[3] namely, name-calling linked to cowardice. They are realized through the noun "chiken" (lines 18, 25, and 27) and the colloquial phrasal verb "chiken out" (lines 05, 07). Additionally, G211 either ignores or openly challenges T211's attempts at resisting this label, using emphatic typography and layout. For instance, in line 03, he weightily loads his apparent lack of understanding by mocking T211's textual rendition of wondering ("Hmm" line 02), which he repeats doubling its duration from two to four "m" characters) and questioning it ("hmmmm???" line 03). Within the same typing turn, G211 engages in the impoliteness strategy of pointed criticism, overtly challenging the relevance of T211's previous turn: "that aint a answer." He similarly weightily loads this use of impoliteness in line 20, when he creates the impression of slow rendition of his previous insult "ur just chiken" (line 18) by starting to repeat it over three consecutive turns: "u/r/a" (you are a). T211's interjection ("Pffftttt," line 21) seems to stop the actual completion of the previous turn—the insulting label chicken is not used again. T211's interjection signals increasing disapproval of G211's other-stance attribution—note T211's mirroring G211's strategy of increasing the number of characters to express emotion, in T211's case one more "f" and one more "t" in line 21 vis-à-vis line 19.

During this relatively brief exchange, too, G211 makes a repeated request to obtain sexual gratification from his target. The head act in this repeated request is a mood derivable: "cum on" (line 14) and "cum on tell me" (line 23). His use of typography here—"cum" instead of "come"—is not linked to dialectal (e.g., northern British English) choice (G211 is North American). Instead, it is a recurrent typographical means to index sexual climax in digital sexual discourse, including in digital sexual grooming. As such, in Extract 4.7 it is likely used by G211 to support the tactic of sexual gratification. However, G211 mitigates the face threat potential of the mood-derivable head act type by, respectively, using an insulting adjective ("silly") that may be construed as a playful term of endearment in close relationships and inserting two consecutive emojis that respectively express positivity and affect: "😄" and "😔" (line 23). Overall, then, in Extract 4.7 G211 indexes his keen interest in

T211—his target-avid stance-taking—through a strategic combination of politeness and impoliteness. To realize the further contact offline (lines 01–08) and sexual gratification (lines 09–27) tactics, G211 manipulates his target into seemingly going along with illegal behavior. He performs playful banter to cloak his harassment under the guise of target avidity and fast and frequent "nice" and "nasty" (politeness-impoliteness) pivoting talk.

4.3 DIGITAL SEXUAL GROOMERS' STYLING OF THEIR TARGET

So far in the chapter, the focus has been on digital sexual groomers' self-styling through three stances: sexual expertise, vulnerable openness, and target avidity. These are performed alongside other-oriented styling work, whereby the groomers ascribe stances to their target (and to their opponents, as we shall see in Section 4.4). As discussed in Chapter 2, levels of presumed entitlement to attribute stances to one's interactants vary across social situations and are aligned to interpersonal power dynamics at play, among other factors. In digital sexual grooming, groomers' self-styling via stances of sexual expertise and emotional openness with a keen interest in their target seemingly makes them presume that they are sufficiently entitled to "speak for" their target, to whom they regularly ascribe "complementary" stances of:

- Keen learning, which constructs the target as being a "good pupil"
- Openness, which constructs the target as being someone who willingly discloses her own emotions; and
- Specialness, which constructs the target as someone who is worthy of the groomer's avidity.

When ascribing the above stances to their target, digital sexual groomers may position themselves as animators and authors of the views expressed. They may use, for example, syntactically self-aligned (first-person singular) statements, such as "i think u r very sexy," and epistemic assertions, such as "I know u'll enjoy it." Often, though, digital sexual groomers position themselves as animators of views that are seemingly authored by their target, stating what her position or view was, is, or will and/or should be. The examples in Extract 4.8 are typical of such a realization of manipulative, other stance-attribution in digital sexual grooming.

Extract 4.8

4.8.1 you want to learn about sex /u r into older guys

4.8.2 most girls your age want to talk about sex with older men

4.8.3 I bet you are fullofpassion dying to be expressed

In these three examples, the targets' identities are constructed through stance-taking acts that present them as being eager pupils ("want to learn"; example 4.8.1) and who, like "most girls [their] age" (example 4.8.2), "want to talk about sex with older men" (example 4.8.2). As such, the stances attributed to the targets appear to be fully aligned to the groomers' wants for adult–child sex ("fullofpassion dying to be expressed," example 4.8.3).

This use of other-stance attribution enables groomers to shift responsibility away from their own illegal and immoral behavior, passing it on to their target. In all three examples in Extract 4.8, for instance, the groomers occupy the production role of animator, as they are the ones typing these interactional turns. Yet the roles of author and principal are differently aligned. In 4.8.3, the groomer presents himself as author, through the first-person singular hypothetical statement "I bet"; he positions the target as the principal, aligning her stance to the ascribed identity of being sexually worthy of his avidity. In 4.8.2, the groomer presents himself implicitly as one of the "older men" being mentioned; that is, he positions himself in the production role of principal. He also implicitly positions his target as the author of the stance he is animating for her (i.e., openness, and in particular talking about sex with adult males), aligning his behavior and therefore hers to normality for the social identity of teenage girls ("most girls your age"). The groomer thus naturalizes an illegal and immoral behavior undertaken by the social identity that he sees himself as a part of: all older men (rather than adult males with a sexual interest in children). He assigns responsibility for that behavior to the social identity that he sees his target as belonging to: namely, teenage girls. It is, he states, "most" such girls who "want to talk about sex with older men." We see here that the individual who is being "spoken for"—the target of digital sexual grooming—is misattributed a stance of normality for a social identity to which she objectively belongs (female teenager). And in example 4.8.1, the groomer extricates himself from the roles of principal (as in example 4.8.2) and author (as in example 4.8.3), which he shifts to his target. It is her who is unambiguously constructed as someone who "want[s] to learn about sex" and who is "into older guys." By doing this, the groomer not only ascribes a set of stances to his target—willingness to learn and communicative openness—but he also manipulates these stances to perform the deceptive trust development and sexual gratification tactics. Specifically, the target's stances become circumscribed to sex: willingness to learn *about sex* and talking *about sex* with older men, even though she neither animates nor authors such stances. This kind of other-stance attribution, which is frequent in digital sexual groomers' manipulative discourse, can be particularly damaging for the target, who may not feel confident enough to challenge the real authorship of the stance.

If recurrently aligned to her, through groomers' avidity and fixated discourse, it may subsequently increase the target's feelings of self-blame.

4.4 DIGITAL SEXUAL GROOMERS' STYLING OF THEIR OPPONENT

As part of their performance of the trust development tactic, digital sexual groomers seek to establish a strong affiliative bond with their target. Crucially, given the illegality and immorality that this tactic ultimately serves (child sexual abuse), their efforts must be hidden from anyone connected with their target, especially their family and friends, who are styled as the groomers' opponents. It is therefore not surprising, for instance, that "mom" is among the second strongest collocate of the highly frequent and dispersed terms "home" and "alone" in the entire Perverted Justice dataset. Similarly, the top collocate of the second-person possessive adjective "your" in the Perverted Justice data set is "mom," with "dad" ranking eleventh. Digital sexual groomers repeatedly ask their target to keep their relationship concealed from these opponents. Given that the target of digital sexual grooming is likely a child living under the care of one or more adults, groomers' opponents are invariably members of the child's social support network—friends, age-appropriate boy/girlfriends, guardians, and family.

One regular way in which digital sexual groomers seek to ensure secrecy of their abusive relationship with their target is by strengthening the groomer–target "we-ness" in their interaction. It is poignant herein, for instance, that the top collocate of the first-person plural possessive adjective "our" in the Perverted Justice dataset is "secret," with (nearly) double the collocational strength of its next five top collocates: "conversation," "relationship," "own," "bodies," and "friendship." Note, moreover, that, apart from "our bodies," these collocations construct a distinctly nonsexual notion of we-ness. This helps give exclusivity through togetherness a false veneer of legality and morality.

Another recurrent way in which digital sexual groomers ensure secrecy is through negative styling of their perceived opponents. This typically consists of digital sexual groomers' use of impoliteness strategies that are generally oriented toward their opponents' quality face. The child targets' support network may become the target of groomers' insults or pointed criticism that construct and other-attribute pejorative stances, such as over-strictness for parents or inattentiveness for boy/girlfriends and also parents. The bond that these opponents may have with the target is also debased, often comparatively—that is, groomers construct the target–opponent bonds as of reduced value vis-à-vis the unique "we-ness" of the groomer–target bond. Let us consider Extract 4.9 in this respect.

Extract 4.9

[The extract occurs approximately in the mid-point of a grooming chatlog lasting slightly over 6 hours across a 39-day time span.]

01	G107	Im nice just have a lot going on in my life right now, how about you?
02	T107	i never get 2 do anythin fun rely/stepmoms a bitch like that
03	G107	that sucks its not even your real mom she shouldn't care or tell you
04		what to do
05	T107	i kno/but my real moms in heaven
06	G107	awww so is my dad
07	T107	oh sorry
08	G107	sorry to hear that/hey, can I ask your height/weight? lol i bet im totally
09		alot bigger than you :-p
10		*[Exchange of turns with G107 asking about T107's mother]*
11	G107	my dad passed 14 years ago/i miss my dad a lot/around the same time
12		as your mom/your dad? where is your dad?
13	T107	japan/hes in the navy
14	G107	so you only live with your step mom?
15	T107	an my step bros
16	G107	she doesnt let ya do shit?
17	T107	tyler is 7 an ryan is 5/ya she lets me do stuff like cook clean an babysit
18		so she can go out w her friends
19	G107	lol ya but nothin for you?/thats dumb/id say maybe i could come over
20		sometime if your babysitting

In Extract 4.9 G107 discloses information that conveys the impression of vulnerability (i.e., his father passing away; see lines 06, 11) in an attempt to generate or strengthen reciprocity, reinforcing this process with empathy tokens ("awww," line 06; "sorry to hear that," line 08) that show a keen interest in T107. Concomitantly, he performs the grooming tactic of mental isolation, seeking to exploit any perceived family relationship rifts in T107's life. T107's criticism and insult directed at her stepmother in line 02 ("i never get 2 do anythin fun rely/stepmoms a bitch like that") is met by G107's empathetic agreement ("that sucks", line 03) and subsequent reference to the flaws in T107s stepmother's (his opponent's) character. This is done via a pragmatically boosted ("not even", line 03) statement that attacks his opponent's social identity face qualities (her not being "your real mom", line 03) and removes any subsequent parenting entitlements ("she shouldn't care or tell you what to do", lines 03-04). A couple of minutes later, having successfully deployed self-disclosure to secure details about T107's appearance (lines 08–09) and physical environment (line 12), G107 reintroduces T107's stepmother in the interaction: "so you only live with your step mom?" (line 14). His next question, she "doesnt let ya do shit?"

(line 16), is semantically a non sequitur to T107's previous turn, which simply answers a question about whom she lives with ("an my step bros", line 15).

In line 16, G107 styles his opponent as someone who prevents T107 from independent action. The stance that is attributed to T017's stepmother here is that of being domineering, which he enacts via the impoliteness strategy of pointed criticism. T107's reply in line 17 that her stepmother "lets me do stuff" spurs G107's on for, as T107's adds, the "stuff" happens to be chores ("like cook clean an babysit") that her stepmother selfishly tasks T107 with "so she can go out w her friends" (line 18). G107's response in lines 19–20 starts with an appreciation token of the target's verbal wit—the initialism for laughing out loud "lol." Immediately after, G107 introduces a shift in key, to serious talk, via the acknowledgment token "ya." This enables him to perform empathy, which he does by showing incredulity at the behavior displayed by his opponent ("but nothin for you?"), before pointedly criticizing it ("thats dumb"). Having thus performed the mental isolation tactic, G107 tentatively resumes the further contact tactic: "id say maybe i could come over sometime" (lines 19–20). To do so he chooses an indirect request head act—the query preparatory "could come over." Moreover, he mitigates the request's potential face threat via two hedges ("maybe" and "sometime") and his hypothetical clauses ("id say..", line 19, and "if your babysitting," line 20). Of course, G107's knowledge of T107's babysitting derives from his seemingly innocent interaction about T107's family environment.

Even when digital sexual groomers do not threaten their perceived opponents' face explicitly, they nevertheless invest significant interactional time and effort in seeking to distance their target from these other individuals in her support networks, as the examples in Extract 4.10 illustrate.

Extract 4.10

4.10.1 i wont be able to see you if you spend weekend at your friends hun

4.10.2 can you keep a secret? i do not want to get when we do it mom and dad
call the cop if find out how old i am

4.10.3 jus tell him [dad] your goin to a friends aunts house

In example 4.10.1, the groomer explicitly states the consequence of the target's noncompliance ("you spend weekend at your friends") with a previous request for them to meet at the weekend: "i wont be able to see you." Within the context of an evolving digital sexual grooming relationship, this constitutes a threat of withdrawal—one that the groomer is unlikely to deliver in practice but that an emotionally invested target, especially if trust has already been built, may believe. In example 4.10.1, the groomer also seeks to minimize the potential face threat to the target behind his threat by closing his turn with the term of endearment "hun," which signals closeness and therefore attends to her positive face needs.

The two other examples in Extract 4.10 concern secrecy. In example 4.10.2, the groomer introduces quite a complex grounding move alongside his conventionally indirect request head act ("can you keep a secret?"). The secret concerns a groomer's planned visit to the target for the purpose of having sex; the grounding move entails a statement of his own needs that "mom and dad [do not] call the cop" upon realizing ("if find out") that a criminal act (age-inappropriate sexual relations—"when we do it") is being committed. Throughout this example, the groomer avoids sexual explicitness repeatedly, using instead euphemisms ("a secret" for hiding information about child sexual abuse, and "find out how old i am" for discovering sexual abuse of a minor) and the vague language approximator quality terms ("do it" in "when we do it" for having sex). Similarly, in example 4.10.3, the groomer uses a discourse marker, the hedge "just," to minimize the potential face-threat of his direct request (a mood derivable head act—"tell him"). This is perhaps unsurprising given that the actual act expressed through the imperative mode seeks to get the target to engage in behavior that is morally questionable (lying to her father), which would lead to legally punitive action for the groomer (having sex with a minor) and to her sexual abuse.

The emphasis placed by digital sexual groomers on being able to access their target alone is shown, among other, by the intensity in their efforts to extract information from the target about their opponents. Extract 4.11 is typical of the battery of quick, successive questions to which digital sexual groomers may subject their target to gain exclusive access to her, which further illustrates their fixated discourse.

Extract 4.11

[The extract reproduces a short fragment from the third day of a grooming interaction lasting approximately 5.5 hours overall.]

01	G589	where is dad???
02	T589	Fla
03	G589	what does mom do???
04	T589	Nurse
05	G589	where???
06	T589	a hospital
07		*[Five further questions–answer exchanges about the schedule of T589's parents,*
08		*resulting in her asking whether G589 is a stalker, which he denies and says he is*
		"just getting info"]
09	G589	what time does mom get off work
10	T589	8
11	G589	so we would have time???

Extract 4.11 resembles an interrogation—one in which G589 seeks to determine his chances of securing exclusive (i.e., without parental supervision) contact offline with T589. While G589 elides the object of the verb "have time (for)???" in his question in line 11, their interactions across previous days have made it ostensive to both i.e., to have sex. Note, too, the strategic shift of footing whereby he positions both as would-be authors of the elided purpose of their offline meeting ("we would . . . "). Shifting volition or decision-making to either their target or to a shared, groomer–target position is characteristic of groomers' attempts at discursively distancing themselves from responsibility for the illegal actions that they are ultimately solely responsible for. G589's questioning style reveals that, at this point in time, he has relegated trust development to the backburner of his grooming tactical toolkit. His questions are not interspersed with, for instance, reciprocal self-disclosures, acknowledgment receipts, evaluation, or any other marker of sociability that may promote interpersonal bonding. Instead, they are focused on fact-finding about his opponent—so much so that T589 asks him if he is a stalker (lines 07–08). Overall, G589 is fixated on isolating the target physically: on securing exclusive physical contact with her, for which finding out in as much detail as possible about her physical environment—including her time home alone from her family—is crucial.

4.5 CONCLUSION

Digital sexual groomers' styling of self and others is critical to their ability to gain, manipulate, and ultimately exploit their target's trust. As this chapter has shown, these individuals seek to lure their target by closely aligning self- and other (target) stances. To do so, they falsely present self and target as fully complementary as regards their (groomers') sexual expertise, communicative openness, and avidity. The groomers display sexual expertise and are willing to share it with the target, who in turn lacks it but is willing to acquire it. The groomers also exploit the cultural rhetoric that digital sharing is good (see Chapter 2): they perform emotional self-disclosure, especially concerning negative, vulnerability-triggering feelings of loneliness and fear, which ignite mutual reciprocity cycles from their target. And they display extreme interest in the target who is ascribed a stance of being worthy of their (sexual) avidity. This requires the performance of complex facework that simultaneously embraces politeness (positive and negative) and impoliteness, with consequent variable levels of non–imposition-based behavior, on the one hand, and encroachment-based behavior, on the other hand. As has been seen in this chapter, fast and frequent pivoting between "nice" and "nasty" talk is a staple of groomers' manipulative work.

Finally, the analysis in this chapter has also shown that digital sexual groomers place considerable emphasis on cultivating a sense of exclusivity with their target. Individuals who may already have an affective bond with her, typically parents and friends, thus become the groomers' opponents—the main obstacle to their exclusivity and secrecy needs. Consequently, groomers invest considerable interactional effort in fact-finding about their opponents and may also cast them in negative and less favorable ways than those used to style themselves and their target. Digital sexual groomers, we have seen throughout the chapter, display fixated discourse, be that in relation to themselves (narcissistic talk), their target (harassment), or their opponents (persistent questioning).

NOTES

1. Their DP_{Norm} values ranged between 0.5 and 0.6, which featured within the top 100 lexically frequent and dispersed terms in the entire dataset.
2. The term "equity rights" is used here in the sense of Spencer-Oatey (2000) to refer to our belief that we are entitled to personal consideration from others—to be treated fairly by them.
3. "Quality face" concerns our wish that others evaluate us positively in terms of our personal qualities (Spencer-Oatey 2000).

CHAPTER 5

Digital Ideological Grooming

Setting the Scene

5.1 INTRODUCTION

On 27 October 2018, 11 people were killed and 6 wounded in a shooting at a synagogue in the Squirrel Hill neighborhood of Pittsburgh, in the United States. The suspected gunman was identified as Robert Bowers, a Pittsburgh resident against whom 29 charges were subsequently brought, including obstructing the exercise of religious beliefs resulting in death, using a firearm to commit murder, weapons offenses, and seriously injuring police officers.[1] Two hours before the shooting, Bowers had posted the following message on the social media platform Gab about the Hebrew Immigrant Aid Society (HIAS): "HIAS likes to bring invaders in that kill our people. I can't sit by and watch my people get slaughtered. Screw your optics, I'm going in."[2]

Bowers's post is representative of the hate-filled group polarization that underpins digital ideological grooming. His post was explicit about both his disdain for the out-group ("invaders . . . that kill") and a deeply held sense of victimization of the social group he saw himself as belonging to ("my people get slaughtered"). While acting alone in the Pittsburgh shooting, subsequent analysis of his Gab account made clear that he had been lured into right wing extremism, including interacting regularly with key white supremacist activists in the United States.

As noted in Chapter 1, extreme ideology groups and their use of the Internet have been extensively researched. This chapter teases out from the consequent literature key findings that help underpin the analysis, in Chapter 6, of digital ideological grooming as a discourse practice. It starts by discussing in Section 5.2 the role of ideology and community-building in

Digital Grooming. Nuria Lorenzo-Dus, Oxford University Press. © Oxford University Press 2023.
DOI: 10.1093/oso/9780190845193.003.0005

digital ideological grooming. Ideology and community are multifaceted phenomena that have been subjected to detailed examination across the social sciences and so Section 5.2 discusses how these concepts are used in this book and their relevance to the analysis of digital ideological grooming. Section 5.3 appraises a key debate in the social sciences literature; namely, the political and/or religious underpinnings of extreme ideology groups. The digital *modus operandi* of political and religious extremist groups are then discussed. Therein the focus is respectively on radical right (Section 5.4) and jihadi (Section 5.5) groups, which represent the most salient—though by no means only—manifestations of contemporary ideological extremism. Section 5.6 then pulls together the key themes identified throughout the chapter.

5.2 IDEOLOGY AND COMMUNITY-BUILDING IN DIGITAL IDEOLOGICAL GROOMING

Ideology designates social representations shared by members of a given group, whether a dominant or a dominated one. These social representations are organized into systems that individuals and groups deploy "in order to make sense of, figure out and render intelligible the way society works" (Hall 1996, 26). These representations are also the fundamental principles that govern social judgment: they "allow people, as group members, to organize a multitude of social beliefs about what is the case, good or bad, right or wrong, for them, and to act accordingly . . . [ideologies] may also influence what is accepted as true or false" (van Dijk 1998, 8). Since ideologies are socially shared mental representations, it is possible—indeed common—for individual members to acquire different versions of these social representations. However, as van Dijk (1998) stresses, individual variation operates within the general parameters shared by the group.

"What do ideologies look like?" van Dijk (1998) asks. His answer is that we do not know. However, he adds, they all too frequently rely on "us-versus-them" discursive strategies, whereby in-group members project self-targeted positive identities, comparing them to other-targeted negative identities. This results in opposition-based boundary setting, which in some cases is openly polarized. The discourse of digital ideological grooming is one such case.

Polarized, us-versus-them discourse operates according to what van Dijk (1998) calls an "ideological square." This comprises four strategies, namely,

1. Emphasize the in-group's good properties/actions
2. Emphasize the out-group's bad properties/actions
3. Mitigate the in-group's bad properties/actions
4. Mitigate the out-group's good properties/actions

A group may favor Strategies 2 and 4 to the point that its discourse becomes openly discriminatory of one or more out-groups. *Othering*—rather than "merely" out-grouping—accurately describes this. Othering individuals and groups means representing them discursively not just as radically different from the in-group but also, and crucially, as deviant and distant—as incompatible strangers (Bauman 1991). The term "othering" has been extensively examined across the social sciences, most often in relation to Western–Asian relations. Said (1997, 2003), for example, argues that the West has systematically othered large parts of Asia, and particularly the Muslim Arab countries of the Middle East, through producing "generalising, irresponsible depictions of Islam to an extent not known in relation to any other group on earth" (Said 1997, xvi). Such depictions fail to acknowledge, let alone highlight, any of their positive traits or actions. A reciprocal form of othering is known as "occidentalism," whereby it is "the West" that is consistently denigrated on grounds of, especially, arrogance (see, e.g., Buruma and Margalit 2004; Sims 2012). Both examples correspond to Strategies 2 and 4 in Van Dijk's ideological square.

Coupland (2010) identifies five partly overlapping discursive means of othering: homogenization, suppression/silencing, pejoration, displaying liberalism, and subverting tolerance. *Homogenization* designates a use of discourse that denies individuals their individuality, often by resorting to social stereotyping. *Suppression* and *silencing* refer to strategies of restricted and zero representation, respectively. Suppression is linked to homogenization in as much as it relies on drawing on a limited set of features of the othered group—a set that suits the othering group's own agendas and priorities. Zero representation entails ghosting certain social groups by making them literally invisible in discourse. *Pejoration* concerns the use of discourse to construct other individuals and groups in a highly negative light. The evaluative loading of the labels and attributes used in pejoration is always context-specific.

Othering is also realized when individuals or groups discursively claim to uphold "liberal" orientations toward those they seek to other. A classic example here is a racist representation accompanied by personal disclaimers à la "I'm not racist but . . ." (see van Dijk 1999). *Tolerance subversion* refers to "discursive work [that] shows that liberalism is over–idealistic or naïve or dull or outmoded" (Coupland 2010, 253). Humor is a widely used strategy for subverting tolerance in discourse. Each of these five discursive means of othering has social exclusion, marginalizing, and discriminatory effects for those whose identities are thus projected. What is more, each of them also contributes to enhancing the internal cohesion and self-worth perception of the in-group as a result of its becoming textually exalted through marked contrast with the othered group (i.e., strategies 1 and 3 in van Dijk's ideological square).

Hogg (2014, see also Hogg et al. 2007; Hogg, Adelman, and Blagg 2010; Hogg and Adelman 2013; Hogg, Kruglanski, and van der Boss 2013) posit uncertainty-identity theory as an explanatory model for polarized social identity construction, which is a staple diet in extreme groups' ideologies. Starting from the observation that extremist groups surge during conditions of acute social uncertainty, he postulates

> (a)that feelings of uncertainty, particularly uncertainty about or relating to who one is and how one should behave, motivate behaviours aimed at reducing uncertainty, and (b) that the process of categorizing oneself and others as members of a group effectively reduces self-uncertainty because it provides a consensually validated social identity that describes and prescribes who one is and how one should behave. (Hogg 2014, 338–339)

While group identification helps resolve uncertainty about one's identity, not all groups are equally effective at doing so. Those with high entitativity fare much better than those with low entitativity. High entitative groups are well-structured, display clear boundaries, and their members are internally homogenous: they share multiple attributes and goals. It is these shared features that are responsible for their groupness—in other words, what makes them "groupy" (Campbell 1958; Hamilton and Sherman 1996). Extreme ideology groups are highly entitative. Their polarized ideology harbors powerful leaders (as identity prototypes) and zealous members while also promoting harshness toward, indeed othering of, dissidents. Under conditions of persistent or severe uncertainty about self-identity, or in the absence of suitable alternative identity choices to draw back on, these groups' chances of luring other individuals toward them increase exponentially (Hogg and Adelman 2013; Hogg et al. 2013).

Highly entitative groups, including extreme ideology groups, invest considerable time and effort in building digital communities, or "affinity spaces" (Gee 2005), through which to consolidate their groupness and learn from each other. These digital communities serve as "echo chambers," in which group members find their ideas supported and amplified by other like-minded members (Koehler 2014). They have clear benefits at individual and group levels. Individual members can learn about, negotiate aspects of, and share knowledge about the group's norms and values. It is their having a common endeavor that binds them together and contributes to the group's high entitativity. At a group (macro-) level, these digital communities offer opportunities to model other extremist groups and their digital communities, as well as to disseminate "best practice" in, for example, recruitment of new members (Maras 2017). Cumulatively, this contributes to the continuing online presence of extreme ideology groups (Clifford and Powell 2019).

Around what kinds of endeavor do members of these extreme ideology, digital communities come together? To answer this question, research has drawn on earlier communities of, broadly speaking, a political nature; specifically, Anderson's classic notion of "imagined political communities." Anderson first developed this notion in the 1980s to conceive of nations. The imagined-ness of these communities derived from the fact that their members never knew, or met, the majority of those with whom they "shared" their nation. Their political nature stemmed from the dominant organizational status of sovereign nation states at the time. As for their community dimension, this captured Anderson's (1983/2016) view that those who formed them were bonded by friendships and common goals.

The type of imagined political communities Anderson theorized were first and foremost created through their members' development of national narratives embedded in time and history. Subsidiary to this were three other actions: establishing threats against boundaries, demonstrating political legitimation and emotional power, and eroding other (previous) imaginings. Obviously much has changed since Anderson first began writing about imagined political communities—including the concept of a single national identity becoming challenged (Blakemore 2016). As we saw in Chapter 2, too, the sharing era (John 2017) has altered how we interact with each other, and globalization has promoted greater cultural diversity. Nevertheless, several studies show that Anderson's notion of imagined political communities remains applicable to contemporary digital spaces beyond nation-states (Christensen 2014), including the kind of digital communities that extreme ideology groups form. Furlow et al. (2014), for instance, found that so-called Islamic State's efforts at restoring the Caliphate in 2014 relied on the construction of an imagined political community that offered social cohesion for its members around their "Muslimness," regardless of whether they knew each other or not, and also of their nationality and ethnicity. This vague, generic construction—the authors argued—was premised on "us-versus-them" rhetorical structures that both enabled diverse audiences to identify with the Caliphate and made it easier to emphasize their irreconcilable differences with the out-group.

Nouri and Lorenzo-Dus (2019) also found Anderson's model to be applicable to digital community-building by the radical right, specifically the groups Britain First and Reclaim Australia. Their analysis of all the Facebook and Twitter content posted by these groups over a 7-month period in 2017 (c. 4.7 million words) revealed the same actions identified by Anderson, albeit in a different configuration—as shown in Figure 5.1.

Establishing threats and boundaries—discursively realized via othering—was Britain First and Reclaim Australia's umbrella action for digital community-building. Seeking to demonstrate political legitimation and emotional power, which the groups' realized via exaltation of their beliefs and hence also discursive polarization—emerged as the groups' main action in support of threat and boundary establishment. Developing national narratives or the writing of time and history, which was the main feature in Anderson's model, were noticeably less important for the two groups examined. In the

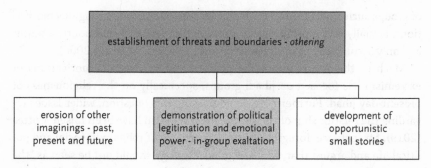

Figure 5.1 Extreme right groups' digital political communities (Nouri and Lorenzo-Dus 2019).

absence of historical evidence on which to graft their own "grand national narratives," Britain First and Reclaim Australia used opportunistic, small stories.[3] The telling of these stories enabled the groups' members to position themselves within the group's ideological discourse and perform their identities as group members. Finally, erosion of other imaginings, which was regarded by Anderson as of equal importance to all but national narrative development, was less salient in these two groups' digital community-building. Muslims and immigrants were not eroded in Britain First and Reclaim Australia's digital discourse. Instead, they were explicitly and regularly denigrated in these groups' social media discourse. What is more, the groups' digital discourse challenged everything and everyone—past, present, and future—who was not ideologically aligned to them: governments, law enforcement, corporations, etc. In doing so, they portrayed a distorted and grossly underdeveloped image of these other imaginings.

5.3 RELIGIOUS AND/OR POLITICAL EXTREMISM

Hitherto we have considered extremist groups as a whole, but it is important to recognize that in academic and policymaking circles there is a vigorous debate about whether they are political and/or religious groups and about the consequences thereof for developing counter-extremism interventions. The grounds on which extremist groups justify the attacks they (may) commit has led some authors to consider them all as being religiously, rather than politically, motivated (e.g., Hoffman 1989; Laquer 2000; Neumann 2009). This resonates with a closely related thesis that terrorism/extremism has evolved in four chronological waves: anarchic, anti-colonial, extreme left wing, and religious, which is the present wave (Rappoport 2004). Other authors, however, posit that extremism has always been—and remains—politically motivated (e.g., Duyvesteyn 2004). Proponents of this perspective note that objectives of groups such as Al Qaeda, which may be seen to epitomize religious motivations, actually relate primarily to consolidating territory and political power and only secondarily to disagreements over religion (Abrahms 2006).

Much of the debate about the political and/or religious motivations of extremism has focused on jihadi groups, specifically on the religiousness of present-day jihad. Furthermore, in addressing this question, wider issues regarding the relationship of the secular West to Islam have been raised. Cottee (2019), for instance, foregrounds the importance of religion in social and political life and argues that, while religious ideology should not be seen as "the sole or exclusive cause of violence carried out in the name of religion," it is nevertheless an element in any causal explanation of its occurrence. Moreover, he cautions that Western scholarship is morally gamed toward minimizing the role of religious ideology in violence because academics are "for the most part liberal-leftist in outlook [and] do not want to denigrate Islam, so they relocate the causal center of gravity away from it" (2018, 448).

Several studies have sought to evidence empirically the political and/or religious underpinning of extremist groups. For example, Mair (2017) examined the content of all the live tweets sent by the jihadi group Al-Shabaab during its 2013 attack on the Westgate shopping mall in Nairobi, Kenya. The analysis revealed a similar number of political and religious content tweets, which made it difficult to ascribe the attack and its perpetrators as being driven primarily by either a political or a religious ideology. As Mair (2017) concluded, for a group that is generally regarded as being religiously motivated, the findings highlight the critical interplay of politics and religion in extremism. This interpretation resonates with studies weighing religion versus political factors in the demise of extremist groups. For instance, Jones and Libicki (2008) examined the dissolving period of 268 such groups and found that, for 43% of them, it was political change in the environment in which they operated that primarily contributed to their end.

This blurring of political and religious motivation within extremist groups is compounded by their tendency to feed off each other in terms of recruitment and violence goals—something referred to as "cumulative extremism" (Eatwell 2006; see also Busher and Macklin 2015). A case in point is the interaction between so-called Islamic State jihadism and the UK radical right group English Defence League. The English Defence League was founded in 2009, as a direct response to a perceived threat from local Islamist groups in the English town of Luton. Between 2009 and 2012, the group inspired a number of similar movements across Europe that campaigned against the perceived Islamification of Western societies that they claimed was triggered by the specific threat of religiously motivated extremism.

When it comes to committing violent acts, there are both similarities and differences in the *modus operandi* of religious and political extremist groups. Pantucci (2018) identified several similarities when analyzing two UK-based attacks in 2018, one by the jihadi group Daesh and the other by the radical right, neo-Nazi group National Action. Both attacks targeted well-known political figures, were partly inspired by other attacks, had an underlying desire for personal revenge, and included evidence of predatory sexual behavior among the group members involved. However, Pantucci (2018) also identified an important difference: whereas the Daesh attack was conducted by an isolated individual, the National Action plot was the collective making of this neo-Nazi group. Furthermore, he noted, this constituted an "almost complete role reversal" for jihadi and radical right extremism vis-à-vis their pre-2010s *modus operandi*. During the mid to late 2000s, Pantucci (2018, 3) noted, the radical right was characterized by isolated individuals who "accumulated massive amounts of weaponry, indulged in anti-social behavior, or sought paedophilic material—all the while showing clear sympathies to the XRW [extreme right wing] cause"; whereas jihad was characterized by "sophisticated networks linked to Al-Qaida affiliates around the world." Isolated loners who latched onto violent Islamist ideology to try to launch attacks were the exception rather than the norm. Pantucci (2018) thus concluded that there are both differences and similarities between jihadi and radical right groups' acts of terror. He also emphasized the constantly evolving "threat picture" that these groups collectively pose: "from one characterised by an external threat touching the UK's shores and using UK nationals, to one of homegrown actors focused on UK interests, to today's threat picture driven by multiple ideologies with competing networks and a broad footprint of isolated adherents conducting attacks without clear direction" (2018, 3).

Using ethnographic methods, Pearson (2020) also found differences and similarities in UK-based jihadi and radical right groups' representation and treatment of men and women. Both movements are homosocial, sharing broadly masculinist and patriarchal ideologies. Yet in radical right groups Pearson (2020, 17) observed, "there is greater diversity [than in jihadi groups] in the gendered approaches of different leaders and groups, and possibilities for women." These possibilities are far from tension-free. On the one hand, women in radical right groups occupy some leadership roles, adopting also some patriarchally typical masculine identities and practices. On the other hand, they support, rather than necessarily contest, patriarchal norms. For their part, women in jihadi groups rebrand the patriarchal value that men must protect women as furthering female agency. Although this does not increase women's position in these groups, let alone challenge patriarchy, it has appeal to both men and women (Pearson 2020, 17–19).

Boundaries between religious and political motivation in extremist ideologies evidently remain difficult to establish. Although jihadi and radical right groups differ regarding a number of operational and ideological factors, they often enjoy a symbiotic relationship in terms of recruitment and evolving *modus operandi*. This is important to our primary concern with digital ideological grooming discourse as it helps inform these groups' strategies, including their members' styling of self and other. The latter is explored in Chapter 6. Next, however, we discuss the digital *modus operandi* of radical right (Section 5.4) and jihadi (Section 5.5) groups.

5.4 RADICAL RIGHT GROUPS' DIGITAL *MODUS OPERANDI*

Radical right groups are generally held to be highly competent digitally (see, e.g., Burris, Smith, and Strahm 2000; Bowman-Grieve 2009; Hainsworth 2016; Rydgren 2017; Conway et al. 2019b). From the early 1980s, they have used and continue to use three digital spaces: Internet forums, blogs, and social media platforms (Ganesh 2019). Internet forums were among the first digital spaces used by radical right groups—such as white supremacists (including members of the Ku Klux Klan) and neo-Nazis—to connect with each other (Zickmund 2002; Daniels 2009). The creation of the best-known radical right website, Stormfront.org, dates to 1995, for instance. In the early 2000s, many radical right groups launched overtly and covertly racist websites, often using blog functionalities. Blogs became appealing to these groups because they reduced access barriers to broad dissemination for individuals, "allowing them to circumvent gatekeepers in the media and to fashion themselves into far-right thought leaders" (Ganesh 2019, 30). *Vlogs*—primarily posted on YouTube—offered them similar opportunities. From around the mid-2010s, blogs became particularly useful as vehicles for radical right groups to spread counter-jihad messages across Europe and North America (Ekman 2015). These blogs both acted as echo chambers for radical right groups and enabled "a 'patchwork' of ideas and texts that reinforce[d] a nativist worldview in which Muslims [were] seen as a monolithic threat to the public in Europe and North America" (Ganesh 2019, 32).

As social media platforms emerged, so did radical right groups' interest in and increased use of them. Ganesh (2019) uses the metaphor of a "swarm" to define the social media networks in which radical right groups are nowadays known to thrive. This swarm includes sites such as 4Chan and Reddit, in which relatively small communities both generate varying content (e.g., memes, images, and videos) and co-ordinate their activities on mainstream social media platforms (e.g., Massanari 2018). This swarm is transnational, with members being able to establish relations globally. Unsurprisingly, therefore, the swarm brings together "a coalition of various toxic [radical right] cultures, including white nationalists, counter-jihad activists and misogynists" (Ganesh 2019, 34). As introduced in Chapter 1, a cross-national (Belgium, France, Germany, Greece, Netherlands, Norway, and United Kingdom) study of extreme ideology groups' use of the social media platform Twitter over a 3-month period in 2018 found Twitter to be used much more by radical right groups than jihadi groups (Nilsen et al. 2020). The study also found that radical right users set up anonymous Twitter accounts through which they shared their worldviews and provided information about themselves to other Twitter users whom they sought to groom ideologically. The main "influencer" in these Twitter radical right networks was former US President Donald Trump.

Across digital spaces, there is a distinctively visual feel to the content posted by radical right groups—something that is shared with jihadi groups (see Section 5.3.2). This is unsurprising given the persuasive power of images (e.g., Messaris and Abraham 2001; Hariman and Lucaites 2007; Zelizer 2010) and the inherent multimodality of digital spaces. Yet research into radical right groups' visual content online is underdeveloped when compared to that into jihadi groups. Extant studies highlight the particular complexity of radical right groups' visual strategies in some digital spaces especially. For example, Prisk (2017) found memes posted by an alt-right group to the image board 4Chan to have such a high level of "hyper-reality"—that is to say, content was so divorced from and in denial of reality—that it was difficult for non-group members to know what many of the memes meant. Doerr (2017) also found that online cartoons posted by three European radical right groups on webpages and blogs included familiar racist symbols while vehemently denying that these symbols held racist connotations. Furthermore, a comparison of Facebook posts (videos, pictures, and graphics) by various radical right groups in Hungary showed that the posts that received most likes and shares were visually sophisticated and tailored their messaging toward a young, tech-savvy audience (Karl 2017).

A case study of how radical right groups tailor their communication strategies to different digital platforms is offered by Nouri, Lorenzo-Dus, and Watkin (2021), who analyzed all the images posted by Britain First during two 4-month periods, in 2017 and 2018, on a mainstream and fringe social media platform, respectively Facebook (n = 731) and Gab (n = 264). The authors found cross-platform differences in both the images' technical properties and their content. Regarding photographic techniques, the group's move from Facebook to Gab in May 2018 showed a marked change in visual style from, respectively, aesthetically polished images, often of Britain, to unedited images of, frequently, identifiable urban spaces in local areas, such as town centers. The group's more "natural" visual style on Gab strengthened the impression of Britain First being a community that is close and familiar to its (target) members. This suited the group's focus on recruitment as it sought to recover from being removed from Facebook (and subsequently Twitter), with its follower count falling from millions on Facebook to just thousands on Gab within a month.

As for image content, the removal of Britain First from Facebook and their migration to Gab resulted in a dual shift. First, the most frequent group of images on Facebook focused on everything that was perceived to be great about being British—that is, on the in-group. On Gab, the most frequent group of images focused on the inner core of the in-group: Britain First's leaders and particularly active members. Second, images related to religion were the second most frequent group on Facebook and Gab, but the framing of these images was different. On Facebook, religion-themed images were polarized, depicting the in-group's religion (Christianity) positively and the out-group religion as Islamic extremism and therefore negatively. On Gab there were no in-group religion-themed images, and the Islam faith was overall depicted negatively. This extension of othering, from Islamic extremism to Islam as a religion, was enabled by platform migration—Gab operates a more lenient policy on monitoring hateful content than Facebook. The evident implications of social media monitoring of these groups' content are discussed further in Chapter 9 as part of broader considerations regarding the regulation of digital (ideological) grooming.

5.5 JIHADI GROUPS' DIGITAL *MODUS OPERANDI*

Jihadi groups are known to fight an ideological as well as a physical war against "the West" and its "nonbelievers." Their ideological war is structured around a tri-tiered information operations architecture comprising a broad membership/supporter base, provincial information offices (known as *wiyalat*), and central media units (Ingram 2015a). The groups' members and supporters disseminate their official communiqués—whether central or local—via those social media platforms over which they have already managed to gain considerable influence (Berger and Morgan 2015; Mair 2017). Provincial information offices tend to disseminate communiqués with a focus on localized issues, resorting to local platforms like posters, billboards, and public events. In contrast, central media units primarily release online messages globally. These messages may be brief (e.g., forum posts, tweets) or lengthy, for example online propaganda magazines such as *Dabiq, Rumiyah* (which replaced Dabiq from September 2016), and *Inspire*. These magazines are disseminated in a variety of ways, including archive sites (Bodo and Speckhard 2017), web forums, filesharing networks (Gambhir 2016), the Dark Net (Stacey 2017), and, primarily, social media (Cunningham, Everton, and Schroeder 2015; Gambhir 2016; Bodo and Speckhard 2017; Grinnell et al. 2018). The so-called Islamic State even tried to sell its free magazine *Dabiq* for profit on the e-retailer Amazon (Masi 2015).

Jihadi groups have been acutely aware of the power of digital spaces to further their goals since the 1990s. Their early digital forays had two purposes. One was their sharing of propaganda as well as the communication of threats and messages. The other was operational: the Internet facilitated their sharing of training material, fundraising, and recruitment (Bindner and Gluck 2019). The first jihadist websites surfaced around 2000 and were followed—indeed, overtaken after a few years—by Internet forums as the principal digital space for meetings and jihadi hubs. The forums also enabled circulation of instructions for building or using weapons, as well as tutorials on committing terrorist acts (Zelin 2013). Jihadi groups' use of social media became common in the 2010s, prompting coinage of the expression "Sheikh Google and LOL jihad," by journalist David Thomson (2014, cited in Bindner and Gluck 2019, 20), to reference a generation of social media–active jihadists who joined the Syrian civil war from 2011.

From the mid-2010s especially, mainstream social media companies started to monitor closely their accounts for jihadi—and other forms of extreme ideology—content. Unsurprisingly, these groups looked for alternative social media homes. For instance, Twitter's account suspension policies, in the late 2010s, resulted in jihadi groups migrating toward Telegram, which is an encrypted messaging application that can be used for one-to-one conversations in groups or in channels that allow users to stream messages to audiences. Moreover, Telegram groups offer interactive and multidirectional communication. All types of media (including large files) can be posted on Telegram—with the application housing a significant jihadi library that includes new and old/recycled documents (Clifford and Powell 2019). These digital affordances have made Telegram and other emergent platforms ideal digital milieus for jihadi and other extreme ideology groups (Bindner and Gluck 2019).

Across digital platforms, jihadi groups are known to base much of their community-building work on motivational frames that emphasize the importance of immediate action and success, typically by respectively highlighting injustice against and exaggerating the successes of the in-group (Andersen and Sandberg 2018). Immediate action activates "hot cognitions," that is, emotional appeals to moral indignation (Gamson 1995). For instance, pictures of Muslim civilians killed across the world are used in online propaganda magazines to activate feelings of moral injustice that may in turn trigger violent "retaliation."[4] As for success exaggeration as a motivational frame, this relies on jihadi groups' glorification of their military advances and conquering of new territories, as well as extreme violence against individuals or groups (e.g., assassinations). According to social movement theory, keenly stressing community success facilitates members' mobilization as it conveys the message that they are joining a winning cause. For instance, the initial military success of the so-called Islamic State caught the global media's eye and led to an increase in the number of foreign fighters that the group was able to recruit to its cause (Rasheed 2015; Andersen and Sandberg 2018).

Ingram (2014, 2015a, 2015b, 2016) argues that jihadi groups synergistically draw on pragmatic and perceptual factors for ideological grooming purposes. Pragmatic factors seek to leverage rational choice-making derived from cost-benefit analyses of alternatives to stability, security, and livelihoods. Perceptual factors seek to leverage choices made according to one's identity;

in the case of jihadi groups, primarily their members' religious identity. The groups differ among themselves in how they deploy such factors. For example, whereas Al Qaeda relies heavily on identity-choice appeals, the so-called Islamic State tends to balance identity and rational appeals.

Also, Al Qaeda and the so-called Islamic State's magazines (respectively *Inspire* and *Dabiq*/Rumiyah) regularly deploy attrition, intimidation, provocation, spoiling, and outbidding tactics. Yet they differ in the frequency of use of some of these. *Inspire* favors attrition; that is, the use of messages that portray Al Qaeda as capable and willing to inflict a high cost on the West unless some of its policies are revoked. In contrast, *Dabiq* favors a combination of intimidation and outbidding strategies that, respectively, seek to prove its ability to destroy their enemies' culture and to draw their recruitment targets away from rival groups by stating the so-called Islamic State's greater commitment to fighting "the West" and their higher fidelity to Islam (Novenario 2016).

Furthermore, Andersen and Sandberg (2018) note a seeming "rhetorical ambiguity" in the so-called Islamic State's digital grooming work. On the one hand, they focus on their attempts at state building, which speaks to the concerns of the Muslim majority and thus fits well with a community rationale. On the other, they promote—via graphic description—excessive violent actions, which appeals to a subcultural minority drawn toward othering and extreme violence. The so-called Islamic State therefore respectively seeks to "attract families to the Caliphate and warriors to fight wars" (2018, 15).

The above differences among jihadi groups are also reflected in their visual messaging, which is a key feature of these groups' digital *modus operandi* (Kovács 2015; KhosraviNik and Amer 2020). Watkin and Looney (2019), for example, identified and examined all the photographic images of children published from 2009 to 2016 in five online jihadi magazines: *Inspire*, *Dabiq*, *Jihad Recollections*, *Azan*, and *Gaidi Mtaani*. The analysis revealed a number of differences among the magazines. First, *Dabiq* and *Gaidi Mtaani* portrayed children as supporting the cause of jihad. However, whereas *Dabiq* chose images of children as fierce and prestigious upholders of jihad, the children always being boys, the children in *Gaidi Mtaani* were depicted as supporting the cause of jihad peacefully. Second, and in contrast to *Dabiq* and *Gaidi Mtaani*, *Inspire* and *Azan* primarily portrayed children as victims of Western-backed warfare. The authors did not identify any child representation patterns in *Jihad Recollections*.

A study of all the images (n = 3,869) in five online magazines published by the jihadi groups Al-Shabaab, Al Qaeda, Taliban in Khurasan, and the so-called Islamic State over a 6-year period (2009–2015) showed that 31% of these images (n = 1,198) depicted ordinary members (i.e., nonleaders) of the respective jihadi groups (Macdonald and Lorenzo-Dus 2021). This was the most frequent category in the dataset under analysis, followed at some distance by images of "the enemy" (14.1% of the total). The images of ordinary jihadi group members constructed the identity of "the good Muslim" based on cumulative stances of fulfillment, respect, and activism. Visual indexes of these stances represented jihad as being significant and worthy of respect, including via depiction of artifacts (e.g., flags), weapons (e.g., guns), and other visual indices of military capability (e.g., transport—motorbikes, horses— and technology—mobile phones, laptops) and religious status (e.g., heaven). Artifacts and weapons focused on the here-and-now, indexing the stance of military activism in accordance with the groups' call to violence on religious grounds. Religious status markers focused on the hereafter, using effects such as superimposing blue sky and clouds and/or giving the individual a heavenly glow to portray their status in the afterlife. Depiction of clothing was also strategic, the prevalence of casual clothing constructing "humility," which expresses knowledge of an attribute revered within this milieu. Cumulatively these images constructed a stance of knowing how to be good members of worthy-of-respect communities—a knowledge that brought a sense of fulfillment to those who possessed it. Yet there were some clear differences between the magazines. For example, *Gaidi Mtaani* placed a greater emphasis on military capability indexes, such as military clothing and military formation, while *Inspire* placed a greater focus on religious status indexes. The most distinctive of the five magazines was *Dabiq*, which had a greater emphasis on positive emotions and (celebratory) salutes, its own flag, and—above all—focused on the communal over the individual.

5.6 CONCLUSION

The unresolved debate regarding the religious and/or political motivations of extremists, together with mutual learning and an often-symbiotic relationship, suggest that the digital *modus operandi* of extremist groups can be expected to exhibit similarities as well as differences. Both jihadi and radical right groups make strategic use of diverse digital spaces, moving across them in agile ways in response to new opportunities and threats. Jihadi and radical right groups also share high entitativity, of which polarized ideology is a *sine qua non*. Indeed, for both jihadi and radical right groups, the dominant objective of their digital communication strategies is community-building as the locus for identity construction, specifically the ideological formation of in-groups that are bound together through their active vilification of out-groups. Such boundary-setting, as we have seen, helps reduce uncertainty about self-identity and thus lures individuals toward them. Furthermore, while the digital community-building activities of jihadi and radical right groups exhibit some continuity with the pre-digital notion of imagined political identities, they also share a key difference: namely, the salience gained by the practice of othering within broader identity construction practices. And it is to the strategic performance of digital ideological groomers' identity—theirs and others' in their discourse—that Chapter 6 next turns.

NOTES

1. https://www.theguardian.com/us-news/2018/oct/27/pittsburgh-synagogue-shooting. Accessed January 2022.
2. https://www.post-gazette.com/news/crime-courts/2018/11/10/Robert-Bowers-extremism-Tree-of-Life-massacre-shooting-pittsburgh-Gab-Warroom/stories/201811080165; and https://www.theguardian.com/us-news/2018/oct/30/pittsburgh-synagogue-shooter-was-fringe-figure-in-online-world-of-white-supremacist-rage. Accessed December 2021.
3. The term "small stories" is used in the sense of Georgakopoulou (2007).
4. For a comprehensive review of the concepts of morality and the moral order across the social sciences, including in linguistics (specifically sociopragmatics) scholarship, see Garcés-Conejos Blitvich and Kádar (2021).

CHAPTER 6

"Let Them Starve, You Idiots!!! Why Feed VERMIN?"

Digital Ideological Grooming Discourse

6.1 INTRODUCTION

This chapter examines digital ideological groomers' styling of themselves, their targets, and their perceived opponents. The focus is on a key aspect of extreme ideology groups' digital *modus operandi*, namely mass sharing of content to create and grow communities of like-minded individuals (Chapter 5). Hence, unlike digital sexual grooming, where the predominant participation framework is one-to-one (groomer–target), the main participation frameworks considered here are one- and many-to-many, with the many being networked publics who interact within continuously expanding contexts (see Chapter 2). The selected content spans radical right and jihadi groups' messaging on "traditional" (blogs, online propaganda magazines) and more recent (social media swarm) digital spaces. The examples covered in the chapter are typical of their authors' ideological grooming practices in the various—and varying—datasets introduced in Chapter 1. The examples therefore reference different degrees of extremism, from weapon use instructions and calls to commit assassinations in the case of some of the jihadi groups through to racial slurs and other forms of verbal denigration in the case of some radical right groups. Across these spaces and examples, the analytic focus is on group members' self- (Section 6.2) and other- (Section 6.3—target focused; Section 6.4—opponent focused) styling within their digital ideological grooming work.

Digital Grooming. Nuria Lorenzo-Dus, Oxford University Press. © Oxford University Press 2023.
DOI: 10.1093/oso/9780190845193.003.0006

6.2 SELF-STYLING IN DIGITAL IDEOLOGICAL GROOMING

Digital ideological groomers style themselves as members of closely knit, highly entitative groups that assert their beliefs in uncompromising ways. Three interrelated stances are at the heart of this self-styling work: broad ("Jack-of-all-trades") expertise (Section 6.2.1), toxic openness (Section 6.2.2), and impatient avidity (Section 6.2.3).

6.2.1 Broad ("Jack-of-all-trades") expertise

Self-styling within digital ideological grooming relies on the performance of stance-taking acts that index expertise. Regardless of whether expertise is held by a single individual, typically the group leader, or the in-group as a whole, digital ideological groomers style themselves as knowledgeable and competent across multiple life domains, from religion and politics through to popular culture and philosophy. One could speak of their expertise stance resembling that of a "Jack-of-all-trades"—a figure of speech with which they are unlikely to self-identify, especially its second part: "master of none." Yet extreme ideology groups regularly deploy topical opportunism to seek to expand their digital supporter base. They latch on to pretty much every aspect of public life, especially if in the news: from chocolate Easter egg sales through to child sexual abuse criminal rings (Brindle and Macmillan 2017; Nouri and Lorenzo-Dus 2019). And when having their say about any such issues, they favor expertise displays.

Stance-taking of broad expertise is frequently activated by digital ideological groomers' use of an educational or instructional frame of talk, of which Extracts 6.1–6.3 are typical. Extract 6.1 comes from Al Qaeda's online magazine *Inspire*; Extracts 6.2 and 6.3 are, respectively, a social media post from a member of Reclaim Australia and part of a blog entry by the leader of the Traditionalist Worker Party.

Extract 6.1 *Inspire* [Issue 4: page 42]

01   Whichever land of jihad you decide to travel to today, the AK will be the
02   standard weapon of choice among the mujahidin. Thus it is imperative to
03   know how to use the weapon. In this series, we will prepare you on the
04   basics of the AK, the weapon's capabilities, how to open the weapon and
05   clean it, shooting positions, the types of bullets and the add-ons.

Extract 6.2 *Reclaim Australia* [Facebook]

01   False doctrine #2 - Multiculturalism.
02   The concept of multiculturalism originally meant to be able to learn
03   from other cultures and expand ones knowledge and experience for the
04   betterment of sharing and understanding between societies and
05   cultures. This has totally changed. Let me give you a case in point
06   —redefining Christmas and NOT displaying Christmas scenes out of
07   'respect' for other cultures—cancellation of ANZAC Day
08   commemorations for the sake of not 'upsetting' those who have NO
09   connection to the bravery and sacrifice for the freedoms we enjoy of
10   those we commemorate.

Extract 6.3 Traditionalist Worker Party [Blog]

01   Just as the male feminists have no sincere intention to actually empower
02   women and no observable effect of doing so, White Saviors also fail to
03   actually empower brown people . . . . White Advocates like myself are
04   the first to highlight the extremely rapid demographic transformation of
05   America . . . White Advocates can help this process along . . . This message
06   is important for us as white advocates to internalize and put into action . . .
07   TMZ tries to shame Alexis Texas for not being color-blind, but interracial
08   porn, as Cleaver states, is "where the Black politics of resentment and the
09   Jewish politics of White Genocide intersect" . . . In case you're still keeping
10   score, the author [TMZ] is proposing "extreme violence" against Whites
11   who attempt to establish safe spaces for themselves to peacefully survive in
12   away from the totalitarian Leftist state which cannot suffer their very
13   existence. This is White Genocide, plain and direct.

The educational frame is most explicit in Extract 6.1, which is part of a section of the magazine titled "Instructional Guide – Training with the AK." Expectedly, the register is that of an instructions' manual seeking to reassure its intended readership (the grooming targets) of the simplicity and accessibility of the learning covered in its contents. This is clearly outlined in Extract 6.1: "we will prepare you on the basics of the AK, the weapons capabilities, how to open the weapon and clean it, shooting positions, the types of bullets and the add-ons" (lines 03–05) The statement of intent "we will prepare you" contributes to conveying a sense of effortlessness on the part of the intended target who are positioned as neophytes to be taught about "the basics of the AK" (lines 03–04). Use of the initialism "AK" to refer to the assault rifle (Automatic Kalashnikov) presumes a certain familiarity with weaponry terminology on the part of the target. Beyond that, however, the Instructional Guide text, including Extract 6.1, is jargon-free. Lay terms—such as "add-ons" (line 05) for additional component parts of the rifle—are used instead.

In the two other extracts, the educational frame entails stating a series of incontrovertible truths and making categorical assertions. In Extract 6.2, a lecture-style explanation of the origin of the "concept of multiculturalism" (line 02) is offered, which is keyed as disproving several untruthful dogmas ("False doctrine #2", line 01). Use of the emphatic adverbial "totally" ("This has totally changed," line 05) highlights a debasement of the original concept: "to be able to learn from other cultures and expand one's knowledge and experience for the betterment of sharing and understanding between societies and cultures" (lines 02–05). The point is further explained through the teaching technique of exemplification ("a case in point," line 05) in the remainder of the post.

In Extract 6.3, the educational frame concerns the distinction between "White saviors" and "White advocates." The former are evaluated in negative terms; the latter—with which the Traditionalist Worker Party post author (the party leader) identifies—are positively appraised. Both evaluations make use of epistemic modality that leaves no room for uncertainty. Thus, white saviors "fail to actually empower" (lines 02–03) those they claim to, in their case "brown people" (line 03)—something that likens them to another out-group—"male feminists" (line 01), who "have no sincere intention to actually empower women and no observable effect of doing so" (lines 01–02). The evaluation is emphasized through gradation (a comparative structure—"just as . . . ") and repetition (of the intensified object clause "to empower"). The actions of those who oppose the author's in-group—here, white advocates—are assertively defined ("This is White Genocide"), with pausing punctuation (comma) being used strategically for emphatic purposes: ", plain and direct" (line 13). This final assertion is presented as being the only possible one on account of previous evidence from external sources ("as Cleaver states, is 'where the Black politics of resentment and the Jewish politics of White Genocide intersect,'" lines 08–09)—more on which later.

Extracts 6.1–6.3 skillfully combine use of impersonal statements and direct forms of address. The impersonal statements present incontrovertible truths that, under the guise of objective definitions, hide evaluative accounts and direct the targets toward vital learning outcomes: "it is imperative to know how to . . . " (lines 02–03, Extract 6.1); "This message is important . . . to internalize and put into action" (lines 05–06, Extract 6.3). Alongside these, second-person deictic pronouns are used where the producer (groomer) engages directly with the intended recipients (target) of the knowledge being imparted: "we will prepare you" (line 03, Extract 6.1), "Let me give you a case in point" (line 05, Extract 6.2), and "In case you're still keeping score" (lines 09–10, Extract 6.3). Ostensibly, this knowledge is not imposed—instead, the rationale for acquiring it is justified. Thus, in Extract 6.1, for example, the imperative of learning to use a weapon, even if only the basics thereof, is presented on practical grounds: it will be valid regardless of "[w]hichever land of jihad you decide to travel to today" (line 01). The knowledge also carries in-group membership benefits: the AK—it is once again unambiguously asserted—"will be the standard weapon of choice" by the aspired-to in-group, "the mujahidin" (lines 01–02). And in Extract 6.3, the conditional clause "In case you're still keeping score" (lines 09–10) presupposes an engaged recipient to whom the choice is ironically given to opt-out of their engagement through the prepositional phrase "in case (+ clause)."

In these extracts "fresh talk" (Goffman 1981) is also used. The text producers are sounding boxes (animators) who offer their views (authors) through the lenses of personal experience (principals), as in "let me give you" (line 05, Extract 6.2) and "White Advocates like myself" (line 03, Extract 6.3). At times they resort to first-person plural deixis. The intrinsic ambiguity of first-person plural pronouns, which can be inclusive or exclusive of one's discourse recipient, makes them particularly helpful devices across a range of contexts in which mobilizing views and building (up) affinity-based communities are at stake. Digital ideological grooming, as discussed in Chapter 5, is a case in point. In Extract 6.1, the "we" in "we will prepare you" (line 03) excludes the grooming target but entails its groomer and those with whom he shares his expertise—the mujahidin in-group. In Extracts 6.2 and 6.3, in contrast, "we" brings the producer and his recipients within the same in-group. In Extract 6.2, it is the in-group that coheres against the "false doctrine" of multiculturalism and its disdain for "the freedoms we enjoy of those we commemorate" (lines 09–10). In Extract 6.3, the in-group comprises "us as white advocates" (line 06)—a strategic personal deictic shift from the previous sentence in which it was only the author ("myself") who self-defined as a white advocate (line 03).

This fluid use of footing (Goffman 1981) supports the "Jack-of-all-trades" expertise stance in digital ideological grooming. As noted earlier, the locus of such expertise can reside in a single person, as Extracts 6.1 and 6.2 have shown. Additionally, the locus of expertise may be fully or partially shifted to an external authority source, which legitimizes the knowledge being imparted, as in the quotation used in Extract 6.3 (lines 01–09). Discourse legitimization entails providing "good reasons, grounds, or acceptable motivations for past or present action" (van Dijk 1998, 255). van Leeuwen (2007, 2008) distinguishes between four main discourse legitimation strategies: moral legitimation, which references value systems; rationalization, whereby legitimation relies on claims of utility; mythopoesis, in which narratives are used, the outcomes of which recompense perceived moral actions and penalize perceived immoral actions; and authorization, which is legitimation by reference to the authority of tradition, custom, law, or persons with authority. This can take the form of a *verbum dicenci* with the relevant authority as subject, such as "The law stipulates that . . .," or a circumstance or attribution, such as "According to x . . ." (van Leeuwen and Wodak 1999), or use of direct quotations. The very practice of quoting recontextualizes—and hence reinterprets—the original text and voice being quoted. Direct quotation is a powerful ideological tool of manipulation in digital environments, where it serves as a "gatekeeping device" that favors particular sources of knowledge and the values that these uphold over other sources and values (Teo 2000, 20). In this sense, it is worth noting that, although quotation misattribution and decontextualization have always existed, they are especially frequent in digital discourse (Schultze and Bytwerk 2012).

It is also worth highlighting the importance of morality-related arguments within practices of legitimation. Morality is a complex phenomenon that has hitherto defied an agreed definition across the many fields of study that have focused on it. From a discourse perspective, Garcés-Conejos Blitvich and Kádar (2021) argue that morality is realized in and through language use when we attribute (non)linguistic good or bad behaviors to others and that these tend to be nonbinary evaluations that usually occur along a cline. Morality evaluations concern "'others' choices that are never independent of the practice and type of relationships we are involved in and are guided by overarching principles that can be subject to discursive struggle" (2021, 390). And the authors stress that morality is crucially linked to impoliteness—many concepts used to describe and make sense of morality (such as fairness/reciprocity, unity, hierarchy, proportionality, authority/respect, and so forth) overlap with concepts used to describe and make sense of (im)politeness, in particular Brown and Levinson's (1978/1987) approach. For example, negative face/politeness is related to autonomy, hierarchy, and respect, and positive face/politeness is related to reciprocity, unity, community, and in-group loyalty.

In digital ideological grooming, legitimation via authorization is often used to index broad expertise stance-taking. For instance, use of direct quotations was frequent in the Traditionalist Worker Party blog—the quotation mark symbol (" . . . ") being among the 180 keywords emerging from a comparison of the blog contents and a reference corpus of Traditionalist Worker Party tweets.[1] With 7,494 occurrences in the blog, the quotation mark symbol was as frequent as all the other keywords, whose combined frequency of use was 7,451 occurrences. This indicates a clear strategic use of external authority sources by the group's leaders—and authors of the blog posts—to legitimize their viewpoints.

Other keywords helped identify who these external sources of expertise were. Many of them corresponded to public figures, past and present, from life domains as varied as philosophy, economics, theology, mythology, and pop culture—the broad parish itself supporting the Jack-of-all-trade-ness, as it were, of the expertise stance in digital ideological grooming. It is worth noting in this regard use of the keyword "philosopher" to refer to numerous public figures whose views were aligned to the Traditionalist Worker Party, regardless of their actual professional status in some cases.

Among the most frequent sources quoted in the Traditionalist Worker Party blog was science fiction author Robert E. Heinlein, whose works were evaluated as upholding the Traditionalist Worker Party's notion of tradition, and linked to the works of the Italian, pro-fascism philosopher Julius Evola, who was also frequently quoted. Other individuals whose work was saliently quoted to legitimize the Traditionalist Worker Party's ideology included former Venezuelan president Hugo Chávez, popular Greek yoga instructor Irene Pappas, and pro-fascism, Russian political analyst Alexander Dugin.

There were several authorities/opinion leaders whose views were also frequently quoted in the Traditionalist Worker Party's blog, but negatively appraised. These included the director of an LGBT Center at Ohio State University (Delfin Bautista) and the founder of the neo-Nazi website The Daily Stormer (Andrew Anglin). Quotes from the works of Bautista were used to legitimate the Traditionalist Worker Party's views on tradition as being diametrically opposed to the religious and/or moral deviance that this author was seen to embody. Negative evaluation of Anglin's quotes may seem surprising given the racist agenda shared by alt-right groups, including the Traditionalist Worker Party and neo-Nazi groups (see, e.g., Berger 2018; Mirrlees 2018). However, the US alt-right—of which the Traditionalist Worker Party is a self-defined member—is a heterogeneous mix of radical right groups rather than a single franchise operation. Outside of their shared aim to secure the dominance of white people and culture across the United States and beyond, US alt-right groups actively seek to carve their own niche in the radical right ideology spectrum, including by ostensibly distancing from each other (Conway 2016; Florido 2016; Berger 2018; Lorenzo-Dus and Nouri 2020). In his capacity as leader of another group in the same overall radical right space, therefore, discrediting Anglin's views would help to legitimize the Traditionalist Worker Party's own ideology.

Extensive referencing and quoting are also used in digital religious grooming, principally from the Quran (Halverson, Bennet, and Corman 2012; Kuznar and Moon 2014; Kuznar 2017). For example, Spier's (2018) analysis of over half a million words from 14 issues (combined) of the online jihadi propaganda magazines *Dabiq* and *Rumiyah* published between July 2014 and April 2016 identified 624 quoted or referenced scripture verses. Approximately 70% of these citations were unique; that is, they were cited only once or twice. The analysis also found that the six most frequently attested Quran verses were quoted a total of 51 times, which accounted for 8.17% of all the cited scripture.

Extract 6.4 illustrates the synergistic use of external authority quotation and the educational frame within broad expertise stance-taking in digital religious grooming. The extract comes from the jihadi online propaganda magazine *Dabiq* and seeks to instruct its intended readership about logistical aspects of the so-called Islamic State's response to a claimed crusade against it. Within it, the text mobilizes two polar religious identities: "muwahhid" and "kafir." The Arabic term "muwahhid" designates a Muslim who abides by the concept of monotheism in Islam ("tawhid") and, as such, believes in Allah as the only God, from whom all legislation should come.[2] A "kafir," in contrast, is a derogatory term for a "nonbeliever," who is defined as someone who does not believe in Allah and is thus presumed to have malicious intentions toward Islam and Muslims.

Extract 6.4 *Dabiq* [Issue 4, page 44]

01 At the point of the crusade against the Islamic State, it is very important that attacks
02 take place in every country that has entered into the alliance against the Islamic State
03 [. . .] Let the muwahhid not be affected by "analysis paralysis" and thus abandon
04 every operation only because his "perfectionism" pushes him toward an operation
05 that supposedly can never fail – one that only exists theoretically on paper. He should
06 be pleased to meet his Lord even if with just one dead kafir's name written in his
07 scroll of deeds, as the Prophet (sallallahu 'alayhi wa wallam) said, *"A kafir and his*
08 *killer will never gather in hellfire."*

In Extract 6.4, legitimation for instructing extreme violence (killing) against kafirs is expressed through an impersonal, third-person statement ("it's very important that," line 01), an impersonally worded volition statement ("let the muwahhid not be . . .," line 03), and, finally, a direct quotation from the Prophet ("*A kafir . . . in hellfire*," lines 07–08). The combination of categorical statements and ultimate religious authority quotations within the teaching being imparted in this extract indexes a stance of, in this case, warcraft and scripture expertise. The latter is made particularly appealing by the promise of salvation that the quotation offers since the killer (the muwahhid) will escape "*hellfire*" (line 08), unlike his kafir victim.

The kind of textually assertive, authority-driven broad expertise stance-taking that Extracts 6.1–6.4 illustrate is mirrored—and hence augmented—visually in digital ideological grooming. In the case of digital religious grooming, one study of photographic images of ordinary jihadis in online propaganda magazines (Macdonald and Lorenzo-Dus 2021; see Chapter 5) showed them—individually or in groups—as being engaged in several activities, the most frequent one being shows of strength. These shows-of-strength images accounted for between 84.5% (*Azan*; n = 93) and 64% (*Inspire*; n = 265) of the total number of the online jihadi images examined. They typically depicted the jihadis adopting intimidating poses as part of some military activity, including saluting or marching. Given the high status of military might among jihadi groups, these images clearly conveyed a highly valued kind of knowledge/expertise: military prowess. The images also displayed a culture of masculinity in which being a "good Muslim" requires being a warrior who fights in a jihad—a mujāhidīn. Men in these groups are visually rendered as tough, resolute, and masculine, consistent with the stereotypical images of masculinity and patriarchy seen to characterize jihadi gender ideology (see Chapter 5). Male honor and in-dividual self-sacrifice are regularly praised (Andersen and Sandberg 2018). In this respect, it is worth noting that the intended readership of jihadi online propaganda magazines is primarily male. Women are described and characterized—rather than directly given a voice or an image—in them (Peresin and Cervone 2015).

Similarly, a study of 995 images posted by the radical right group Britain First across Facebook and Gab revealed a tendency to post images of the in-group that projected shows of strength, typically large groups of members in street marches, leafleting, and so forth, often surrounded by symbols that con-veyed political officialdom, such as flags and other products bearing the group's logo (Nouri, Lorenzo-Dus, and Watkin 2021). The images thus showcased com-petence at being a member of a strong, internally cohesive, highly entitative group. Across many of these images, the group's leaders were centrally posi-tioned, flanked by menacing-looking supporters—their collective facial expres-sions frequently conveying anger. As in the case of the intimidating-looking jihadis, such shows of strength imagery not only support a particular construc-tion of expertise but also speak to a second, interrelated stance in digital ide-ological groomers' self-styling: namely, toxic openess, which is discussed next.

6.2.2 Toxic openness

The legitimation strategy of mythopoesis plays a key part in the performance of toxic openness in digital ideological groomers' self-styling. Through mytho-poesis an individual's story can be presented "as evidence for a general norm of behaviour" (van Leeuwen and Wodak 1999, 110). Mythopoesis is one of the most important legitimation strategies in racist and anti-Semitic discourses (van Leeuwen and Wodak 1999), of which a number of extreme ideology groups feed and where primarily negative stories are functionalized to support such discourses. For instance, in a study of legitimation strategies in online jihadi propaganda magazines by Lorenzo-Dus, Kinzel, and Walker (2018), mythopoesis was the most frequent strategy used in *Inspire* (37% of total) and *Dabiq* (32% of total) to justify violence against apostates ("murtaddin"), with the second most frequent strategy being authorization (29% of the total in *Inspire*; 16% of the total in *Dabiq*).

In digital ideological grooming, moreover, it is first-person, emotional stories that tend to be used for legitimizing viewpoints. These stories thus index a stance of openness. Use of personal experience via emotional storytelling may seem counter-intuitive given that extreme ideology groups, which tend to be male-dominated (Pearson 2020), display high levels of toxic masculinity. Alongside violence, toxic masculinity is after all characterized by a disdain for communicative openness about one's feelings (Karner 1996; Haider 2016). However, the kind of emotions favored for disclosure in digital ideological grooming typically revolve around anger, including accounts of anger-fueled violence. Anger is indeed the one emotion that, far from being stigmatized in toxic masculinity, is elevated above any other (Parent, Gobble, and Rochlen 2019). Importantly, anger is always externally directed within the self-disclosing narratives of digital ideological groomers (see Section 6.4). It is always others who are held responsible for inflicting varying forms of damage on individuals and/or members of the in-group and thus "deserve" the in-group's anger displays. In other words, digital ideological groomers' toxic openness stance-taking helps to construct a distinctive blame maker (in-group)–blame taker (out-group) discourse, one in which the blame makers are also the victims of wrongdoing. The resulting narratives are therefore also manipulative disclosures of inner struggle.

Let us consider Extract 6.5, which comes from an interview with a member of the jihadi group Al-Sham that was originally posted on the group's website.[3]

Extract 6.5

01 Question: What was it that made you take that step toward hijrah?
02 Answer: living in the UK is very difficult, I felt as if I was imprisoned, you know.
03 You can't really express your feelings, in case you're being watched by the
04 secret services or suspicion could be raised about you, it's very difficult for
05 someone who has such passion for the Muslim Ummah to be able to
06 express his feelings. . . . Watching videos of innocent and helpless Muslims getting
07 tortured by the regime, similar to Iraq, Burma and other Muslim countries;
08 alongside these I was inspired by a few Mashaikh who would always talk
09 about the situation of the Muslim Ummah and had links with Jihad.

In Extract 6.5, the jihadi relays a first-person narrative of suffering, rich in emotional language, to legitimize a practice within jihad: hijrah (Muslim conquest via emigration). There is no evidence in the extract—or throughout the full interview—of his having been either incarcerated or under police surveillance. Yet these are the precise simile ("as if I was imprisoned," line 02) and contextual framing ("in case you're being watched," line 03) that he activates at the onset of his narrative. He repeats—thus emphasizing—his predicament in the UK as being one of emotional restraint born out of fear of institutions ("the secret services," line 04). This conjures up an image of censorship or worse at the heart of a democratic country. The image is further embellished by relaying other sources of inner struggle for him, namely "[w]atching videos of innocent and helpless Muslims getting tortured by the regime, similar to Iraq, Burma and other Muslim countries" (lines 06–07), an activity that, presumably, was self-selected rather than imposed upon him and that "inspired" (line 08) him, alongside the words of others ("a few Mashaikh," line 08) about "the situation of the Muslim Ummah" (lines 08–09), to undertake hijrah. Although clearly edited before publishing, the extract retains elements of orality, such as the tag "you know," which follows immediately from the first self-disclosing statement: "as if I was imprisoned, you know" (line 02). This seeks to authenticate the performance of a "naturally occurring" self-disclosing chat with an interviewer that, both parties know, will be subsequently digitally shared.

Narrative self-disclosing of inner struggle and victimization serves to legitimize group practices (hijrah, in Extract 6.5) in digital ideological grooming. The risk that such narratives may weaken digital ideological groomers' shows of strength is limited by their authors' stated desire to put an end to the wrongdoing they claim to endure—something that is further explored in Section 6.2.3 under the stance of impatient avidity. Mythopoesis in digital ideological grooming thus often relies on the *topos* of "savior," whereby the "victim" is also presented as strong, capable and keen to "defend the man/woman on the street" (Wodak 2015, 10). In doing so, these individuals construct "a Robin Hood-like figure," providing their targets with "an 'idol' to aspire to" (Wodak 2015, 10–21). Typically, it is the groups' leaders who play this part. However, ordinary group members also take it upon themselves to narrate stories in which they fight against perceived injustices—again from within a stance of toxic openness. Thus, in Extract 6.5 for example, an ordinary jihadi appears fearful of the enemy but he counters this feeling through his emotional staunchness to the Muslim Ummah, which ultimately helped him conquer his fear. His is, therefore, a moral tale that rewards the overcoming of inner struggle, presenting it as an experiential journey for others to emulate. Emulatibility, as discussed in Chapter 2, is a key determiner of engagement/influence across social media, one that lends itself well to the manipulative practice of digital ideological grooming.

Extracts 6.6.1 (part of a Traditionalist Worker Party blog) and 6.6.2 (a Reclaim Australia social media [Facebook] post) further illustrate this feature of digital ideological groomers' toxic openness in relation to a recurrent *topos* in radical right discourse: immigration is negative.

Extract 6.6.1 Traditionalist Worker Party [Blog]

```
01   My Irish and Swedish ancestors felt no more and no less commonality with
02   each other than with the Tlingit or the Kogi or the Malians or the
03   Vietnamese. . . . They also did not work with the same gods or share the
04   same rituals. Some of the Daoine Sidhe came across the ocean on ships with
05   my great grandparents (my father heard a Bean-Sidhe wailing the night my
06   great-grandmother died) just as the Orisha traveled from Africa to the
07   Americas in slave ships and across Damballah's rainbow bridge. But the next
08   generation had to cease acknowledging their presence if they wanted to be
09   admitted to white society. I did not say, "How dare you! Don't you know the
10   scientists have proven that we are all the same, we share the same DNA!?" I
11   simply acknowledged and respected that, despite our friendship, there was a
12   cultural barrier between us
```

Extract 6.6.2 Reclaim Australia [Facebook post]

```
01   I came out from England when I was 11 years old my parents both got jobs straight
02   away and always had to work hard we never got any help from the government . . .
03   The migrants that came to this country in the 50s were the people who helped this
04   country become what it is today. . . . Not like the ones that are coming today want
05   everything and expect it and who have no respect for us and the country that has
06   extended the welcome mat to them
```

Multiculturalism is the primordial focus of denigration in the discourse of radical right groups, where it is seen as a threat to the "purity" of those who founded a particular nation, which the in-groups represent (Nouri and Lorenzo-Dus 2019; Wodak 2020). This makes immigrants a threat per se: they bring along and also bring about their culture when they enter the in-groups' territory. This is expressed in Extract 6.6.1 in terms of there being a "cultural barrier" (line 12) between people from different countries, races, and cultures. Upon narrating his realization of this scientifically proven fact (lines 09–11), the author of Extract 6.6.1—and leader of the Traditionalist Worker Party—deploys the kind of covert or subtle xenophobia that avoids explicit incitement of violence against out-groups. In the context of race, and drawing on Bauman's (2000) notion of liquid modernity, Weaver (2010) coins the term "liquid racism." This refers to the kind of racism that is generated by "ambiguous cultural signs" that nevertheless encourage the development of "entrenched sociodiscursive positioning alongside reactions to racism when reading these signs." The ambiguity of liquid racism rests in its combination of "signs of older racisms alongside those of political and social issues that are not necessarily racist" (Weaver 2010, 678). Liquid racism is not an enfeebled or challenged residue of racism. Instead, it is a treacherous manifestation of racism, its power lying in the strategic use of ambiguity to weaken different arguments against claims of racism.

This is precisely what happens in Extract 6.6.1. The adverbial "simply" naturalizes white supremacism by explicitly referring to racial difference (line 11), which is not a racist claim per se. What is ambiguously claimed, though, is the concept of racial superiority, specifically the superiority of the white race. The concessive clause "despite our friendship" (line 11) downplays interracial affective social bonds vis-à-vis an assumed "cultural barrier" (line 12), the existence of which is constructed as uncontestable—to be "simply acknowledged and respected" (line 11), despite any evidence. The possibility that such evidence may exist is snubbed through *keying*—a performance that involves self-quoting to mock others' anger ('"How dare you!' . . .," line 09) in the face of fake self-ignorance ("Don't you know . . . ?," line 09).

In digital political grooming, moreover, multiculturalism is constructed as being a case of failed immigration. By failed immigration, radical right groups really mean immigrants' presumed unwillingness to assimilate to the host country, "insisting" instead in bringing about their own culture and/or making "unreasonable demands" of their host. This is typically appraised as indexing disrespect toward a generous and benign host. In Extract 6.6.2, for example, a marked evaluative contrast is created between good immigration in the past and bad, present-day immigration. In the author's legitimizing narrative, he positions himself as the offspring of respectful immigrants who contributed to the host country by "work[ing] hard" (line 02). His first-person story presents Australia as a generous host that is being disrespected by present-day immigrants who "have no respect for us and the country that has extended the welcome mat to them" (lines 05–06), including being institutional sponges in constant need of "help from the government" (lines 02–03). Through first-person narratives such as this one, digital political groomers project stances of toxic openness within which they are legitimated as understandingly angry victims of others' wrongdoing.

6.2.3 Impatient avidity

A third stance that supports digital ideological groomers' self-styling—complementing those of "Jack-of-all-trades" expertise and toxic openness—is impatient avidity. This entails their regular performance of keenness to uphold and/or reinstate the values of the in-group, be these values linked to religion, race, tradition, politics, and so forth. This is a point of difference with avidity stance-taking in digital sexual grooming where, as we saw in Chapter 4, the target was the object or cause of groomers' keen interest. In digital ideological grooming avidity is instead manifested in terms of urgent calls to action in the face of threats to the in-group by other groups, constructed as a threatening "other," and their values. Therefore, this stance also works alongside styling of perceived opponents, which is considered in Section 6.4.

Urgent calls to action are addressed to the target of digital ideological grooming, who may be either already a member of the in-group or someone the group seeks to bring in. These calls to action are discursively constructed as a necessary, indeed the only, option available to the in-group given the severity and/or long-standing nature of the threat posed by their opponents. The examples in Extract 6.7 (from social media posts by different radical right groups) and Extract 6.8 (from the file-sharing site justpaste.it[4]) are typical of digital ideological groomers' stance of impatient avidity.

Extract 6.7

6.7.1 Bandera Vecinal [Twitter]
Unite NOW to fight for the country corrupt populists who govern since 1983 have destroyed the country.[5]

6.7.2 Bandera Vecinal [Twitter]
PREACHING OF NATIONALISM NO LONGER STOPS!!!!!!!!!!!!!!!!!!![6]

6.7.3 Britain First [Facebook]
Why moan why not confront them and do something bout it enough is enough

6.7.4 Britain First [Facebook]
Defend our country people now because our government wont How come we have all these police for our marches but not for the Muslims n Islamic.

6.7.5 Traditionalist Worker Party [blog]
We may have originated in England, Ireland, Italy, or Russia, but we've become Amerikaners, the primordial ethnogenetic soup from which an entirely new nation must be born in the wake of this failed "American" experiment.

The examples in Extract 6.7 illustrate some of the regular devices used to index the stance of impatient avidity in digital ideological grooming. In 6.7.2, for example, emphatic typography—specifically use of capitalization and multiple exclamation marks—serves to stress that the group's proselytization goal is unstoppable. For their part, in examples 6.7.1 and 6.7.4, indexing impatient avidity is achieved through interactional directness in the form of mood derivable (imperatives) request head acts to join the in-group, which is further emphasized through both temporal adverbials that signal urgency ("NOW") and support (grounding) moves. In example 6.7.1, the grounding is provided via an elided causative connector: "(because) the corrupt populist who govern since 1983 have destroyed the country." In example 6.7.4, the grounding is prefaced by the same causative connector ("because"), this time explicitly pointing to the government's failure to "defend our country." This is presented as an incontrovertible truth, further justified through a rhetorical question that positions the in-group as the recipients of unfair treatment, namely having police attend their marches, vis-à-vis the "Muslims n Islamic" out-group, whose marches are not policed. The author of example 6.7.5 uses deontic modality, oriented toward obligation (must) rather than permission (may), to justify the birth of "an entirely new nation," which "must be born" from evolutionary superiority ("we've become Amerikaners, the primordial ethnogenetic soup"), regardless of ancestry ("We may have originated in England, Ireland, Italy, or Russia"—but note they are all originally European, white-race nations). And in example 6.7.3, the importance of the cause being avidly pursued is stressed through a two-part rhetorical question that criticizes current behavior by the target/in-group ("moan"), advocating instead confrontation as the "something bout it" that must be done. This is reinforced with the idiomatic expression "enough is enough," which categorically closes off the post and buttresses its author's impatient avidity.

Extract 6.8 comes from an interview of an Al Qaeda member. He is responding to a question about his understanding of jihad.

Extract 6.8 *Inspire*

01 There is no Muslim who sees America violating sanctity, killing children and women
02 and yet hesitates in fighting them. If an American comes at your doorstep, that is by
03 all means a test to your faith and loyalty. Therefore, this is a golden chance to avenge
04 your fellow Muslims by this American soldier who practices crime against the Muslim
05 nation in Afghanistan, Iraq, Somalia, Syria and among other Islamic Countries. Oh,
06 and what triumph for one who Allah eased his way avenging his fellow Muslims.

In Extract 6.8, the interviewee adopts the broad expertise stance, drawing on an educational frame. He makes use of generalization ("There is no Muslim who sees . . . and yet hesitates . . .," lines 01–02), legitimization by authority ("Allah eased his way," line 06) and exemplification ("If an American comes at your doorstep . . .," line 02). Use of "you" in the latter sentence has the additional advantage of ambiguously indexing direct interpellation (you as the target reader of this interview) or self-disclosure (generic you, but also modestly implying his own actions over time), thus potentially appealing to the openness stance, too. The point nevertheless remains crystal clear: there is "a golden chance" (line 03) that must be taken now "to avenge your fellow Muslims" (lines 03–04) and that carries a similarly clear reward: "triumph" (line 06) in the afterlife. He thus performs a stance of impatient avidity— a religious fervor that does not contemplate any degree of hesitation, just as (government) inertia was not an option for the radical right extremists. Action—here "avenging" one's in-group ("fellow Muslims," line 06)—is called for instead. It is worth noting that the violence being called for is euphemistically referenced as "avenging" (line 06). This contrasts markedly with the alleged actions by the out-group that must be avenged, which are not only stated but described in ways that intend to generate sympathy for the in-group as victims. Thus, the out-group—the generic "America" (line 01) or the pseudo-personalized "American" (line 02)/"American soldier" (line 04) in Extract 6.8—is denigrated on counts of despicable, repeated actions "violating sanctity, killing children and women" (line 01) and "practi[sing] crime against the Muslim nation in Afghanistan, Iraq, Somalia, Syria and among other Islamic Countries" (lines 04–05). Such clear othering of out-groups is characteristic of—indeed crucial to—digital ideological grooming, as will be shown in Section 6.4.

6.3 STYLING THE TARGET OF DIGITAL IDEOLOGICAL GROOMING

Despite comprising networked publics, and hence varied selves that may only come together in fleeting moments digitally, the target in digital ideological grooming is styled as a homogeneous entity that embodies a single, shared stance: needing help. The target of digital ideological grooming must be saved by the groomer who, as seen in Section 6.2, has the broad expertise, toxic openness, and impatient avidity to do so. Within this savior *topos*, digital ideological grooming swivels strategically between intra-group affiliation (groomer = target) and disaffiliation (groomer has superior knowledge to the target, and they are therefore not aligned, yet). In other words, "selective dissociation" (García Bedolla 2003) from the target, and the stances the target is seen to perform, may be enacted within an otherwise associative discourse. Selective dissociation occurs when individuals temporarily or permanently detach themselves from the representation of in-group members because of some objectionable trait or behavior that these members are believed to have. Selective dissociation tends to be discursively realized through impoliteness strategies of seeking disagreement with, and explicit distancing from, the target (Garcés-Conejos Blitvich 2018). Let us next consider Extracts 6.9 and 6.10, which respectively illustrate this in the context of radical right and jihadi grooming discourse.

Extract 6.9

6.9.1 Reclaim Australia (Facebook)
wake up australia islam is not a race it's a sick ideology. It's starting.
6.9.2 Britain First (Facebook)
Let them [Muslims] starve, you idiots!!! Why feed VERMIN?

Extract 6.10 *Dabiq* [issue 7; page 75]

```
01   O Muslims, O you who claim to be from the Ummah of Muhammad (sallallahu
02   'alayhi wa sallam), do you not see the religions of kufr gathering against the
03   Muslims just as the beasts gather to feed upon their prey? . . . Our children have
04   been dismembered by bombardment everywhere. The chastity of our sisters has
05   been violated. Our lands and wealth have been stolen. Yet you do not do anything!
06   How do you live with these criminals, the enemies of Allah and His Messenger,
07   while they wage war against Islam and the Muslims?
```

Extracts 6.9 and 6.10 are typical of styling the target as requiring help, specifically needing to be awakened from apathy and enlightened (Extract 6.9) and/or spurred to retaliate after long-endured humiliation (Extract 6.10). The target may thus be attributed negative stances that range from ignorance/apathy ("wake up . . . islam is not . . . it's . . .," example 6.9.1; "do you not see . . . ?," Extract 6.10, line 02) and stupidity ("you idiots!!!," example 6.9.2) to insincerity ("you who claim . . .," Extract 6.10, line 01) and unresponsiveness ("Yet you do not do anything!," Extract 6.10, line 05). These pointed criticisms and insults are direct and unmitigated, constituting instances of impoliteness oriented toward the target's quality face. The accusation of inaction, for instance, is emphasized through use of a challenging question ("how do you live with these criminals . . . ?," Extract 6.10, line 056) in the wake of a damming, rhetorical list of three atrocities committed by the enemy against the in-group: "our children . . . dismembered by bombardment everywhere . . . chastity of our sisters . . . violated . . . our land and wealth . . . stolen" (lines 03–05). A strategic shift of footing is used in this list of three, whereby the author goes from addressing the target directly (I-to-you [target]: "you who claim . . . do you not see," lines 01–02) to speaking on behalf of the in-group (I + you [target] as a collective, victimized "we" ["Our children . . . our sisters . . . Our lands and wealth"], lines 03–05) and then back to direct interpellation ("Yet you do not do anything! How do you live with . . .," lines 05–06).

The opponent is also overtly criticized and insulted within the same texts: "[Islam] is a sick ideology" (example 6.9.1); "Why feed VERNIM?," where vermin's anaphoric referent is the out-group (them—Muslims; example 6.9.2); "these criminals, the enemies of Allah and His Messenger . . . " (Extract 6.10, line 06). Criticizing/insulting both target and opponent within the same messages may risk alienating the former and, hence, jeopardize the grooming potential of these posts. Yet the stances attributed to the target in these cases are the components of a change process—from ignorance to knowledge; from apathy to action—that digital ideological groomers seek to trigger through these otherwise openly aggressive and target face-threatening messages. In contrast, the negative stances attributed to the out-group concern immutable properties—they are part of its "essence" (being a sick ideology, for example, in example 6.9.1). Thus, although selective dissociation processes are conflictual, relying as they do on impoliteness strategies, there is further nuance to them. The target being selectively disassociated from is nevertheless either perceived to be one of us (i.e., part of the in-group) or wanted to become one of us. This may explain why, on balance, selective dissociation relies more on strategies that emphasize the positive and mitigate the negative characteristics of the in-group than on strategies that emphasize the negative and mitigate the positive characteristics of the out-group (Garcés-Conejos Blitvich 2018).

Emphatically attributing positive stances to the target is, unsurprisingly, a recurrent feature of digital (ideological) grooming. Unlike in digital sexual grooming, in digital ideological grooming praise does not tend to be directly addressed at the target at an individual level. Instead, the in-group's virtues as a homogeneous community of like-minded persons are often extolled. This is where processes of groomer–target affiliation are at their most obvious. Let us consider some typical images posted by Britain First, on Facebook (Figures 6.1 and 6.2) and Gab (Figures 6.3 and 6.4). A cutout technique for picture alteration has been applied to Figures 6.3 and 6.4 to preserve the anonymity of the individuals depicted therein (see Chapter 1). Images were posted in color but are reproduced in black and white here with textual description of their color properties whenever this is is relevant to the analysis.

All four images concern the in-group: its members (potential [Figure 6.3] or actual [Figure 6.4] ones); its culinary culture (fish and chips—Figure 6.1) and its landscape (English countryside—Figure 6.2). Technically, the images in Figures 6.1 and 6.2 are more polished than the images in Figures 6.3 and 6.4. Figures 6.1 and 6.2 appear to have been photo-edited, including use of textual overlay, and have a clear aesthetic value that contributes to their social media sharing "worthiness" (Bednarek and Caple 2017; Nouri, Lorenzo-Dus, and Watkin 2021). Their aesthetics relies on the deployment of bright colors, such as lush green for the grass and bright blue for the sky in Figure 6.2, to highlight the stereotypical beauty of English rural life. Their aesthetics also relies on a particular choice of composition, whereby the

Britain First
@BritainFirst

SHARE IF YOU SHARE IF YOU
LOVE TRADITIONAL BRITISH
FOOD!

SHARE IF YOU ENJOY

Figure 6.1 Britain First (Facebook).

realms of the material and the immaterial are connected, and the immaterial is idealized.

Thus, in Figure 6.1, the material realm of food—fish and chips served in newspaper wrapping—is connected to the immaterial realm of feelings ("LOVE") and national ancestry ("TRADITIONAL BRITISH"), which is textually laced above the image and typographically emphasized through capitalization and punctuation (use of the exclamation mark). In Figure 6.2, the material realm of a rural village is connected to the realm of national aesthetics ("A BEAUTIFUL COUNTRY"), which is again textually embedded and typographically emphasized, including by using contrasting white text over a black banner capitalization and emphatic punctuation. In both cases, the connections are channeled through strategic composition: the food container in Figure 6.1 is tilted upward, toward the textual messages that represent the idealized, immaterial realm; the church spire in the village depicted in Figure 6.2 points to the sky, the metaphorical home of heaven. In both cases, the material realm has been carefully arranged to highlight social class aesthetics. Although wrapping fish and chips in newspaper sheets is associated with nonaffluency, the food wrapping is carefully arranged inside a basket, accompanied by a sauce container and a fabric (not paper) napkin that has

Figure 6.2 Britain First (Facebook).

been laid over a tablecloth (bottom right corner). These all visually index an aspirational social class status for the "ordinary folk" targeted by Britain First for recruitment. Similarly, the village depicted in Figure 6.2 appeals to idyllic representations of rural tranquility and natural beauty that index social class upward mobility aspirations—the grass is not only lush green but seems immaculately kept; the buildings are of natural stone, unblemished and perfectly maintained despite the passage of time. Completing the aesthetics are the inviting rolling hills, framed by white fluffy clouds that enable the sun to get through to the ground. In both images the message is uplifting. The in-group has class and beauty, rooted in tradition and history, and this message is to be shared, as per the instructional textual overlay in the lower part of the images.

The choice of aesthetics in Figures 6.3 and 6.4 is different from that in Figures 6.1 and 6.2. While continuing to depict a positive image of the in-group, the original images did not make (obvious) use of photo-editing. Instead, they appeared naturally occurring, those in the frame either being unaware of their being photographed (Figure 6.3) or posing without photographic

Figure 6.3 Britain First (Gab).

filters (Figure 6.4). Both images are typical of Britain First's technical change in visual style when migrating from Facebook to Gab, as noted in Chapter 5. Many of the group's photos on Facebook were stock or collage images, mostly unattributed and often seemingly out of context, with captions or textual overlay being added to fit the group's messaging at that point in time, as in Figures 6.1 and 6.2. The group's photos on Gab, in contrast, were technically simpler, with little or no editing and a much less frequent use of text overlaying—they often appeared to have been "just snapped" and uploaded to the site immediately. This shift from polished to "rough" aesthetics was not accidental. The connotation of authenticity that the latter visual look carries (Dahlgreen 2000; Lorenzo-Dus 2009) dovetailed nicely with the group's move at the time to a social media home, Gab, that parades an anti-establishment, "for and by the people"[7] ethos, to which the targeted in-group is expected to easily relate. Relatability, as discussed in Chapter 2, is both multifaceted and crucial to digital engagement and influence. The images in Figures 6.3 and 6.4 are illustrative of what, to explain the performance of authenticity in digital spaces, Abidin (2017, 1) terms "calibrated amateurism"—a "practice and aesthetic in which actors in an attention economy labor specifically over crafting contrived authenticity that portrays the raw aesthetic of an amateur." Calibrated amateurism works such that the impression is created that the self is somehow less filtered and planned; that is, it helps to construct digital engagement and influence through authenticity and relatability.

Figure 6.4 Britain First (Gab).

Differences in aesthetics aside, Britain First's images of the in-group remained unquestionably positive across Facebook and Gab. Figures 6.1 and 6.2 are typical of the group's marked preference for images that flaunt "the British nation"—be that its culinary traditions (Figure 6.1) or its rural landscape (Figure 6.2). Indeed, out of a total of 731 images posted by Britain First on Facebook over the 4-month period immediately preceding their ban from that social media platform, 242 (33%) were idyllic images of the British nation (Nouri, Lorenzo-Dus, and Watkin 2021). These images became much less frequent during the 4 months following the group's migration to Gab, representing only 9% (23) of the 264 images posted. Nevertheless, images that highlighted positive attributes of the in-group remained salient. In Figure 6.3, for instance, it is the in-group's activists that are shown off, specifically their on-the-ground leafleting and supporter recruitment. Whereas the original photograph may be technically natural, it is thematically assembled to style the target in a calculated way. Stereotypes abound: the frail elderly lady who requires a walking frame; the strong, white male Britain First activist, centrally framed as he stands—leaflets in hand—listening attentively to the elderly male.

Nouri, Lorenzo-Dus, and Watkin (2021) also identified a concomitant shift whereby images of Britain First as a group—that is, images of activist and affiliated members—increased sharply as the group moved from Facebook, where they accounted for 24% of the total, to Gab, where they accounted for 66%. These images often communicated a sense of male camaraderie, of brotherhood, as in Figure 6.4, where one of the group's leaders (in an orange t-shirt), on the left side of the picture, poses in close physical proximity to an affiliated group member, arms around each other's back, hand-gesturing victory, and smiling broadly to camera. This kind of positive visual styling of the in-group—within groomer–target affiliation processes—as a closely knit male group is a recurrent feature of digital ideological grooming.

Let us next consider Extract 6.11, from the Facebook page of the radical right group British Patriotic Resistance. The group's Facebook page primarily consists of selected news items posted from the official group's account that list supposed wrongdoings against the British nation by numerous out-groups. These news items expectedly trigger varying amounts of discursive engagement from group members, typically resulting in an escalation of verbal aggression against one or more of the out-groups. Interspersed within this othering discourse, one also finds the kind of in-group affiliation shown below.

Extract 6.11

[The extract reproduces an interaction between five group members. One of them (BPR) posts from the official group account and is therefore likely one of its leaders, or at least a core member. M1–M4 are group members, their account names being all male. The extract includes all the content posted on its Facebook page by the group over four consecutive days in the autumn of 2017.]

01	Day 1 - 18:56	BPR	astalavista baby
02	Day 1 - 18:59	M1	have a safe evening to you all 🖤
03	Day 1 - 18:59	M2	and you xxx
04	Day 1 - 19:04	BPR	i don't go out much these days so much pain tragic
05			death of my brother who dies 3 months ago I am not
06			cannot even want the television, not too worry
07			thanks xx [M1]
08	Day 1 - 19:06	M3	TWAT. Sentence is too short/Lock him up with me for
09			10 minutes/I'll meter out some [English town] justice
10	Day 1 - 19:13	BPR	they know nothing about the word #HONOUR
11			smelly fucking scum
12	Day 1 - 22:35	BPR	eye, me too [M3]
13	Day 1- 23:16	M4	Kill
14	Day 2 - 02:24	M1	stay safe if your on your way home from a night club,
15			so many nounces about

16	Day 2 – 2:33	BPR	respect this country or leave, i came home this eve-
17			ning all i hear are voices unknown too me spitting
18			on our pavements just stay very safe #nfse
19	Day 2 – 20:55	M1	GREETINGS
20	Day 3 – 9:02	M1	stay safe in these troubled times #NFSE
21	Day 3 – 10:53	BPR	Greetings, stay safe and sound on the streets
22			wake up defy these thugs
23	Day 4 – 00:49	BPR	how,s everyone doing? as always i ask because i care
24			stay safe

In Extract 6.11 the in-group members bond around the notion of watching over each other as members of an affectively close community, specifically being concerned about their safety when going out at night. As per the grooming potential of high entitativity in extreme ideology groups discussed in Chapter 5, this may appeal to targets as potential recruits who, were they to join, would be welcomed by such a close-knit group. The in-group's closeness is further indexed by the insistence of the advice to "stay safe," which is stated seven times in this brief sequence—3 times by BPR (lines 18, 21, and 24), 3 times by M1, who is one of its most active members in the dataset for this radical right group (lines 02, 14, and 20) and once by M3 (an implicit reply to M1 in line 03). The insistence to stay safe is justified on grounds of an external danger in general ("these troubled times," line 20) and in relation to a specific out-group ("nounces," line 15; "voices unknown too me", line 17, "thugs," line 18) that lurk in big numbers out there in the night ("on your way home from a night club, so many nounces about," lines 14–15; the message itself being posted short of 2:30 AM) and whose behavior is uncivil toward the target's physical territory ("voices unknown too me spitting on our pavements," lines 17-18—note the use of first person plural determiner—"our"—in relation to the town's asphalted roads). BPR adds a painful self-disclosure narrative (lines 04–06) to justify why he need not worry about staying safe in the streets at night: "i don't go out much these days so much pain tragic death of my brother who dies 3 months ago I am not cannot even want the television," despite brushing off—in typical toxic masculinity style—any potential emotional leakage and additional concern for him ("not too worry") from his fellow group members.

This personal experience narrative triggers an extreme violence–advocating sequence (lines 08–18)—involving BPR, M3, and M4—that stands out in stark contrast both to the preceding polite farewell exchange (lines 01–03) and the subsequent repeated expressions of care and concern for members' safety (lines 19–24). Within the sequence, criticism is first levied against the judiciary via impersonal ("Sentence is too short," line 08) or generic, third-person plural ("they know nothing about the word #HONOUR," line 10) assertions. Insults are next levied against the individual convicted for, it is implied, the death of BPR's brother ("TWAT," line 08) and/or the judiciary ("smelly fucking scum," line 11). And extreme violence is advocated as the alternative: "Lock him up with me for 10 minutes / I''ll meter out some [English town] justice" (M3, line 08–09). This last step is endorsed by BPR through an agreement turn directly addressed at M3 (line 12). He also uses linguistic accommodation, ty-pographically representing "yes" in a dialectal pronunciation /ai/ (which he spells as "eye"), which is characteristic of the accent in the English area being referenced.

While easily retrievable from M3's posts, advocating use of extreme violence—murder—remains to this point implicit. But in line 13, M4 joins the sequence to explicitly and categorically avow it: "Kill." Having reached its vio-lence climax, the intensity of this sequence reduces to insults and criticism, as noted above ("nounces," "spitting"), before morphing to calls for action from BPR ("wake up defy these thugs," line 22) and a return to in-group camara-derie through, again, the advice for members to stay safe (line 24) and overt expressions of affection ("as always i ask because i care"—line 23). BPR justi-fies his speech act (asking) through an explicit reference to feelings of concern that, like his asking, are persistent ("as always"). In-group members, whether actual like M1–M4 here or social media lurkers being targeted for ideological grooming, may thus feel that they matter to the group, including its caring elite/inner circle. In this extreme violence–advocating sequence, this elite's call for action carefully avoids explicit violence, inciting violence instead in metaphorical ("wake up") and/or generic ("defy") terms. The target of digital ideological grooming is thus positioned as part of a close community of like-minded individuals who, in the face of external "threat" to it, must act. Action entails protecting themselves and challenging the out-group. The inner group manipulates the targets into thinking that the decision to act is their own, rather than the result of ideological grooming—a clear example of manufac-turing consent.

6.4 STYLING THE OPPONENT IN DIGITAL IDEOLOGICAL GROOMING

The emphasis on styling the opponent is much greater in digital ideological grooming than it is in digital sexual and, as we shall see in Chapter 8, com-mercial grooming. The remainder of this chapter examines othering as the main discursive strategy for styling the opponent in digital ideological groom-ing. As discussed in Chapter 5, othering dehumanizes an individual or a group on the basis of perceived negative attributes and behaviors by that individual or group. The range of stances constructed for the other—the opponent in digital ideological grooming—varies. A large-scale survey of online othering practices by radical right groups, for instance, revealed blacks, Jews, Muslims, immigrants and refugees, the LGBTQ community, and women to be the most frequently denigrated social identities. Black people were customarily positioned as criminals, uncivilized and lazy, in addition to the dehumanizing metaphors of African men as animals[8]; Jews were positioned as globalists scheming behind the scenes, Shylocks (i.e., devious merchants and usurers), and Holocaust deniers; Muslims were denigrated as being terrorists and responsible for a clash of civilizations—Muslim men being othered as misogynist and sexually deviant; immigrants and refugees were othered on basis of stances of moral (un-)deservedness, especially in terms of access to welfare and housing; LGBTQ individuals were attributed stances of sin, sexual deviancy, and degeneration; and women were othered on grounds of sexual promiscuity/prostitution, of being two-faced, untrustworthy, and only interested in money and status (Conway 2019; see also Pohjonen 2018).

Alongside these regularly targeted out-groups, extreme ideology groups develop their own hierarchies of othering, as it were. For example, jihadi groups primarily position themselves in opposition to—and other—either a "far" out-group (i.e., the West) or a "near" out-group (rival jihadi groups). Lorenzo-Dus and Macdonald (2018) found 91.79% and 73.58% of all the references to the West in, respectively, the online jihadi propaganda magazines *Inspire* and *Dabiq* (2009–2015) to entail othering. The higher presence of West-othering language in *Inspire* reflected Al Qaeda's (the group behind this magazine) prioritizing the far over the near enemy. For its part, the so-called Islamic State's prioritizing of the near enemy explains the comparatively lower frequency of othering the West in *Dabiq*.

Their study also found strategically convenient reference to "the West" in both online magazines, which used it as a catch-all term for multiple extralinguistic entities. The West was used to refer more frequently to America, Western troops/armies, and Western allies in *Inspire* than in *Dabiq*. Conversely, more frequent references to Western leaders and crusaders were made in *Dabiq* than in *Inspire*. These reflected and helped to construct Al Qaeda's focus on nation state–level policies and, in contrast, the so-called Islamic State's focus on public figures. For both groups, however, the most frequent extralinguistic referent for the West was the absence of a specific extralinguistic entity (23.1% *Dabiq*; 26.3% *Inspire*). Moreover, Lorenzo-Dus and Macdonald's (2018) analysis revealed that the West was primarily denigrated in *Dabiq* (41.1%) and *Inspire* (61.8%) by attributing to it a stance of immorality. Two other negative stances were also attributed to the West, in different descending order of frequency by the magazines: arrogance (*Dabiq* 19.2%; *Inspire* 9.5%) and violence (*Dabiq* 11.5%; *Inspire* 9.7%).

While some radical right groups express most contempt toward Muslims as an out-group, others do so toward "progressive" individuals and political groups. Even when one such group, say Muslim immigrants, is singled out for othering, its identity boundaries and internal composition are fluidly constructed such that they support particular in-group values and proposed actions. Typical of this is radical right groups' distinguishing between "good" and "bad" immigrants on the basis of a *sui generis* notion of "respect" toward the in-group's territory. Thus, as we saw in Extract 6.8, in-group members who are second- or third-generation immigrants selectively disassociated from current immigrants who, unlike them, "disrespected" the in-group's home. As also seen in Extract 6.11, all this othering simultaneously supports intra-group identity construction through its differentiation and disaffiliation from the out-group.

As for the actual discursive means for styling the opponent in digital ideological grooming, these include a combination of the othering strategies of, principally, homogenization, suppression, and pejoration (see Chapter 5). Within pejoration, it is impoliteness strategies oriented toward either the out-group's quality/social face or equity rights that are most frequently deployed. In Lorenzo-Dus and Macdonald's (2018) analysis, a number of impoliteness strategies for othering the West in *Dabiq* and *Inspire* were identified. These were primarily oriented toward threatening the quality and social face needs of the opponent, comprising insults, challenges/unpalatable questions, and pointed criticism/complaints. Within these face-oriented strategies, direct insults were hardly ever used—they accounted for less than 3% in *Inspire* and were not used at all in *Dabiq*. Challenging and asking unpalatable questions (e.g., " . . . why are Muslims getting angrier and angrier about how the West arrogantly pushes and shoves?" [*Dabiq*]) were also infrequently used. In contrast, pointed criticism and complaints accounted for 41.3% and 38.5%, respectively, of the total. Pointed criticism and complaints were mainly realized via third-person negative references, such as "the West is hiding behind a nigab of human rights, civil liberties, women's rights, gender equality and other rallying slogans while in practice it is being imperialistic, intolerant, chauvinistic and discriminating against the Muslim population of Western countries" [*Inspire*]. The preference for criticism over insults in these online jihadi magazines may owe to genre conventions. The articles published in *Dabiq* and *Inspire* either reported events (i.e., they were "news articles") or explained particular religious concepts (i.e., they were "theological articles"). In both genres, journalistic or scholarly voice was respectively adopted, and this did not entail the use of insulting interpellations.

Quality/social face-oriented impoliteness is also salient in radical right groups' digital grooming discourse. The examples in Extracts 6.12 are typical of the use of insults (6.12.1 and 6.12.2) and pointed criticism/complaints (6.12.3).

Extract 6.12

6.12.1 Jair Bolsonaro (Facebook)

Marlon Furtado you are another son of a bitch thief who tries at all costs to keep this mafia to continue this pilfering. Fuck you sucker and take that woman with you[9]

6.12.2 English Patriotic Resistance (Facebook)

Absolute Animals...Vile..Evil...Put them all in one place..on islamic soil.... and let them destroy each other . . . ALL spineless gutless politically correct wimps need to be GONE and let's give these bastards a REAL War....

6.12.3 Bandera Vecinal (Facebook)

where is democracy? ah it's for those who block the streets destroy our city and then one has to take care of the costs not to speak of the super crooks who plundered the country and are running again to hold public office. LONG LIVE THE HOMELAND!!!!![10]

In these examples, more than one opponent per post is being othered through a combination of insults and criticism/complaints. In example 6.12.1, the insults are addressed at a spiritual leader in Brazil (Marlon Furtado) and an undefined group that this individual allegedly supports and which is labeled as "mafia." In example 6.12.2, the opponents are two large groups: Muslims living in the UK (described as "Absolute Animals . . . Vile..Evil") and British people who disagree with the in-group's view on those Muslims (described as "ALL spineless gutless politically correct wimps"). In example 6.12.3, it is public officials seeking re-election who are insulted as "super crooks." In all three examples, the insults are accompanied by a negative description of the out-groups' behaviors (e.g., "continue this pilfering" in example 6.12.1; "destroy each other" in example 6.12.2; and "plunder(ing) the country" in example 6.12.3). It is the opponent's wrongdoing that thus legitimizes the in-group's actions, such as mass extradition ("Put them all in one place..on islamic soil") and "give these bastards a REAL War," in example 6.12.2.

Example 6.12.3 also contains criticism of, and complaint against, the in-group's opponents. The opening utterance ("where is democracy?") is clearly both an unpalatable and a rhetorical question. Its answer is keyed as exaggeration through a paralinguistic rendition of obviousness ("ah"). What follows is a criticism of the government in Argentina for being selectively democratic—which is tantamount to not being democratic. Democracy is heralded as something positive that only violent groups—those who "block the streets, destroy our city"—have access to under this government's regime. Complaining ensues, specifically about others—though this is impersonally constructed ("one has to")—needing to absorb the financial consequences of these groups' vandalism. Further criticism is then emphatically ("not to speak of") levied against a new opponent at this stage: corrupt individuals ("super crooks") running for public office despite having previously plundered the country. The example concludes with a typographically (capitalization, multiple exclamation marks) emphatic defense of national identity, "LONG LIVE THE HOMELAND!!!!!," which is thereby aligned to the in-group.

Relationship Regulation Theory (Rai and Fiske 2011, 2012, 2016; see Garcés-Conejos Blitvich and Kádár 2021 for an overview) posits that there are four key moral motives that drive social relations, namely unity, hierarchy, equality, and proportionality. In Extract 6.12, the in-group activates their *sui generis* version of the motives of unity, equality, and proportionality. *Unity* refers to the need to support the integrity of social groups and is guided by a sense of common fate and responsibility. *Equality* is directed toward implementing social relations based on balance and reciprocity; *proportionality* "toward calculating in accord with ratios or rates for otherwise distinct goods to ensure that rewards or punishment for each party are proportional to their costs, contribution, effort, merit or guilt" (Rai and Fiske 2011, 64). The behaviors being evaluated in examples 6.12.1 - 6.12.3 are presented as concerning groups (in- and out-groups) as opposed to individuals therein: they are therefore discursively constructed through the moral motive of unity. In the examples, moreover, the in-groups attribute unwarranted bad behaviors to the out-groups: the latter's pilfering, destroying, and so forth are one-sided (no triggering action by the in-groups is stated, for instance) and therefore in breach of the moral motive of equality, which the in-group must reinstate. The way to do so relies on the moral motive of proportionality: mass extradition, war, and so forth are the in-group's view of proportionate response. The in-groups, furthermore, use impoliteness (insults, pointed criticism, etc.) to uphold moral values (see Kádár and Márquez-Reiter 2015; Garcés-Conejos Blitvich and Kádár 2021)—clearly, their own version thereof. In digital ideological grooming (not unlike in other discourse polarization contexts), the opponent always exhibits the less moral behavior (Garcés-Conejos Blitvich 2009, 2010; Garcés-Conejos Blitvich and Kádár 2021).

As discussed in Chapter 5, juxtaposition of out-group denigration and in-group exaltation is characteristic of digital ideological grooming, a form of polarized argumentation that is often multimodally constructed. Consider, in this regard, the image reproduced in Figure 6.5, which was posted on Facebook by Britain First in support of their views on refugees. The 2 photographs in Figure 6.5 are unattributed, stock images: the one in the lower half of the image is used, for example, in resource materials for promoting equality, diversity, and inclusion in secondary schools in the United Kingdom.

In Figure 6.5 the out-group (top half of the image) is negatively portrayed, being reduced to the stance of unruliness, which is visually indexed via a hoard of predominantly angry young males that the caption identifies as refugees to be stopped ("FB.COM/STOPTHEREFUGEES"). In contrast, the in-group (bottom half of the image) is positively rendered—here as a group of smiling, peaceful elderly people, predominantly female. Skin color

Figure 6.5 Britain First (Facebook).

differences between the in- and out-groups are highlighted: all the members of the in-group are Caucasian (fair-skinned and, with one exception, blue-eyed); all the members of the out-group are brown-skinned and eyed. Background color supports this light–dark contrast, which has established metaphorical connotations of respectively good and evil: the in-group wear white or very light colored clothing; the out-group wear predominantly nonwhite clothing; image brightness is higher in the in-group than in the out-group photograph. Superimposed text uses a rhetorical question—in large, color-contrasting capital lettering—that challenges current support for both groups. This support is assumed to be diverted from the in-group to the out-group, and this is presented as binary "x (out-group) instead of y (in-group)." The image is accompanied by a caption, "IT'S WRONG!", which reinforces the answer to the rhetorical question through use, once again, of expressive typography (capitals and an exclamation mark sign) and assertive evaluation (a categorical affirmation of erroneousness). In addition to obvious othering of refugees as a group, Figure 6.5 is an example of liquid racism in as much as discrimination of refugees on racial grounds is not explicit. Instead, Britain First "simply" makes the case against supporting refugees whose behavior is threatening (angry) over support of people whose behavior is the antithesis of threatening (smiling). It just so happens, as it were, that both groups are visually—rather than verbally—racialized as well as age-stereotyped and are representative, respectively, of the out- and the in-group.

As well as impoliteness oriented to quality and/or social face, digital ideological grooming regularly entails equity rights-oriented impoliteness toward perceived opponents. In Lorenzo-Dus and Macdonald's study (2018), threats to "the West" were the second and third most frequently used impoliteness strategy, respectively, in *Dabiq* and *Inspire* after criticism and, in the case of *Inspire*, also exclusion. As noted by Culpeper (2011, 252) threats are coercive in that they seek "a realignment of values between the [threat] producer and the target such that the producer benefits or has their current benefits reinforced or protected." In digital ideological grooming, such realignment of values is often used to legitimize violent behavior, once more using impoliteness to activate the moral motives of unity, equality, and proportionality. Consider the examples in Extract 6.13.

Extract 6.13

6.13.1 So-called Islamic State [*Dabiq*]
        Perhaps once there was a chance that an attack inside the West or on Western borders by the Islamic State could be averted through negotiations, but no longer.
6.13.2 Al Qaeda [*Inspire*]
        The West has been plundering our wealth for centuries. Now it is the time for payback. In Sha'Allah, the chickens will come home to roost.

Whether literally "an attack inside the West or on Western borders," (example 6.13.1) or a metaphorically articulated attack ("the chickens will come home to roost," example 6.13.2), the in-group (as a social grouping with a common fate rather than a set of individuals) presents violence toward their opponent (the out-group) as the only—and urgent—form of action. Thus, "negotiations" are "no longer" (example 6.13.1) an option. Nor can the in-group, within the moral motive of equality, continue to endure centuries-long "plundering [of its] wealth." Instead, and as per the moral motive of proportionality, acting "now" is called for (example 6.13.2). Example 6.13.2 is typical of how this imperative for violence is constructed as a form of *distributive justice*—a case of "payback" within the moral motive of proportionality. Distributive justice refers to the principle of "fair allocation of benefits, a fair distribution of responsibilities, and recognition of performance or effort" (Tedeshi and Felson 1994, 218). As we have seen, in digital ideological grooming it is often used to legitimate violence. When violence concerns future actions, distributive justice is used within equity-oriented impoliteness; specifically, threats. In the case if jihadi groups, these threats are often authority-endorsed (note the customary "God willing," "In Sha'Allah," in extract 6.13.2), compelling the grooming targets to respond to calls that are therefore constructed as urgent, legitimate call for violence aligned to in-group identity/membership. Through this lens, for instance, becoming a foreign fighter or lone wolf terrorist becomes obligatory for any true jihadi (Ingram 2016).

Threats can be conditional and nonconditional (see Martínez-Cabeza 2009; Culpeper Iganski, and Sweiry 2017). The former are embedded within implicated or explicated statements that the threats may dissipate, were the threat's target to change its *modus operandi*. In the latter, which Extracts 6.13.1 and 6.13.2 illustrate, the threat will continue regardless of whether the behavior that "led" to it is corrected. Although *Dabiq* and *Inspire* made use of both threat types, *Dabiq* favored nonconditional over conditional threats, in contrast to *Inspire* (Lorenzo-Dus and Macdonald 2018). In both cases, threats were constructed as reaction rather than initiation moves that would not only deliver upon the in-groups' opponents what they rightly deserved (distributive justice) but would also put targets on their path to redemption were they to join the groomers and, ultimately, their maximum religious/divine authority. These threats were also presented as helpful warnings to the targets of digital religious grooming "about the danger posed by fellow Muslims who fail to heed the 'true' interpretations of Islam and encouraged to respond to global injustices perpetrated by the crusaders" (Kirke 2015, 295).

Insincere displays of liberalism (see Chapter 5) are also used in digital ideological grooming to other the out-group(s), albeit that less saliently than pejoration in the case, especially, of jihadi groups. Insincere liberalism displays feature less frequently in digital political than religious grooming, possibly due to the lower purchase of the concept of fair retribution in Christianity (the religion of the in-group) than Islam. Moreover, liberalism is politically respected in the democratic societies in which radical right groups operate. As for the related othering strategy of subverting tolerance (see Chapter 5), this is commonplace in digital ideological grooming, especially in the discourse of radical right groups. Herein, others' (typically, mainstream political groups') views or actions toward the out-group are constructed as being too lenient and, hence, both ineffective and responsible for further victimization of the in-group. As Extract 6.14 illustrates, political correctness is often seen as the root cause of such "pernicious" tolerance.

Extract 6.14 Bandera Vecinal (Facebook)

Jjajaajajaja!!! party-cracy unites against Biondini whose only crime is to be a nationalist and to tell some truths that make 'political correctness people' uncomfortable.[11]

The author of the post reproduced in Extract 6.14 denigrates the out-group, through belittling and verbal wit. Individuals who uphold different views to those upheld by the leader of the Argentinean neo-Nazi party Bandera Vecinal, Alejandro Biondini, are patronized through the label "political correctness people," which is itself placed inside quotation marks to cast doubt about it genuinely signifying correctness in politics. The message positions these people as being "uncomfortable" with the "truths" that the in-group tells. These individuals, most parties (and their followers) in the country, are also denigrated through the label "party-cracy" (*partidocracia* in Spanish). Party-cracy is an example of word formation via blending that is here used to characterize nondemocratic values. It is a combination of (the initial part of) the word (political) party (*partido*, part) and the Greek origin suffix -cracy (*krátos*), which means rule and strength. As such, it conveys that alignment not to the people's will, as per the broad meaning of the term "democracy," but to political parties' will, specifically all but the in-group's political party. In other words, it disparages the out-group's values. Word formation through blending is a form of verbal wit, which is itself both associated with humor and a widely used strategy for subverting tolerance in discourse. Word formation— whether via blending or other processes—also contributes to developing the in-group's "own language code" as a mechanism to reinforce in-group membership and exclude out-groups. In this sense, as Pohjonen (2018) notes, radical right groups favor nuanced linguistic forms, including irony, jokes, innuendo, metaphors (see also Brindle 2016), and double meanings, over explicitly identifiable linguistic markers or features of othering. Their use of "hateful codes" is regarded as especially problematic as it creates a sense of community among those who have the knowledge to decode it (Conway 2019).

6.5 CONCLUSION

Digital ideological grooming relies, first and foremost, on argumentative polarization of a wide range of social identities that are reduced to being part of either an in- or out-group—an "us or them." In-group/out-group boundaries are clear-cut and result in social identities that are constructed as being diametrically opposed. High entitativity, which is known to increase recruitment potential online and requires such clear-cut boundary setting, defines the in-group. Self-styling in digital ideological grooming supports this through regular stance-taking of broad ("Jack-of-all-trades") expertise, toxic openness, and impatient avidity. Broad expertise enables having a say about any— ideally topical—issue, piggybacking on it as a means to present the in-group's ideology. It often takes the form of teaching or instruction giving that goes to considerable lengths to minimize the learning load on the target. And it makes salient use of quotation or referencing of external sources to justify and legitimize the in-group's ideology. Toxic openness relies on mythopoesis, specifically first-person storytelling that highlights stereotypically masculine emotions such as anger. The groomers' anger is rooted in perceived victimization and supports a logic of retaliation—of distributive justice in, especially, jihadi groups—against the out-group. The *topos* of savior is thus a feature in digital ideological grooming, with the task at hand being an urgent one in the face of prolonged, other-inflicted suffering. Impatient avidity, a pressing call to action, thus becomes the third, interrelated stance contributing to digital ideological groomers' self-styling.

In digital ideological grooming, groomer and target are regularly constructed as part of the same in-group, one to which the target may already belong (but perhaps not yet be sufficiently committed) or may join. This in-group is styled through stances that complement those by the groomers for they are indeed at times seen as the same entity. Overall, the virtues and strengths of in-group as target are profusely extolled. Yet, at times, selective dissociation processes are also enacted, whereby the target is presented as not quite where it needs to be ideologically and shown the pathways to getting there. Apathy and/or accepting victimization are the stances thereby attributed to the in-group as target.

As for the styling of opponents in digital ideological grooming, this is pervasive and varied. Both jihadi and radical right groups' messaging constructs multiple out-groups, strategically aligned to particular goals, be it recruitment of Muslims globally to the call for jihad or the spread of false choices between supporting out-groups (e.g., refugees) at the expense of vulnerable in-groups (e.g., the elderly). These opponents are explicitly othered, primarily through denigration via face-oriented and equity rights–oriented impoliteness. Insults/criticism/complaints and threats are, respectively, recurrent realizations thereof, often serving a manipulative use of notions such as distributive justice or an imperative to act urgently in the face of long-endured in-group victimization.

NOTES

1. Keyness rank 136; keyness measure used: log ratio; log ratio value: 8.27.
2. http://www.salafi-dawah.com/who-is-the-muwahhid.html.
3. http://fursanshammedia.net/2017/01/14/fursan-al-sham-media-interview-with-abu-bakr-al-britani/.
4. The site became the object of global attention after so-called Islamic State supporters started to use it for disseminating information about the group.
5. *Unanse YA a luchar por el país los corruptos populistas que gobiernan desde 1983 han destruido el país.*
6. *LA PREDICA DEL NACIONALISMO YA NO SE DETIENE!!!!!!!!!!!!!!!!!!*
7. Gab homepage: https://gab.com/. Accessed July 2022.

8. Dehumanizing metaphors are used across several discourses for othering purposes, such as anti-immigration discourses in the UK press (see, e.g., Mussolf 2015) and misogynous discourses in Twitter (see, e.g., Demjén and Hardaker 2016). For the use of binary metaphors in jihadi discourse, see also Patterson (2022).
9. *Marlon Furtado tu é outro filho da puta bandido que tenta a todo custo manter essa máfia para continuar na maracutaia! Vai se fuder ô seu otário e leva junto a grelo duro!*
10. *donde esta la democracia? ah es para los que cortan las calles destruyen nuestra ciudad y despues hay que hacerse cargo de los costos ni hablar de los super chorros que saquearon el pais y estan postulandose nuevamente para ejercer un cargo publico. VIVA LA PATRIA!!!!!*
11. *Jjajaajajaja!!! la partidocracia se une contra Biondini cuyo único delito es ser Nacionalista y decir algunas verdades que a la "correccion politica" le incomodan.*

CHAPTER 7

Digital Commercial Grooming

Setting the Scene

7.1 INTRODUCTION

I keep hearing this argument come up when people talk about drug prohibition: legalize, regulate and tax it. On the surface it sounds like a good idea. . . . Here's the rub: the drug war is an acute symptom of a deeper problem, and that problem is the state. If they "legalize, regulate and tax" it, it's just one more part of society under their thumb, another productive sector that they can leech off. . . . Here's my point: Silk Road is about something much bigger than thumbing your nose at the man and getting your drugs anyway. It's about taking back our liberty and our dignity and demanding justice. . . . If prohibition is lifted, where will you be? . . . I know where I'll be. I won't rest until children are born into a world where oppression, institutional violence and control, world war, and all the other hallmarks of the state are as ancient history as pharaohs commanding armies of slaves. . . . Hold on to what you DO have and stand for the freedom you deserve!

William Ross Ulbricht (Silk Road forum, 29 April 2012)

These are the views of the creator of the crypto-drug market Silk Road, on the long-standing debate about drug legalization. Ulbricht originally posted them on one of the site's forums, from where he regularly self-proclaimed and promoted Silk Road's libertarian ideology. His prolific postings in Silk Road were subsequently quoted and widely shared across social media and websites, such as www.evolveandascend, from which they are cited here. Ulbricht carefully cultivated an anti-establishment, hero-like image. Yet behind this veneer of kind-hearted heroism lay a hugely profitable enterprise, including for himself. The site traded successfully from 2011 until 2014, when it was permanently shut down by the US Federal Bureau of Investigation (FBI). Ulbricht was convicted in 2015 and incarcerated in 2017 on charges of money laundering,

Digital Grooming. Nuria Lorenzo-Dus, Oxford University Press. © Oxford University Press 2023.
DOI: 10.1093/oso/9780190845193.003.0007

computer hacking, and conspiracy to traffic narcotics and fraudulent identity documents online.

Silk Road offers a valuable case study for the interrogation of digital commercial grooming insofar as it was the first large-scale cryptomarket that exploited notions of grassroot community and libertarianism to lure individuals into purchasing and selling narcotics and other illegal goods in unregulated, illicit digital markets. In Ulbricht's words quoted above, a relentless desire ("I won't rest until . . .") to save the world from "oppression, institutional violence and control, world war, and all the other hallmarks of the state" and to "stand for the freedom you deserve!" justified this crypto-drug market. Such dual emphasis on commerce and grassroot community is at the heart of the digital commercial grooming practices that Silk Road set up, perfected and ultimately bequeathed to successor crypto-drug markets. This chapter examines the "community of interest" (boyd 2002) logic that underpins digital commercial grooming in crypto-drug markets (Section 7.2). It also appraises their internal technical (Section 7.3) and social (Section 7.4) structures as these reflect and support particular self- and other- styling practices therein.

7.2 CRYPTO-DRUG MARKETS: MORE THAN AN EBAY FOR DRUGS

Drugs have been bought and sold online for several decades. The first documented online drug transaction—specifically, cannabis—took place between university students at Stanford and Massachusetts Institute of Technology in the 1970s. However, the origins of today's burgeoning crypto-drug market date back to 2009, with a few websites that operated inconspicuously, such as The Drug Store and Farmer's Market (Bewley-Taylor 2017). Other crypto-drug markets soon followed. They became less discreet, seemingly disregarding the risk of state intervention (Mounteney, Oteo, and Griffiths 2016). The most notable example—and soon to position itself as the "sector leader"—was Silk Road.

Silk Road was founded in February 2011. During the first two and a half years of trading, it grew exponentially: from approximately 340 product listings in May 2011 to approximately 13,000 listings in October 2013. Although most of these listings were narcotics, other illicit goods and services were also traded throughout this period, such as computer hacking and forgery services, malicious software, and pirated media content.[1] On 2 October 2013, the FBI arrested Ulbricht and took down the Silk Road site. Just over 1 month later, on 6 November 2013, the site was relaunched under the name Silk Road 2.0 and with a new administrator. In December of the same year this administrator handed control of the market to his former deputy, Blake Benthall, who went by the username of Defcon. Benthall was arrested on 6 November 2014, when the FBI seized the Silk Road 2.0 site, this time alongside other crypto-drug markets.

A plethora of crypto-drug markets have come and gone since the early days of Silk Road 1.0—some lasting only a few days, others running longer and centralizing the crypto-drug market economy. Out of 19 live crypto-drug markets in 2016, for example, three (Alphabay, Nucleus, and Dream Market) accounted for 65% of all drug listings (Kruithof et al. 2016). The continuing growth of crypto-drug markets is noteworthy both in terms of sales and revenues and also their resilience to law enforcement's persistent interdiction efforts. As noted in the 2021 UNODC World Drug Report, vendors in crypto-drug markets "play a cat-and-mouse game with law enforcement," for example by "marketing their products as 'research chemicals' or advertising 'custom synthesis', whereby clients can request substances not included on a list of available products" (2021, 24). This is a legitimate practice in the pharmaceutical industry, but it is misused by traffickers in crypto-drug markets.

According to DarknetLive, a news and information website for the Dark Net, in 2019 there were approximately 30 cryptomarkets worldwide. This is despite rolling law enforcement operations and consequent shutdown of many such markets.[2] In addition to the high-profile operations resulting in the seizures of Silk Road 1.0 and 2.0, for instance, in 2017, the FBI and Europol closed the large-scale AlphaBay and Hansa cryptomarkets. Law enforcement operations have evolved over time—with mixed results. The 2017 interdictions newly combined tactical attacks on the websites, psychological manipulation, and undercover operatives (Afilipoaie and Shortis 2018) to undermine users' trust in crypto-drug markets. This paid off in the operations' immediate aftermath, with users of the resulting crypto-drug market leader at the time, Dream Marketplace, becoming more cautious about trading in fear that the market could be yet another law enforcement-run set-up (Afilipoaie and Shortis 2018). Yet sales soon returned to pre-interdiction levels, demonstrating crypto-drug markets' resilience to law enforcement interdiction activity as vendors quickly migrate to clone marketplaces from which they continue plying their trade (Dittus 2017). Spagnoletti, Ceci, and Bygstad (2021) recorded the existence of 122 crypto-drug markets between October 2013 and April 2018. This "hydra effect" (Maddox 2020) also results in so-called *target hardening*, whereby vendors spur market innovation aimed at reducing detection (Bouchard 2007). An "enforcement-innovation paradox" thus ensues whereby each enforcement activity increases the resources and skills that are required to prosecute the next. If crypto-drug markets continue to innovate to avoid interdiction, "we can also expect future market takedowns to net diminishing intelligence returns" (Horton-Eddison et al. 2021).[3]

How big a problem are crypto-drug markets for law enforcement and governments across the globe, then? Not too big, one may argue, in quantitative terms. As introduced in Chapter 1, crypto-drug markets constitute a small proportion of the overall drug market. They are also less global than their digitalness may suggest, geographically clustering in a few European countries,

Australia, and the United States (Hall and Antonopoulos 2016; Barratt, Ferris, and Winstock 2014; Barratt and Aldridge 2016). However, crypto-drug markets pose a significant challenge in qualitative terms for they have transformed the overall criminal space of drug trafficking worldwide (Aldridge and Décary-Hétu 2014; Hall, Koenraadt, and Antonopoulos 2017; Masson and Bancroft 2018, UNODC World Drug Report 2021). Specifically, these markets have enabled and accelerated the establishment of global networks of offenders: vendors and buyers of narcotics who, once online, conduct a range of illicit activities on an unprecedented scale and with a higher degree of freedom than through conventional, interpersonal criminal networks (Martin 2014).

A positive, myth-making narrative about crypto-drug markets has emerged, too, in no small part fueled by certain sectors of the media. At the time Silk Road 1.0 traded, for instance, the leading business magazine *Forbes* described Ulbricht as "Julian Assange with a hypodermic needle" (Greenberg 2013). Such myth-making presents crypto-drug sites as "transparent, economically motivated markets that place a premium on quality, service and stealth" (Masson and Bancroft 2018, 78). Crypto-drug markets have indeed been described as an e-Bay for drugs, as if they were devoid of illicitness and/or unethical principles (Barratt 2012). Upon creating Silk Road, for example, Ulbricht called it a "kind of anonymous amazon.com" (Bitcointalk.org, 2011). This implied that, as with the online retailer Amazon, individuals buying drugs in Silk Road customarily were also the end-user of the products bought. Yet the commercial reality of Silk Road and other crypto-drug markets is far less benign as regards the profile of those accessing and trading in the drugs being sold, as well as regarding the sales methods used therein.

An early study of supply and demand on Silk Road 1.0 found most drug purchases to be for small amounts, suggesting personal use rather than distribution (Christin 2013). Subsequent studies, though, revealed a pattern of drug trafficking similar to that found in face-to-face drug markets whereby a large number of transactions involving small amounts of drugs, typically single grams of cocaine or heroin stamps, is complemented by a lesser number of transactions that involve large quantities of drugs for distribution. Between 31% and 45% of all Silk Road 1.0 revenue, for instance, was generated by drug dealers sourcing stock on the site to resell it offline (Aldridge and Décary-Hétu 2014).

Orsolini et al. (2015) identify two types of crypto-drug market user. One type buys drugs for recreational use and tends to be an economically stable, well-educated Caucasian male who views these markets as offering the opportunity to avoid the potential legal and social risks of face-to-face street deals. The other type comprises individuals with limited financial resources and no health insurance who therefore shop in these markets for primarily prescription drugs. To these two types a more recent user profile has been added, namely enterprising local street dealers who resell face to face on the street the drugs bought on crypto-drug markets (Aldridge and Askew 2016; Aldridge and Decary-Hetu 2016; Pergolizzi et al. 2017). Individuals' transition from buying drugs for personal use in crypto-drug markets to buying them to resell on the street often develops through an intermediary stage: "social dealing." This refers to the practice of buying drugs online for both personal use and for friends and acquaintances. As Demant, Munksgaard, and Houborg (2018, 46) put it, social dealers' logic is that "[s]ince it takes just as long to order one gram of MDMA[4] as it does to order 10 grams, and the risk of the package being seized may be the same, [they] may as well order for friends."

A comprehensive report about crypto-drug markets (Mounteney, Oteo, and Griffiths 2016) found them to be strongly anchored in offline drug markets, with their users still likely to become victims and perpetrators of violence connected with face-to-face drug transactions. The violence that is associated with offline drug markets does not only arise as a function of their illegality, but it is also culturally, politically, and socially conditioned (Bourgois 2003; Johnson et al. 2006). Therefore, for as long as these external conditions remain unchanged, Mounteney, Oteo, and Griffiths (2016) concluded, the possibility that cryptomarkets may reduce violence and conflict in the drug trade overall remains limited.

Moreover, crypto-drug markets are far from violence- or conflict-free spaces themselves. In them, harm to users often manifests in nonphysical forms, via different forms of blackmail—from damage to reputation through to "doxing" (hacking and then threatening to expose the users' identity)—as well as via frequent instances of theft and fraud. Crypto-drug markets therefore need to be understood as a transformative *criminal* innovation in individuals' and organized groups' handling of the drugs trade, rather than simply an eBay for drugs (Aldridge and Decary-Hetu 2014; Demant, Munksgaard, and Houborg 2018; Weber and Kruisbergen 2019; Kethineni and Cao 2020). They operate in the absence of formal rules and sociolegal legitimacy. They thrive despite conflicting goals among internal and external actors, such as police operations, hacker attacks, and opportunistic behaviors by their own administrators and/or vendors. For instance, of the 122 crypto-drug markets identified in the period from October 2013 until April 2018 by Spagnoletti, Ceci, and Bygstad (2021), 9 markets were closed by law enforcement and 42 were closed by administrators with exit scams, whereby they continued to receive payments for new orders after stopping order shipping.

Several arguments are levied in favor of crypto-drug market legalization. One of them is that the actual drugs traded therein are neither necessarily more convenient to obtain nor significantly more potent/cheaper than in the so-called *meatspace*—the term given by crypto-drug market users to the offline world of face-to-face drug exchanges (see Barratt, Allen, and Lenton 2014; Barratt, Ferris, and Winstock 2014; van der Gouwe, Brunt, and Van Laar 2017). In other words, the argument goes, crypto-drug markets neither facilitate drug use nor make it less safe for users. Another argument levied in favor of crypto-drug market legalization is that these spaces trade primarily in so-called "soft" drugs, like cannabis and MDMA. A global, online survey of 15,000 people about drug use in 2012 showed MDMA to be the most popular drug bought on Silk Road 1.0 in the three countries where the market had the most customers (i.e., the United States, the United Kingdom, and Australia; see Barratt, Ferris, and Winstock 2014). A subsequent study of visible listings on the Silk Road website showed that the vast majority of sales were, in decreasing order of revenue, for cannabis, MDMA, and psychedelics. The study also found that drugs associated with dependence, harmful use, and chaotic lifestyles (i.e., heroin, methamphetamine, and crack cocaine) neither featured frequently nor generated significant revenue for the market (Aldridge and Décary-Hétu 2014).

An examination of the drug types discussed across the Silk Road 1.0 and Silk Road 2.0 forums confirms this predominance of soft drugs. As shown in Table 7.1, MDMA and LSD were, in decreasing order of frequency, the top two drug types that members of the Silk Road community discussed the most, with their comparative frequencies of use being quite similar across Silk Road 1.0 and 2.0. It is worth noting, however, that the hard drug type cocaine ranked fifth in Silk Road 1.0 and in Silk Road 2.0; its colloquial synonym "coke" ranking fourth in Silk Road 1.0 and third in Silk Road 2.0.

Soft and hard drugs were sold in Silk Road, then, with a preference for soft drugs. This may support arguments in favor of decriminalizing crypto-drug markets. As discussed, counterarguments may also be levied referencing the regular presence of different forms of (virtual) violence in these markets as well as their anchorage in "traditional," street-based drug trafficking. Transcending what remains an unresolved academic debate and policy/regulatory issue, though, crypto-drug markets clearly are more than simply an online retail space for drugs. Buying drugs for personal use does happen in them, as do social dealing and sourcing stock for reselling on the streets. This

Table 7.1 FIVE MOST FREQUENTLY MENTIONED DRUG TYPES IN THE SILK ROAD 1.0 AND 2.0 FORUMS

Silk Road 1.0		Silk Road 2.0	
Drug Type (lemma)	Frequency	Drug Type (lemma)	Frequency
MDMA	648.656	**MDMA**	698.881
lsd	484.607	**lsd**	402.366
weed	387.204	**coke**	388.417
coke	252.464	**weed**	369.894
cocaine	213.988	**cocaine**	293.254

Frequency normalized to per million words.

chapter next examines crypto-drug markets' technical affordances and how these shape and reflect digital commercial grooming practices therein.

7.3 THE TECHNICAL STRUCTURE OF CRYPTO-DRUG MARKETS

As introduced in Chapter 1, crypto-drug markets are located within the Dark Net, which is itself located within the Deep Web. The latter is the largest part of the Internet, estimated at 96% of all networked pages (Epstein 2014) and is not accessible through traditional search engines such as Google or Yahoo. This Deep Web includes raw information, for example databases, file-sharing websites that use standard Internet protocols (e.g., Kazaa), military networks (e.g., Secret Internet Protocol Router Network) that are structurally detached from the public Internet, large amounts of social networking site content (e.g., nonpublic Facebook content), and so forth (Mansfield-Devine 2009). A small part of the Deep Web hosts hidden Internet services that can only be accessed via specific anonymizing portals, such as Tor (The Onion Routing). While not particularly difficult to use, accessing these portals requires a certain level of technical competence. Dark Net users typically communicate with each other via Pretty Good Privacy (PGP) data encryption that provides end-to-end cryptographic privacy and authentication—each user has a unique PGP key (Cox 2016). This technically enabled anonymity is a magnet for illicit activity, including drug dealing, as transactions are not linked to searchable identities (Kethineni and Cao 2020).

A crucial feature of crypto-drug markets is their chosen payment method, specifically the technical infrastructure that supports transactions therein. This must appear—and be—secure for users, which means that it must be resilient both to fraud from users and/or external parties and to detection by law enforcement. To achieve such resilience, as discussed in Chapter 1, crypto-drug markets make use of encrypted crypto-currencies, such as Bitcoin and Monero. They also use a sophisticated technical mechanism for holding funds in deposit until transactions are finalized. This third-party mechanism—or *escrow*—seeks to build trust in the marketplaces, which is central to attracting vendors and buyers. Centralized escrow services, in which the market sites act as the escrow, were regularly used in the first wave of crypto-drug markets, from 2011 to 2013. Since approximately 2014, and in the wake of several exit scams in which market administrators closed the sites and absconded with the funds, a decentralized, multisignature escrow model was developed and became the industry standard (Horton-Eddison 2018). The move from centralized crypto-drug markets to decentralized peer-to-peer (P2P) trade platforms and the use of chat applications, such as Telegram, are further causes for concern. As Horton-Eddison et al. (2021) argue, in the absence of centralized control over the systems for payments, disputes, and reviews, and an active discussion forum space, vendors may see little incentive for being honest about the quality and consistency of their products. All in all, the technical affordances of crypto-drug markets are focused on generating trust in these illicit transactional spaces online by showing resilience to those who may seek to interdict them and/or exploit them for their own gain.

7.4 THE SOCIAL STRUCTURE OF CRYPTO-DRUG MARKETS

While, as per their name, crypto-drug markets are trading digital spaces, they make every effort to show that they are not only economically motivated. To support this, they seek to demonstrate that they are chiefly concerned with community-building around a common endeavor. These markets thus place considerable emphasis on the formation of "communities of interest" (boyd 2002); that is, social structures bound together by their members' interest, in this case in drugs. Community members join a social circle by virtue of buying and selling drugs in these markets as well as their sharing in the sites' forums or bulletin boards of their experiences as buyers and sellers. Across all these practices, commerce remains the basis for community members' interaction. In Silk Road, for example, community-building under the values of libertarianism was the main legitimation for achieving economic gain.

Ethnographic analysis of crypto-drug market users reveals that they regularly share "professionalized knowledge" about, among other, overdose risks and various aspects of drug safety with other members of their community (Masson and Bancroft 2018, 82). The markets operate like "affinity spaces" (Gee 2005), in which learning happens in a nonhierarchical way: "the whole continua of people from new to experienced, from unskilled to highly skilled, from minorly integrated to addicted, and everything in between, is accommodated in the same space" (2005, 225). Knowledge sharing in crypto-drug markets thus takes the form of "broscience." A portmanteau of "brother" and "science," the term broscience was first used to refer to male online circles interested in athletic, body-building practices. It is nowadays also used in relation to other online affinity spaces, such as discussion forums in crypto-drug markets, in which members learn about drugs from each other. Their broscience discourse expresses a certain distrust of experts and authorities that provide official drug information as these are perceived to lack the specialist knowledge that the broscience community possesses and uses to keep its drug-using members safe (Sumnall, Evans-Brown, and McVeigh 2011; Bilgrei 2018).

Broscience also serves a less altruistic end: namely, to boost sales in crypto-drug markets. For instance, analysis of the discourse of a subset of 315 listings of several drug types (crystal meth, heroin, ecstasy pills, LSD, DMT, benzodiazepines, and cocaine) on Silk Road 1.0 and 2.0 revealed that broscience discourse was ostensibly about harm reduction yet actually functioned as drug quality product advertising: vendor profiles exhorted potential new customers to be cautious precisely because their products were so good (Aldridge and Askew 2016). Vendors therefore strategically selected the type of information and level of detail that they provided in their profile pages. In the case of cocaine, for example, there was an absence of harm reduction information about snorting, even though this was the route of administration that vendors could, from the product sold, assume would be used by most buyers. As Aldridge and Askew (2016) note, vendors could have provided advice about alternative nostrils use, rinsing nasal passages after use, and other forms of harm reduction linked to drug use, which none of them did. Thus, the ostensive goal of communicating product quality was to share selectively harm reduction advice within the cryptomarket community; the covert goal was to increase sales revenue and, in turn, enhance vendors' reputation.

A key aspect of crypto-drug markets' community-building concerns their morality claims. These are typically framed within a strong libertarian ideology, as in Ulbricht's quote at the start of the chapter illustrate. When first established, Silk Road traded in a wide range of illicit items and services, including drugs, fake IDs, hacking manuals, criminal guidebooks, weapons, and money laundering. It subsequently claimed to remove "anything whose purpose is to harm or defraud" from its listing, rebranding itself as a crypto-drug market with a moral edge over its competitors (Afilipoaie and Shortis 2015). Symptomatic of this was its creator's pseudonym—Dread Pirate Roberts— chosen by Ulbricht after the fictional character in the 1970s novel The Princess Bride and its film adaptation. This hero-like character was feared for his swordsmanship. Yet he turned out to be a series of individuals passing the name and fearsome reputation to chosen successors to scare their opponents into surrender without engaging in combat. These opponents typically represented the establishment. By choosing this trading pseudonym, therefore, Ulbricht sought to emphasize the nonviolent, anti-establishment ideology of Silk Road.

Ulbricht's libertarian ideology was specifically driven by *agorism*, a radical anarchist philosophy that advocates that all relations between people are to be conducted on the basis of voluntary exchanges; that is, a kind of sharing economy that seeks to bypass any form of centralization from institutions. Indeed, Ulbricht claimed to conceive of the Silk Road crypto-drug market as a peaceful means to dismantle the state and of its members as constructive activists working toward a more permissive and egalitarian digital reality against the coercion of the state (Munksgaard and Demant 2016). As he argued in one of the forum posts on the Silk Road 1.0 site (February 2012),

The great thing about agorism is that it is a victory from a thousand battles. Every single transaction that takes place outside the nexus of state control is a victory for those individuals taking part in the transaction. So there are thousands of victories here each week, and each one makes a difference, strengthens the agora, and weakens the state.

Ulbricht was right that each transaction made a difference, albeit in a different sense to that in his quote: every product purchase on Silk Road certainly made a financial difference to him. As the site's main executive, he took a 10–20% commission of the selling price on every single transaction that went through the site's escrow service—a far from insignificant $US18 million in personal benefits over a 2 -year period (*United States v. Ulbricht* court case, 2014).[5] Moreover, every single transaction on Silk Road benefited disproportionately an elite group of vendors who monopolized this highly lucrative marketplace. The top 1% of the most successful Silk Road 1.0 vendors processed 51.5% of all the transactions (Soska and Christin 2015). This is typical of cryptomarkets overall, which are top-heavy competitive settings in which 90% of drug dealers occupy peripheral roles (Paquet-Clouston, Décary-Hétu, and Morselli 2018). In these markets, new vendors encounter high barriers to sales, having first to demonstrate their trustworthiness to other members of the cryptomarket community (Décary-Hétu et al. 2019).

In addition to being a monopolized market, and clearly contrary to Ulbricht's utopian claims of egalitarianism, Silk Road operated according to fraudulent economic principles and made regular use of coercion (Pace 2017). For example, Silk Road implemented five-star vendor ratings similar to those found in many other Clear Net markets. In principle, this simply sought to assess vendors' reputation: the quality of their products, shipping times, and stealth and their customer service. The rationale was that the Silk Road community would use the reputation system for market self-regulation, shunning those vendors who provided low quality service and helping buyers to make "informed" decisions about purchasing from particular vendors, drug purity, and so forth. In practice, though, Silk Road used extortion to turn its vendor reputation system into manageable assets. Vendors regularly collected buyer addresses rather than destroy them after product shipping. They then used this information about buyers to blackmail them for high vendor ratings. Some vendors even forced buyers to grant higher ratings as a condition of sale. Scams were also commonplace, especially *whitewashing*, whereby after developing a good reputation through the bogus rating system, a vendor would take numerous payments from buyers and close his or her account without sending the goods. Another regular tactic was the use of "quick buy" programs, where attractive markdowns would be offered by vendors with good reputation ratings to lure new buyers before accepting payment and immediately disappearing—only to reappear under a different vendor username. These vendor scams are an example of the kind of fraudulent economic practices' that, coupled with ineffective regulation, user anonymity, and the profit motive, underpinned social structures in Silk Road (Pace 2017). Ulbricht himself was repeatedly blackmailed using some of these practices. During his judicial trial, the prosecution referred to his responding through violent counter-measures, including hiring hit men to identify and murder scamming vendors who threatened to release thousands of buyer addresses (Pace 2017).

Silk Road was far from unique in its abuse of vendor reputation systems. Most reviews and ratings in crypto-drug markets are known to be commissioned and therefore rigged. For example, a section of the social media platform Reddit—titled the Dark Net Markets Sub-Reddit—contains guidance on how to write helpful reviews in cryptomarkets. This includes covering the main areas of interest to users (communication, product, price and market), including images, and formatting the review clearly (Mounteney, Oteo, and Griffiths 2016). And in a study about reputation systems in the crypto-drug market Hansa, Espinosa (2019) found that sellers with more positive reputation profiles (the majority, in any case) charged significantly higher prices for especially sought-after drugs like weed, hash, and ecstasy. Overall, then, crypto-drug markets manipulate reputation systems and social structures such as escrow to achieve economically motivated goals. They are indeed indicative of digital grooming practices that—under the pretense of hierarchy-free affinity, conviviality, and broscience—consistently rely on fraudulent, often coercive, practices of manipulation.

7.5 CONCLUSION

There are commonalities between crypto-drug markets and Clear Net shopping platforms: both are digital marketplaces reliant on vendor reputation systems and both use a number of mainstream marketing techniques. Nevertheless, the media-fueled image of crypto-drug markets as an e-Bay for drugs is misleading. Crypto-drug markets exploit the very economic theories of cooperation and freedom they claim to abide by—Silk Road's self-professed libertarianism may be aptly described as a form of "greenwashing advertising," for instance. These markets' faux libertarianism, moreover, often lures individuals into becoming not only (more frequent) consumers of illicit drugs but also to develop a "career" as drug dealers. Crypto-drug buyers progressively source stock intended for social dealing and wholesale offline distribution (Aldridge and Décary-Hétu 2016). If a comparison is to be made, therefore, crypto-drug markets resemble traditional drug markets: both operate according to economic principles of coercion. Crypto-drug markets are intertwined with organized crime, even if the percentage of the total drug trade represented by crypto-drug market trade is not at present large enough to impact the profits of the larger organized criminal groups. Were crypto-drug market turnover to increase substantively, organized crime would likely annex these marketplaces. And since criminal groups already use private servers and protected networks for communicating, they may relatively easily move into managing their own cryptomarkets (Mounteney, Oteo, and Griffiths 2016).

The sociotechnical affordances that underpin crypto-drug markets reflect and shape the kind of digital grooming practices undertaken in them. These affordances seek to enhance a sense of trust in the marketplaces and those who use them, especially vendors. Trust is crucially linked to risk (Chapter 2). Technically, therefore, crypto-drug markets seek to minimize the risk of detection from law enforcement and scamming by users through third-party payment services such as escrow. Socially, they operate vendor reputation systems that, while largely fraudulent, purportedly demonstrate to potential and extant buyers the quality of the products sold, the efficiency and stealth of the transactional services provided, and the bona fide identity of those selling the drugs. These systems are crucial to vendors' styling of themselves, their "brand" (and those [not] associated with it) within the marketplace, which Chapter 8 will explore.

NOTES

1. US Attorney's Office (05/02/2015), Ross Ulbricht, the creator and owner of the Silk Road website, found guilty in Manhattan federal court on all counts. https://www.fbi.gov/contact-us/field-offices/newyork/news/press-releases/ross-ulbricht-the-creator-and-owner-of-the-silk-road-website-found-guilty-in-manhattan-federal-court-on-all-counts. Accessed January 2022.
2. https://www.nytimes.com/2019/06/11/technology/online-dark-web-drug-markets.html.
3. https://www.swansea.ac.uk/media/Drug-Crypto-Markets_FINAL_June_2021.pdf. Accessed January 2022.
4. MDMA stands for methylenedioxy methamphetamine, a drug commonly known as "ecstasy."
5. https://www.publicsafety.gc.ca/cnt/rsrcs/pblctns/2019-r004/2019-r004-en.pdf. Accessed January 2022.

CHAPTER 8

"Your DrugBuddy"

Digital Commercial Grooming Discourse

8.1 INTRODUCTION

In 2018, the US cable and satellite business news television channel CNBC published an investigative report about crypto-drug markets. Entitled "How Bitcoin Is Fueling America's Opioid Crisis," the report evidenced how these markets had financed a "deadly wave of fentanyl flooding into the country."[1] More interestingly for our purposes, it also described these crypto-drug markets as large-scale criminal spaces, arguing—as also discussed in Chapter 7—that fraudulent practices commonly lurked beneath their veneer of libertarianism. This chapter examines these markets from the perspective of digital commercial grooming, focusing on what is widely regarded as the flagship of crypto-drug markets: Silk Road.

Drug selling on the Dark Net, as an individual or on behalf of a drug trafficking outfit, is illegal and entails luring others (buyers) into unregulated, illicit spaces online. These vendors may therefore be considered digital commercial groomers, with customers in turn being the target of their grooming practices. However, determining who is grooming whom in crypto-drug markets like Silk Road is not as straightforward as it is, for instance, in digital sexual grooming. As argued in Chapter 7, buyers in crypto-drug markets may be involved in wholesale drug distribution on- and offline. This means that they, too, may engage in digital commercial grooming practices, seeking to lure other individuals into the same buying and selling cycle they have become a part of. Moreover, as also discussed in Chapter 7, users' interrelations in Silk Road—and other crypto-drug markets—operate according to community-of-interest principles. These make anyone interacting within these digital spaces an in-group member for as long as they abide by the community's rules of

Digital Grooming. Nuria Lorenzo-Dus, Oxford University Press. © Oxford University Press 2023.
DOI: 10.1093/oso/9780190845193.003.0008

engagement. If and/or when they fail to do so, and as per the markets' self-regulation efforts, community members become its opponents. This fluidity of members' positionings accounts for the *sui generis* grooming practices that characterize crypto-drug markets like Silk Road.

As in the case of digital sexual (Chapter 4) and ideological (Chapter 6) grooming, the analysis of digital commercial grooming in this chapter is structured around examination of self- (Section 8.3) and other- (Section 8.4, target; Section 8.5, opponent) oriented styling. Prior to this analysis, Section 8.2 explores continuity and change in the Silk Road site across the 4-year period during which it traded, first as Silk Road 1.0 (2011–2013) and, following FBI interdiction, as Silk Road 2.0 (2013–2014). This enables a better understanding of the underpinning of digital commercial grooming in this crypto-drug market.

8.2 CONTINUITY AND CHANGE IN SILK ROAD

As discussed in Chapter 7, crypto-drug markets exploit what may be termed a morality of exchange ethos; that is to say, they rely on ideological values, specifically of community-based libertarianism, to legitimate drug trafficking. These markets thus evidence transactional (commerce) and social (community) goals, which their digital architecture reflects and further supports. Figure 8.1 represents schematically this architecture for the Silk Road marketplace.

As Figure 8.1 shows, the Silk Road site included a wiki page and a support page, accessible as clickable hyperlinks from the vendor profile pages.[2] The two main components of the site were the vendor profile pages and the forum pages, which were primarily oriented to the market's commercial and community goals, respectively. As digital genres, forum pages differ considerably from vendor profile pages in terms of content, layout, and participation framework. In Silk Road, the forums operated as "affinity spaces" (Gee 2005) in which multiple participants generated, maintained, contended, and shared knowledge about drug use and drug dealing. The forums ranged from tens to hundreds of words per post across threads, the duration and number of participants of which fluctuated considerably, too. Using John's (2017— see Chapter 2) theory of digital sharing, one may see these forums as trading in abstract objects of sharing; namely, in the discursive sharing of members' personal experiences of, and advice about, drug use/selling, as well as of their views on a wide range of topics pertinent to the Silk Road community. Collectively, the forums promoted the market's morality of exchange ethos, with Ulbricht himself hosting a "libertarian book club" within one of them (Ormsby 2014).

For their part, the Silk Road vendor profile pages mainly operated as retail spaces. The vendors who managed these pages made regular use of established marketing techniques ranging from advertising free samples of products for

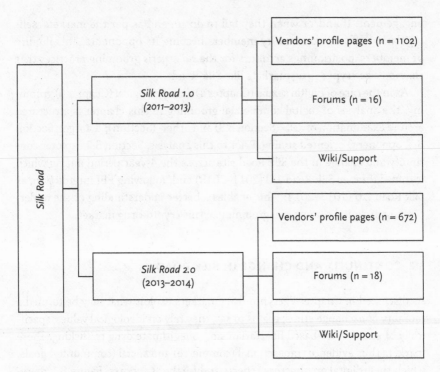

Figure 8.1 The digital architecture of Silk Road.

bulk purchases to publicizing one-off or special deals, loyalty discounts for repeat customers, and promotions during festive seasons. Prize-draws and raffles were also common, with prizes tending to be a particular number of bitcoins and winners' names being announced on the profile pages. As such, and again in John's (2017) terms, the vendor profile pages traded in concrete objects of sharing; that is, in actual illegal goods, such as narcotics and related paraphernalia (e.g., disposable needles). As the analysis in this chapter will show, though, some of the profiles also referenced abstract objects of sharing, principally stories about vendors' experiences as drug users/dealers. The vendor profile pages adopted a "one-to-many" participation framework: a vendor would address potential buyers, often using "for-anyone-as-someone" forms of talk (Scannell 2000). The vendor profile pages were of varying length—ranging from approximately 200 to more than 1,000 words—yet followed a template layout, which is reproduced in Figure 8.2.

Running vertically, from top to bottom, the profiles contained branding (the Silk Road logo, the DPR [Dread Pirate Roberts] avatar, and a hyperlink to messaging from him), a row of statistics ("messages," "orders," account'), and clickable functionality ("Shop by Category", "Search," "Go," "Logout," and the shopping cart icon). Under the vendors' username, an instructional hyperlink invited direct contact with them ("send a message.") before providing information about

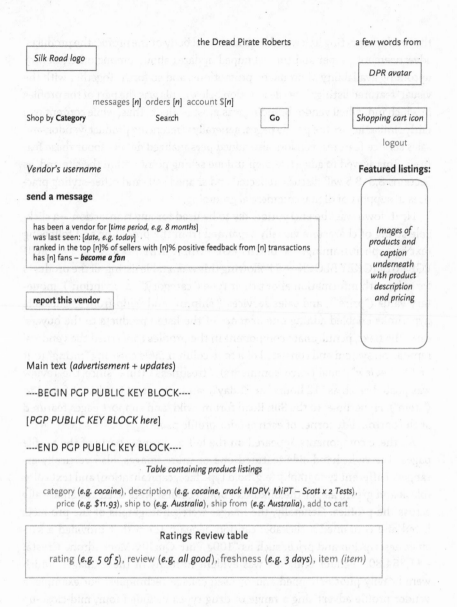

the Dread Pirate Roberts   a few words from

Silk Road logo

DPR avatar

messages [n] orders [n] account $[n]

Shop by **Category**   Search   Go   Shopping cart icon

logout

Vendor's username   **Featured listings:**

send a message

has been a vendor for [*time period, e.g. 8 months*]
was last seen: [*date, e.g. today*]
ranked in the top [n]% of sellers with [n]% positive feedback from [n] transactions
has [n] fans – ***become a fan***

Images of products and caption underneath with product description and pricing

report this vendor

Main text (*advertisement + updates*)

----BEGIN PGP PUBLIC KEY BLOCK----

[*PGP PUBLIC KEY BLOCK here*]

----END PGP PUBLIC KEY BLOCK----

Table containing product listings

category (*e.g. cocaine*), description (*e.g. cocaine, crack MDPV, MiPT – Scott x 2 Tests*),
price (*e.g. $11.93*), ship to (*e.g. Australia*), ship from (*e.g. Australia*), add to cart

Ratings Review table

rating (*e.g. 5 of 5*), review (*e.g. all good*), freshness (*e.g. 3 days*), item (*item*)

community forums | wiki | support

Figure 8.2 Template Silk Road vendor profile page (*n* = specific amount; italicized text added for illustrative purposes).

them. This consisted of the period of time vendors had been trading in Silk Road, their most recent transaction therein, and a couple of Silk Road "clout" (popularity) indexes, such as their feedback-based ranking and number of followers ("fans"). Two links were then provided for profile viewers, as potential customers, to become a vendor's fan and to report them for bad practice. Below the vendor reporting link was the main textual body of the profile: the products' advertisement proper and time-stamped updates about, among other, new or upcoming availability of products, promotions, and so forth. Together with the visual "featured listings" (see description below), this was the part of the profiles in which individual vendor branding was most evident. Thus, while content was fairly similar across the profile pages, generally referencing product, vendor, and sales service features, vendors also added personalized details about these features. This served to advertise their unique selling point within the site and, as Sections 8.3–8.5 will discuss, reflected and shaped self- and other-styling practices in support of digital commercial grooming.

Next down was the encryption key to be used for any transaction—a clickable string of characters visually separated from the preceding and following text by explicit framing: "----BEGIN PGP PUBLIC KEY BLOCK---- . . . ---END PGP PUBLIC KEY·BLOCK----." Following this was a table listing all the products for sale, with information about their type ("category," "description"), monetary value ("price"), and sales services ("ship to" and "ship from"). Clickable hyperlinks enabled adding one or more of the listed products to the buyers' cart. The next, penultimate component in the profiles concerned the vendors' reputation system and consisted of a four-column table covering "rating" (out of 5), "review" (qualitative comments), "freshness" (time since the review was posted, such as "12 hours" or "1 day"), and the actual product referred to ("item"). Hyperlinks to the Silk Road forum, wiki, and support pages featured at the bottom left corner of each vendor profile page.

All these components appeared on the left and center parts of the profile pages. The right-hand side featured one or more images, also vertically arranged. Different typography (e.g. bold type face, capitalization) and text color (black and green, as per the Silk Road brand colors) were used systematically across the profiles. Generally, the images were photographs of the products listed and contained a clickable caption beneath them that provided a succinct description and price, such as "100g Pure Quality Mephedrone Crystal - $1,364.80." Vendor branding was evident in many of these images, which were heavily photo-shopped and/or used collage techniques. For example, a vendor profile advertising a range of drug types included four, mid-close-up photographs of a smiling Pope Francis looking at the camera, waving with his right hand. Each image contained an in-text caption: a speech bubble advertising a different drug type, such as "The spirit of the coke as it is!" and a product placement box, such as "eztest for OPIATES."

The overall structure of the Silk Road site reproduced in Figure 8.1 and the template in Figure 8.2 remained constant throughout its lifespan, its main components being present in Silk Road 1.0 and Silk Road 2.0. Yet there were several changes—as well as certain continuities—in the forums and the vendor profile pages before and after the market was seized by the FBI in 2013. The number and subject matter of the forums was similar across Silk

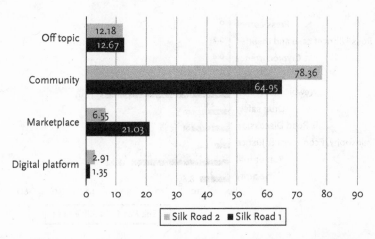

Figure 8.3 Distribution (%) of posts per forum cluster in Silk Road 1.0 and Silk Road 2.0.

Road 1.0 and 2.0: 16 and 18, respectively, with the 16 with forums in Silk Road 1.0 also featuring in Silk Road 2.0. However, their relative popularity in terms of number of posts per forum changed, as shown in Figure 8.3.

The forums in Silk Road 1.0 and 2.0 have been grouped into four broad thematic clusters in Figure 8.3: "Digital platform," "Marketplace," "Community," and a single forum (named "Off topic"). The "Digital platform" cluster included three (Silk Road 1.0: "technical support," "customer support," and "bug reports") and two (Silk Road 2.0: "customer support" and "bug reports") forums in which users discussed the technical affordances of the crypto-drug market as a digital platform, including requesting and offering assistance to navigate the Silk Road 1.0 and 2.0 sites. These forums were the least popular across Silk Road 1.0 and Silk Road 2.0, comprising approximately 12% of all posts in both sites.

The "Marketplace" forum cluster comprised five forums (Silk Road 1.0: "vendor roundtable," "feature requests," "product offers," "product requests," "shipping"; Silk Road 2.0: "feature requests," "product offers," "product requests," "shipping," "bounties") in which users discussed various aspects of the activity of buying and selling drugs, from product placement techniques through to shipping methods. The frequency of posts submitted to this cluster of forums decreased by almost two-thirds to 6.55% in Silk Road 2.0, from 21.03% in Silk Road 1.0. This was likely due to the discontinuing of the "vendor roundtable" forum in Silk Road 2.0, which at 8% in Silk Road 1.0 had been the most popular forum within the "Marketplace" cluster. Its replacement forum in Silk Road 2.0—"bounties"—generated only five posts.

The most popular forum cluster—"Community"—comprised 7 (Silk Road 1.0: "security," "legal," "rumor mill," "philosophy, economics, and justice," "drug safety," "newbie discussion," and "Silk Road discussion") and 10 (Silk Road 2.0: the seven sub-forums in Silk Road 1.0 plus "press corner,"

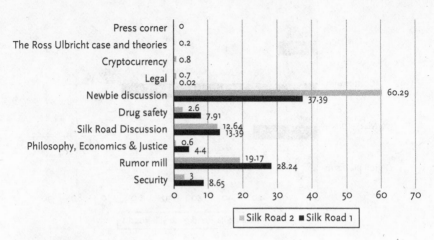

Figure 8.4 Distribution (%) of forums within the "Community" cluster across Silk Road 1.0 and Silk Road 2.0.

"cryptocurrency," and "The Ross Ulbricht case & theories") forums, in which a wide range of issues related to the community's endeavors were discussed. Community was already salient in Silk Road 1.0, where posts within this cluster accounted for 64.95% of the total. Users' discussion in these forums rose to 78.36% of the total of all posts in Silk Road 2.0. Figure 8.4 shows the forum distribution, by percentage number of posts, within the "Community" cluster across Silk Road 1.0 and Silk Road 2.0.

As can be seen in Figure 8.4, the relative distribution of use of the different forums within the "Community" cluster remained relatively stable across Silk Road 1.0 and Silk Road 2.0. In descending order, the top three forums—hosting, by some difference, the highest proportion of posts—were "newbie discussion," "rumor mill," and "Silk Road discussion." The most popular forum ("newbie discussion") experienced a marked increase over time—from 37.39% (Silk Road 1.0) to 60.29% (Silk Road 2.0). This forum primarily contained advice to individuals who were new to drug selling in the site, the emphasis being on their joining a community of supportive, like-minded individuals bound together by their shared interest in the world of drugs. Three other forums experienced a noticeable decrease from Silk Road 1.0 to Silk Road 2.0: "rumor mill" went from 28.24% to 19.17%, "drug safety" from 7.91% to 2.6%, and "security" from 8.65% to 3%. The two new forums established in Silk Road 2.0 did not really take off, the most popular of them ("cryptocurrency") reaching only 0.8% of the total percentage of posts.

Continuity and change across Silk Road 1.0 and 2.0 were also evident in the vendor profile pages. Analysis of a randomly selected set of 400 such profiles, half from Silk Road 1.0 (154,153 word tokens) and half from Silk Road 2.0 (148,813 word tokens), identified three broad thematic categories: namely, product, vendor, and sales service. Their distribution of use is shown in Figure 8.5.

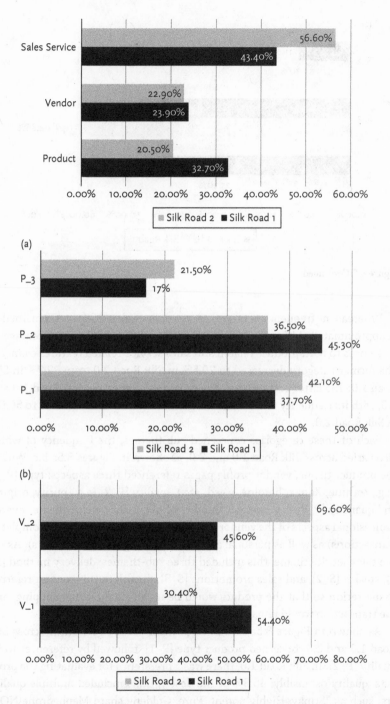

Figure 8.5 Distribution (%) of thematic categories referenced in vendor profiles in Silk Road 1.0 (*n* = 200) and Silk Road 2.0 (*n* = 200). (a) Distribution (%) of product-related features in vendor profiles in Silk Road 1.0 and 2.0. (b) Distribution (%) of vendor-related features in Silk Road 1.0 and 2.0. (c) Distribution (%) of sales service-related features in Silk Road 1.0 and 2.0.

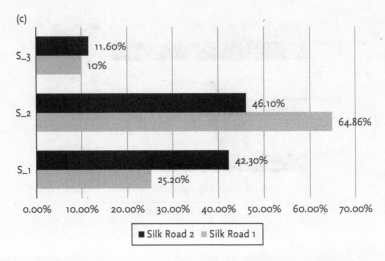

(c)

S_3	11.60% / 10%
S_2	46.10% / 64.86%
S_1	42.30% / 25.20%

■ Silk Road 2   ■ Silk Road 1

Figure 8.5 Continued

Whereas the frequency of references to vendor-related features remained—at approximately 23%—stable across Silk Road 1.0 and 2.0, the percentage of references to both product-related and sales service-related features changed. The former category decreased to 20.5% in Silk Road 2.0 from 32.7% in Silk Road 1.0. The latter category was the most frequent across Silk Road 1.0 and 2.0, with its frequency of use increasing from 43.4% in Silk Road 1.0 to 56.6% in Silk Road 2.0.

Each of these categories concerned sub-themes, the frequency of which also varied across Silk Road 1.0 and 2.0, as shown in Figures 8.5a,b,c. Within the product theme, vendor profile pages referenced three aspects: type [P_1] (e.g., cocaine, Xanax, heroine, weed, etc.), quality [P_2] (e.g., purity, origin), and quantity [P_3] (e.g., weight, number of pills). The vendor theme covered professional aspects of the vendor's identity ([V_1], e.g., number of completed transactions) as well as personal aspects ([V_2], e.g., drug use habits). As for the sales service theme, this included three sub-themes: delivery method [S_1], stealth [S_2], and sales promotions [S_3]. Stealth in this context referred to discretion so that the product would be undetected during shipping, and the transaction would remain secure from interdiction.

As shown in Figure 8.5a, the most product-related references across Silk Road 1.0 and 2.0 concerned product type [P_1], followed by references to its quality [P_2]. In Silk Road 1.0, there was a preference for evaluating the products' quality ostensibly: 45.3% of the descriptions included multiple qualifiers, such as "Stinky, Highly potent, Pure, Goldeny shard Mephedrone NOW IN – Feels just like the pre-ban," with 37.7% being less evaluative (e.g., " 'social' coke.") This trend changed in Silk Road 2.0, in which moderately evaluative statements (42.1%) were slightly more frequent than those that extolled the qualities of the products being advertised (36.5%). As regards vendor-related references (Figure 8.5b), in Silk Road 1.0 there was a slight prevalence of professional (V_1 54.4%) over personal (V_2 45.6%) features. The opposite was the case in Silk Road 2.0, in which professional details accounted for 30.4% of all vendor references, the remaining 69.6% being references to personal attributes. Within the sales service theme (Figure 8.5c), the relative frequency of references to delivery method vis-à-vis those related to stealth changed noticeably from Silk Road 1.0 to Silk Road 2.0. In Silk Road 1.0, references to stealth (S_2, 64.86%) were more frequent than to delivery method (S_1, 25.2%). In contrast, the frequency of use of both sub-themes was similar in Silk Road 2.0, with delivery method (S_1 46.10%) being only slightly more frequently referenced than stealth (S_2 42.3%). Sales promotions were comparatively less frequent across Silk Road 1.0 (S_3 11.6%) and Silk Road 2.0 (S_3 10%).

The picture that emerges from the analysis of forum and vendor profiles across Silk Road 1.0 and 2.0 is that of an agile crypto-drug market that, in the face of law enforcement interdiction, maintained its core digital architecture but adapted its grooming style from a transactional to a social goal orientation. Within the forums, the emphasis shifted from discussion of commerce-based topics (e.g., shipping methods and stealth), as it was launched and traded under Silk Road 1.0, to community-based ones (e.g., support for newcomers) post interdiction and re-launching as Silk Road 2.0. This pattern was mirrored in the vendor profile pages. In Silk Road 1.0, vendors prioritized transactional themes, stressing the quality of their products and the stealth of their own retail site and commercial *modus operandi* therein. In Silk Road 2.0, vendors became less effusive about the quality of their products, yet they also increased the frequency of references to personal aspects of their vendor identities, including sharing experiences about their own drug use—more on that topic in Section 8.3.2. Vendor profile pages in Silk Road 2.0 were also comparatively more oriented to delivery methods over stealth within the sales service theme. This may have been the result of perceived lower risk of scam following Silk Road 2.0's introduction of a strengthened, decentralized escrow system (see Chapter 7). An increase in social orientation was also observed in the Silk Road 2.0 forums, in which the frequency of posts within the "Community" cluster was noticeably higher than in Silk Road 1.0.

It is important to stress, notwithstanding the above changes, that both transactional and social goals were present in both Silk Road 1.0 and Silk Road 2.0; that is to say, the crypto-market operated from beginning to end as a community of interest as opposed to simply as either a crypto-drug market or an online community. Nevertheless, sight must not be lost that, ultimately, Silk Road 1.0 and 2.0 were digital spaces that facilitated drug trafficking, enticed a consumer base for their products, and often encouraged buyers to become traders. Inevitably, perhaps, vendor and/or buyer malpractice vis-à-vis Silk Road's libertarian ethos was commonplace. This assumed significant importance given the centrality of social trust within the marketplace. Analysis consequently moves now to examining self- and other-styling practices for digital commercial grooming in Silk Road 1.0 and 2.0. Unless otherwise stated, the results reported and discussed in the remainder of this chapter apply to both Silk Road 1.0 and 2.0 and are therefore referenced as "Silk Road." The examination of self- (Section 8.3) and other- (Sections 8.4 and 8.5) styling is informed by discourse analysis of the same 400 vendor profile pages referenced above. The discussion draws also on corpus-assisted discourse study (CADS) of the entirety of the Silk Road forums (see Chapter 1).

8.3 SELF-STYLING IN DIGITAL COMMERCIAL GROOMING

Self-styling in digital commercial grooming evinces the same broad stances identified in sexual and ideological grooming; namely, expertise, openness, and avidity. Likewise, digital commercial grooming features particular nuances in stance-taking. In Silk Road, expertise was constructed as specialist knowledge about drug dealing (in the vendor profile pages especially) and drug use (Section 8.3.1). The stance of openness was framed in terms of sharing personal experiences of resilience against perceived continuing market crises triggered by internal (vendor scams) and external (law enforcement interdiction) challenges (Section 8.3.2). And the avidity stance was cast as a keen interest in the Silk Road community as both customers and fellow libertarians (Section 8.3.3).

8.3.1 Drug expertise

As shown in Section 8.2, one of the three thematic categories referenced in the Silk Road profile pages was the vendor themselves. Within this category, vendors adopted an expertise stance. The actual expertise being brought to bear concerned drug use and dealing, and it rested on 4 attributes: experience, personal commitment, reliability, and knowledge about drugs. Let us take each of these in turn.

Experience as a proxy for expertise was typically constructed through explicit references to years of drug selling—a piece of information that the vendor profile page template required ("has been a vendor for [period of time]"; see Figure 8.2). Additional textual references to drug selling experience were included in the profile pages. As seen in Figure 8.5b, the references were more frequent in the Silk Road 1.0 (54.4% of all references to themselves as vendors) than the Silk Road 2.0 (30.4%) vendor profiles. This may have owed to a perceived need, as the market emerged, to establish one's commercial credentials. Extracts 8.1 and 8.2 are typical of the emphasis on demonstrating experience in drug selling in, respectively, the Silk Road 1.0 and 2.0 vendor profile pages.

Extract 8.1 Silk Road 1.0

01   We are new to Silk Road but definitely not to the pharmaceutical business.
02   With over 23 years in discreet medical sales, we have access to almost any
03   medication made both here in the states and through various other countries.

Extract 8.2 Silk Road 2.0

01   We are experienced users and sellers, not quite a year on the Silk Road. We
02   have been dealing for over many years – online and offline. We have started
03   our personal journey by deep seeking of the Self and now we are committed to
04   provide the best quality for really good prices for you.
05   We personally know the people who synthesize all our products, so we
06   guarantee they come straight from the sources and you are about to
07   experience the purity of each substance

Both extracts show the importance of possessing experience in the drug-dealing business. If this could not be demonstrated through years of trading in Silk Road (or other crypto-drug markets), then alternative sources of experience must be provided. This was the case of the two vendors in the above extracts, who overtly acknowledged that they were either "new to" (Extract 8.1, line 01) or "not quite a year on the Silk Road" (Extract 8.2, line 01) at the time they created their profile pages. To compensate for this, Extract 8.2's vendor claimed being "experienced" (line 01) sellers—as well as drug users—on account of "dealing for over many years – online and offline" (line 02). Similarly, Extract 8.1's vendor countered inexperience in Silk Road with an emphatic ("definitely," line 01) claim to more than two decades of commercial experience in the presupposed relevant and related "pharmaceutical business" (line 01). The illegality of this experience was alluded to through a reference to discretion ("discreet medical sales," line 02) and, therefore, knowing how to keep customers' identities private (i.e., hidden from law enforcement). Protecting users' identity from detection, as we shall see in Section 8.3.3, also indexed the stance of community avidity in digital commercial grooming.

Both extracts, too, illustrate vendors' emphasis on displaying personal commitment to the drug trade profession in Silk Road. As shown in Figure 8.5b, personal commitment references were more frequent in the Silk Road 2.0 (69.6% of all references to themselves as vendors) than the Silk Road 1.0 (45.6%) vendor profiles examined. Across the two sites, though, the same discourse features were regularly used to index such personal commitment. One was a marked use of first-person social deixis, with a balance between singular and plural deictic pronouns. First-person social deixis accounted for 89% of all the sentences that referenced vendor activities in the 400 vendor profiles examined, the remaining 11% of them using passive voice structures instead (e.g. "product is shipped within 3–5 working days").

Another discourse feature regularly deployed to index personal commitment entailed highlighting vendors' direct involvement in all things narcotics, as it were. In Extract 8.2, for example, the vendor's opening statement referenced experience not only in drug dealing but also in drug use: "we are experienced users and sellers" (line 01). This was described in experiential terms, as a "personal journey" (line 03) and "deep seeking of the Self" (line 03). The vendor also emphasized a hands-on, no-intermediary approach to commercial activity and flow: "We personally know the people who synthesize all our products" (line 05). This was in turn linked to another expertise-indexing trait: product quality ("purity of each substance," line 07).

Reliability is key in the business world—it contributes to the impression of professional expertise, enhancing brand trust (Sohn and Kim 2020). Unsurprisingly, therefore, vendor profile pages often referenced reliability, which primarily concerned the sales services features of stealth and delivery methods. Statements of intent, such as "I will deliver orders promptly, and with no externally identifying features or return address" (see Extract 8.3 for the complete advertising text) are typical of how vendors sought to construct a stance of expertise via commercial reliability in Silk Road. As we saw in Figure 8.5c, the frequency of references to sales services increased from 43.4% of the total number of references in Silk Road 1.0 to 56.6% in Silk Road 2.0. Within these sales service references, stealth was much more frequently mentioned in Silk Road 2.0 (43% of all sales service-related references) than in Silk Road 1.0 (25.2%). For its part, delivery—and specifically speed of delivery after purchase—was referenced more frequently in Silk Road 1.0 (74.86%) than in Silk Road 2.0 (57.7%). In other words, prior to the market being interdicted, vendors constructed sales service reliability by highlighting efficient, fast delivery within a cryptomarket environment that was presumed to be broadly safe. When reality—in the form of the FBI's takedown of the marketplace—proved otherwise, reliability through stealth became a more salient feature of vendors' discursive construction of drug expertise.

The fourth attribute used to index expertise in Silk Road was knowledge, specifically displays of knowledge about drugs: from drug purity and value for money to harm minimization and legal matters linked to drug use. In the vendor profile pages, such knowledge was often claimed via unsubstantiated, factual assertions, as in Extract 8.3.

Extract 8.3 Vendor profile (Silk Road 1.0)

01   Hello.

02   I am [vendor's username]

03   I sell official Ez-Test drug test kit range from the Netherlands manufac-

04   tured to the Australian Silk Road community. These kits are not illegal to

05   buy or sell, and are available to buy on the clearnet.

06   BUT using and possessing illegal drugs is illegal, so technically, actually

07   "using" these kits is illegal. For this reason, many users do not want to buy

08   with a credit card, or have kits delivered to them by name, or risk being

09   flagged by customers if inspected. That's why I sell them here, in the spirit

10   of Silk Road and the anonymous economy.

11   I have also started selling clean disposable needles for injecting, including

12   alcohol swabs, pure water and filters. These things can also be acquired

13   through most pharmacies as part of the needle exchange program but re-

14   quire a physical visit which may make some people uncomfortable. If you

15   buy needles from Silk Road, please dispose of them responsibly. Do not

16   reuse or share needles – they are very cheap so just stock up.

17   I will deliver orders promptly, and with no externally identifying features

18   or return address. Post parcels have tracking to confirm delivery for buyer

19   and seller but no signature is required.

20   Silk Road is already much safer than street sourcing drugs because the

21   community test, and share their results on the forums and vendor feed-

22   back areas. Responsible vendors can also maintain a testing regime for

23   their products and use positive results as part of their Silk Road marketing!

24   Please be safe and take care out there.

25   Your DrugBuddy

26   UPDATE: Thanks for the positive feedback everyone. I really appreciate it.

In Extract 8.3, the vendor displayed knowledge of legal matters around obtaining and using the "Ez-Test drug test kit range," his main listed product: "These kits are not illegal to buy or sell. . . . BUT using and possessing illegal drugs is illegal, so technically, actually 'using' these kits is illegal" (lines 04–07). This was presented as factual information, without referencing its source. The display of legal knowledge continued in relation to another product listed in his profile page: "clean disposable needles for injecting, including alcohol swabs, pure water and filters" (lines 11–12). He referenced both a licit ("most pharmacies as part of the needle exchange program," line 13) and an illicit ("Silk Road," line 15, generally) alternative for purchasing this product. Once again, the source of this knowledge was not referenced. The impression was given of a confident vendor who was categorically certain about the products they traded in and did not therefore need to support their knowledge through other sources.

In Silk Road, knowledge displays about drugs were often linked to vendors' dispensing of advice. Likely driven by the mercantile logic that the customer is always right, in the vendor profile pages advice-giving was generally worded in indirect terms. In Extract 8.3, for example, the vendor's reference to the licit procedure for purchasing disposable needles included a caveat: "but require a physical visit, which may make some people uncomfortable" (lines 13–14). The wording was overtly oriented toward saving the customer's negative face through use of possibility-indexing modality ("may make") as well as referencing the customer generically ("some people"). Whenever the vendors used directness to dispense their advice, such as through the imperative "dispose," "Do not reuse or share," and "stock up" (lines 15–16), negative politeness (use of hedging particles, "please" and "just") and positive politeness (the grounding move "they are very cheap so") strategies served to soften the potential face-threatening force of these imperatives.

Similarly, the dispensation of advice in the forums was both recurrent and mainly based on the use of negative politeness strategies. Unlike in the vendor profile pages, though, knowledge in the forums was generally constructed as stemming from internal (e.g., acquired through experience and personal commitment, as seen in Extracts 8.1 and 8.2) and/or external sources (e.g., scientific community, other drug users). The forums provided a broscience discourse of expertise about drugs (see Chapter 7), with their members regularly styling themselves as belonging to an informed community who supported each other around a wide range of aspects relating to drug use, from the pros and cons of its legalization through to critiquing drug taxonomies around "old-fashioned," "state-imposed" binaries of hard versus soft drugs. Extract 8.4 is typical of the use of academic references of knowledge as part of the broscience discourse of Silk Road forums. It reproduces two consecutive forum posts by two forum members, FM01 and FM12, from a multiparty discussion thread about health risk minimization in "soft drug" use, specifically cannabis.

Extract 8.4 Silk Road 1.0

FM12	01	What is your opinion on long term cannabis use? Admittedly,
	02	I have been a daily heavy consumer for over 10 years. I am specif-
	03	ically interested in decreasing cognition or other complications.
FM01	04	If I remember correctly some studies show that the use of cannabis
	05	reduces the threat of alzheimers. In 2007, Ohio State University
	06	researchers published a paper stating that medications which can
	07	stimulate cannabinoid receptors in the brain "may provide clinical
	08	benefits in age-related diseases that are associated with brain in-
	09	flammation, such as Alzheimer 's disease."

In Extract 8.4, one of the most active forum members, FM01, was asked by Silk Road self-identified new member FM12 about FM01's opinion "on long term cannabis use" (line 01), offering his (FM12's) personal experience ("I have been a daily heavy consumer for over 10 years," line 02) in a pseudo-confessional manner ("Admittedly," line 01). The question, initially worded in general terms, was next rephrased "specifically" (lines 02–03) as an inquiry about "decreasing cognition or other complications" (line 03), the register used ("decreasing cognition") keying the inquirer as scientifically aware. FM01's response was keyed as scientifically informed, too. Following what—given the specificity of the subsequent content—may be regarded as a formulaic expertise boasting avoidance device ("If I remember correctly," line 04), FM01 proceeded to provide scientific evidence regarding the benefits of cannabis use. His response moved from generic ("some studies" . . . "the use of cannabis," line 04) to specific: he referred to "a paper" published in a specific year by a research team within a specific university ("In 2007, Ohio State University researchers," lines 05–06). His technical account of the paper's results was directly rendered via the *verbum dicendi* "state" (line 06) and the use of direct quotation ("may provide clinical benefits in age-related diseases that are associated with brain inflammation, such as Alzheimer's disease," lines 07–09). The citation method was not academic (i.e., neither a page number for the quote nor a citation of the actual publication were provided). Yet the register clearly was, even when FM01 was not directly quoting from the paper, as in "medications which can stimulate cannabinoid receptors in the brain" (lines 06–07).

8.3.2 Resilience openness

Another stance used regularly in digital commercial grooming for self-styling was openness. In the Silk Road forums, this was discursively indexed by the sharing of negative experiences and, crucially, lessons learned. These were overall uplifting narratives in which the community members presented themselves as willing to share the ups and downs of their drug journeys, with an emphasis on happy endings. The ups served to demonstrate their ultimately having learned to master drug use/dealing (i.e., they indexed resilience). The downs in turn were offered as both further evidence of resilience and as ways of helping other community members through sharing non–imposition-based advice on what to avoid. In the vendor profile pages, the stance of openness also entailed uplifting journeys of drug use and/or successful experiences of drug dealing in which any occasional set-back ultimately contributed to resilience building. This is illustrated in Extracts 8.5.1 and 8.5.2, which respectively come from the updates sections within a Silk Road 1.0 and 2.0 vendor profile.

Extract 8.5.1 Silk Road 1.0

```
01    2/19/13: Closing up shop until I can reliably connect to SR. This is ridiculous,
02    apologies to anyone who has been affected by this. Haven't been able to
03    get on since after Thursday or so for more than a page load or two, tops.
04    And it can take an hour to send each message. The effect this is having on
05    my personal life and job is too severe of an impact when I have to sit here
06    clicking refresh and waiting 3 minutes then trying again and again and again
07    . . . So frustrating when you strive for professionalism and perfection like me!
```

Extract 8.5.2 Silk Road 2.0

```
01    April 19, 2014: Got sick and it turned into a week hospital stay. we just got
02    home and its midnight and this was our first order of business. we will be
03    going through all orders and emails tomorrow and making all right plus
04    extras. we will go through as orders and emails were received. if you will
05    give us a chance to make this right you will be rewarded but if you need to
06    cancel than no hard feelings.
```

In the above extracts, the two vendors shared personal experiences linked to a specific aspect of their professional activity: namely, difficulty in processing online orders. Both vendors projected "affective face" (Partington 2006), which is based around the impression of being normal, in this case experiencing—like everyone else—difficulties while doing one's job. In doing so, both vendors disclosed their emotions. In Extract 8.5.1, the vendor overtly acknowledged "[t]he effect this is having on my personal life and job is too severe of an impact" (lines 04–05) and described the resulting internal state as one of exasperation ("So frustrating," line 07). Crucially in terms of self-styling, such a state was presented as responsible for undermining his aspired-to commercial self: "when you strive for professionalism and perfection like me!" (line 07). Note the use of the present tense in "strive for," which conveys resilience in the face of challenge, here having to suspend his business temporarily ("Closing up shop until I can reliably connect to SR," line 01). This may be seen as an appeal for sympathy, which would support the overall grooming goal. Moreover, his negative emotional state (frustration) did not interfere with his professionalism/perfection aim in terms of customer relations. Thus, he provided an early, explicit apology to potential and existing customers ("apologies to anyone who has been affected by this," line 02), to whom he also offered a fulsome explanation. This included a time frame ("Haven't been able to get on since after Thursday or so," lines 02–03) and details of the technical challenge he faced: "for more than a page load or two, tops. And it can take an hour to send each message. . . . I have to sit here clicking refresh and waiting 3 minutes then trying again and again and again" (lines 03–06).

In Extract 8.5.2, the vendor shared a personal experience narrative of ill health to justify the professional challenge he was facing—again, an appeal to sympathy in support of his overall grooming goal. He minimized the seriousness of his illness, succinctly and nonchalantly moving from his "g[etting] sick" (line 01) to this "turn[ing] into a week hospital stay" (line 01). He then shifted attention to the professional resilience that he was nevertheless able to display, performing a strategic shift of footing: from first-person singular to first-person plural deixis. This framed the remainder of the experience being shared in business-like terms: from an individual who fell ill (author, animator, principal) to the sounding-box (animator) of a business that was committed to moving on (author, principal). He thus referred to prompt reaction business capability ("we just got home and its midnight . . . we will be going through all orders and emails tomorrow," lines 01–03). He also referred to business principles of customer fairness and incentivization: their requirements would be processed methodically ("as orders and emails were received," line 04) and customers would be compensated for any inconvenience caused by means of either product rewards ("making all right plus extras . . . you will be rewarded," lines 03–05) or no-penalty cancellations ("if you need to cancel than no hard feelings," lines 05–06). Sharing of experiences such as those in the two extracts was thus strategically used in the vendor profile pages to index a stance of openness about a vital aspect of successful enterprising: resilience in the face of inevitable and varied challenges.

8.3.3 Community avidity

A third, regularly adopted stance for self-styling in Silk Road entailed showing a keen interest in the Silk Road community. This was presented as deep concern for protecting Silk Road users' interests, be those linked to anonymity/stealth (i.e., remaining undetected by law enforcement), wellbeing (i.e., drug use safety), or finance (i.e., making money from sales and/or not being scammed as buyers and sellers). While this stance was often orientated to users as fellow libertarians within the community, it clearly also benefitted Silk Road's transactional (commercial) goals and thus orientated to Silk Road users as customers, too. We saw in Extract 8.2, for instance, that a vendor overtly expressed their desire to facilitate their targets' "personal journey" of drug use. And in Extract 8.3, another vendor made an explicit point of noting how he sought to minimize any inconvenience to his potential customers, such as feeling uncomfortable by having to pay a "physical visit" to a pharmacy to buy disposable needles or buying a legal drug test kit through means other than his site. The vendor justified his concern about the customer's needs for anonymity on grounds of Silk Road's libertarianism: "That's why I sell them here, in the spirit of the anonymous economy" (lines 09–10).

Safeguarding users from "the establishment" and, in turn, preserving libertarian principles were indeed commonly referenced across Silk Road. Vendors primarily talked about drug "communities" and "community members," rather than about narcotic "markets" and "customers" (or similarly commercial labels). In Extract 8.3, for instance, the product being sold was "manufactured to the Australian Silk Road community" (lines 03-04); that is, tailored to the needs of the membership base this vendor was seeking to attract. The vendor was far from alone in explicitly showing concern for the wellbeing of community members. Variations of his pre-closing statement "Please be safe and take care out there" (line 24) were recurrent across the vendor profiles—as well as the forum posts. So were thanking statements for (repeated) custom and positive vendor ratings, of which the update in Extract 8.3 is typical: "Thanks for the positive feedback everyone. I really appreciate it" (line 26). The following message was placed just above that vendor profile by the market's administrator:

Extract 8.6 Silk Road 1.0

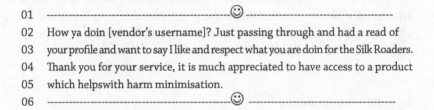

```
01   -----------------------------------------☺-------------------------------------
02   How ya doin [vendor's username]? Just passing through and had a read of
03   your profile and want to say I like and respect what you are doin for the Silk Roaders.
04   Thank you for your service, it is much appreciated to have access to a product
05   which helpswith harm minimisation.
06   -----------------------------------------☺-------------------------------------
```

As argued in Chapter 7, the libertarian ethos promoted within Silk Road was subservient to commercial interests and entailed regular coercion of those who bought drugs therein. Yet the market worked hard to create the impression that it was keenly focused on its customers as fellow members in an affinity space (the Silk Road marketplace) that provided equal opportunities for learning and sharing experiences about a common endeavor: drug use/trading. In Extract 8.6, this impression came from none other than Dread Pirate Roberts, its administrator. In a direct, one-to-one message to the vendor, Ulbricht explicitly and positively evaluated ("I like and respect," line 03) his drug selling approach as a "service" (line 04) to the community ("the Silk Roaders," line 03) through "harm minimisation" (line 05).

In keeping with the egalitarian ethos of the community, the message also minimized power-imbalance between Ulbricht and the vendor. What in essence constituted an instance of the top layer of management running spot checks on his business was instead presented as Ulbricht's "Just passing through" (line 02) and "hav[ing] a read of your profile" (lines 02–03). Ulbricht also expressed his appreciation of the vendor through a repeated thanking statement: "Thank you for your service, it is much appreciated" (line 04). Two smiley emoticons (☺; lines 01 and 06) at the start and end visually framed Ulbricht's message, further keying it as friendly and interpersonally close. The register was informal, too. Note the use of a casual greeting formula in line 02, in which the spelling was typographically rendered to show relaxed pronunciation: "ya," for the pronoun "you," and g-dropping in "doin" (also repeated in his endorsement of the vendor's activities in line 03).

Community avidity stance-taking thus entailed the strategic placing of Silk Road members' interests at the heart of commercial activity through referencing a discourse of libertarianism. In doing so, drug use risk minimization was a frequent *topos*, as we have seen. Indeed, taking drugs was often presented as contributing to the targets' wellbeing. In their profiles, many vendors relied on a "physical and spiritual wellness" *topos* to support drug use risk minimization. Consider the following extract from a Silk Road 2.0 vendor profile. The text appeared immediately after the product's description as "BEST QUALITY," "REALLY GOOD PRICES."

Extract 8.7 Silk Road 2.0

01 What you may expect. and more: BELIEVE IT OR NOT,
02 OR JUST TRY – ALL OF OUR STUFF IS BLESSED
03 BY THE FIVE'TH DIMENSIONAL ENERGY AND KEEPS VIBRATIONS OF LOVE TO
04 LEAD YOUR SPIRIT STRAIGHT TO THE LIGHT and to develop the brightness
05 possibilities of your life potential at any given moment.
06 Please do remember – all psychedelics turn off curtains of ignorance and what
07 you see is your mind with no resistance, possibly unlimited. Please notice to
08 whom this happens. Please find your way to the heart!

Extract 8.7 presented illegal activity (purchasing through an illegal Dark Net market) and consuming psychedelic drugs as enlightening ("turn off curtains of ignorance," line 06), cognitively liberating ("your mind with no resistance," line 07), affectively rewarding ("KEEPS VIBRATIONS OF LOVE," line 03; "find your way to the heart!," line 08), and, ultimately, spiritually transcending ("LEAD YOUR SPIRIT STRAIGHT TO THE LIGHT," lines 03–04). Such manipulative reframing was realized either through factual statements that presented "incontrovertible truths" about drug use or through conventionally mitigated ("please," line 06) imperatives. Only once was epistemic modality used that introduced possibility, as opposed to certainty, when it came to the "possibly unlimited" (line 07) liberation of the mind through drug use. As per the conventions of the advertising genre, vendors self-styled themselves as totally focused on their customers' perceived needs. These reflected and further constructed a grooming discourse around drug use that highlighted its benefits (Extract 8.7) and either simply silenced its dangers (Extract 8.7) or underscored vendors'—and the market's—efforts to ensure health risk minimization (e.g., Extracts 8.3 and 8.6).

8.4 STYLING THE TARGET IN DIGITAL COMMERCIAL GROOMING

Two stances were regularly attributed to the targets of digital commercial grooming in Silk Road: savviness and niceness. As Extracts 8.8.1–8.8.3 illustrate, drug users/buyers were discursively constructed as belonging to an informed community whose members were most capable of making their own decisions about a range of drug-related issues, including how to remain both anonymous when purchasing drugs and safe when dosing. They were also talked about and/or to as being, essentially, a nice, polite group of people.

Extract 8.8.1 Silk Road 2.0

01   I'm a guy from Germany just trying to give it a try to be a good Silk Road
02   member and contribute to this wonderful, clever platform

Extract 8.8.2 Silk Road 2.0

01   My goal is to offer competitive pricing along with excellent customer
02   service and fast professional shipping. I will be specializing in prescription
03   meds and weed. I am very excited and proud to be part of such a smart
04   community

Extract 8.8.3 Silk Road 2.0

01   We have noticed that the people of silk road compared to people from
02   similar forums such as topix are on a much higher level, and courtesy in
03   general. You have been super kind and friendly . . . a really big THANK YOU
04   to the people of the Silk Road community

The vendors in the above examples described Silk Road users in face-enhancing, indeed flattering, terms that highlighted their know-how: as a "clever" (Extract 8.8.1, line 02), "smart" (Extract 8.8.2, line 03) community, as a group that was "on a much higher level" (Extract 8.8.3, line 02) than "the people from similar forums such as topix" (Extract 8.8.3, lines 01–02). Not only was this community drug-savvy but also "super kind and friendly" (line 03), displaying "courtesy in general" (8.8.3, lines 02–03), which made Silk Road a "wonderful . . . platform" (Extract 8.8.1, line 02)—a place where a vendor would thus be "very excited and proud to be part of" (Extract 8.8.2, line 03). Such positive, other-stance attribution clearly served as a marketing strategy whereby vendors strived to meet the high demands of their smart target/customers. In Extract 8.8.1 the vendor thus referred to his "just trying to give it a try" (line 01)—it designating "be[ing] a good Silk Road member and contribut[ing]" (lines 01–02) to the "wonderful, clever platform" (line 02). In Extract 8.8.2, similarly, the vendor's commercial goal— "to offer competitive pricing along with excellent customer service and fast professional shipping" (lines 01–02)—preceded his overt statement of excitement and pride "to be part" (line 03) of an intelligent community—the implication here being that the community appreciated and deserved that goal being fulfilled.

In addition to being positively appraised as savvy and nice, drug users/buyers in Silk Road were both deferentially addressed as customers and treated with in friendly interactions as fellow community members, of which Extracts 8.9 (8.9.1 and 8.9.2) and 8.10 are, respectively, typical.

Extract 8.9.1 Silk Road 2.0

01   If you have any problems, I apologise, and just PM me. We appreciate that you stay
02   polite; then we can work it out.

Extract 8.9.2 Silk Road 2.0

01   It would be most appreciated if you could please finalize once you have the
02   item and are happy with it. We do put a fair bit of effort into the shipping
03   (labels, some degree of stealth) and always try ensure it gets to you ASAP.
04   Thank you for your custom.

Extract 8.10 Silk Road 1.0

01   We're not hippies, we came a little late, but we're close. You help us
02   reinvigorate the psychedelic scene when buying our products. Get your
03   friends for an Acid Test. Like Austin Powers said, let our trips be:
04   [username], baby!

The vendors in the two examples in Extract 8.9 made marked use of negative face-saving work when addressing their target. The impression being conveyed was that Silk Road community members must be treated with respect and their freedom of choice, as customers, must be recognized. In Extract 8.9.1, an apology in principle, as opposed to relating to a specific offense, was offered: "if you have any problems, I apologise" (line 01), and practical redress thereof was also provided that was oriented to minimizing any perception of hassle being caused to the target: "just PM me" (line 01). Having proffered this explicit, personal apology, the vendor shifted footing to express gratitude from a corporate "we" subject position. Herein he attributed the stance of niceness to his targets as customers, showing appreciation of their politeness: "We appreciate that you stay polite" (lines 01–02). He maintained plural social deixis to, once again, minimize any potential negative face threat of an already hypothetical problem: "then we can work it out" (line 02). In this last statement, "we" became referentially ambiguous: it could be interpreted as including or excluding the targets.

In Extract 8.9.2, the vendor also went to considerable lengths to heed the target's negative face needs within his request for prompt payment upon satisfactory receipt of purchased drugs. The request contained a query preparatory ("you could . . . finalize once . . . ," line 01), the deference-indexing of which was strengthened by a thanking statement that made use of a conditional clause ("It would be most appreciated if . . .," line 01) and the negative politeness marker "please" (line 01). It was also further justified via a grounding move that emphasized the vendor's commitment to providing a high-level, prompt service to the target: "We do put a fair bit of effort . . . and always try to ensure it gets to you ASAP" (lines 02–03). Target deference was further conveyed through what may be described as a formulaic closing-cum-thanking statement in commercial transactions: "Thank you for your custom" (line 04).

Alongside presenting customers as worthy of deference, a stance of fellow community members (of "Silk Roaders," in the words of administrator Ulbricht in Extract 8.6) was also regularly constructed for the targets of digital commercial grooming. This assumed no power asymmetry between vendors and buyers and was discursively indexed through interpersonal closeness, mainly positive politeness geared toward highlighting sameness/like-mindedness. Informal greeting formulae, such as "hi," "greetings," and "hey there!," were commonplace in forum posts and vendor profile pages. Verbal wit was also frequent, as were the use of directness, as illustrated in Extract 8.10, in which target support of the vendor's implicit goal to "reinvigorate the psychedelic scene" (line 02) was presupposed ("You help us," line 01) and linked to the concrete action of "buying [the vendor's] products" (line 02). Social deixis was once more strategically mobilized in this extract to support such other-stance attribution. Thus, first-person plural pronouns shifted from being used to refer to the vendor only, excluding the target ("We're not hippies. . . . You help us . . . our products. Get your friends. . . .") to being inclusive of the target: "Like Austin Powers said, let our trips be: [username] baby!" (lines 03–04). The intertextual film reference in this statement entailed a play of words as the vendor's username was a clipping of two words, the last one of which is the ending "-delic," and thus resembles one of the main character's catch terms in the Austin Power films: "shagadelic." This is an example of product placement targeting a particular customer profile with whom identification—on the basis of shared cultural references—was promoted. The vendor also sought to get his targets to lure others to using drugs: "Get your friends for an Acid Test" (lines 02–03)—the kind of social dealing activity that, as was shown in Chapter 7, makes cryptomarkets grooming spaces rather than just an e-Bay for drugs.

As the extracts examined thus far show, targets were generally styled through other-attributed stances of being savvy customers and socially (i.e., community-wise) "nice" and supportive of the Silk Road marketplace. However, in approximately one-fifth of the vendor profile pages analyzed, of which Extracts 8.11.1–8.11.3 are typical, targets were attributed negative stances as customers and community members.

Extract 8.11.1 Silk Road 1.0

01   I go through the trouble of trying to ship same day/next day please show me the
02   same by finalizing immediately once you receive your package. Its disrespectful
03   making me wait 17 fucking days to get paid go neck yourself.

Extract 8.11.2 Silk Road 2.0

01   I am not out to scam anyone, selectively or otherwise. Any PMs or forum posts
02   stating/suggesting that i am scammer will result in your account being banned from
03   purchasing from me in the future and your username will be shared with the other
04   vendors of the site so they do not have to deal with any of your potential allegations
05   and to prevent you from ruining the reputation of other vendors

Extract 8.11.3 Silk Road 2.0

01   Holding my feedback 'hostage', claiming I didn't send you the right quantity,
02   threatening me in another way, or claiming you never received your package when

03   DCN says otherwise will not work out in your favour. I'm an honest businessman
04   looking for straightforward transactions and don't want to deal with immature
05   bullshit.

Extracts 8.11.1–8.11.3 constitute instances of selective dissociation (see Chapter 6) in which individuals—here Silk Road vendors—distanced themselves from the representation of the in-group as being underserving of Silk Road community membership. In the extracts, the undesirable traits and behaviors attributed to these members of the Silk Road community were being "disrespectful" (line 03) customers who made committed vendors ("I go through the trouble of trying to ship same day/next day," lines 01–02) wait for payment for a comparatively speaking unreasonable period of time ("17 fucking days," line 03), in Extract 8.11.1; spreading lies about the vendor on "PMs or forum posts" (line 02), specifically "stating /suggesting that [he is a] scammer" (Extract 8.11.2, line 02); and engaging in dishonest transactional activity as buyers (Extract 8.11.3). This included lying about product delivery ("claiming you never received your package," line 02) despite evidence to the contrary ("when DCN says otherwise," line 03) and refusing to provide expected positive feedback in the vendor's page ("Holding my feedback 'hostage,'" line 01) on false accounts ("claiming I didn't send you the right quantity," line 01). In all three extracts, moreover, selective dissociation entailed presenting vendor and buyer as being diametrically opposed: vendor's commitment to shipping efficiency versus buyer's protracted payment (Extract 8.11.1); vendor's honest intentions toward buyers versus buyer's underhanded goal to ruin vendor's reputation (Extract 8.11.2); vendor's commercial integrity ("an honest businessman looking for straightforward transactions," lines 03–04) versus buyer's "immature bullshit" (Extract 8.11.3, line 05).

Chapter 7 discussed vendors' use of coercive behavior, including violent extortion practices, to secure positive ratings that they could list on their profile pages. Sabotaging of the market's reputation system was known to the community and, as Section 8.5 will discuss, made such vendors part of the internal opponent to digital commercial grooming. Extract 8.11.3 illustrates an inverse situation, whereby the vendors appraised targets' behavior as being coercive ("threatening me," line 02) whenever they withheld the expected positive feedback.

These vendors' use of selective dissociation gave them an opportunity to assert the self-regulatory principles of Silk Road, including via publicly shaming "misbehaving" members. As in other digital spaces (see Garcés-Conejos Blitvich 2022a, 2022b), shaming discourses in Silk Road supported—and further constructed—situated constructions of morality and internal regulation by the community. Thus, in Extract 8.11.2, the vendor threatened to share the transgressing customer's username "with the other vendors of the site" (line 04), which would be tantamount to commercially blacklisting them. This action was legitimated not in terms of personal retaliation but as part of the market's internal monitoring and implementation of its rules: "so they [the other vendors on Silk Road] do not have to deal with any of your potential allegations and to prevent you from ruining the reputation of other vendors" (lines 04–05). The vendor in Extract 8.11.3 similarly referenced the negative consequences for the customer were he to continue disregarding the market's rules of engagement, albeit that the vendor's threat was here presented in a more veiled manner: "will not work out in your favour" (line 03).

8.5 STYLING THE OPPONENT IN DIGITAL COMMERCIAL GROOMING

Digital commercial grooming is primarily concerned with self- and target-styling. This is to be expected given the community of interest essence of crypto-drug markets in general and Silk Road's digital architecture in particular, its main components being oriented to self-advertising (vendor profile pages) and community members' discussion (forums). Despite this, discursive work in both vendor profile and member forum pages went into styling those perceived to challenge the market and/or their users. These opponents were of two main types: external and internal. The former was the establishment, often conceptualized in generic terms. The latter were fraudulent vendors.

The establishment is a dominant group or elite that holds power across one or more life domains. In Silk Road, this dominant group was the state and the life domains under its power were mainly those of the economy and the law. As discussed in Chapter 7, Silk Road was established as a community of interest. The life domain of interest to this community was drug using and dealing, which its members wanted to run free from any kind of external influence. An anti-establishment ideology, libertarianism, encapsulated this want for a free-market society in which all relations between individuals and groups would be conducted as voluntary exchanges. Indeed, Ulbricht established Silk Road with the explicit intent of dismantling the state through digital commercial disruption. As part of the grooming goal, therefore, Silk Road created a sense of togetherness against this external authority (the state), which was constructed as wishing the community harm.

Ulbricht—and other community members—were at times explicit in their disdain for the state, with the opening quote in Chapter 7 being a case in point. Therein, Ulbricht attributed to the state the stance of "leeching off a productive sector" (drug trading), its "hallmarks" being "oppression, institutional violence and control, world war," among other. Generally, though, moderate and/or veiled (implicit) criticism was favored over overt impoliteness and/or any form of hate speech when it came to styling the state as the external opponent of Silk Road. Consider Extract 8.12.

Extract 8.12 Silk Road Discussion Forum (Silk Road 1.0)

Author	Topic: Acknowledging Heroes (Read 45685 times)
Dread Pirate Roberts	Acknowledging heroes
Administrator	On: February 27, 2012, 04:36am
Hero Member	UPDATE: Specific listings can be made stealth now as
▆ ▆ ▆ ▆ ▆	well. From the Seller's Guide:
	Quote

[Dread Pirate Robert's avatar]

" When listing or editing an item, you may also control its visibility . . .

Posts: 608

There are heroes among us here at Silk Road. Every day they risk their lives, fortunes, and precious liberty for us. . . . Of course I am talking about our vendors. . . . They risk so much already and being in the spotlight, while good for business, also poses the risk of becoming a target for law enforcement.

At the request of some of our top vendors, we are implementing a new feature called Stealth Mode. From the Seller's Guide:

Quote

Karma: +648/-140 as you wish

" Stealth Mode allows you to run your business our of view of the general public. Whether your sales are growing faster than you can expand your infrastructure to keep up, or you just don't want to be in the public eye any more. . . .

Our aim is to give our vendors the ability to control the growth and visibility of their business and take on the level of risks they are comfortable with.

In the post reproduced in Extract 8.12, Ulbricht was sharing the news (hence the "UPDATE" framing) of a novel technical feature in the site—"Stealth Mode"—that would enable vendors to select whom to make their trade visible to. This information was already available in the Sellers' Guide, from which Ulbricht included two direct quotations, visually indexing them via explicit labelling as such ("Quote"), large type face quotation marks, different font color (dark green) and size, and use of bordering lines. Ulbricht used the post to promote the new feature as well as to eulogize vendors in his market, whom he labeled "heroes" and, as per the post's topic, thought to be in need of community recognition for the risks they took by simply running their business. In van Dijk's (1998) ideological square terms (see Chapter 5), Ulbricht's post applied the in-group exaltation discourse strategies of maximizing its members'—here, vendors'—good properties or actions and minimizing its bad properties or actions. Reference to vendors' daily "risking their lives, fortunes, and precious liberty for us" presented their unstated, personally lucrative, and often coercive business as responding to their willing sacrifice for the Silk Road community. In this regard it is worth reminding ourselves that Ulbricht personally took a 10–20% percentage mark-up on every transaction each of these "heroes" conducted on his site (Chapter 7).

Ulbricht's post also stated that the market's aim was to yield to these heroes "the ability to control the growth and visibility of their business and take on the level of risks they are comfortable with." This non-imposition approach no doubt served as a marketing ploy for, ultimately, "Stealth Mode" sought to prevent law enforcement from detecting Silk Road's successful vendors and therefore also to safeguard the market's—and Ulbricht's—finances. The out-group threatening the market, law enforcement at this point, was either mentioned in passing, in risk rather than actuality terms ("the risk of becoming a target for law enforcement"), or hinted at through a general reference to anyone outside of Silk Road ("the public"). Both instances styled a very real opponent to the site's very existence—law enforcement—in mild negative terms.

In contrast to the above, overt face threat characterized the styling of Silk Road's internal opponent: fraudulent vendors. Unlike misbehaving drug users/buyers who were selectively disassociated from but remained community members, fraudulent vendors were styled as an out-group—as individuals who infiltrated the marketplace with the sole purpose of hurting its members. As discussed in Chapter 2, trust is a central aspect of the digital mediation of grooming. In the case of crypto-drug markets, trust is constructed as a *sine qua non*. In a forum post, published after a Silk Road 1.0 outage raised concerns among users that he might have run off with the funds stored on the site, Ullbricht stated,

Extract 8.13 Silk Road 1.0 (Dread Pirate Roberts, 17 November 2012)

01   I know this whole market is based on the trust you put in me and I don't take that lightly.

02   It's an honor to serve you and though you don't know who I am, and have no recourse if

03   I were to betray you, I hope that as time goes on I will have more opportunities to

04   demonstrate that my intentions are genuine and no amount of money

05   could buy my integrity. . . .

Ulbricht's post was unequivocal about the foundational status of trust in Silk Road, specifically members' trust in its leadership, and his not "tak[ing] that lightly" (line 01). Addressing members' suspicion about his intentions as the site's administrator, he asserted these to rest on integrity over financial reward: "my intentions are genuine and no amount of money could buy my integrity" (lines 04–05)—something that, in the face of rumored betrayal, he "hoped [to have] more opportunities to demonstrate" (line 03). The post thus prioritized the social-based over the system-based dimension of digital trust in Silk Road.

As discussed in Chapter 2, social-based trust refers to how individuals express the level of connection that they feel to a certain individual or social group, and systems-based trust refers to how much faith individuals invest in the functionality of technological systems based on the systems' known technological affordances. When styling fraudulent vendors as opponents in Silk Road, it was precisely their betrayal of social-based trust that members homed in on. For instance, a keyword analysis of the lemma "vendor" across the Silk Road 1.0 and 2.0 forums showed that it was similarly used, principally collocating with trust-related terms. In Silk Road 1.0, key "vendor" collocates included "trust," "reputable," "favorite," "established," "rogue," and "top"; in Silk Road 2.0, they included "reputable," "reliable," "trust," "legit," "trustworthy," and "honest."[3] Qualitative examination of numerous concordance lines for each of these collocations confirmed community members' interest in determining vendors' trustworthiness and publicly naming and shaming those who engaged in fraudulent activity in the site. Consider Extract 8.14, which is part of a lengthy forum post in which members were discussing how reliable—or otherwise—customer reviews on vendors' profiles were.

Extract 8.14 Silk Road 1.0

01   We have been told that in these forums there are a couple of people bashing

02   our integrity . . . we must say that was very disrespectful and pretty much just

03   made up lies and rumors . . . to you cowards that bashed our name in the
04   forum grow up and act like adults maybe even try to get a life as you are all just
05   cowards acting brave behind a screen and yes it does make us furious that we
06   work so hard . . . so to the cowards take your business elsewhere . . . 'so
07   before you talk lies about honest people just know that you never know
08   whom you are talking lies about you pathetic cowards.

In Extract 8.14 this forum member expressed unmitigated anger ("yes it does make us furious," line 05) at competitor vendors' "bash[ing their] name" (line 03) in the forums. These competitors, who were instructed to "take [their] business elsewhere" (line 06), were said to be engaging in "talk[ing] lies about honest people" (line 07) who "work so hard" (line 06). Their behavior was described as "very disrespectful" (line 02) and unsubstantiated ("just made up lies and rumors," lines 02–03). A stance of cowardice was explicitly, repeatedly, and emphatically attributed to them. This entailed directly ("you cowards," line 03; "you are all just cowards," line 04–05; "you pathetic cowards," line 08) and indirectly ("to the cowards," line 06) addressed name-calling. It also included belittling of the opponent, whose cowardice was evaluated as "pathetic" (line 08) and who was instructed to "grow up an act like adults maybe even try to get a life" (line 04). Impoliteness was, in short, overtly resorted to when styling vendors who were believed to have transgressed the community's norms, here as regards untruthfully bad-mouthing other vendors.

In a digital space where trust was paramount, such transgressions were not taken lightly. Vendors considered to have misbehaved were, as discussed, named and shamed in the forums. When no identifying details of the "transgressors" were available, as was the case in Extract 8.14, this did not prevent unmitigated criticism still being levied against suspects in general terms. The impression was clearly conveyed that Silk Road was capable of self-regulation. This argument was internally useful as a means to generate social-based trust especially. It also affirmed the community's libertarianism as self-regulation obviated any need for external oversight.

8.6 CONCLUSION

Silk Road was interdicted after 3 years of trading (as Silk Road 1.0), resurfaced within a month of being taken down (as Silk Road 2.0), and continued to trade for a further year until it was permanently shut down. Throughout this time, the site's main components, its vendor profiles and community forum pages, exhibited considerable continuity in terms of marketing techniques and topics. Yet there was a progressive move, following the first interdiction, toward emphasizing community-based goals, including sharing "best practice" about drug use and dealing, over commercial goals. In other words, libertarianism as a legitimating force for illicit commerce became progressively rooted in this market's digital grooming practices.

When it came to self-styling, Silk Road vendors went to considerable lengths to show their keen interest in their customers, which they typically presented as seeking to protect the Silk Road community from being tracked by law enforcement, scammed by other vendors, and being subject to drug-related harm. As part of their self-styling as experts, Silk Road users—vendors in particular—regularly shared externally (i.e., scientific) and internally (i.e., personal experience) sourced knowledge about drug use and drug dealing. And by constructing a stance of openness, specifically through stories of resilience, Silk Road users displayed business acumen (especially in the vendor profile pages) and their broscience (particularly in the forums) disposition. These three stances worked synergistically and, alongside target-styling, were crucial to the market's grooming discourse.

Styling of the target relied on stances of drug savviness and niceness that catered to projected identities of, respectively, Silk Road customers and fellow community members. The targets of digital commercial grooming were herein related to via deference (as customers) and interpersonal closeness (as fellow community members). In some cases, selective dissociation practices were applied whereby vendors would use impoliteness toward those buyers who did not abide by the commercial rules of the site (e.g., by delaying payment or withholding expected favorable vendor ratings). As an illicit digital market, Silk Road was itself the target of efforts aimed at detecting and exploiting its activity. Law enforcement and fraudulent vendors were constructed as being behind such efforts and, therefore, styled as its opponents. Law enforcement represented the state and, as such, constituted a direct challenge to Silk Road's libertarian ethos. Styling of this enemy was primarily undertaken in the site's forums, often instigated by Ulbricht himself, and generally made use of moderate face threat. In contrast, fraudulent vendors were othered through impoliteness strategies that were primarily oriented toward face (insults) and equity (belittling) rights. The strength of expression against these internal opponents was legitimated on community-based grounds, mainly lack of integrity as vendors (e.g., scams) and not being respectful to other market users. Needless to say, their fraudulent practices damaged more than social ties among this community, harming also its commercial underpinnings.

NOTES

1. https://www.cnbc.com/2018/04/13/how-bitcoin-and-cryptocurrencies-are-fuel ing-americas-opioid-crisis.html. Accessed January 2022.
2. The files corresponding to the wiki and support pages could not be retrieved from the Silk Road Archive dataset and are thus not included in the analysis offered here.
3. The statistical analysis was conducted using log-likelihood with 3-left to 3-right word span and a frequency of 5 for both node collocate and collocate alone.

CHAPTER 9

Digital Grooming

Applications to Daily Life

Because, you see, humans live by beliefs. And beliefs can be manipulated. The power to manipulate beliefs is the only thing that counts.
Michael Ende, *The Neverending Story* (1997)

9.1 INTRODUCTION

This chapter has two foci: bringing together the main findings of this book's discourse analytic study of digital grooming (Section 9.2) and discussing the potential (Section 9.3) and actual (Section 9.4) applications of such findings to what we may call, for want of a better term, "daily life." In Section 9.2, the book's key findings are revisited against the approach to digital grooming provided in Chapter 2. Then, cast against a backdrop of increasing digital grooming, Section 9.3 introduces and discusses some of the principal disruption practices used by manifold agents ranging from law enforcement to technology companies. These are not always specifically geared toward digital grooming, but to the broader concept of online harms. In UK proposed legislation, the concept covers illegal content and behavior online, such as digital sexual and ideological grooming, alongside currently legal but unethical and/or immoral content and behavior, such as disinformation, and trolling.[1] When discussing these attempts at countering online harms, Section 9.3 highlights the unique, yet hitherto only recent and hence developing, part that linguistics (especially discourse-based approaches) can play. This is illustrated via a case study of an academia–practitioner project aimed at detecting and preventing digital sexual grooming: Project DRAGON-S (Section 9.4).

Digital Grooming. Nuria Lorenzo-Dus, Oxford University Press. © Oxford University Press 2023.
DOI: 10.1093/oso/9780190845193.003.0009

9.2 DIGITAL GROOMING: APPLYING A DISCOURSE LENS

As introduced in Chapter 1, at the time of writing there is only one other book on the concept of grooming: Robin Dunbar's (1996) *Grooming, Gossip and the Evolution of Language*. Dunbar's book connects grooming and strategic language use. In doing so, the author focuses on what may be considered benign uses of grooming, such as forming groups, improving group efficiency around various tasks, and deriving a sense of community and individual wellbeing. Dunbar nevertheless acknowledges that grooming can be, and is, "easily used for evil," listing goals such as "to outwit and bamboozle, to lay propaganda trails to mislead, or to inveigle and cajole" (1996, 171). The analyses offered in the preceding chapters of *Digital Grooming* include those very goals and more: to isolate but also to build trust; to extort, but also to offer advice; and so forth. As discussed in Chapter 2, the analyses offered in *Digital Grooming* have not sought to identify and/or quantify, list-like, discourse strategies for each of those goals, let alone for digital grooming as a whole. Rather, they have foregrounded an identity approach to digital grooming, focusing on self- (groomer) and other- (target and opponent) styling through recurrent stance-taking. This approach flows from an understanding of the concept of digital grooming as comprising three core, interrelated dimensions: digital mediation, manipulation, and identity construction. Let us revisit each of these in turn.

9.2.1 The "digitalness" of digital grooming

Digital grooming is inevitably shaped by—and shapes—the digitally mediated spaces in which it occurs. Chapter 2 proposed three features as being crucial to shaping such spaces: sharing, trust, and engagement. The subsequent analyses of digital sexual, ideological, and commercial grooming offered in Chapters 4, 6, and 8 confirmed the importance of each of these features and offered fresh insights into their actual entextualization within the practice of digital grooming.

Digital grooming exploits the digital sharing era in which we are said to live, specifically the positive cultural rhetoric about sharing concrete (e.g., pictures, files) and abstract (e.g., advice, opinions, personal experiences) objects online. Across sexual, ideological, and commercial digital grooming contexts, communicative openness—and the consequent sharing of primarily abstract objects digitally—emerges as one of three stances that digital groomers regularly adopt to achieve their manipulative goals. Digital sexual groomers frequently engage in self-disclosing talk via which they share feelings of vulnerability, typically loneliness and fear; digital ideological groomers regularly self-disclose feelings, too, primarily of anger; and digital commercial groomers often talk about their experiences of market resilience in the face of external (state) and/or internal (competitor vendors) risks to their commercial and community focused endeavors. Self-disclosure, particularly when emotionally charged, triggers reciprocity, which helps advance digital grooming goals, for instance, enhancing feelings of target–groomer in-groupness and trust.

Trust development is frequently manipulated through—among other things—sharing in digital grooming. In digital sexual grooming, as Chapter 4 showed, this primarily works at the level of interpersonal relations between the groomer and the target, so that the latter may, for instance, interpret the groomer's framing of child sexual abuse as signaling romantic involvement on his part or feel safe enough to share sexual content (images, textual accounts) with him. In digital ideological grooming, (reciprocal) sharing aids deceptive trust development through homogenizing social groups (see Chapter 6). It is not therefore merely the case that in-groups and out-groups are presented as diametrically opposed in digital ideological grooming, though this is crucial to identity construction (Section 9.2.3), but that these groups are constructed as being internally uniform, too. Such group homogenizing contributes to developing high entitativity, facilitating identification, and helping to dispel doubts about "fit" and "belonging." In digital commercial grooming, system-based (technical) and social-based (community) dimensions of trust go hand in hand. As we saw in Chapters 7 and 8, crypto-drug markets invest significant technical resource in developing digital affordances, such as escrow, aimed at reducing the risk of their users being scammed by other users and/or being detected by law enforcement. Risk and trust are, as discussed in Chapter 2, the flip sides of the same coin: reducing risk and enhancing trust, and vice versa. Additionally, and as the analysis of Silk Road vendor profiles in Chapter 8 demonstrated, vendors invest considerable communicative resource in proving their trustworthiness through stance-taking aligned to expertise and community avidity in particular.

Digital grooming requires gaining access to, and then being able to continuously engage, targets online—and such engagement may extend to the "offline" realm, too. As introduced in Chapter 2, the permeability of the online/offline realms in our lives means that most of us nowadays conceive of digital media as situated actions we take in our lives to achieve specific goals, rather than as a textual repository of actions we take elsewhere (Jones, Chik, and Hafner 2018). Target engagement is enabled via different participation frameworks in digital grooming, ranging from one-to-one interaction, in the case of digital sexual grooming, to one-to-many, specifically for-anyone-as-someone structures, in the case of vendor profiles within digital commercial grooming. Shifting across participatory frameworks is both frequent and partly determined by digital affordances within and across platforms. Thus, for instance, some digital sexual groomers may first use a scatter-gun approach, based on an anyone-as-someone participation framework within a particular social media platform and then shift to a one-to-one participation framework when migrating to a different platform. Similarly, as Chapters 5 and 6 discussed, the digital *modus operandi* of extreme ideology groups varies and evolves rapidly depending on sociodigital contextual factors.[2] Othering of opponents as part of digital ideological grooming, for instance, is more frequent and explicit in social media platforms that have less strict content monitoring policies than in those that are known to clamp down on community standard/policy violations. Proposed legislation, such as the UK Online Safety Bill (2022), introduces a higher level of accountability for digital providers regarding harmful content featured in their products—including produsers' content—as well as "safety by design" principles into their business. The priority categories of harmful content, which encompass those covered in digital grooming in this book, include criminal offenses (e.g., child sexual exploitation and abuse, terrorism, hate crime, and the sale of illegal drugs and weapons), harmful content and activity affecting children (e.g., pornography), and harmful content and activity that is legal when accessed by adults but which may be harmful to them (e.g., content about eating disorders, self-harm, or suicide).[3]

9.2.2 A *sui generis* form of manipulation

Digital grooming entails communicative manipulation. The distinctiveness of digital grooming within the broader notion of manipulation stems from the fact that digital grooming practices lie outside, or at the boundaries of, the law, and transgress "the moral order" (see below). The illegality and immorality of online child sexual abuse and exploitation; incitement of extreme violence against others on grounds of their religion, race, nationality, and so forth; and trafficking of narcotics are far from mere secondary considerations in relation to the kind of manipulation practices that characterizes digital sexual, ideological, and commercial grooming. For digital groomers, the stakes of getting things wrong, as it were, are very high in terms of social and legal sanction. This, as shown in Chapters 4, 6, and 8, shapes their discourse. Chapter 4, for instance, highlighted the salience of secrecy-seeking within digital sexual groomers' tactic of isolation. These groomers construct the groomer–target relationship as being exclusive/special and deceptively use that specialness as the reason why it must be kept hidden from others with whom the target in particular has other relationships, typically her support network. The reality, of course, is far more sinister because secrecy guarantees continuing target abuse and groomer stealth. In digital ideological grooming, as shown in Chapter 6, calls to extreme violence (e.g., individual assassination, group extermination) are often accompanied by elaborate legitimation work based on appeals to authority and mythopoesis primarily. Similarly, as Chapters 7 and 8 showed, Silk Road mobilized a whole philosophy—agorism—as a kind of macro-legitimation strategy for the digital commercial grooming of the market's users. The illegality of running a highly lucrative commercial operation was thereby counteracted, if not altogether silenced.

While cybercrime provides a distinctive edge to digital grooming vis-à-vis manipulation, there are commonalities, too. Two of the four overall features of manipulation identified in Chapter 2 are particularly salient in digital grooming: covertness and intentionality/interest. At a global (or macro) level, covertness features across all cases of digital grooming examined in this book—the illegality and/or immorality of the behaviors involved making this a *sine qua non* therein. There are also some instances where covertness is attempted at the local (or micro) level, too. As noted earlier, attempts at keeping the digital interaction between digital sexual groomers and their targets exclusive (i.e., hidden from the targets' support networks) are a case in point. Similarly, morality-based justifications for inciting violence in digital ideological grooming may be regarded as efforts to neutralize the illegality of the actions referenced on grounds of distributive justice (i.e., perceived fairness through "payback"). And the kind of detailed justifications for purchasing drugs in a cryptomarket on grounds of convenience, product quality, and service stealth, for example, also signal locally instantiated covertness in what remains illicit and often coercive commercial practice.

Intentionality, specifically a misalignment of groomer and target interests, is also salient in digital grooming. Given the illegality and/or immorality of the behaviors being pursued, the targets' interests cannot be seen to be aligned to those of the groomers. This, of course, is not to say that groomers always present their work in zero-sum game terms ("by going along with my intentions, I'll benefit and you'll lose"). Instead, and as part of their covertness work, digital groomers strive to present full alignment between their own and their targets' interests. This, as we saw across the chapters, is particularly evident in terms of other-stance attribution, specifically groomers' attribution of stances to their targets that are compatible with those they (the groomers) attribute to themselves. In the case of digital sexual grooming, for example, the targets are attributed stances of keen learning about sex with adults. Moreover, such a stance is presented not just as being compatible with the groomers' stance of sexual expertise but also as being a natural activity for the target, as something that all children engage in. In digital ideological and commercial grooming, a strong sense of groomer–target alignment—including in terms of interests—is forged, too. In digital ideological grooming, this frequently revolves around othering: identifying one or more out-groups and cohering around their discursive denigration, exclusion, and so forth. In digital commercial grooming, it is often a case of sharing best practice about drug use and drug selling via broscience discourse. At the same time, though, in both ideological and commercial digital grooming, groomers use selective disassociation processes that mis-align their and their targets' interests.

The two other features of manipulation identified in Chapter 2, namely coercion/power asymmetry and falsity/insincerity, are comparatively less salient across the three digital grooming contexts than covertness and intentionality/interest. Coercion and power asymmetry feature in some but not all cases of digital grooming examined in this book. Indeed, they are infrequent in the instances of digital ideological grooming considered in Chapter 6. Therein, targets are exhorted to act in particular ways, including violently, as part of a kind of social media/digital collective outcry in the face of in-group long-endured victimization, rather than as targeted coercion.[4] The screen-based nature of the data examined in this book makes it impossible to determine whether such exhortative illocutionary acts have a "successful" perlocutionary effect on their targets. As noted in Chapters 1 and 2, moreover, the link between online encouragement of extremism, including via online propaganda, and offline extremism is the subject of considerable debate. Coercion, in the form of threats and harassment primarily, does feature in digital sexual grooming. Herein, the adult–child relationship already carries along power asymmetry, too, making any coercive acts particularly difficult for targets to resist. In digital commercial grooming, coercion tends to operate at a macro-level in the sense that, as discussed in Chapter 7, it is primarily linked to widespread and well-known rigging—through for instance threats and extorsion—of the market's review system.

Importantly, across the digital grooming contexts examined, coercion tends to be sugar-coated through facework that relies on positive and negative politeness strategies. In digital commercial grooming, the target is the customer and, as per the mercantile principle par excellence, therefore always right: targets are told they are smart and nice and reminded that it is their decision ultimately to buy what from whom. In digital sexual grooming, this comes from frequent pivoting between "nice" and "nasty" talk, which is cognitively very difficult for children to make sense of and may trigger particularly acute feelings of self-blame. Target praise is also frequent, as is seemingly yielding actional power over to her. Additionally, a strong sense of target–groomer togetherness—indeed identification—is frequently fostered across all three contexts of digital grooming. At the macro-level, of course, constructing target–groomer togetherness/identification is one of the chief means via which consent is manufactured. This makes the concealment of coercion, rather than coercion per se, a staple diet of digital grooming.

As for falsity/insincerity, this is present in some of the contexts examined in the book. In the case of digital ideological and commercial grooming, falsity lies primarily in misinformation about a wide range of facts: levels of state support for migrants, drug product quality, and so forth. The analysis of

digital sexual grooming, for its part, unveils some instances of identity deception. For example, there were some clear contradictions within some of the
chat logs examined regarding the groomer being both a minor and working in
a relatively senior role (as opposed to an apprenticeship position, for example).
Digital sexual groomers' deception about their motives cannot really be determined from screen-based datasets only: Are their references to love and friendship (partly) genuine?; Do their motives change throughout the course of the
grooming interaction? These are questions that textual analysis on its own
cannot answer—and answering them has in fact not been attempted across the
pages of *Digital Grooming*. Nevertheless, they are questions worthy of further
investigation, regardless of how uncomfortable the answers may be at a societal
and/or personal level e.g., the possibility that digital sexual groomers may hold
romantic and friendship feelings towards their targets.

As noted in Chapter 2, a number of linguistic studies have identified structures and discursive strategies used within and across manipulation contexts,
primarily those linked to institutions such as the media or politics. It is perhaps unsurprising, therefore, that many of these strategies also feature in the
digital grooming datasets examined in this book. In digital sexual groomers'
discourse, they include the use of implicatures and vague language markers;
argumentative reframing of sex as romance and/or as beneficial to the target;
"fresh talk" (Goffman 1981), especially emotional self-disclosure; banter and
(humorous) self-deprecation; fast pivoting between politeness and impoliteness toward the target; fixated discourse, including through batteries of
questions; regular use of push-pull structures (assertiveness-tentativeness;
sexual explicitness-implicitness); and prevalence of first-person social deixis
(narcissistic discourse). Strategies frequently seen in digital ideological
groomers' discourse entail polarized argumentation; assertiveness (incontrovertible truths, expressive typography); verbal wit; in-group language
codes; politeness (groomer- or target-oriented) and impoliteness/othering
(opponent-oriented); selective dissociation (from the target); fresh talk, especially anger-fueled moral tales; and extensive legitimation via authority and
mythopoesis. As for digital commercial grooming, recurrent strategies include
use of first-person social deixis and commissive speech acts that highlight personal commitment to a particular service or product, blending of directness
and indirectness, use of for-anyone-as-someone participation frameworks,
references to academic studies, argumentative reframing (drugs as good/drug
trading as beneficial to society), politeness (target-oriented) and impoliteness
(opponent-oriented), selective dissociation (from the target), and fresh talk,
especially resilience tales.

Understanding of digital grooming as a discourse practice is enhanced by being
able to identify these strategies and the recurrence of some of them across the
three contexts of digital grooming examined in this book. However, because the
same strategies may be deployed in nongrooming—nonmanipulative—discourse

contexts, there is, as discussed in Chapter 2, limited utility in adopting a strategy-based analytic approach to digital grooming. And this is why this book has instead adopted an identity-foregrounded approach to the practice of digital grooming, specifically one that revolves around examining groomers' self- and other-styling through stance taking.

9.2.3 An identity-foregrounded approach to digital grooming

The analyses offered in Chapters 4, 6, and 8 show that, when it comes to self-styling, digital sexual, ideological, and commercial groomers have more in common than not. Three stances—expertise, openness, and avidity—scaffold the discursive crafting of their identities during the practice of digital grooming. *Expertise* refers to discursive displays of skill or knowledge, which are presented as being superior to those of the target and the opponent. As noted in Chapter 2, this stance rests on placing a positive value on the self on grounds of competence. In the cases of digital sexual and commercial grooming, expertise is confined to subject matter, respectively, sex and drugs. Yet, in the case of digital ideological grooming, expertise stance-taking is broad and superficial—a Jack-of-all trades expertise display, that, in the case of radical-right groups in particular, piggybacks on topical news as a means to build a broad support base on which to advance their digital grooming.

The stance of *openness* exploits the principle of reciprocity as a means to promote closeness between—indeed homogenizing—groomer and target. Across the three digital grooming contexts examined, this stance relies on emotional release—albeit that the emotions foregrounded therein vary. Digital sexual groomers primarily disclose their emotional vulnerabilities, genuine or otherwise, often linking them to feelings of loneliness or fear. Digital ideological groomers favor the disclosure of anger, which they connect to victimization. And digital commercial groomers primarily tell tales of personal and professional resilience: stories in which, despite a number of difficulties, they pull through and deliver on their customer-cum-community commitments. The stance of openness is arguably the most obvious manifestation—indeed exploitation—of the positive cultural rhetoric around both digital sharing (John 2017) and digital relatability (Abidin 2017, 2018; Kanai 2019).

Digital groomers also engage in self-styling via a stance of *avidity*, discursively demonstrating a keen interest in, or enthusiasm about, something or someone. In digital sexual and commercial grooming, the "beneficiary" of such keen interest is, respectively, the child and the drug community. In digital ideological grooming, it is the extreme ideology group's values that are constructed as being worthy of the groomers' avidity. Avidity stance-taking helps digital groomers to style themselves as selfless individuals whose actions—proposed and/or undertaken—place their targets at the heart of all decision-making. As previously discussed, the lack of alignment between groomer and target interests makes this a fallacious line of argumentation.

Alongside self-styling via stances of expertise, openness, and avidity, digital grooming entails attributing stances to those who are positioned as the targets and the opponents of digital grooming. The stances attributed to the targets of digital grooming are generally complementary with those the digital groomers self-attribute. Thus, as discussed in Chapter 4, the targets in digital sexual grooming are attributed stances of keen learning about sex, which complement the groomers' self-styling as sexual experts; willing (emotional) self-disclosure, which supports groomer tactics of developing trust, sexual gratification, and isolation; and specialness, which complements the groomers' avidity stance. In digital ideological and commercial grooming, the targets are mainly constructed as being part of a homogenous in-group, which the groomers' self-styling epitomizes. The positive attributes of the targets are thus exalted. In digital ideological grooming, they are, for example, host-respecting, typically second (or later) generation immigrants (radical right groups), or good Muslims (jihadi groups). In digital commercial grooming, they are smart, polite customers. In both cases, however, selective dissociation may also be used, whereby the targets are neither praised nor respected but criticized for failing to uphold the values of the groomer/the groomer's group. Selective dissociation is, however, a transient state. The groomers' negative other-stance attribution in these instances tends to be a matter of the target "not yet" upholding treasured values rather than being incapable of doing so. In other words, the targets are positioned as some kind of "work in progress"—their digital groomers' work in progress. A case in point are the calls for urgent action by digital ideological groomers, whereby the targets are exhorted to wake up from their apathy and/or victimization and join the in-group's call to arms, literally and/or metaphorically speaking.

Attributing stances to the opponents of digital grooming is always a case of out-grouping. In digital commercial and ideological grooming, moreover, it is a blatant case of othering. In these contexts, and especially in digital ideological grooming, the opponent is constructed as the reason for all the humiliation, wrongdoing, suffering, and so forth that the groomer and target so unjustly endure. Groomer–target and opponent thus adopt subject positions of, respectively, blame-maker (the victimized in-group) and blame-taker (the victimizing out-group) (Angouri and Wodak 2014). Within these positionings, temporality matters: the in-group's victimization is long-endured but also finite through adopting the groomers' "instructional frames" that call for "more traditional violent extremist views (e.g., Nazi or neo-Nazi) [as well as] more radical populist views around, particularly, anti-immigration and Islam" (Conway 2019, 12).

A plethora of impoliteness strategies are deployed when styling the opponent in digital ideological grooming. These are primarily oriented toward the opponents' face and equity rights. Digital ideological groomers seek to draw their target in by foregrounding the uncertainty and chaos created by their opponents. The groomer–target bond is promoted though hate of the opponent (othering); social identity/group identification is relentlessly sought. In digital sexual grooming, the opponents are generally individuals whom—the groomers know—are emotionally and physically close to the targets, typically their families and friends. As such, although other-stance attribution to these opponents remains critical of them, the intensity of the criticism is lower than in digital ideological and commercial grooming. Instead, most of the discursive work aimed at positioning these opponents concerns keeping them at an arm's length of the groomer–target relationship. Secrecy from these opponents is what matters most.

All in all, what clearly emerges from the analysis of self- and other-styling in digital grooming is an attempt at identity homogenization. On the one hand, digital groomers' manipulative discourse seeks to construct them and their targets as inhabiting a perfectly aligned ideological, affective, and overall identity space. The better aligned they are, the more likely it is that they will see themselves as being dis-aligned from other, equally homogenously constructed identities: their opponents'. Digital grooming thus works at the fundamental level of subject positioning vis-à-vis multiple sociocultural dimensions: religion, immigration, nationalism, sexual relationships, commerce, community-building, and so forth. The alignments being sought all entail transgression of legal systems and/or moral orders.

In this sense, it is worth noting that whereas legal systems determine what constitutes rule-breaking or otherwise, the moral order is a considerably more slippery entity. In ethnomethodology, Harold Garfinkel (1967, 225) described the moral order as the "rule governed activities of everyday life" that members of society would perceive as "normal courses of action." In other words, like the legal system, the moral order is socially constructed, but, unlike the legal system, what is and is not a normal course of action is only to a much lesser extent culturally, ideologically, and, especially, situationally predetermined. Moreover, unlike the legal system, the moral order is not always articulated in textual frameworks, such as bills and laws, being instead often manifested in terms of reciprocity arrangements (Malinowski 1926/1932; Culpeper and Tantucci 2021).

The link between moral orders and reciprocity "applies to both negative and positive behaviours" (Culpeper and Tantucci 2021, 146) in terms of, respectively (legal, societal), punishment and gratification. This is evident within the digital grooming contexts examined in this book. For instance, reframing of sexual activity between an adult and a minor as something beneficial—bringing gratification—to groomer *and* target aids digital sexual grooming, and the principle of fair retribution is a salient legitimation strategy within digital religious grooming. In both cases, while positive and negative behaviors are invoked, an underlying attempt at stabilizing the groomer–target relationship is attempted based on reciprocity within a locally negotiated moral order (Gouldner 1960; Culpeper and Tantucci 2021; Garcés-Conejos Blitvich and Kádar 2021).

9.3 APPLYING RESEARCH FINDINGS TO DAILY LIFE: A FOCUS ON DIGITAL GROOMING AND OTHER ONLINE HARMS

The idea that academic research findings have applications beyond academia's so-called ivory tower is not new in linguistics. Almost three decades ago, Brumfit (1995, 27) defined the discipline of applied linguistics as "the theoretical and empirical investigation of real-world problems in which language is a central issue." Three observations are in order. First, the world of research findings, to which findings generated within applied linguistics theoretical and empirical studies belong, is real, too, rather than fictional or otherwise separated from a presumed real "real-world," as it were—hence the use of quotation marks around the commonly used expression "real-world" here. Second, the term "problems" in Brumfit's quote above need not be equated with problematic matters but rather with conundrums or puzzles that we all, as members of society, may experience at different levels: personal, interpersonal, community, societal, and so forth. Third, the term "applied" need not be exclusive of theoretical investigation—Brumfit speaks of theoretical and empirical investigations, for instance. In other words, just because it is *appliable* (i.e., amenable of being applied), applied linguistics need not shy away from theory—or even metatheory—endeavors.

This last aspect is the subject of some debate within linguistics scholarship. For instance, Haugh (2018) calls for a "metatheory turn" in im-politeness studies such that empirical work leads to refinement of theories and models about im-politeness notions. In contrast, Bousfield (2018) cautions against lapsing into "unfettered academic 'navel gazing' with an over focus on a 'metatheory'—in effect arguing repeatedly over what the terms [politeness and impoliteness] themselves mean both to academics and lay users of language." He sees such navel gazing as academically risky "against the backdrop of a world and of research funding systems increasingly impatient for results, critical of the presumed value of research, and sceptical of the actual or potential applicability of much Humanities and Social Sciences findings." (2018, 233). What really seems to be at stake here is generating findings, including metatheoretically based ones, that are *appliable* at some level within as well as beyond academia—of generating findings of relevance to society; that is to say, to one or more of us. What "appliability" and "relevance" mean cannot be predetermined and made valid across all possible research conundrums and puzzles.

Digital grooming, as we have seen in this book, is a "real-world" challenge that has language use as its core. Given its exponential increase over time, as discussed in Chapter 1, attempts at combating digital grooming and other forms of online harm are expectedly—and thankfully—not in short supply. Such attempts are spearheaded by multiple actors, ranging from regulators, law enforcement, and technology companies to third-sector organizations, academia, and grassroot movements. It is also worth noting that some state actors, for example the European Union,[5] are proposing legislative requirements that the technology industry better prevent online harm, including by applying safety-by-design principles. As for what the actual attempts entail, they tend to fit into one or more of the following approaches: redirection, counter-messaging, one-to-one dialogue, disruption, and education (Henschke and Reed 2021).[6]

Redirection entails targeting Internet produsers who are detected to be searching for online harmful material and substituting content, including advertisements, that promotes nonharmful alternatives and is linked to the original searches. In the case of digital ideological grooming, this may consist of curated YouTube videos that debunk violent jihad themes used for recruitment. In the context of adults searching for child sexual abuse material (CSAM) online, redirection may also entail providing information about available support. An example of such support is the UK-based Lucy Faithfull Foundation's "Get Help" program, which includes resources (such as a website, telephone helpline, and a secure chat service) for people "troubled by their sexual thoughts about children and young people, their family and friends, and professionals working with these groups."[7]

The *counter-messaging* approach seeks to reduce the demand side of online harmful content by disseminating messages that counter the impact of such content. It is known to be primarily used to reduce the impact of extreme ideology propaganda by raising awareness of government actions, correcting misinformation, disseminating messages about social inclusion, and debunking the myths in extreme ideology groups' narratives. *One-to-one dialogue* entails detecting produsers of online harmful content and reaching out to them, offering to engage in an online dialogue with them. As Henschke and Reed (2021, 4) note, the approach requires a specialized skills set and often entails credible messengers—such as former extreme ideology group members/leaders—joining online spaces under a pseudonym and building up relationships with individual produsers in those spaces in order to get them to discuss their extremist ideas with a view to changing them.

The last two approaches—disruption and education—are possibly the most widely known. *Disruption* seeks to reduce the supply of the content by removing it and/or hiding it to prevent access to it. For instance, operated by the

Canadian Centre for Child Protection, Project Arachnid was launched in 2017, as a tool to combat CSAM on the Internet. When CSAM or harmful-abusive content is detected, the Arachnid tool sends a removal request to the hosting provider. Through curbing the public availability of such content, this project contributes to breaking the cycle of abuse for survivors.[8] Also, Europol's Internet Referral Unit (IRU) monitors and identifies extremist content online, and then shares this information with partner organizations including social media companies and other Internet providers who may then remove the content from their platform themselves. In some cases, content removal goes hand in hand with account suspension. A high-profile case in point concerns Facebook's decision in March 2018 to ban the radical-right group Britain First from using its platform, reasoning that the group had repeatedly posted content that incited hatred against minority groups.[9] At the time, Britain First had more than 2 million likes and 1.8 million followers on Facebook,[10] making it the "second most liked Facebook page in the politics and society category in the UK—after the royal family."[11] Another high-profile case concerns Twitter's announcement in July 2020 that it would take a harder line against conspiracy theory and extreme ideology content, evidenced in its subsequent banning of multiple "QAnon"-related accounts.[12]

A *hiding* strategy within disruption is used, among other technology companies, by Google and YouTube for content that does not violate their policies but may be regarded as being offensive. In such cases, the company may place that content behind an interstitial warning and also ensure that the content will not be recommended or become eligible for user comments or endorsements, meaning it will not be further monetized. This also means the content generates less engagement and thus becomes harder to find.

Nuance is called for when it comes to applying content removal/hiding strategies to disruption of online harms. Research cautions against a one-size-fits-all approach and advocates interventions that target digital platforms on the basis of how they are being exploited specifically, for example, to host content or signpost content elsewhere online (Alexander and Braniff 2018). This is particularly important, Nouri, Lorenzo-Dus, and Watkin (2021) further argue, in terms of potential tradeoffs. While removing extreme ideology groups from a social media platform reduces the groups' ability and opportunity to disseminate their grooming messages and recruit, it is also known to push the groups and their recruits to other platforms that present law enforcement with more challenges in terms of account monitoring activity (Conway et al. 2019a; Clifford and Powell 2019; Macdonald et al. 2019a; Whittaker 2019).

Other factors are crucial, too, when it comes to implementing measures such as account suspension and content removal in relation to digital ideological grooming. Timing, for example, is critical: poorly timed takedowns can prevent law enforcement and intelligence services from identifying behaviors that could lead to arrests and prosecutions (Alexander and Braniff 2018; Nouri, Lorenzo-Dus, and Watkin 2021). Decisions regarding what kind of content to remove are also key. Generally, these decisions favor removal of violent content over content that is nonviolent while still promoting extreme ideologies, including othering and hate speech. Yet extreme ideology groups have become most adept at circumventing detection of violent content (Doerr 2017; Weirman and Alexander 2020) and, nonviolent material can be just as manipulative as violent content, being also more resilient to removal because it is less graphic. As seen in Chapter 6, for instance, some of the content these groups post uses "liquid racism." In other cases, the content seemingly engages with mundane, nonviolent topics. Britain First's strategy for increasing its presence and reach on Facebook, for example, included continuing posting about widely different topics and varying levels of violence, ranging from Islamophobia through to mere support for the British monarchy and army (Nouri and Lorenzo-Dus 2019). By doing this, the group sought to widen their support base and emphasize the sheer amount of Facebook activity they were capable of generating. This in turn served to manipulate the algorithms of Facebook to increase the frequency with which the group's account content appeared on a person's feed or wall (Brindle and MacMillan 2017).

Disruption through account suspension/content removal approaches has also been tried and tested in relation to digital commercial grooming. As noted in Chapter 7, for some time law enforcement operations were chiefly aimed at closing cryptomarkets—effectively removing access to content. In 2017, two law enforcement operations—"Operation Bayonet" (targeting the AlphaBay cryptomarket) and "Operation GraveSac" (targeting the Hansa cryptomarket)—introduced an important strategic shift: they focused on breaking trust, rather than take-down, within these cryptomarket communities during and after the operations. The combination of suspension/removal and trust-undermining tactics was overall successful, even if the markets continued to trade elsewhere (Afilipoaie and Shortis 2018; Horton-Eddison et al. 2021).

As for *education-based approaches* to tackling online harmful content, these seek to empower produsers about their digital choices, including how these relate to their offline choices. As discussed throughout the book, the online and offline realms are interlocked in our daily experiences. Yet, when it comes to online harms, there is still a belief in some cases that these pose a lesser risk than those that happen offline. Hamilton-Giachritis et al. (2021a), for instance, found that some child safeguarding practitioners still perceive digital sexual grooming and other forms of technology-assisted child sexual abuse as less serious than offline child sexual grooming/abuse. Such perception may lead to victims of offline offending being prioritized for support when compared to those who suffer digital sexual grooming, despite evidence that clearly demonstrates the impacts of the latter to be no less than those of the former (Chapter 4).

Academic research findings underpin several attempts across the above five approaches to countering online harms. Arguably, most (and the most widely known) research into combating online harms, specifically focused on detection thereof, comes from artificial intelligence (AI).[13] Undoubtedly, AI-based detection of online harm has proved beneficial to key actors, especially law enforcement and technology companies. Yet AI is neither the silver bullet nor the panacea to detection. Well-known examples of relatively straight-forward fooling of AI algorithms include such models being unable to detect 300,000 of the 1.5 million copies of the 2019 Christchurch extremist attack video on Facebook within 24 hours of the crime.[14] As discussed in Chapter 5, extreme ideology groups constantly improve their own tactics. Jihadi ideology groups, for example, are well-known for bypassing AI monitoring of their social media content through a range of tactics, such as image distortion; hijacking hashtags; posting standards-violating content in comments, rather than in main posts; and "blank screening" video previews (Bindner and Gluck 2019). The groups adapt their tactics to the particular digital affordances of given platforms. Binder and Glick (2019), for instance, show that jihadi ideology groups try to avoid AI-based detection on Telegram by, among other measures, distorting the names of their channels and deploying bots to provide new links to channels and URL shorteners (named "permanent" or "eternal" links) to redirect content to the latest available page once a previous link has been deleted. Weimann and Ben Am (2020) also note the limitations of AI-based detection methods used by mainstream social media platforms like Facebook or Twitter of radical right groups' "dog whistling tactic." This refers to such groups continually developing coded messages that they communicate, in plain sight, through words, phrases, iconography, and other visual cues that are commonly understood by a particular group of people only. Human moderation of digital grooming content is a more reliable—though by no means infallible—alternative to AI-based detection in terms of accuracy, but there are clearly important issues of moderator wellbeing, as well as scalability.

Faced with, at the time of writing at least, evolving—rather than fully proofed—AI models of online harms detection, one should continue to make room for research findings from other disciplines within the behavioral and social sciences. Herein, linguistics, especially research that either relies only on or integrates qualitative analysis methods, such as (corpus-assisted) discourse studies (CA)DS, is a disciplinary newbie, when compared to work undertaken within criminology and psychology. However, there is considerable added value of such discourse-based research, which comes from its ability to provide nuanced, richly contextualized understandings of online harmful content that, for the main part, comes in textual (discourse) format—be those words, images, videos, music, or, indeed most frequently, a combination thereof.

The findings presented across the chapters of this book—and by extension in discourse-based research into digital grooming and other forms of online harms—are applicable to disruption and education approaches in several ways. Among them, regarding *Digital Grooming* specifically, are the similarities and differences across digital sexual, ideological, and commercial grooming, which is something that, as noted in Chapter 1, has been hypothesized but not hitherto empirically demonstrated. As the analyses offered in Chapters 4, 6, and 8 show, digital groomers resort to the same main stances for self-styling: expertise, openness, and avidity. At the same time, and as discussed in Section 9.2, each of these stances is to some extent differently "flavored" in digital sexual, ideological, and commercial grooming. That being the case, disruption and education approaches to countering each of these manifestations of digital grooming need to be tailored to them while also being mindful of broad-based manipulation "principles" around self-styling.

Also, discourse-based research can add fresh insights into psychologically and criminogenically informed profiling of digital groomers and their targets. For example, a number of models of digital sexual grooming have been developed since the early 2000s. As discussed in Chapter 3, these models have identified a set of groomer goals, from deriving sexual gratification from the interaction online with the target to isolating the target emotionally and physically from her support networks. The goals have been primarily derived either through macro-level (topic/thematic) or micro-level (single- word) analyses of digital sexual grooming chat logs. Being able to identify these goals in interaction has proved invaluable in many respects, including debunking the myth that digital sexual grooming develops through sequential phases that go from nonsexual to sexual content.

Since approximately the second half of the 2010s, discourse-based research has emerged that significantly enhances this body of work through descriptions of, for example, the rhetorical moves typically used by digital sexual groomers (Chiang and Grant 2017, 2018). These, in turn, have been used to provide linguistics training, including in speech acts and other discourse analysis concepts, to undercover law enforcement officers who may infiltrate an online child sexual offending group or assume a victim's or an offender's identity online (Grant and MacLeod 2020). Discourse-based research has also encompassed use of CADS methods to identify recurrent phrases used by digital sexual groomers to achieve each of their goals (Lorenzo-Dus, Kinzel, and Di Cristofaro 2020; Lorenzo-Dus, Evans, and Mullineux-Morgan 2023).

Education-based approaches to combating digital grooming—and more broadly online harms—can also benefit considerably from the nuanced analysis that discourse-based approaches provide. An area in which this has been recently and successfully applied is the evaluation and further development of strategic communications to prevent and counter ideological extremism. This work is recognized as being of critical importance by, among other, the United

Nations Security Council (Resolution 2354, 2017), the US State Department's Global Engagement Centre, and the UK Foreign Office's support of the Global Coalition Against Daesh (HM Government 2018). An early example of this work is the study by Allendorfer and Herring (2015), who used multimodal methods to compare the rhetorical strategies used in jihadi propaganda videos and US government counter-messaging videos. Their analysis was able to show that the success of the jihadi videos resulted partly from their ability to properly identify and appeal to the values of their intended online audience, which the US government videos were unable to do. Another example worthy of mention is Whittaker and Elsayed's (2019) analysis, which integrated quantitative (cluster) and qualitative (thematic) examination of counter-messaging from 10 multimessage social media campaigns against Islamist propaganda between 2014 and 2017. Their findings showed a prioritization of offensive messages over defensive ones, a targeting of less extreme audiences, and a correlation between increased negative counter-messaging and more extreme audience targets. The research also found a difference between Arabic-language messages, which favored identity appeals in their target audience, and English-language messages, which favored pragmatic appeals.

There is no shortage of education-based programs in relation to digital sexual grooming and other forms of online child sexual abuse and exploitation (OCSAE). The benefits of these programs have been attested (see, e.g., Bond and Dogaru's [2019] positive evaluation of the training provided by the UK-based NGO Marie Collins Foundation, in partnership with the telecommunications company British Telecom, for practitioners working with children who have been sexually abused or exploited online).[15] However, there is a real shortage of content within these programs about the communicative mechanisms that shape such abuse. Education-based programs do, for example, regularly mention that digital sexual groomers build trust in their targets; some programs go a bit further, noting that groomers build trust by, for instance, reframing sexual abuse as romantic love and by paying compliments to their targets. Yet trust is quite a general and abstract concept, romantic love can take many communicative manifestations, and compliments can cover many topics (not necessarily all oriented toward sexual or physical attributes). Education-based work to counter digital sexual grooming and other forms of OCSAE needs to delve deeper, in appropriate ways, into the communicative *modus operandi* of groomers as well as targets' own communicative behaviors during digital sexual grooming (Lorenzo-Dus 2021a). Knowing that, in their digital engagement with targets, groomers typically adopt stances of target avidity, expertise, and openness—as well as more fine-grained details of the kind of linguistic realizations that may be aligned to such stances—can empower decision-making by children and those adults whose role it is to keep children safe online (i.e., by all of us). With this in mind the chapter turns next to a research project that places discourse analysis at the heart of collaborative efforts to combat digital sexual grooming: Project DRAGON-S.[16]

9.4 PROJECT DRAGON-S (DEVELOPING RESISTANCE AGAINST GROOMING ONLINE: SPOT AND SHIELD)

Project DRAGON-S is research project led by myself and supported by the Safe Online initiative at End Violence[17] that aims to improve the safeguarding of children against digital sexual grooming. DRAGON-S is headquartered in Swansea University, Wales, in partnership with Toulon University, France, and involves close collaboration with academic and practitioner experts— including child-protection NGOs, policymakers, and law enforcement agencies—in Australia, Canada, New Zealand, and the United States, as well as the UK. DRAGON-S brings together expertise in linguistics, AI, psychology criminology, public policy, software development, and user experience testing in order to develop two ethically responsible tools to help detect (DRAGON-Spotter) and prevent (DRAGON-Shield) digital sexual grooming.

DRAGON-Spotter integrates prior knowledge about digital grooming discourse into AI (Deep Learning) architectures. This is an important point of departure from prevalent approaches to AI-based detection of digital sexual grooming that frequently either take off-the-shelf AI algorithms and train them on large textual datasets or support such algorithms with the results of textual analyses derived from use of sentiment and/or topic modeling tools. Moving away from decontextualized word-level analysis, the prior knowledge embedded within DRAGON-Spotter comes from quantitative and qualitative linguistic analysis of a large dataset of digital interaction between groomers and their child targets.

Over a 6-year period, this linguistic analysis has used a range of techniques.[18] In the early work, digital discourse analysis was conducted of a subset of digital sexual chatlogs, focusing on the groomers' discourse. This initial analysis spurred several lines of further inquiry. For example, speech act analyses were subsequently conducted of groomers' use of compliments, sexual requests, and threats, and through examination of facework. The analysis also encompassed groomers' use of other-stance attribution, as well as self-styling (e.g., reframing of sexual expertise as being beneficial to the target) and other discourse features discussed in Chapter 6. Moreover, topic management analysis of groomer and child target discourse was undertaken. This paved the way for, to my knowledge, the first discourse analysis of children's communicative behavior during digital sexual grooming, including their use of speech acts and relational work when, for example, refusing to (or agreeing to and also initiating) exchange of sexual images, discussing sexual acts, furthering digital contact, and so forth.

In other work contributing to DRAGON-Spotter, CADS methods were used. For example, the entire Perverted Justice database was interrogated, which resulted in identification of a set of 70 language structures (three-word collocations) that were statistically salient within groomers' discourse in terms of frequency and dispersion. Fewer than half of these structures contained sexually explicit words, and a considerable number used romance/friendship words, such as "love" and "like." Multiple extended concordance lines containing these 70 structures were selected, and each was manually mapped to its primary grooming tactic (e.g., "wish + could + help" for deceptive trust development, or "home + alone + weekend" for further contact offline). Importantly, the analysis indicated limitations of chat classifiers for digital sexual grooming detection that assign primacy to sexually explicit language. Digital groomers were shown to use sexual implicitness—as opposed to sexual explicitness—across many of the recurrent linguistic structures and their associated grooming goals. Groomers' use of vague language for communicating sexual intent was further examined using keyword in context (KWIC) techniques (see Chapter 1). And a keyword (groomer–child target) comparative analysis was also conducted that evidenced a clear misalignment as regards groomer–child goals as well as a marked during-interaction power imbalance in addition to the preexisting power inequality between them. The knowledge about digital sexual grooming resulting from the above studies is not only comprehensive but, through the integration of qualitative and quantitative analysis, richly contextualized and eminently *appliable* to detection and prevention technology development in Project DRAGON-S.

DRAGON-Spotter is designed to support law enforcement agents' efficient triaging of high volumes of suspicious chatlogs that they regularly monitor. It identifies those chatlogs that contain a high probability of containing digital sexual grooming content and pinpoints use of particular groomer tactics therein. This approach is at the core of the emerging field of *explainable AI*, including active machine learning methodologies, as a result of which algorithms become less of a black box and more of an accountable decision-making process that integrates human expert review.

DRAGON-Shield is a digital learning portal that relays knowledge, in lay terms, to child safeguarding practitioners about groomers' tactics and children's communicative behaviors during digital sexual grooming. It does so through a series of interactive modules, the first of which provides an overview of digital sexual grooming as a discourse practice. The remaining modules delve deeper into each of its communicatively evidenced groomer tactics: trust development, sexual gratification, and so forth (see Chapter 3).

The idea for DRAGON-Shield emerged from an academia (Swansea University)–third-sector (NSPCC Wales) collaboration in 2016–2019 within a project funded by the UK government-sponsored Digital Economy Research

Centre CHERISH-DE.[19] During 2016–2017, we co-created a prototype: the *Stop TIME Online* anti-digital sexual grooming resource. This drew on consultations with approximately 100 selected individuals in Wales: children and cross-sector child safeguarding practitioners. As per its name, Stop TIME Online was constructed around the idea of time: specifically, that children should feel empowered to pause it while being online to make informed decisions about their digital relationships. As such, it was inspired by a rights-based approach to children's (digital) lives.

Stop TIME Online was produced as a physical (i.e., paper-based) pack (see Figure 9.1) with the option of digitalization in the future—which DRAGON-Shield has implemented. The pack comprised of two sections, each of which

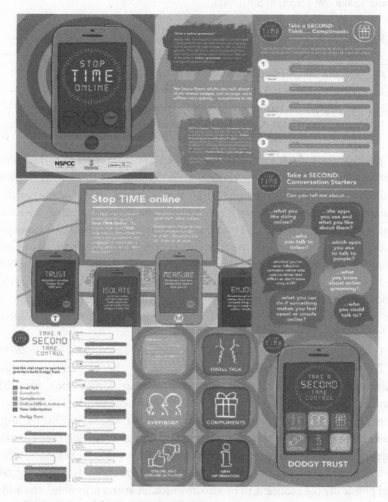

Figure 9.1 Overview of the Stop TIME Online resource.

used time-related acronyms, TIME and SECOND. The first section, also labeled Stop TIME Online, was housed in a folder that translated research findings about groomer tactics into lay language. TIME thus worked as an acronym for these tactics: Trust (Deceptive Trust Development), Isolate (Isolation), Measure (Compliance Testing), and Enjoy (Sexual Gratification). This section of the pack also contained a case study example provided by a UK-based child helpline. Signposting information was printed in the folder, which contained activities for practitioners to deploy during their therapeutic work with children.

The Stop TIME Online resource focused on the groomer tactic of seeking to establish and maintain deceptive trust (see Chapters 3 and 4). The pack illustrated how this is broken down into sub-tactics that, when translated into lay terms, make the acronym SECOND:

S   Small Talk

E   Everybody (talking about relationships)

C   Compliments (offering praise and other gifts)

O   Online and offline activities (discussing hobbies, activities, and so forth)

N   New information (exchanging personal information, including images)

D   These are the five sub-tactics that digital sexual groomers use to build "Dodgy Trust"

This was framed within the phrase "Take a SECOND, Take Control," which further underpinned the key concept that children are in control to pause and take their time online to make informed decisions, in this case, regarding trusting others online. The pack contained "conversation starters" for therapeutic work with children, an emotions' barometer for children to register and discuss their feelings about the contents covered in the therapeutic session, an activity sheet to complete with the practitioner facilitating the session, and involving a transcript example of how groomers use language to develop "dodgy trust," a series of questions regarding the use of each groomer sub-tactic, a full example transcript to consolidate learning/allow the sub-tactics to be identified, and an answer sheet.

Evaluation of the Stop TIME Online resource was undertaken in 2018–2020. It entailed extensive consultation about the resource's functionality: approximately 120 child safeguarding practitioners took part. The results confirmed the added value (indeed uniqueness) of a digital sexual grooming prevention tool centered on communicative behavior. The consultation exercise reinforced the need for and viability of extending the resource's scope to all groomer tactics and to children's communicative behavior, too. It also indicated a significant appetite for the resource to be delivered digitally and physically (i.e., content to be also downloadable and printable), the added value of using actual language examples, and the need to incorporate a users' guide. Moreover, the feedback led to identification of opportunities for using the resource as part of one-to-one and/or group elements of wider intervention programs with child age groups 8–17.

DRAGON-Shield integrated and further developed all this invaluable research and feedback. Crucially, it incorporates across all its modules the perspective of adults with lived experience of digital sexual grooming as well as signposting safeguarding protocols and support around practitioner wellbeing. Regarding the latter, DRAGON-Shield seeks to mitigate the effects on its research team and end-users of sustained exposure to digital sexual grooming content, be that screen- and/or user-based. This builds on previous research into the negative impact that repeated, extended exposure to digital sexual grooming (and other online harmful content) can have, as discussed in Chapter 1.

9.5 CONCLUSION

I started this book by describing the primarily personal research quest that inspired it—a quest that sought to understand through discourse analysis the workings of digital grooming. As the quest developed and the chapters were drafted and re-drafted, I kept returning to identity as being the kernel of the manipulative discourses I was examining. Throughout the pages of this book, I have therefore focused on digital groomers' styling of themselves and others—their targets and their opponents.

As with many projects, the further my research for this book developed, so it became evident how it also related to other channels of inquiry beyond its scope but inherently linked to its arguments. For instance, the analyses offered and conclusions drawn across the pages of *Digital Grooming* can be used to investigate other manifestations of digital grooming, such as Ponzi schemes, in which fraudulent activity is communicatively reframed against the target's best interest as being licit. They can also be extended to consideration of how groomers, targets, and opponents dialogically relate with each other's stances and acts of styling. After all, and as Mead (1974, 182) argued, "[t]he self is not something that exists and then enters into relationship with others, but it is, so to speak, an eddy in the social current and so still a part of that current."

Finally, as readers of *Digital Grooming* reach its end, it is my fervent hope that they feel not only informed but also inspired to debate, challenge, and build on its arguments and conclusions. For my part, its research and writing have led me into unforeseen and rich interdisciplinary collaborations in investigating and combatting nefarious digital practices. I have been fortunate, too, to gain invaluable insights from a host of practitioners who work daily to combat online harms—my admiration for them all has increased every step of the way. Just as importantly, through work such as Project DRAGON-S, I have been able to lead and learn from committed, professional, and inspiring cross-disciplinary academic teams. Together, I hope we have been able to demonstrate the value of applying discourse-based analyses to daily life challenges.

NOTES

1. https://www.gov.uk/government/consultations/online-harms-white-paper/outcome/online-harms-white-paper-full-government-response. Accessed April 2022.
2. See KhosraviNik (2017a, 2017b) for a discussion of the interplay of the social and the digital in social media discourse, including local contexts of production and consumption of meaning, contexts of mediation and distribution, digital practice as meaning-making (e.g., likes, shares, etc.), technological fore-/backgrounding, promotion and suppression, and genre specifications.
3. https://bills.parliament.uk/bills/3137/publications. Accessed April 2022.
4. This situation is likely different in one-to-one participatory frameworks linked to digital ideological grooming typically covered within radicalization, which this book has not examined.
5. https://ec.europa.eu/info/law/better-regulation/have-your-say/initiatives/12726-Fighting-child-sexual-abuse-detection-removal-and-reporting-of-illegal-content-online_en.
6. These are derived from practice in relation to ideological extremism but some of them are also applicable to other forms of online harmful content, including digital sexual and commercial grooming.
7. https://www.lucyfaithfull.org.uk/get-support-support-for-those-concerned-about-thoughts.htm. Accessed January 2022.
8. httpps://projectarachnid.ca. Accessed January 2022.
9. http://www.wired.co.uk/article/facebook-britain-first-far-right-extremism-ban. Accessed January 2022.
10. *Extreme Far Right Groups' Use of Social Media: A Focus on Britain First and Reclaim Australia*. Cyberterrorism Project Research Report (No. 7). Available at: http://www.cyberterrorism-project.org/wp-content/uploads/2013/03/Far-Right-Project-Report-Nov2017.pdf. Accessed January 2022.
11. Hope not Hate (2018). Britain First. Available at http://www.hopenothate.org.uk/research/the-hate-files/britain-first/. Accessed January 2022.
12. https://www.wired.com/story/twitter-cracks-down-qanon-policy/. Accessed January 2022.
13. The studies are too numerous to list but see, e.g., Cano et al. (2014), Bogdanova et al. (2014), Preuß et al. (2021), and Milon-Flores and Cordeiro (2022) in the context of digital sexual grooming, and, Jaki et al. (2018), Fernandez et al. (2019), Nerurkar et al. (2020), and Mackey et al. (2020) in the context of digital ideological grooming.
14. https://www.theguardian.com/world/2019/mar/17/facebook-removed-15m-videos-new-zealand-terror-attack. Accessed January 2022.
15. https://www.mariecollinsfoundation.org.uk/cpp. Accessed January 2022.
16. https://www.swansea.ac.uk/project-dragon-s/. Accessed January 2022.

17. https://www.end-violence.org/safe-online. Accessed January 2022.
18. Published work includes, e.g., Lorenzo-Dus, Izura, and Tattam (2016); Lorenzo-Dus and Kinzel (2019, 2021); Lorenzo-Dus, Kinzel and Di Cristofaro (2020); Lorenzo-Dus, Evans, and Mullineux-Morgan (2023).
19. https://www.swansea.ac.uk/science/computationalfoundry/cherish-de/. Accessed January 2022.

REFERENCES

Abidin, Crystal. 2017. "#familygoals: Family Influencers, Calibrated Amateurism, and Justifying Young Digital Labor." *Social Media & Society*, 3(2): 1–15.

Abidin, Crystal. 2018. *Internet Celebrity. Understanding Fame Online*. London: Emerald Publishing.

Abrahms, Max. 2006. "Why Terrorism Does Not Work." *International Security*, 31(2): 42–78.

Addawood, Aseel, Adam Badawy, Kristina Lerman, and Emilio Ferrara. 2019. "Linguistic Cues to Deception: Identifying Political Trolls on Social Media." *Proceedings of the Thirteenth International AAAI Conference on Web and Social Media* (ICWSM 2019). https://www.aaai.org/ojs/index.php/ICWSM/article/view/3205/3073.

Afilipoaie, Alois, and Patrick Shortis. 2015. "From Dealer to Doorstep: How Drugs Are Sold on the Dark Net." *Global Drug Policy Observatory Situation Analysis*. https://www.swansea.ac.uk/media/From-Dealer-to-Doorstep-%C3%A2%C2%80%C2%93-How-Drugs-Are-Sold-On-the-Dark-Net.pdf.

Afilipoaie, Alois, and Patrick Shortis. 2018. "Crypto-market Enforcement: New Strategy and Tactics." *Policy*, 54: 87–98.

Agha, Asif. 2003. "The Social Life of Cultural Value." *Language and Communication*, 23: 231–273.

Agha, Asif. 2007. "Recombinant Selves in Mass-mediated Spacetime." *Language and Communication*, 27: 320–335.

Aldridge, Judith, and Rebecca Askew. 2016. "Delivery Dilemmas: How Drug Crypto-market Users Identify and Seek to Reduce Their Risk of Detection by Law Enforcement." *International Journal of Drug Policy*, 41: 101–109.

Aldridge, Judith, and David Décary-Hétu. 2014. "'Not an 'Ebay for Drugs': The Cryptomarket 'Silk Road' as a Paradigm Shifting Criminal Innovation." https://ssrn.com/abstract=2436643 or http://dx.doi.org/10.2139/ssrn.2436643.

Aldridge, Judith, and David Décary-Hétu. 2016. "Hidden Wholesale: The Drug Diffusing Capacity of Online Drug Cryptomarkets." *International Journal of Drug Policy*, 35: 7–15.

Alexander, Audrey, and William Braniff. 2018. "Marginalizing Violent Extremism Online." *Lawfare Blog*. https://www.lawfareblog.com/marginalizing-violent-extremism-online.

Allendorfer, William, and Susan Herring. 2015. "ISIS vs the US Government: A War of Online Video Propaganda." *AoIR Selected Papers of Internet Research*, 5. https://journals.uic.edu/ojs/index.php/spir/article/view/8698.

Alshech, Eli. 2014. "The Doctrinal Crisis within the Salafi-Jihadi Ranks and the Emergence of Neo-Takfirism." *Islamic Law and Society*, 21(4): 419–452.

Alty, A., and Rodham, K. 1998. "The Ouch! Factor: Problems in Conducting Sensitive Research." *Qualitative Health Research*, 8: 275–282.

Anafo, Comfort, and Richmond Ngula. 2020. "On the Grammar of Scam: Transititvity, Manipulation and Deception in Scam Emails." *Word*, 66: 16–39.

Andersen, Jan Christoffer, and Sveinung Sandberg. 2018. "Islamic State Propaganda: Between Social Movement Framing and Subcultural Provocation." *Terrorism and Political Violence*, 32(7): 1506–1526.

Anderson, Benedict. 1983/2016. *Imagined Communities: Reflections on The Origin and Spread of Nationalism*. London: Verso.

Androutsopoulos, Jannis. 2008. "Potentials and Limitations of Discourse-centered Online Ethnography." *Language@Internet*, 5. https://www.languageatinternet.org/articles/2008/1610.

Androutsopoulos, Jannis. 2013. "Online Data Collection." In *Data Collection in Sociolinguistics: Methods and Applications*, edited by Christine Mallinson, Becky Childs, and Gerard Van Herk, 236–249. London: Routledge.

Androutsopoulos, Jannis. 2014a. "Moments of Sharing: Entextualization and Linguistic Repertoires in Social Networking." *Journal of Pragmatics*, 73: 4–18.

Androutsopoulos, Jannis. 2014b. "Languaging when Contexts Collapse: Audience Design in Social Networking." *Discourse Context & Media*, 4–5: 62–73.

Androutsopoulos, Jannis, and Michael Beisswenger. 2008. "Introduction: Data and Methods in Computer-mediated Discourse Analysis." *Language @ Internet*, 5: 2. https://www.languageatinternet.org/articles/2008/1609.

Angouri, Jo, and Ruth Wodak. 2014. "They Became Big in the Shadow of the Crisis: The Greek Success Story and the Rise if the Far Right." *Discourse & Society*, 25(4): 540–565.

Arundale, Robert B. 2006. "Face as Relational and Interactional: A Communication Framework for Research on Face, Facework, and Politeness." *Journal of Politeness Research*, 2(2): 193–216.

Augestad Knudsen, Rita. 2020. "Measuring Radicalisation: Risk Assessment Conceptualisations and Practice in England and Wales."*Behavioural Sciences of Terrorism and Political Aggression*, 12(1): 37–54.

Babchishin, Kelly M., R. Karl Hanson, and Chantal A. Hermann. 2011. "The Characteristics of Online Sex Offenders: A Meta-analysis." *Sexual Abuse*, 23(1): 92–123.

Bachenko, Joan, Eileen Fitzpatrick, and Michael Schonwetter. 2008. "Verification and Implementation of Language-based Deception Indicators in Civil and Criminal Narratives." *Proceedings of the 22nd International Conference on Computational Linguistics*, 41–48.

Baker, Paul, and Jesse Egbert (Eds.). 2016. *Triangulating Methodological Approaches in Corpus Linguistic Research*. New York and London: Routledge.

Baker, Paul, Costas Gabrielatos, Majid KhosraviNik, M. Krzyżanowski, Tony McEnery, and Ruth Wodak. 2008. "A Useful Methodological Synergy? Combining Critical Discourse Analysis and Corpus Linguistics to Examine Discourses of Refugees and Asylum Seekers in the UK Press." *Discourse & Society*, 19(3): 273–306.

Baker, Paul, Costas Gabrielatos, and Tony McEnery. 2013. *Discourse Analysis and Media Attitudes: The Representation of Islam in the British Press*. Cambridge: Cambridge University Press.

Baker, Paul, and Erez Levon. 2015. "Picking the Right Cherries? A Comparison of Corpus-based and Qualitative Analyses of News Articles About Masculinity." *Discourse & Communication*, 9(2): 221–236.

Baker, Paul, Rachel Vessey, and Tony McEnery. 2021. *The Language of Violent Jihad*. Cambridge: Cambridge University Press.

Baker, Stephanie Alice, and Chris Rojek. 2020. "The Belle Gibson Scandal: The Rise of Lifestyle Gurus as Micro-Celebrities in Low-Trust Societies." *Journal of Sociology*, 56(3): 388–404.

Barak, Azy, and Orit Gluck-Ofri. 2007. "Degree and Reciprocity of Self-Disclosure in Online Forums." *CyberPsychology & Behavior*, 10 (3): 407–417.

Barker, Chris, and Dariusz Galasinski. 2001. "Language, Culture, Discourse." In *Culture Studies and Discourse Analysis: A Dialogue on Language and Identity*, edited by Chris Barker and Dariusz Galasinski, 4–27. London: Sage.

Barratt Monica, and Judith Aldridge. 2016. "Everything You Always Wanted to Know About Drug Cryptomarkets but Were Afraid to Ask." *International Journal of Drug Policy*, 35: 1–6.

Barratt, Monica, Mathew Allen, and Simon Lenton. 2014. "'PMA Sounds Fun': Negotiating Drug Discourses Online." *Substance Use & Misuse*, 49(8): 987–998.

Barratt, Monica, Jason Ferris, and Adam Winstock. 2014. "Use of Silk Road, the Online Drug Marketplace, in the United Kingdom, Australia and the United States." *Addiction*, 109(5): 774–783.

Barrio, Rafael, Govezensky Tzipe, Robin Dunbar, Gerardo Iñiguez, and Kimmo Kaski. 2015. "Dynamics of Deceptive Interactions in Social Networks." *Journal of the Royal Society Interface*, 12: 20150798. http://dx.doi.org/10.1098/rsif.2015.0798.

Barta, Kristen, and Gina Neff. 2015. "Technologies for Sharing: Lessons from Quantified Self About the Political Economy of Platforms." *Information, Communication & Society*, 19(4): 518–531.

Barton, David, and Carmen Lee. 2013. *Language Online: Investigating Digital Texts and Practices*. London: Routledge.

Bartlett, Jamie. 2014. *The Dark Net: Inside the Digital Underworld*. Brooklyn, NY: Melville House.

Bakir, Vian, Eric Herring, and David Miller. 2018. "Organised Persuasive Communication: A New Conceptual Framework for Research on PR, Propaganda and Promotional Culture." *Critical Sociology*, 45(3): 311–328.

Barratt, Monica. 2012. "Silk Road: Ebay for Drugs." *Addiction*, 107(3): 683–683.

Baryshevtsev, Maxim, and Matthew McGlone. 2018. "Pronoun Usage in Online Sexual Predation." *Cyberpsychology, Behavior, and Social Networking*, 21(2): 117–122.

Bauman, Richard, and Charles Briggs. 1990. "Poetics and Performance as Critical Perspectives on Language and Social Life." *Annual Review of Anthropology*, 19: 59–88.

Bauman, Zygmunt. 1991. "The Social Manipulation of Morality: Moralizing Actors, Adiaphorizing Action." *Theory, Culture & Society*, 8(1): 137–151.

Bauman, Zygmunt. 2000. *Liquid Modernity*. Cambridge: Polity Press.

Baumgarten, Nicole, Eckhard Bick, Klaus Geyer, Ditte Iversen, Andrea Kleene, Ann Lindo, Jana Neitsch, Olver Niebuhr, Rasmus Nielsen, and Esben Petersen. 2019. "Towards Balance and Boundaries in Public Discourse: Expressing and Perceiving Online Hate Speech." *RASK: International Journal of Language and Communication*, 50: 87–108.

Bazarova, Natalya. 2012. "Public Intimacy: Disclosure Interpretation and Social Judgments on Facebook." *Journal of Communication*, 62(5): 815–832.

Bednarek, Monika, and Helen Caple. 2017. *The Discourse of News Values: How News Organizations Create Newsworthiness*. Oxford: Oxford University Press.

Bell, Allan. 1984. "Language Style as Audience Design." *Language in Society, 13*: 145–204.

Benveniste, Emile. 1966. "Problèmes de Linguistique Générale, 1 vol." *Les Etudes Philosophiques, 21*(3): 237–250.

Benwell, Bethan, and Elizabeth Stokoe. 2006. *Discourse and Identity*. Edinburgh: Edinburgh University Press.

Berger, Jonathon, and Jonathon Morgan. 2015. "The ISIS Twitter Census: Defining and Describing the Population of ISIS Supporters on Twitter." https://www.brookings.edu/wp-content/uploads/2016/06/isis_twitter_census_berger_morgan.pdf.

Berger, Jonathon. 2018. "The Alt-Right Twitter Census: Defining and Describing the Audience for Alt-Right Content on Twitter." VOX-POL. https://www.voxpol.eu/download/vox-pol_publication/AltRightTwitterCensus.pdf

Bewley-Taylor, David. 2017. "Narcotics Anonymous: Crypto-Drug Markets Adapt to Law Enforcement Intervention." *Jane's Intelligence Review, 29*(6): 50–53.

Bilgrei, Ola Røed. 2018. "Broscience: Creating Trust in Online Drug Communities." *New Media & Society, 20*(8): 2712–2727.

Billig, Michael, and Cristina Marinho. 2014. "Manipulating Information and Manipulating Power: Examples from the 2004 Portuguese Parliamentary Celebration of the April Revolution." *Critical Discourse Studies, 11*(2): 158–174.

Bindner, Laurence, and Raphael Gluck. 2019. "Jihadist Extremism. *Extreme Digital Speech: Context, Responses and Solutions*," 19–26. VOX-Pol Network of Excellence. https://www.voxpol.eu/download/vox-pol_publication/DCUJ770-VOX-Extreme-Digital-Speech.pdf.

Bitcointalk.org. Accessed June 2022.

Black, Pamela, Melissa Wollis, Michael Woodworth, and Jeffrey T. Hancock. 2015. "A Linguistic Analysis of Grooming Strategies of Online Child Sex Offenders: Implications for our Understanding of Predatory Sexual Behavior in an Increasingly Computer-mediated World." *Child Abuse & Neglect, 44*: 140–149.

Blommaert, Jan. 2015. "Chronotopes, Scales, and Complexity in the Study of Language in Society." *Annual Review of Anthropology, 44*: 105–116.

Bloomberg, Jason 2017. "Using Bitcoin or Other Cryptocurrency to Commit Crimes? Law Enforcement is onto You." *Forbes*. https://www.forbes.com/sites/jasonbloomberg/2017/12/28/using-bitcoin-or-other-cryptocurrency-to-commit-crimes-law-enforcement-is-onto-you/#776e383c3bdc.

Blum-Kulka, Shoshana, Juliane House, and Gabriele Kasper. 1989. *The CCSARP Coding Manual: Cross-Cultural Pragmatics: Requests and Apologies*. In *Cross-Cultural Pragmatics: Requests and Apologies*, edited by Shoshana Blum-Kulka, Juliane House, and Gabriele Kasper, 273–294. Norwood, NJ: Ablex.

Bogdanova, Dasha, Paolo Rosso, and Thamar Solorio. 2014. "Exploring High-level Features for Detecting Cyberpedophilia." *Computers, Speech, and Language, 28*(1): 108–120.

Bolander, Brooke, and Miriam Locher. 2014. "Doing Sociolinguistic Research on Computer-mediated Data: A Review of Four Methodological Issues." *Discourse, Context & Media, 3*: 14–26.

Bolander, Brooke, and Miriam Locher. 2020. "Beyond the Online Offline Distinction: Entry Points to Digital Discourse." *Discourse, Context & Media, 35*: 100383.

Bond, Emma, and Christian Dogaru. 2019. "An Evaluation of an Inter-disciplinary Training Programme for Professionals to Support Children and Their

Families Who Have Been Sexually Abused Online."*British Journal of Social Work*, 49(3): 577–594.

Borum, Randy. 2011. "Radicalization into Violent Extremism: A Review of Social Science Theories." *Journal of Strategic Security*, 4(4): 7–36.

Botsman, Rachel. 2012. "The Currency of the New Economy Is Trust." *TED Talks*. https://www.youtube.com/watch?v=kTqgiF4HmgQ

Botsman, Rachel, and Roo Rogers. 2010. *What's Mine Is Yours: The Rise Of Collaborative Consumption*. New York: Harper Business (also TED Talk 2012 www.ted.com/talks/rachel-botsman).

Bouchard, Martin. 2007. "On the Resilience of Illegal Drug Markets." *Global Crime*, 8(4): 325–344.

Bourgois, Philippe. 2003. *In Search of Respect: Selling Crack in El Barrio*. Cambridge: Cambridge University Press.

Bousfield, Derek. 2018. "Face(t)s of Self and Identity in Interaction." *Journal of Politeness Research*, 14(2): 225–243.

Bouvier, Gwen, and David Machin. 2018. "Critical Discourse Analysis and the Challenges and Opportunities of Social Media." *Review of Communication*, 18(3): 178–192.

Bowman-Grieve, Lorraine. 2009. "Exploring 'Stormfront': A Virtual Community of the Radical Right." *Studies in Conflict & Terrorism*, 32(11): 989–1007.

Boyd, Josh. 2002. "In Community we Trust: Online Security Communication at eBay." *Journal of Computer-Mediated Communication*, 7(3): JCM736.

boyd, Danah. 2002. *Faceted ID/Entity: Managing Representation in a Digital World*. Unpublished MA thesis. MIT.

boyd, Danah. 2008. "Why Youth (Heart) Social Network sites: The Role of Networked Publics in Teenage Social Life." In *Youth, Identity, and Digital Media*, edited by David Buckingham, 119–142. Cambridge, MA: MIT Press.

boyd, Danah. 2010. "Social Network Sites as Networked Publics: Affordances, Dynamics, and Implications." In *A Networked Self: Identity, Community, and Culture on Social Network Sites*, edited by Zizi Papacharissi, 47–66. London: Routledge.

Boyd, Michael. 2014. "(New) Participatory Framework on YouTube? Commenter Interaction in US Political Speeches." *Journal of Pragmatics*, 72: 46–58.

Brayda, Winsome, and Travis Boyce. 2014. "So You Really Want to Interview Me?: Navigating 'Sensitive' Qualitative Research Interview." *International Journal of Qualitative Methods*, 13: 318–334.

Brechwald, Whitney, and Mitchell Prinstein. 2011. "Beyond Homophily: A Decade of Advances in Understanding Peer Influence Processes." *Journal of Research on Adolescence*, 21(1): 166–179.

Brewer, John. 1990. "Sensitivity as a Problem in Field Research: A Study of Routine Policing in Northern Ireland." *American Behavioral Scientist*, 33(5): 578–593.

Brezina, Vaclav, Tony McEnery, and Stephen Wattam. 2015. "Collocations in Context: A New Perspective on Collocation Networks." *International Journal of Corpus Linguistics*, 20(2): 139–173.

Briggs, Peter, Walter T. Simon, and Stacy Simonsen. 2011. "An Exploratory Study of Internet-initiated Sexual Offenses and the Chat Room Sex Offender: Has the Internet Enabled a New Typology of Sex Offender?" *Sexual Abuse*, 23(1): 72–91.

Brindle, Andrew. 2016. "Cancer Has Nothing on Islam: A Study of Discourses by Group Elite and Supporters of the English Defence League." *Critical Discourse Studies*, 13(4): 444–459.

Brindle, Andrew, and Corrie MacMillan. 2017. "Like & Share if You Agree." *Journal of Language Aggression and Conflict*, 5(1): 108–133.

Broome, Laura, Cristina Izura, and Jason Davies. 2020. "A Psycho-linguistic Profile of Online Grooming Conversations: A Comparative Study of Prison and Police Staff Considerations." *Child Abuse & Neglect*, 109: 104647.

Broome, Laura, Cristina Izura, and Nuria Lorenzo-Dus. 2018. "A Systematic Review of Fantasy vs. Contact Driven Internet Initiated Sexual Offences: Discrete or Overlapping Typologies?" *Child Abuse and Neglect*, 79: 434–444.

Brown, Penelope, and Stephen Levinson. 1987. *Politeness. Some Universals in Language Usage*. Cambridge: Cambridge University Press.

Brumfit, Christopher. 1995. "Teacher Professionalism and Research." In *Principle and Practice in Applied Linguistics*, edited by Guy Cook and Barbara Seidlhofer, 27–42. Oxford: Oxford University Press.

Bruns, Axel. 2008. *Blogs, Wikipedia, Second Life, and Beyond: From Production to Produsage*. Bern: Peter Lang.

Bucholtz, Mary. 2004. "Styles and Stereotypes: The Linguistic Negotiation of Identity Among Latin American Youth." *Pragmatics*, 14(2–3): 127–147.

Bucholtz, Mary. 2009. "From Stance to Style: Gender, Interaction and Indexicality in Mexican Immigrant Youth Slang." In *Stance: Sociolinguistic perspectives*, edited by Alexandra Jaffe, 146–170. Oxford: Oxford University Press.

Bucholtz, Mary, and Kira Hall. 2004. "Language and Identity." In *A Companion to Linguistic Anthropology*, edited by Alessandro Duranti, 369–394. Oxford: Blackwell.

Bucholtz, Mary, and Kira Hall. 2005. "Identity and Interaction: A Sociolonguistic Cultural Approach." *Discourse Studies*, 7(4–5): 585–614.

Burris, Val, Emmery Smith, and Ann Strahm. 2000. "White Supremacist Networks on the Internet." *Sociological Focus*, 33(2): 215–235.

Buruma, Ian, and Avishai Margalit. 2004. *Occidentalism: A Short History of Anti-Westernism*. London: Atlantic Books.

Busher, Joel, and Graham Macklin. 2015. "Interpreting "Cumulative Extremism": Six Proposals for Enhancing Conceptual Clarity." *Terrorism and Political Violence*, 27(5): 884–905.

Butler, Judith. 1990. "Gender Trouble, Feminist Theory, and Psychoanalytic Discourse." *Feminism/Postmodernism*, 327: 324–340.

Butler, Judith. 2004. *Undoing Gender*. London: Routledge.

Cameron, Deborah. 2000. *Good to Talk?: Living and Working in a Communication Culture*. Thousands Oaks, CA: Sage.

Campbell, Donald. 1958. "Common Fate, Similarity, and Other Indices of the Status of Aggregates of Persons and Social Entities." *Behavioural Science*, 3: 14–25.

Cano Basave, Amparo Elizabeth, Miriam Fernandez, and Harith Alani. 2014. "Detecting Child Grooming Behaviour Patterns on Social Media." In *Social Informatics*, edited by L. M. Aiello and D. McFarland, 412–427. Cham: Springer. https://doi.org/10.1007/978-3-319-13734-6_30 412-427

Carbaugh, Donald. 1988. *Talking American: Cultural Discourses on Donahue*. Thousands Oaks, CA: Sage.

Castells, Manuel. 2002. *The Rise of the Network Society* (3rd ed.). Hoboken, NJ: Blackwell Publishing.

Cha, Meeyoung, Hamed Haddadi, Fabricio Benevenuto, and Krishna Gummadi. 2010. "Measuring User Influence in Twitter: The Million Follower Fallacy." In *Proceedings of the Fourth International AAAI Conference on Weblogs and Social Media*, edited by Tumasjan, A., T. O. Sprenger, P. G. Sandner, and I. M. Welpe, 10–17. Menlo Park: AAAI Press.

Chertoff, Michael. 2019. "A Public Policy Perspective of the Dark Web." *Journal of Cyber Policy*, 2(1): 26–38.

Chiang, Emily. 2020. "Dark Web: Study Reveals how New Offenders Get Involved in Online Paedophile Communities." *The Conversation*. https://theconversation.com/dark-web-study-reveals-how-new-offenders-get-involved-in-online-paedophile-communities-131933.

Chiang, Emily. 2021. "'Send Me Some Pics': Performing the Offender Identity in Online Undercover Child Abuse Investigations." *Policing: A Journal of Policy and Practice*, 15(2): 1173–1187.

Chiang, Emily, and Tim Grant. 2017. "Online Grooming: Moves and Strategies." *Language and Law/ Linguagem e Direito*, 4(1): 103–141.

Chiang, Emily, and Tim Grant. 2018. "Deceptive Identity Performance: Offender Moves and Multiple Identities in Online Child Abuse Conversations." *Applied Linguistics*, 40(4): 1–25.

Chiluwa Isioma M., and Innocent Chiluwa. 2020. "We Are a Mutual Fund: How Ponzi Scheme Operators in Nigeria Apply Indexical Markers to Shield Deception and Fraud on Their Websites." *Social Semiotics*. doi:10.1080/10350330.2020.1766269.

Chiu, Ming Ming, Kathryn Seigfried-Spellar, and Tatiana Ringenberg. 2018. "Exploring Detection of Contact vs. Fantasy Online Sexual Offenders in Chats with Minors: Statistical Discourse Analysis of Self-disclosure and Emotion Words." *Child Abuse & Neglect*, 81: 128–138.

Christensen, Gitte. 2014. *Is the EU a Failed Imagined Community*? MA dissertation, University of Rudar.

Christin, Nicolas. 2013. "Traveling the Silk Road: A Measurement Analysis of a Large Anonymous Online Marketplace." *Proceedings of the 22nd International Conference on World Wide Web*, 213–224. https://doi.org/10.1145/2488388.2488408.

Clifford, Bennet, and Helen Powell. 2019. "De-platforming and the Online Extremist's Dilemma." *Lawfare Blog*. https://www.lawfareblog.com/de-platforming-and-online-extremists-dilemma.

Conway, Maura. 2016. "Violent Extremism and Terrorism Online in 2016: The Year in Review." VOX Pol. https://ec.europa.eu/home-affairs/sites/homeaffairs/files/news/docs/year_in_review_2016_en.pdf.

Conway, Maura. 2019. "We Need a 'Visual Turn' in Violent Online Extremism Research." *VOX-Pol Blog*. https://www.voxpol.eu/we-need-a-visual-turn-in-violent-online-extremism-research/

Conway, Maura, Moign Khawaja, Suraj Lakhani, Jeremy Reffin, Andrew Robertson, and David Weir. 2019a. "Disrupting Daesh: Measuring Takedown of Online Terrorist Material and its Impacts." *Studies in Conflict and Terrorism*, 42: 141–160.

Conway, Maura, Ryan Scrivens, and Logan Macnair. 2019b. *Right-Wing Extremists' Persistent Online Presence: History and Contemporary Trends*. The Hague: ICCT.

Cornejo, Marcela, Gabriela Rubilar, and Pamela Zapata-Sepulveda. 2019. "Researching Sensitive Topics in Sensitive Zones: Exploring Silences, 'the Normal,' and Tolerance in Chile." *International Journal of Qualitative Methods*, 18: 1–11.

Cottee, Simon. 2019. *ISIS and the Pornography of Violence*. London: Anthem Press.

Coupland, Justine, and Nikolas Coupland. 2009. "Attributing Stance in Discourses of Body Shape and Weight Loss." In *Stance: Sociolinguistic Perspectives*, edited by Alexandra Jaffe, 227–250. Oxford: Oxford University Press.

Coupland, Nikolas. 1985. "'Hark, Hark, the Lark': Social Motivations for Phonological Style-Shifting." *Language & Communication*, 5(3): 153–171.

Coupland, Nikolas. 2001. "Dialect Stylization in Radio Talk." *Language in Society*, 30(3): 345–375.

Coupland, Nikolas. 2007. *Style: Language Variation and Identity*. Cambridge: Cambridge University Press.

Coupland, Nikolas. 2010. "'Other' Representation." In *Society and Language Use*, edited by Jürgen Jaspers, Jan-Ola Östman, and Jef Verschueren, 242–260. Amsterdam: John Benjamins.

Coupland, Nikolas. 2014. "Social Context, Style, and Identity in Sociolinguistics." In *Research Methods in Sociolinguistics: A Practical Guide*, edited by Janet Holmes and Kirk Hazen. 290–303. New York: John Wiley & Sons.

Cox, Joseph. 2016. "Confirmed: Carnegie Mellon University Attacked ToR, Was Subpoenaed by Feds." Vice. https://www.vice.com/en/article/d7yp5a/carnegie-mellon-university-attacked-tor-was-subpoenaed-by-feds.

Culpeper, Jonathan. 1996. "Towards an Anatomy of Impoliteness." *Journal of Pragmatics*, 25(3): 349–367.

Culpeper, Jonathan. 2011. *Impoliteness: Using Language to Cause Offence*. Cambridge: Cambridge University Press.

Culpeper, Jonathan, Paul Iganski, and Abe Sweiry. 2017. "Linguistic Impoliteness and Religiously Aggravated Hate Crime in England and Wales." *Journal of Language, Aggression and Conflict*, 5(1): 1–29.

Culpeper, Jonathan, and Vittorio Tantucci. 2021. "The Principle of (Im)Politeness Reciprocity." *Journal of Pragmatics*, 175: 146–164.

Cunningham, Daniel, Sean F. Everton, and Robert Schroeder. 2015. *Social Media and the ISIS Narrative*. White Paper. Monterey, CA: Defense Analysis Department, Naval Postgraduate School. http://hdl.handle.net/10945/53059.

Dahlgren, Peter. 2000. "The Internet and the Democratization of Civic Culture." *Political Communication*, 17(4): 335–340.

Daniels, Jessie. 2009. *Cyber Racism: White Supremacy Online and the New Attack on Civil Rights*. Lanham, MD: Rowman & Littlefield.

Davey, Jacob, and Julia Ebner. 2017. *The Fringe Insurgency: Connectivity, Convergence and Mainstreaming of the Extreme Right*. Institute for Strategic Dialogue. http://www.isdglobal.org/wp-content/uploads/2017/10/The-Fringe-Insurgency-221017.pdf.

Davis, Dorian, and Aram Sinreich. 2020. "Beyond Fact-Checking: Lexical Patterns as Lie Detectors in Donald Trump's Tweets." *International Journal of Communication*, 14: 5237–5260.

Dayrell, Carmen, Ram-Prasad Chakravarthi, and Gwen Griffith-Dickson. 2020. "Bringing Corpus Linguistics into Religious Studies: Self-Representation Amongst Various Immigrant Communities with Religious Identity." *Journal of Corpora and Discourse Studies*, 3: 96–121.

Décary-Hétu, David, Masarah Paquet-Clouston, and Judith Aldridge. 2016. "Going International? Risk Taking by Cryptomarket Drug Vendors." *International Journal of Drug Policy*, 35: 69–76.

Décary-Hétu, David, Masarah Paquet-Clouston, Martin Bouchard, and Carlo Morselli. 2019. *Patterns in Cannabis Cryptomarkets in Canada in 2018*. Ottawa: Public Safety Canada/Sécurité publique Canada.

De Fina, Anna. 2020. "The Negotiation of Identities." In *Interpersonal Pragmatics*, edited by Miriam Locher and Sage Graham, 205–224. Berlin: Mouton de Gruyter.

De Fina, Anna, Deborah Schiffrin, and Michael Bamberg. 2006. *Studies in Interactional Sociolinguistics, 23: Discourse and Identity*. Cambridge: Cambridge University Press. https://doi.org/10.1017/CBO9780511584459.

De Hart, Dana, Gregg Dwyer, Michael C. Seto, Robert Moran, Elizabeth Letourneau, and Donna Schwarz-Watts. 2017. "Internet Sexual Solicitation of Children: A Proposed Typology of Offenders Based on Their Chats, e-mails, and Social Network Posts." *Journal of Sexual Aggression*, 23(1): 77–89.

De Saussure, Louis. 2005. "Manipulation and Cognitive Pragmatics." In *Manipulation and Ideologies in the Twentieth Century*, edited by Louis de Saussure and Peter Schulz, 113–145. Amsterdam and Philadelphia: John Benjamins.

De Saussure, Louis, and Peter Schulz (Eds.). 2005. *Manipulation and Ideologies in the Twentieth Century*. Philadelphia: John Benjamins.

Demant, Jakob, Rasmus Munksgaard, and Esben Houborg. 2018. "Personal Use, Social Supply or Redistribution? Cryptomarket Demand on Silk Road 2 and Agora." *Trends in Organized Crime*, 21: 42–61.

Demjén, Zsofia, and Clare Hardeker. 2016. "Metaphor, Impoliteness and Offence in Online Communication." In *The Routlege Handbook of Metaphor and Language*, edited by Elena Semino, 353–367. London: Routledge.

Deumert, Ana. 2014. *Sociolinguistics and Mobile Communication*. Edinburgh: Edinburgh University Press.

Dittus, Martin. 2017. A Distributed Resilience Among Darknet Markets? *Oxford Internet Institute*, November 9, 2017. https://www.oii.ox.c.uk/blog/a-distributed-resilience-among-darket-markets/

Doerr, Nicole. 2017. "Bridging Language Barriers, Bonding Against Immigrants: A Visual Case Study of Transnational Network Publics Created by Far-Right Activists in Europe." *Discourse & Society*, 28(1): 3–23.

Du Bois, John. 2007. "The Stance Triangle." In *Stancetaking in Discourse. Subjectivity, Evaluation, Interaction*, edited by Robert Englebretson. 139–182. Philadephia: John Benjamins.

Dunbar, Robin. 1996. *Grooming, Gossip and the Evolution of Language*. Cambridge, MA: Harvard University Press.

Dutton, William, Ginette Law, Gillian Bolsover, and Soumitra Dutta. 2013. "The Internet Trust Bubble. Global Values, Beliefs and Practices." World Economic Forum. http://www3.weforum.org/docs/WEF_InternetTrustBubble_Report2_2014.pdf.

Duyvesteyn, Isabelle. 2004. "How New Is the New Terrorism?" *Studies in Conflict and Terrorism*, 27(5): 439–454.

Dynel, Marta. 2014. "Participation Framework Underlying YouTube Interaction." *Journal of Pragmatics*, 73: 37–52.

Dynel, Marta. 2017. "Participation as Audience Design." *In Pragmatics of Social Media*, edited by Christian R. Hoffmann and Wolfram Bublitz, 61–82. Berlin: Mouton de Gruyter.

Easton, David. 1958. "The Perception of Authority and Political Change." In *Authority, Nomos I*, edited by Karl Friedrich, 170–196. Cambridge, MA: Harvard University Press.

Eatwell, Roger. 2006. "Community Cohesion and Cumulative Extremism in Contemporary Britain." *The Political Quarterly*, 77(2): 204–216.

Eckert, Penelope. 2000. *Linguistic Variation as Social Practice*. Oxford: Blackwell Publishers.

Eckert, Penelope. 2001. "Style and Social Meaning." In *Style and Sociolinguistic Variation*, edited by Penelope Eckert and John Rickford, 119–126. Cambridge: Cambridge University Press.

Eckert, Penelope. 2006. "Communities of Practice." *Encyclopedia of Language and Linguistics*, 2: 683–685.

Eckert, Penelope, and Jon Rickford (Eds.). 2001. *Style and Sociolinguistic Variation*, Cambridge: Cambridge University Press.

Edwards, John. 2009. *Language and Identity: An Introduction*. Cambridge: Cambridge University Press.

Eelen, Gino. 2001. *A Critique of Politeness Theories*. Manchester: St. Jerome Publishing.

Egan, Vincent, James Hoskinson, and David Shewan. 2011. "Perverted Justice: A Content Analysis of the Language Used by Offenders Detected Attempting to Solicit Children for Sex." *Antisocial Behavior: Causes, Correlations and Treatments*, 20(3): 272297.

Eisenlauer, Volker. 2014. "Facebook as a Third Author: (Semi-)Automated Participation Framework in Social Network Sites." *Journal of Pragmatics*, 72: 73–85.

Elliott, Ian, and Anthony Beech. 2009. "Understanding Online Child Pornography Use: Applying Sexual Offense Theory to Internet Offenders." *Aggression and Violent Behavior*, 14(3): 180–193.

Ende, Michael. 1997. *The Neverending Story*. London: Puffin Books.

Enke, Nadia, and Niels Borchers. 2019. "Social Media Influencers in Strategic Communication: A Conceptual Framework for Strategic Social Media Influencer Communication." *International Journal of Strategic Communication*, 14(4): 261–277.

Epstein, Zach. 2014. "How to Find the Invisible Internet." BGR. https://news.yahoo. com/invisible-internet-162645102.html?guccounter=1&guce_referrer=aHR0 cHM6Ly93d3cuZ29vZ2xlLmNvbS8&guce_referrer_sig=AQAAAMQaDFHmKBdX90wvpFbAaTw5aryNMyYGWLh9L7lzIaLoEyxRSIqHyvJmfyB3jOkshfKnx6mvSH8iKu9vO1OuCeSIkzKjKdKpqv3RwZmYjzvJiFho7TKCRkokxPKIvKiqemW7zTq0jFqOWjICjZxwcO3JSGEf03S9Jbf-M8BYOi9s.

Espinosa, Romain. 2019. "Scamming and the Reputation of Drug Dealers on Darknet Markets." *International Journal of Industrial Organization*, 67: 102523.

Fairclough, Norman. 1995. *Media Discourse*. London: Lawrence Erlbaum Associates.

Ferguson, Kate. 2016. "Countering Violent Extremism Through Media and Communication Strategies: A Review of Evidence." *Reflections*, 27: 28. http://www.dmef orpeace.org/peacexchange/wp-content/uploads/2018/10/Countering-Violent-Extremism-Through-Media-and-Communication-Strategies.pdf.

Fernandez, Miriam, Antonio González-Pardo, and Harith Alani. 2019. "Radicalisation Influence in Social Media." *Journal of Web Science*, 6. http://oro.open.ac.uk/ 66155/

Fisher, David. 1984. "A Conceptual Analysis of Self-Disclosure." *Journal for the Theory of Social Behaviour*, 14(3): 277–296.

Florido, Adrian. 2016. "The White Nationalist Origins of the Term 'Alt-Right': And the Debate Around It." www.npr.org/ 2016/11/27/503520811/the-white-nationalist-origins-of-the-term-alt- right-and-the-debate-around-it?t=1534781671383.

Foster, Jennifer, and Bryce Hagedorn. 2014. "Through the Eyes of the Wounded: A Narrative Analysis of Children's Sexual Abuse Experiences and Recovery Process." *Journal of Child Sexual Abuse*, 23(5): 538–557.

Foucault, Michel. 1988. *The Care of the Self*. London: Allen Lane.

Furlow, R. Bennett, Kristin Fleischer, and Steven Corman. 2014. "De-Romanticizing the Islamic State's Vision of the Caliphate." Center for Strategic Communication.

http://csc.asu.edu/2014/10/28/de-romanticizing-the-islamic-states-vision-of-the-caliphate-2/

Gabrielatos, Costas. 2018. "Keyness Analysis." In *Corpus Approaches to Discourse: A Critical Review*, edited by Charlotte Taylor and Anna Marchi, 225–258, London: Routledge.

Gabrielatos, Costas, and Anna Marchi. 2012. "Keyness: Appropriate Metrics and Practical Issues." Paper presented at Corpus-Assisted Discourse Studies International Conference. Bologna, Italy.

Gambhir, Harleen. 2016. *The Virtual Caliphate: ISIS's Information Warfare*. Washington, DC: Institute for the Study of War.

Gamson, William. 1995. "Constructing Social Protest." *Social Movements and Culture*, 4: 85–106.

Ganesh, Bharath. 2019. "Right-Wing Extreme Digital Speech in Europe and North America." In *Extreme Digital Speech: Contexts, Responses, and Solutions*, edited by Bharath Ganesh and Jonathan Bright, 89–97. Vox-Pol Network of Excellence. https://www.voxpol.eu/download/vox-pol_publication/DCUJ770-VOX-Extreme-Digital-Speech.pdf.

Garcés-Conejos Blitvich, Pilar. 2009. "Impoliteness and Identity in the American News Media: The "Culture Wars." *Journal of Politeness Research*, 5(2): 273–303.

Garcés-Conejos Blitvich, Pilar. 2010. "A Genre Approach to the Study of Im-politeness." *International Review of Pragmatics*, 2(1): 46–94.

Garcés-Conejos Blitvich, Pilar. 2013. "Face, Identity, and Im/politeness: Looking Backwards, Moving Forwards: From Goffman to Practice Theory." *Journal of Politeness Research*, 9(1): 1–33.

Garcés-Conejos Blitvich, Pilar. 2018. "Globalization, Transnational Identities, and Conflict Talk: The Superdiversity and Complexity of the Latino Identity." *Journal of Pragmatics*, 134: 120–133.

Garcés-Conejos Blitvich, Pilar. 2022a. "Going into the Mob: A Netnographic, Casestudy Approach to Online Public Shaming." In *Analysing Digital Discourse: Practices of Convergence and Controversy*, edited by Marjut Johansson, Sanna-Kaisen Tanskanen, and Jan Chovanec. 247–274. London: Palgrave Macmillan.

Garcés-Conejos Blitvich, Pilar. 2022b. "Moral Emotions, Good Moral Panics, Social Regulation, and Online Public Shaming." *Language and Communication*, 84: 61–75.

Garcés-Conejos Blitvich, Pilar, and Dániel Kádar. 2021. "Morality in Sociopragmatics." In *The Cambridge Handbook of Sociopragmatics*, edited by Michael Haugh, Dániel Kádar, and Marina Terkourafi, 385–407. Cambridge: Cambridge University Press.

Garcés-Conejos Blitvich, Pilar, and Maria Sifianou. 2017. "(Im) politeness and Identity." In *The Palgrave Handbook of Linguistic (Im) Politeness*, edited by Jonathan Culpeper, Michael Haugh, and Daniel Kádár. 227–256. London: Palgrave Macmillan.

García Bedolla, Lisa. 2003. "The Identity Paradox: Latino Language, Politics and Selective Dissociation." *Latino Studies*, 1(2): 264–283.

Garfinkel, Harold. 1967. *Studies in Ethnomethodology*. Hoboken, NJ: Prentice-Hall.

Gaudette, Tiana, Ryan Scrivens, and Vivek Venkatesh. 2020. "The Role of the Internet in Facilitating Violent Extremism: Insights from Former Right-wing Extremists." *Terrorism and Political Violence*: 1–18.

Gee, James Paul. 2005. "Semiotic Social Spaces and Affinity Spaces: From the Age of Mythology to Today's Schools." In *Beyond Communities of Practice: Language*,

Power and Social Context, edited by David Barton and Karen Tusting, 214–232. Cambridge: Cambridge University Press.

Georgakopoulou, Alexandra. 2007. *Small Stories, Interaction and Identities*. Philadelphia: John Benjamins.

Georgakopoulou, Alexandra. 2017. "Whose Context Collapse?": Ethical Clashes in the Study of Language and Social Media in Context." *Applied Linguistics Review*, 8(2–3): 169–189.

Goffman, Erving. 1956/1967. *The Presentation of Self in Everyday Life*. New York: Doubleday.

Goffman, Erving. 1974. *Frame Analysis: An Essay on the Organization of Experience*. London: Harper and Row.

Goffman, Erving. 1981. *Forms of Talk*. Philadelphia: University of Pennsylvania Press.

Gouldner, Alvin. 1960. "The Norm of Reciprocity: A Preliminary Statement." *American Sociological Review*, 25(2): 161–178.

Gottschalk, Petter. 2011. "Characteristics of the Internet and Child Abuse." In *Internet Child Abuse: Current Research and Policy*, edited by Julia Davidson and Peter Gottschalk, 27–51. London: Routledge Taylor & Francis Group.

Grassmuck, Volker Ralf. 2012. "The Sharing Turn: Why We Are Generally Nice and Have a Good Chance to Cooperate Our Way Out of the Mess We Have Gotten Ourselves Into." In *Cultures and Ethics of Sharing / Kulturen und Ethiken des Teilens*, edited by Wolfgang Sützl, Felix Stalder, Ronald Maier, and Theo Hug, 17–34. Innsbruck: Innsbruck University Press.

Greenberg, Andy. 2013. "Meet the Dread Pirate Roberts, the Man Behind Booming Black Market Drug Website Silk Road." *Forbes*. https://www.forbes.com/sites/andygreenberg/2013/08/14/meet-the-dread-pirate-roberts-the-man-behind-booming-black-market-drug-website-silk-road/?sh=47dbafc8b735.

Grinnell, Daniel, Stuart Macdonald, and David Mair. 2017. *The Response of, and on, Twitter, to the Release of Dabiq Issue 15*. Paper presented at the 1st European Counter Terrorism Centre conference on online terrorist propaganda, April 10–11, 2017, The Hague. https://www.europol.europa.eu/publications-documents/response-of-and-twitter-to-release-of-dabiq-issue-15.

Grinnell, Daniel, Macdonald, Stuart, David Mair, and Nuria Lorenzo-Dus. 2018. "Who Disseminates *Rumiyah*? Examining the Relative Influence of Sympathiser and Non-sympathiser Twitter Users." Paper presented at the 2nd European Counter Terrorism Centre Advisory Group Conference. Europol Headquarters, The Hague.

Gwern Branwen, Nicolas Christin, David Décary-Hétu, Rasmus Munksgaard Andersen, StExo, El Presidente, Anonymous, Daryl Lau, Sohhlz, Delyan Kratunov, Vince Cakic, Van Buskirk, Whom, Michael McKenna, and Sigi Goode. "Dark Net Market Archives, 2011–2015." July 12, 2015. https://www.gwern.net/DNM-archives

Graham, Todd, and Scott Wright. 2013. "Discursive Equality and Everyday Talk Online: The Impact of 'Superparticipants.'" *Journal of Computer-Mediated Communication*, 19(3): 625–642.

Grant, Tim, and Nicki Macleod. 2020. *Language and Online Identities: The Undercover Policing of Internet Sexual Crime*. Cambridge: Cambridge University Press.

Gries, Stefan T. 2008. "Dispersions and Adjusted Frequencies in Corpora." *International Journal of Corpus Linguistics*, 13(4): 403–437.

Gries, Stefan T. 2010. "Useful Statistics for Corpus Linguistics." *A Mosaic of Corpus Linguistics: Selected Approaches*, 66: 269–291.

Habeck, Mary. 2006. *Knowing the Enemy: Jihadist Ideology and the War on Terror*. New Haven, CT: Yale University Press.

Haciyakupoglu, Gulizar, and Weiyu Zhang. 2015. "Social Media and Trust during the Gezi Protests in Turkey." *Journal of Computer-Mediated Communication*, 20(4): 450–466.

Haider, Syed. 2016. "The Shooting in Orlando, Terrorism or Toxic Masculinity (or Both?)." *Men and Masculinities*, 19(5): 555–565.

Hainsworth, Paul. (Ed.) 2016. *The Extreme Right in Europe and the USA*. London: Bloomsbury Publishing.

Halavais, Alexander. 2019. "Overcoming Terms of Service: A Proposal for Ethically Distributed Research." *Information, Communication and Society*, 22: 1567–1581.

Hall, Stuart. 1996. "The Problem of Ideology: Marxism Without Guarantees." In *Stuart Hall: Critical Dialogues in Cultural Studies*, edited by David Morley and K. H. Chen, 25–46. London: Routledge.

Hall, Stuart, and Paul Du Gay, eds. 1996. *Questions of Cultural Identity*. London: Sage.

Hall, Alexandra, and Georgios A. Antonopoulos. 2016. *Fake Meds Online: The Internet and the Transnational Market in Illicit Pharmaceuticals*. New York: Springer.

Hall, Alexandra, Rosa Koenraadt, and Georgios A. Antonopoulos. 2017. "Illicit Pharmaceutical Networks in Europe: Organising the Illicit Medicine Market in the United Kingdom and the Netherlands." *Trends in Organized Crime*, 20(3): 296–315.

Halonen, Mia, and Sirpa Leppanen. 2017. "Pissis Stories: The Self and the Other as Gendered, Sexualized and Class-based Performance on Social Media." In *Social Media Discourse, (Dis)identifications and Diversities*, edited by Sirpa Leppanen, Elyna Westinnen, and Samu Kytola, 39–61. London: Routledge.

Halverson Jeffrey, R. Bennet Furlow, and Steven Corman. 2012. "How Islamic Extremists Quote the Qur'an." Center for Strategic Communication, Arizona State University. http://csc.asu.edu/wp-content/uploads/pdf/csc1202-quran-verses.pdf.

Hamilton, David, and Steve Sherman. 1996. "Perceiving Persons and Groups." *Psychological Review*, 103(2): 336–355.

Hamilton-Giachritsis, Catherine, Elly Hanson, Helen Whittle, and Anthony Beech. 2017. "Everyone Deserves to Be Happy and Safe: A Mixed Methods Study Exploring how Online and Offline Sexual Abuse Impact Young People and how Professionals Respond to it." NSPCC Report. https://learning.nspcc.org.uk/media/1123/impact-online-offline-child-sexual-abuse.pdf.

Hamilton-Giachritsis, Catherine, Elly Hanson, Helen Whittle, Filipa Alves-Costa, Andrea Pintos, Theo Metcalf, and Anthony Beech. 2021a. "Technology-Assisted Child Sexual Abuse: Professionals' Perceptions of Risk and Impact on Children and Young People." *Child Abuse and Neglect*, 119(1): 104651.

Hamilton-Giachritsis, Catherine, Elly Hanson, Helen Whittle, Filipa Alves-Costas, and Anthony Beech. 2021b. "Technology-Assisted Child Sexual Abuse in the UK: Young People's Views on the Impact of Online Sexual Abuse." *Children and Youth Services Review*, 119: 105451.

Hariman, Robert, and John L. Lucaites. 2007. *No Caption Needed: Iconic Photographs, Public Culture, and Liberal Democracy*. Chicago: University of Chicago Press.

Harris, Sandra. 2001. "Being Politically Impolite: Extending Politeness Theory to Adversarial Political Discourse." *Discourse & Society*, 12(4): 451–472.

Haugh, Michael. 2018. "Afterword: Theorizing (Im) Politeness." *Journal of Politeness Research*, 14(1): 153–165.

Haugh, Michael, and Wei-Lin Melody Chang. 2015. "Troubles Talk, (Dis) Affiliation and the Participation Order in Taiwanese-Chinese Online Discussion Boards." In *Participation in Public and Social Media Interactions*, edited by Marta Dynel and Jan Chovanec, 99–133. Amsterdam and Philadelphia: John Benjamins.

Hendriks Friederike, Dorothe Kienhues, and Rayner Bromme. 2015. "Measuring Laypeople's Trust in Experts in a Digital Age: The Muenster Epistemic Trustworthiness Inventory (METI)." *Plos One, 10*. https://doi.org/10.1371/journal.pone.0139309.

Henschke, Adam, and Alastair Reed. 2021. "Toward an Ethical Framework for Countering Extremist Propaganda Online." *Studies in Conflict and Terrorism*, 1–18. https://doi.org/10.1080/1057610X.2020.1866744.

Herbert, Robert. 1991. "The Sociology of Compliment Work: An Ethnocontrastive Study of Polish and English Compliments." *Multilingua, 10*(4): 381 – 402.

Heritage, John. 1985. "Analyzing News Interviews: Aspects of the Production of Talk for an 'Overhearing' Audience." In *Handbook of Discourse Analysis, vol. III: Discourse and Dialogue*, edited by Teun Van Dijk, 95–117. London: Academic Press.

Herman, Edward, and Noam Chomsky. 1988. *Manufacturing Consent: The Political Economy of the Mass Media*. New York: Random House.

Herring, Susan. 2004. "Computer-mediated Discourse Analysis: An Approach to Researching Online Behavior." In *Designing for Virtual Communities in the Service of Learning*, edited by Sasha A. Barah, Rob Kling, and James H. Gray, 338–376. New York: Cambridge University Press.

Herring, Susan. 2013. "Discourse in Web 2.0: Familiar, Reconfigured, and Emergent." In *Georgetown University Round Table on Languages and Linguistics 2011: Discourse 2.0: Language and New Media*, edited by Deborah Tannen and Anna Marie Trester, 1–25. Washington, DC: Georgetown University Press.

Herring, Susan. 2019. "The Co-Evolution of Computer-Mediated Communication and Computer-mediated Discourse Analysis." In *Analyzing Digital Discourse: New Insights and Future Directions*, edited by Patricia Bou-Franch and Pilar Garcés-Conejos Blitvich, 25–53. London: Palgrave.

Himelboim, Itai, Eric Gleave, and Marc Smith. 2009. "Discussion Catalysts in Online Political Discussions: Content Importers and Conversation Starters." *Journal of Computer Mediated Communication, 14*(4): 771–789.

HM Government. 2018. "CONTEST. The United Kingdom's Strategy for Countering Terrorism." https://assets.publishing.service.gov.uk/government/uploads/system/uploads/attachment_data/file/716907/140618_CCS207_CCS0218929798-1_CONTEST_3.0_WEB.pdf.

Hoffman, Bruce. 1989. *Inside Terrorism*. New York: Columbia University Press.

Hoffmann, Christian R. 2012. *Cohesive Profiling: Meaning and Interaction in Personal Weblogs*. Amsterdam and Philadelphia: John Benjamins Publishing.

Hogg, Michael. 2014. "From Uncertainty to Extremism: Social Categorization and Identity Processes." *Current Directions in Psychological Science, 23*(5): 338–342.

Hogg, Michael, and Janice Adelman. 2013. "Uncertainty–identity Theory: Extreme Groups, Radical Behavior, and Authoritarian Leadership." *Journal of Social Issues, 69*(3): 436–454.

Hogg, Michael, Janice Adelman, and Robert Blagg. 2010. "Religion in the Face of Uncertainty: An Uncertainty-identity Theory Account of Religiousness." *Personality and Social Psychology Review, 14*: 72–83.

Hogg, Michael, Aire Kruglanski, and Kees van der Boss. 2013. "Uncertainty and the Roots of Extremism." *Journal of Social Issues, 69*(3): 404–418.

Hogg, Michael, David Sherman, Joel Dierselhuis, Angela T. Maitner, and Graham Moffitt. 2007. "Uncertainty, Entitativity and Group Identification." *Journal of Experimental Social Psychology*, 43(1): 135–142.

Holt, Thomas J., Russell Brewer, and Andrew Goldsmith. 2019. "Digital Drift and the 'Sense of Injustice': Counter-Productive Policing of Youth Cybercrime." *Deviant Behavior*, 40(9): 1144–1156.

Horgan, John. 2014. "What Makes a Terrorist Stop Being a Terrorist?" *Journal for Deradicalization*, 1: 1–4.

Horton, Donald, and Richard Whol. 1956. "Mass Communication and Parasocial Interaction: Observations on Intimacy at a Distance." *Psychiatry*, 19: 215–229.

Horton-Eddison, Martin. 2018. "Evolving Reality: The Strategic Shift in Crypto-Drug Market Enforcement." Intersessional of the 62nd session of the Commission of Narcotic Drugs, United Nations Office on Drugs and Crime, 1–4, United Nations Office on Drugs and Crime, Vienna, Austria.

Horton-Eddison, Martin. 2020. "Seoul Searching: South Korea's AI Counter-cryptomarket Capability and Associated Privacy Dilemmas." *GDPO Working Paper Series*, 6(April). https://www.swansea.ac.uk/media/Seoul-Searching-V4-23042020.pdf.

Horton-Eddison, Martin, and Mateo Di Cristofaro. 2017. "Hard Interventions and Innovation in Crypto-drug Markets: The Escrow Example." *Global Drug Policy Observator.* Policy Brief. https://www.swansea.ac.uk/media/Hard-Interventions-and-Innovation-in-CryptoDrug-Markets-The-escrow-example.pdf.

Horton-Eddison, Martin, Patrick Shortis, Judith Aldridge, and Fernando Caudevilla. 2021. "Drug Cryptomarkets in the 2020s: Policy, Enforcement, Harm and Resilience." *Global Drug Policy Observatory*,. Policy Brief. https://www.swansea.ac.uk/media/Drug-Crypto-Markets_FINAL_June_2021.pdf.

Hoskins, Andrew. 2016. "Archive me! Media, Memory, Uncertainty." In *Memory in a Mediated World*, edited by Andrea Hajek, Christine Lohmeier, and Christian Pentzold, 13–35. London: Palgrave Macmillan.

Hymes, Dell. 1974. *Foundations of Sociolinguistics: An Ethnographic Approach*. Philadelphia: University of Pennsylvania Press.

Iedema, Rick. 2003. "Multimodality, Resemiotization: Extending the Analysis of Discourse as Multisemiotic Practice." *Visual Communication*, 2(1): 29–56.

Inches, Giacomo, and Fabio Crestani. 2012. "Overview of the International Sexual Predator Identification Competition at PAN-2012." In *CLEF* (Online working notes/labs/workshop|), 30. http://ceur-ws.org/Vol-1178/CLEF2012wn-PAN-InchesEt2012.pdf.

Ingram, Haroro J. 2014. "Three Traits of the Islamic State's Information Warfare." *The RUSI Journal*, 159(6): 4–11.

Ingram, Haroro J. 2015a. "The Strategic Logic of Islam State Information Operations." *Australian Journal of International Affairs*, 69(6): 729–752.

Ingram, Haroro J. 2015b. "An Analysis of the Taliban in Khurasan's Azan (Issues 1–5)." *Studies in Conflict and Terrorism*, 38(7): 560–579.

Ingram, Haroro J. 2016. "An analysis of Islamic State's *Dabiq* magazine." *Australian Journal of Political Science*, 51: 458–477.

Irvine, Judith. 1985. "Status and Style in Language." *Annual Review of Anthropology*, 14: 557–581.

Irvine, Judith. 2001. "Style as Distinctiveness: The Culture and Ideology of Linguistic Differentiation." In *Natural Histories of Discourse*, edited by Penelope Eckert and John Rickford, 21–43. Cambridge: Cambridge University Press.

Jackson, Sharon, Kathryn Backett-Milburn, and Elinor Newall. 2013. "Researching Distressing Topics: Emotional Reflexivity and Emotional Labour in the Secondary Analysis of Children and Young People's Narratives of Abuse." *SAGE Open*, 3.2. doi:10.1177/2158244013490705.

Jaffe, Alexandra (Ed.). 2009. *Stance: Sociolinguistic Perspectives*. Oxford: Oxford University Press.

Jaffe, Alexandra. 2011. "Sociolinguistic Diversity in Mainstream Media: Authenticity, Authority and Processes of Mediation and Mediatization." *Journal of Language and Politics*, 10(4): 562–586.

Jaki, Sylvia, Tom De Smedt, Maja Gwóźdź, Rudresh Panchal, Alexander Rossa, and Guy De Pauw. 2018. "Online Hatred of Women in the Incels. me Forum: Linguistic Analysis and Automatic Detection." *Journal of Language Aggression and Conflict*, 7(2): 240–268.

Jenkins, Henry (with Ravi Purushotma, Margaret Weigel, Katie Clinton, K., and Alice Robison). 2009. *Confronting the Challenges of Participatory Culture: Media Education for the 21st Century*. Cambridge, MA: MIT Press.

Jenkins, Henry. 2014. "Rethinking 'Rethinking Convergence/culture.'" *Cultural Studies*, 28(2): 267–297.

John, Nicholas. 2012. "Sharing and Web 2.0: The Emergence of a Keyword." *New Media & Society*, 15(2): 167–182.

John, Nicholas. 2013. "Sharing, Collaborative Consumption and Web 2.0." *MEDIA@ LSE Electronic Working Papers*, 26. https://www.lse.ac.uk/media-and-communications/assets/documents/research/working-paper-series/EWP26.pdf.

John, Nicholas. 2017. *The Age of Sharing*. London: Polity Press.

Johnson, B. M., and H. Plant. 1996. "Collecting Data from People with Cancer and Their Families: What Are the Implications?" In *Nursing Research: An Ethical and Legal Appraisal*, edited by L. De Raeve, 85–100. London: Bailliere Tindall.

Johnson, Sharon, Catherine Striley, and Linda Cottler. 2006. "The Association of Substance Use Disorders with Trauma Exposure and PTSD Among African American Drug Users." *Addictive Behaviors*, 31(11): 2063–2073.

Johnstone, Barbara, and Scott Kiesling. 2008. "Indexicality and Experience: Exploring the Meanings of /aw/-monophthongization in Pittsburgh." *Journal of Sociolinguistics*, 12: 5–33.

Joleby, Malin, Carolina Lunde, Sara Landström, and Linda S. Jonsson. 2021. "Offender Strategies for Engaging Children in Online Sexual Activity." *Child Abuse & Neglect*, 120: 105214.

Jones, Rodney. 2004. "The Problem of Context in Computer-Mediated Communication." In *Discourse and Technology: Multimodal Discourse Analysis*, edited by Philip Levine and Rod Scollon, 20–33. Washington, DC: Georgetown University Press.

Jones, Rodney. 2020. "Accounting for Surveillance." *Journal of Sociolinguistics*, 24(1): 89–95.

Jones, Rodney. 2017. "Surveillant Landscapes." *Linguistic Landscape*, 3(2): 149–186.

Jones, Rodney, Alice Chik, and Christoph A. Hafner. 215. *Discourse and Digital Practices*. London and New York: Routledge.

Jones, Seth G., and Martin C. Libicki. 2008. *How Terrorist Groups End: Lessons for Countering al Qa'ida*. Santa Monica, CA: RAND Corporation.

Joseph, John. 2004. *Language and Identity: National, Ethnic, Religious*. London: Palgrave.

Kádár, Dániel, and Márquez-Reiter, Rosina. 2015. "(Im)politeness and (Im)morality: Insights from Intervention." *Journal of Politeness Research*, 11(2): 239–260.

Kanai, Akane. 2019. *Gender and Relatability in Digital Culture. Managing Affect, Intimacy and Value*. London: Palgrave Macmillan.

Karl, Philipp. 2017. "Hungary's Radical Right 2.0." *Nationalities Papers*, 45(3): 345–355.

Karner, Tracy. 1996. "Fathers, Sons, and Vietnam: Masculinity and Betrayal in the Life Narratives of Vietnam Veterans with Post Traumatic Stress Disorder." *American Studies Journal*, 37: 63–98.

Katz, Carmit, and Zion Barnetz. 2016. "Children's Narratives of Alleged Child Sexual Abuse Offender Behaviors and the Manipulation Process." *Psychology of Violence*, 6(2): 223–232.

Kennedy, Helen. 2006. "Beyond Anonymity or Future Directions for Internet Identity Research." *New Media and Society*, 8: 859–876.

Kethineni, Sesha, and Cao, Ying. 2020. "The Rise in Popularity of Cryptocurrency and Associated Criminal Activity." *International Criminal Justice Review*, 30(3): 325–344.

KhosraviNik, Majid. 2017a. "Social Media Critical Discourse Studies (SM-CDS)." In *Routledge Handbook of Critical Discourse Studies*, edited by John Floredew and John Richardson, 582–591. London: Routledge.

KhosraviNik, Majid. 2017b. "Right Wing Populism in the West: Social Media Discourse and Echo Chambers." *Insight Turkey*, 19(3): 53–68.

KhosraviNik, Majid, and Mohammedwesam Amer. 2022. "Social Media and Terrorism Discourse: The Islamic State's (IS) Social Media Discursive Content and Practices." *Critical Discourse Studies*, 19(2): 124–143.

Kiesling, Scott. 2009. "Style as Stance." In *Stance: Sociolinguistic Perspectives*, edited by Alexandra Jaffe, 171–194. Oxford: Oxford University Press.

Kiesling, Scott. 2013. "Constructing Identity." In *The Handbook of Language Variation and Change*, edited by J. K. Chambers and Natalie Shilling, 448–467. Oxford: Blackwell.

Kim, Chung, Donchul Han, and Seung-Bae Park. 2001. "The Effect of Brand Personality and Brand Identification on Brand Loyalty: Applying the Theory of Social Identification." *Japanese Psychological Research*, 43(4): 195–206.

Kimmage, Daniel. 2008. *The Al-Qaeda Media Nexus: The Virtual Network Behind the Global Message*. Washington, DC: Radio Free Europe.

Kimmage, Daniel, and Kathleen Ridolfo. 2007. *Iraqi Insurgent Media: The War of Images and Ideas*. Washington, DC: Radio Free Europe.

Kinzel, Anina. 2021. *The Language of Online Child Sexual Groomers: A Corpus Assisted Discourse Study of Intentions, Requests and Grooming Duration*. PhD dissertation. Swansea University.

Kirke, Xander. 2015. "Violence and Political Myth: Radicalizing Believers in the Pages of *Inspire* Magazine." *International Political Sociology*, 9(4): 283–298.

Kiyimba, Nikki, and Michelle O'Reilly. 2016. "The Risk of Secondary Traumatic Stress in the Qualitative Transcription Process: A Research Note." *Qualitative Research*, 16: 468–476.

Kloess, Juliane A., Catherine E. Hamilton-Giachritsis, and Anthony R., Beech. 2019. "Offense Processes of Online Sexual Grooming and Abuse of Children via Internet Communication Platforms." *Sexual Abuse*, 31(1): 73–96.

Koehler, Daniel. 2014. "The Radical Online: Individual Radicalization Processes and the Role of the Internet." *Journal for Radicalization*, 15(1): 116–134. https://journals.sfu.ca/jd/index.php/jd/article/view/8/8.

Kontostathis, April, Lynne Edwards, Jen Bayzick, Amanda Leatherman, and Kristina Moore 2009. "Comparison of Rule-Based to Human Analysis of Chat Logs."

Communication Theory, 8(2) 1–12. https://april-edwards.me/KontostathisM
SMFinal.pdf.

Kovács, Arpad. 2015. "The 'New Jihadists' and the Visual Turn from al-Qa'ida to ISIL/
ISIS/Da'ish." *Bitzpol Affairs*, 2(3): 47–69.

Kroker, Arthur. 2014. *Exits to the Posthuman Future*. Cambridge: Polity Press.

Krone, Tony. 2004. "A Typology of Online Child Pornography Offending." *Trends and
Issues in Crime and Criminal Justice, 279*: 1–6.

Kruithof, Kristy, Judith Aldridge, David Décary-Hétu, Megan Sim, Elma Dujso, and
Stijn Hoorens. 2016. *Internet-Facilitated Drugs Trade: An Analysis of the Size,
Scope and the Role of the Netherlands*. Santa Monica, CA: RAND Corporation.
https://www.rand.org/pubs/research_reports/RR1607.html.

Kundnani, Arun. 2012. "Radicalisation: The Journey of a Concept." *Race & Class*,
54(2): 3–25.

Kurzon, Dennis. 1998. "The Speech Act Status of Incitement: Perlocutionary Acts
Revisited." *Journal of Pragmatics*, *29*(5): 571–596.

Kusmierczy, Ewa. 2014. "Trust in Action: Building Trust Through Embodied Negotiation of Mutual Understanding of Job Interviews." In *Trust and Discourse: Organ-
isational Perspectives*, edited by Katja Pelsmaekers, Jacobs Geerts, and Craig
Rollo, 11–44. Philadelphia: John Benjamins.

Kuznar, Lawrence. 2017. "The Stability of the Islamic State (IS) Narrative: Implications
for the Future." *Dynamics of Asymmetric Conflict*, *10*(1): 40–53.

Kuznar Lawrence, and William H. Moon 2014. "Thematic Analysis of ISIL Messaging."
In *Multi-Method Assessment of ISIL*, edited by Michael Nagata et al., 47–54.
Arlington, VA: Strategic Multilayer Assessment (SMA) Periodic Publication.
https://digitalcommons.chapman.edu/cgi/viewcontent.cgi?referer=https://
scholar.google.com/&httpsredir=1&article=1030&context=sociology_articles.

Labov, William. 1972. *Language in the Inner City*. Philadelphia: University of Pennsylvania Press.

Lane, Scott, and Don Cherek. 2000. "Analysis of Risk Taking in Adults with a History of
High Risk Behavior." *Drug and Alcohol Dependence, 60*(2): 179–187.

Lanning, Ken. 2019. "The Evolution of Grooming: Concept and Term." *Journal of Interpersonal Violence, 33*(1): 5–16.

Laquer, Walter. 2000. *The New Terrorism: Fanaticism and the Arms of Mass Destruction*.
New York: Oxford University Press.

Lee, Seunghyeon, Changhoon Yoon, Heedo Kang, Yeonkeun Kim, Yongdae Kim,
Dongsu Han, Sooel Son, and Seungwon Shin. 2019. "Cybercriminal Minds: An
Investigative Study of Cryptocurrency Abuses in the Dark Web." *Network and
Distributed Systems Security (NDSS) Symposium*. https://www.ndss-symposium.
org/wp-content/uploads/2019/02/ndss2019_09-1_Lee_paper.pdf.

Leech, Geoffrey. 1976. *Semantics*. Harmondsworth: Penguin Books.

Le Page, Robert, and Andree Tabouret-Keller. 1985. *Acts of Identity: Creole-Based
Approaches to Language and Ethnicity*. Cambridge: Cambridge University Press.

Leppänen, Sirpa, and Sanna Tapionkaski. 2021. "Intersectionality and Multimodality
in Social Media." In *Routledge Handbook of Language, Gender and Sexuality*, edited
by Jo Angouri and Judith Baxter, 543–556. London: Routledge.

Lewicki, Roy, Edward Tomlison, and Nicole Gillespie. 2006. "Models of Interpersonal
Trust Development: Theoretical Approaches, Empirical Evidence, and Future
Directions." *Journal of Management*, *36*(2): 991–1022.

Li, Xiaofan, and Andrew B. Whinston. 2020. "Analyzing Cryptocurrencies." *Information
Systems Frontiers, 22*(1): 17–22.

Lippman, Walter. 1925. *The Phantom Public*. Piscataway, NJ: Transaction Publishers.

Lindsay, James. 2003. "Ibn 'Asakir (1105–1176): Muslim Historian and Advocate of Jihad against Christian Crusaders and Shi'ite Muslims." *Middlebery College, Rohatyn Center for International Affairs, Working Paper Series*, 11: 1–31.

Liu, Dan, Ching Yee Suen, and Olga Ormandjieva. 2017. "A Novel Way of Identifying Cyber Predators." *arXiv preprint arXiv:1712.03903*.

Locher, Miriam. 2008. "Relational Work, Politeness and Identity Construction." In *Handbooks of Applied Linguistics. Volume 2: Interpersonal Communication*, edited by Antos Gerd, Eija Ventola, and Tilo Weber, 509–540. Berlin and New York: Mouton de Gruyter.

Locher, Miriam. 2020. "Moments of Relational Work in English Fan Translations of Korean TV Drama." *Journal of Pragmatics*, 170: 139–155.

Locher, Miriam, Brooke Bolander, and Nicole Höhn. 2015. "Introducing Relational Work in Facebook and Discussion Boards." *Pragmatics*, 25: 1–21.

Locher, Miriam, and Richard Watts. 2005. "Politeness Theory and Relational Work." *Journal of Politeness Research*, 1(1): 9–33.

Locher, Miriam, and Richard Watts. 2008. "Relational Work and Impoliteness: Negotiating Norms of Linguistic Behaviour." In *Impoliteness in Language. Studies of its Interplay with Power in Theory and Practice*, edited by Derek Bousfield and Miriam Locher, 77–99. Berlin: Mouton de Gruyter.

Lorenzo-Dus, Nuria. 2009. *Television Discourse. Analysing Language in the Media*. Basingstoke, UK: Palgrave Macmillan.

Lorenzo-Dus, Nuria. 2021a. "Online Child Sexual Grooming: Abuse and Manipulation Through Communication." *Hwb: Views from the Experts*. https://hwb.gov.wales/zones/keeping-safe-online/views-from-the-experts/online-child-sexual-grooming-abuse-and-manipulation-through-communication/

Lorenzo-Dus, Nuria. 2021b. "'It's the Subtle Language That Gets to You': Understanding and Managing Researcher Exposure to Online Child Sexual Grooming Content.' Presented at 8th annual BAAL Language and New Media SIG Event Focus on the Researcher: Dealing with Distressing Data.

Lorenzo-Dus, Nuria, and Sadiq Almaged. 2021. "Poverty and Social Exclusion in Britain: A Corpus-assisted Discourse Study of Labour and Conservative Party Leaders' Speeches, 1900–2014." In *The Discursive Construction of Economic Inequality: CADS Approaches to the British Media*, edited by Eva Gómez-Jiménez and Michael Toolan, 13–32. London: Bloomsbury Publishing.

Lorenzo-Dus, Nuria, and Matteo Di Cristofaro. 2016. "#Living/minimum Wage: Influential Citizen Talk in Twitter." *Discourse, Context & Media*, 13: 40–50.

Lorenzo-Dus, Nuria, and Matteo Di Cristofaro. 2018. "'I Know This Whole Market Is Based on the Trust You Put in Me and I Don't Take That Lightly': Trust, Community and Discourse in Crypto-drug Markets." *Discourse & Communication*, 6: 608–626.

Lorenzo-Dus, Nuria, Craig Evans, and Ruth Mullineux-Morgan. 2023. *When Chat Entraps: Online Grooming Discourse*. Cambridge: Cambridge University Press (Cambridge Elements).

Lorenzo-Dus, Nuria, and Cristina Izura. 2017. "'Cause Ur Special': Understanding Trust and Complimenting Behaviour in Online Grooming Discourse." *Journal of Pragmatics*, 112: 68–82.

Lorenzo-Dus, Nuria, Cristina Izura, and Rocío Pérez-Tattam. 2016. "Understanding Grooming Discourse in Computer-mediated Environments." *Discourse, Context and Media*, 12: 40–50.

Lorenzo-Dus, Nuria, and Anina Kinzel. 2019. "'So Is Your Mom as Cute as You?': Examining Patterns of Language Use by Online Sexual Groomers." *Journal of Corpora and Discourse Studies*, 1: 4–39.

Lorenzo-Dus, Nuria, and Anina Kinzel. 2021: "'We'll Watch TV and Do Other Stuff': A Corpus-assisted Discourse Study of Vague Language Use in Online Child Sexual Grooming." In *Exploring Discourse and Ideology Through Corpora*, edited by Miguel Fuster-Márquez José Santaemilia, Carmen Gregori-Signes, and Paula Rodríguez-Abruñeiras, 189–210. Bern: Peter Lang.

Lorenzo-Dus, Nuria, Anina Kinzel, and Matteo Di Cristofaro. 2020. "The Communicative Modus Operandi of Online Child Sexual Groomers: Recurring Patterns in Their Language Use." *Journal of Pragmatics*, 155: 1–19.

Lorenzo-Dus, Nuria, Anina Kinzel, and Luke Walker. 2018. "Representing the West and 'Non-believers' in the Online Jihadist Magazines *Dabiq* and *Inspire*." *Critical Studies on Terrorism*, 11(3): 521–536.

Lorenzo-Dus, Nuria, and Stuart Macdonald. 2018. "Othering the West in the Online Jihadist Propaganda Magazines *Inspire* and *Dabiq*." *Journal of Language Aggression and Conflict*, 6(1): 79–106.

Lorenzo-Dus, Nuria, and Lella Nouri. 2021. "The Discourse of the US Alt-Right Online: A Case Study of the Traditionalist Worker Party Blog." *Critical Discourse Studies*, 4: 410–428.

Lorenzo-Dus, Nuria, Laura Mercé Moreno-Serrano, Sergio Maruenda-Bataller, and Carmen Pérez-Sabater. 2022. "Ciberacoso Sexual a Menores (*Online Grooming*) y Pandemia: Actuar con el Lenguaje ante la Vulneración de los Derechos de la Infancia. *Signo y Seña*, 40: 166–187.

Luchjenbroers, June, and Michelle Aldridge-Waddon.2011. "Paedophiles and Politeness in Email Communications: Community of Practice Needs That Define Face-Threat." *Journal of Politeness Research*, 7(1): 21–42.

Luhmann, Niklas. 1988. "Law as a Social System." *Northwestern University Law Review*, 83(1&2): 136–151.

Macdonald, Stuart. 2017. "Radicalisers as Regulators: An Examination of *Dabiq* Magazine." In *Terrorists' Use of the Internet: Assessment and Response*, edited by Maura Conway, Lee Jarvis, and Orla Lehane. 146–157. Amsterdam: IOS Press.

Macdonald, Stuart, Sara Correia, and Amy-Louise Watkin. 2019a. "Regulating Terrorist Content on Social Media: Automating and the Rule of Law." *International Journal of Law in Context*, 15: 183–197.

Macdonald, Stuart, Daniel Grinnell, Anina Kinzel, and Nuria Lorenzo-Dus. 2019b. "A Study of Outlinks Contained in Tweets Mentioning *Rumiyah*." *RUSI*. https://rusi.org/publication/other-publications/study-outlinks-contained-tweets-mentioning-rumiyah.

Macdonald, Stuart, and Nuria Lorenzo-Dus. 2021. "Visual Jihad: Constructing the "Good Muslim" in Online Jihadist Magazines." *Studies in Conflict & Terrorism*, 5: 363–386.

Macdonald, Stuart, and Nuria Lorenzo-Dus. 2020. "Intentional and Performative Persuasion: The Linguistic Basis for Criminalising the (Direct and Indirect) Encouragement of Terrorism." *Criminal Law Forum*, 31: 473–512.

Mackey, Tim Ken, Jiawei Li, Vidya Purushothaman, Matthew Nali, Neal Shah, Cortni Bardier, Mingxiang Cai, and Bryan Liang. 2020. "Big Data, Natural Language Processing, and Deep Learning to Detect and Characterize Illicit COVID19 Product Sales. Infoveillance Study on Twitter and Instagram." *JMIR Public Health Surveillance*, 6(3): 10.2196/20794.

Maddox, Alexia. 2020. "Disrupting the Ethnographic Imaginarium: Challenges of Immersion in the Silk Road Cryptomarket Community." *Journal of Digital Social Research*, 2(1): 20–38.

Maillat, Didier. 2013. "Constraining Context Selection: On the Pragmatic Inevitability of Manipulation." *Journal of Pragmatics*, 59: 190–199.

Maillat, Didier, and Steve Oswald. 2009. "Defining Manipulative Discourse: The Pragmatics of Cognitive Illusions." *International Review of Pragmatics*, 1: 348–370.

Mair, David. 2017. "#Westgate: A Case Study. How Al-Shabaab Used Twitter during an Ongoing Attack." *Studies in Conflict and Terrorism*, 40: 24–43.

Malinowski, Bronislaw. 1926/1932. *Crime and Custom in Savage Society*. London: Trubner.

Manes, Joan, and Nessa Wolfson. 1981. "The Compliment Formula." In *Volume 2 Conversational Routine*, edited by Florian Coulmas, 115–132. The Hague: Mouton De Gruyter.

Maras, Marie-Helen. 2017. "Social Media Platforms: Targeting the 'Found Space' of Terrorists." *Journal of Internet Law*, 2: 3–9.

Marsh-Rossney, Rosie, and Lorenzo-Dus, Nuria. 2022. "A Discourse Analysis of Sexual Identity Construction by Offenders in Online Paedophile Communities." Paper presented at EPICS X Conference, Seville, Spain.

Martellozzo, Elena. 2012. *Online Child Sexual Abuse: Grooming, Policing and Child Protection in a Multimedia World*. London: Routledge.

Martínez-Cabeza, Miguel. 2009. "Dangerous Words: Threats, Perlocutions and Strategic Actions." In *Cognitive Approaches to Language and Linguistic Data*, edited by Wieslaw Olesky and Piotr Stalmaszcyk, 269–284. Frankfurt: Peter Lang.

Marwick, Alice, and Danah boyd. 2011. "I Tweet Honestly, I Tweet Passionately: Twitter Users, Context Collapse, and the Imagined Audience." *New Media & Society*, 13: 114–133.

Masi, Alessandria. 2015. "ISIS Propaganda Magazine Dabiq for Sale on Amazon, Gets Taken Down," *International Business Times*. http://www.ibtimes.com/isis-pro paganda-magazine-dabiq-saleamazon-gets-taken-down-1961036

Massanari, Adrienne. 2018. "Rethinking Research Ethics, Power, and the Risk of Visibility in the Era of the 'Alt-Right' Gaze." *Social Media and Society*, 4(2): 2056305118768302.

Masson, Kimberly, and Angus Bancroft. 2018. "'Nice People Doing Shady Things': Drugs and the Morality of Exchange in the Darknet Cryptomarkets." *International Journal of Drug Policy*, 58: 78–84.

Massullo Chen, Gina. 2017. *Nasty Talk: Online Incivility and Public Debate*. London: Palgrave Macmillan.

Mautner, Gerlinde. 2019. "A Research Note on Corpora and Discourse: Points to Ponder in Research Design." *Journal of Corpora and Discourse Studies*, 2: 2–13.

McElvaney, Rosaleen. 2015. "Disclosure of Child Sexual Abuse: Delays, Non-Disclosure and Partial Disclosure. What the Research Tells us and Implications for Practice." *Child Abuse Review*, 24(3): 159–169.

McGeeney, Ester, and Elly Hanson. 2017. *Digital Romance: A Research Project Exploring Young People's Use of Technology in Their Romantic Relationships and Love Lives*. London: National Crime Agency and Brook. https://www.basw.co.uk/system/files/resources/basw_85054-7.pdf.

Mead, George Herbert. 1974. *Self, Language, and the World*. Austin: University of Texas Press.

Meraz, Sharon, and Zizi Papacharissi. 2013. "Networked Gatekeeping and Networked Framing on# Egypt." *International Journal of Press/Politics*, (2): 1–29.

Messaris, Paul, and Linus Abraham. 2001. "The Role of Images in Framing News Stories." In *Framing Public Life: Perspectives on Media and our Understanding of the Social World*, edited by Stephen D. Reese, Oscar H. Gandy, and August E. Grant, 215–226. London: Lawrence Earlbaum Associates.

Metzger, Miriam, and Andrew Flanagin. 2013. "Credibility and Trust of Information in Online Environments: The Use of Cognitive Heuristics." *Journal of Pragmatics*, 59: 210–220.

Metzger, Miriam, Andrew Flanagin, and Ryan Medders. 2010. "Social and Heuristic Approaches to Credibility Evaluation Online." *Journal of Communication*, 60(3): 413–439.

Mey, Jacob. 2001. *Pragmatics: An Introduction* (2nd ed.). London: Wiley Blackwell.

Meyrowitz, Joshua. 1985. *No Sense of Place: The Impact of Electronic Media on Social Behavior*. New York: Oxford University Press.

Mills, Sara. 2003. *Gender and Politeness*. Cambridge: Cambridge University Press.

Milon-Flores, Daniela F., and Robson L. F. Cordeiro. 2022. "How to Take Advantage of Behavioral Features for the Early Detection of Grooming in Online Conversations." *Knowledge-Based Systems*, 240: 108017.

Milton, Daniel. 2016. *Communication Breakdown: Unraveling the Islamic State's Media Efforts*. West Point, NY: Combating Terrorism Center.

Mirrlees, Tanner. 2018. "The Alt-Right's Discourse on 'Cultural Marxism': A Political Instrument of Intersectional Hate." *Atlantis: Critical Studies in Gender, Culture & Social Justice*, 39(1): 49–69.

Moisie, Evangelina. 2019. "'County Lines': The Modern Cyber Slaves of Britain's Drug-Trafficking Networks." RUSI. https://rusi.org/explore-our-research/publicati ons/commentary/county-lines-modern-cyber-slaves-britains-drug-trafficking- networks.

Montgomery, Martin. 2007. *The Discourse of Broadcast News: A Linguistic Approach*. London: Routledge.

Morrison, Sarah Elizabeth, Caroline Bruce, and Sarah Wilson. 2018. "Children's Disclosure of Sexual Abuse: A Systematic Review of Qualitative Research Exploring Barriers and Facilitators." *Journal of Child Sexual Abuse*, 27(2): 176–194.

Mouffe, Chantal. 2005. *The Return of the Political*. London and New York: Verso.

Mounteney, Jane, Alberto Oteo, and Paul Griffiths. 2016. *The Internet and Drug Markets: Shining a Light on These Complex and Dynamic Systems*. European Monitoring Centre for Drugs and Drug Addiction: Insights 21. Luxembourg: Publications Office of the European Union, 13–17. http://www.emcdda.europa.eu/system/ files/publications/2155/TDXD16001ENN_FINAL.pdf.

Mullineux-Morgan, Ruth, and Lorenzo-Dus, Nuria. 2021. "'He Says I Have to Do Anything He Says Else He's Coming to My House': A Discourse Im-politeness Approach on Children's Perspectives on Coercion in Online Child Sexual Grooming." Paper presented at the 8th New Zealand Discourse Conference. https:// www.canterbury.ac.nz/arts/nzdc8/

Mungan, Murat, and Jonathan Klick. 2014. "Forfeiture of Illegal Gains, Attempts, and Implied Risk Preferences." *Journal of Legal Studies*, 43(1): 137–153.

Munksgaard, Rasmus, and Jakob Demant. 2016. "Mixing Politics and Crime: The Prevalence and Decline of Political Discourse on the Cryptomarket." *International Journal of Drug Policy*, 35: 77–83.

Mussolf, Andreas. 2015. "Dehumanizing Metaphors in UK Immigrant Debates in Press and Online Media." *Journal of Language Aggression and Conflict*, 3(1): 41–56.

Nerurkar, Pranav, Sunil Bhirud, Dhiren Patel, Romaric Ludinard, Yann Busnel, and Saru Kumari. 2020. "Supervised Learning Model for Identifying Illegal Activities in Bitcoin." *Applied Intelligence* https://doi.org/10.1007/s10489-020-02048-w

Nettel, Ana Laura, and Georges Roque. 2012. "Persuasive Argumentation versus Manipulation." *Argumentation, 26*: 55–69.

Neumann, Peter R. 2009. *Old and New Terrorism*. Cambridge: Polity Press.

Neumann, Peter. R. 2013. "The Trouble with Radicalisation." *International Affairs, 89*(4): 873–893.

Nie, Norman, and Lutz Erbring. 2002. "Internet and Society: A Preliminary Report." *IT & Society, 1*(1): 275–283.

Nie, Norman, Sunshine Hillgus, and Lutz Erbring. 2002. "Internet Use, Interpersonal Relations and Sociability: A Time Diary Study." In *The Internet in Everyday Life*, edited by Barry Wellman and Caroline Haythornthwaite, 213–243. London: Blackwell.

Nightingale, Elena, and Baruch Fischhoff. 2002. Adolescent Risk and Vulnerability: Overview. *Journal of Adolescent Health, 31*(1): 3–9.

Nilsen, Anna B., Nathalie Paton, Mark Dechesne, Alexandros Sakellariou, Grant Helm, Ahmed Baky, Liam Monsel, and Danielle Soskin. 2020. "Cross-National Level Report on Digital Sociability and Drivers of Self-Radicalisation in Europe." http://www.dare-h2020.org/uploads/1/2/1/7/12176018/d5.3_cross_country_report.pdf.

Nosek, Margaret A., Catherine Clubb Foley, Rosemary B. Hughes, and Carol A. Howland. 2001. "Vulnerabilities for Abuse Among Women with Disabilities." *Sexuality and Disability, 19*(3): 177–189.

Nouri, Lella, and Nuria Lorenzo-Dus 2019. "Investigating Reclaim Australia and Britain First's Use of Social Media: Developing a New Model of Imagined Political Communities Online." *Journal for Deradicalization, 18*: 1–37.

Nouri, Lella, Nuria Lorenzo-Dus, and Amy-Louise Watkin. 2021. "Impacts of Radical Right Groups' Movements Across Social Media Platforms: A Case Study of Changes to Britain First's Visual Strategy in its Removal from Facebook to Gab." *Studies in Conflict & Terrorism*, 1–27. doi:10.1080/1057610X.2020.1866737.

Novenario, Celine Marie. 2016. "Differentiating Al Qaeda and the Islamic State Through Strategies Publicized in Jihadist Magazines." *Studies in Conflict & Terrorism, 39*(11): 953–967.

Obar, Jonathan. 2015. "Big Data and the Phantom Public: Walter Lippmann and the Fallacy of Data Privacy Self-management." *Big Data & Society, 2*(2): 2053951715608876.

Ochs, Elinor. 1992. "Indexing Gender." In *Rethinking Context: Language as an Interactive Phenomenon*, edited by Alexandro Duranti and Charles Goodwin, 335–358. Cambridge: Cambridge University Press.

O'Connell, Rachel. 2003. *A Typology of Child Cyberexploitation and Online Grooming Practices*. Cyberspace Research Unit. PhD dissertation, University of Central Lancashire.

O'Keefe, Daniel J. 2006. "Persuasion." In *The Handbook of Communication Skills*, edited by Owen Hargie. 333–352. London: Routledge.

Ogiermann, Eva, and Garcés-Conejos Blitvich, Pilar. 2019. "Im/politeness Between the Analyst and Participant Perspectives: An Overview of the Field." In *From Speech Acts to Lay Understanding of Politeness: A Mulitlingual and Multicultural Perspective*, edited by Eva Ogiermann and Pilar Garcés-Conejos Blitvich, 1–24. Cambridge: Cambridge University Press.

Olson, Loreen, Joy Daggs, Barbara Ellevold, and Teddy Rogers. 2007. "Entrapping the Innocent: Toward a Theory of Child Sexual Predators' Luring Communication." *Communication Theory*, 17(3): 231–251.

Ormsby, Eileen. 2014. *Silk Road*. Sydney: Macmillan.

Orsolini, Laura, Gabriele Duccio Papanti, Giulia Francesconi, and Fabrizio Schifano. 2015. "Mind Navigators of Chemicals' Experimenters? A Web-based Description of e-psychonauts." *Cyberpsychology, Behavior, and Social Networking*, 18(5): 296–300.

Pace, Jonathan. 2017. "Exchange Relations on the Dark Web." *Critical Studies in Media Communication*, 34(1): 1–13.

Page, Ruth. 2020. "Relatability and the Shared Stories of Social Media Influencers." Paper presented at the Second International Conference on Internet Pragmatics (Netpra2). https://www2.helsinki.fi/sites/default/files/atoms/files/page_abstract.pdf.

Pantucci, Raffaello. 2018. "A Tale of Two Terrors: The British Extreme Right Organises while Islamists Scatter." *RUSI*, 38(6): 1–3.

Papacharissi, Zizi, and Maria de Fatima Oliveira. 2012. "Affective News and Networked Publics: The Rhythms of News Storytelling on #Egypt." *Journal of Communication*, 62(2): 266–282.

Paquet-Clouston, Masarah, David Décary-Hétu, and Carlo Morselli. 2018. "Assessing Market Competition and Vendors' Size and Scope on AlphaBay." *International Journal of Drug Policy*, 54: 87–98.

Pardo, María Laura. 2001. "Linguistic Persuasion as an Essential Political Factor in Current Democracies: Critical Analysis of the Globalization Discourse in Argentina at the Turn and at the End of the Century." *Discourse & Society*, 12(1): 91–118.

Parent, Mike, Teresa Gobble, and Aaron Rochlen. 2019. "Social Media Behavior, Toxic Masculinity, and Depression." *Psychology of Men & Masculinities*, 20(3): 277–287.

Partington, Alan. 2006. *The Linguistics of Laughter. Laughter-Talk at the White House*. London: Routledge.

Partington, Alan. 2010. "Modern Diachronic Corpus-Assisted Discourse Studies (MDCADS) on UK Newspapers: An Overview of the Project." *Corpora*, 5(2): 83–108.

Partington, Alan, Alison Duguid, and Charlotte Taylor. 2013. *Patterns and Meanings in Discourse: Theory and Practice in Corpus-Assisted Discourse Studies (CADS)*. Amsterdam: John Benjamins.

Partington, Alan, and Charlotte Taylor. 2018. *The Language of Persuasion in Politics: An Introduction*. London: Routledge.

Patterson, Katie J. 2022. "Dualisms in Jihad: The Role of Metaphor in Creating Ideological Dichotomies." *Journal of Language Aggression and Conflict*. doi.org/10.1075/jlac.00075.pat.

Pearson, Elizabeth. 2020. "Gendered Reflections? Extremism in the UK's Radical Right and al-Muhajiron Networks." *Studies in Conflict and Terrorism*, 1–24. doi:10.1080/1057610X.2020.1759270.

Pennebaker, James W., Roger J. Booth, Ryan L. Boyd, and Martha E. Francis. 2015b. *Linguistic Inquiry and Word Count: LIWC2015: Operator's Manual*. Austin: University of Texas at Austin. https://s3-us-west2.amazonaws.com/downloads.liwc.net/LIWC2015_OperatorManual.pdf.

Pennebaker, James W., Ryan L. Boyd, Kayla Jordan, and Kate Blackburn, 2015a. *The Development and Psychometric Properties of LIWC2015*. Austin: University of

Texas at Austin. https://repositories.lib.utexas.edu/bitstream/handle/2152/31333/LIWC2015_LanguageManual.pdf.

Pérez de Ayala, Soledad. 2001. "FTAs and Erskine May: Conflicting Needs?—Politeness in Question Time." *Journal of Pragmatics*, 33(2): 143–169.

Pergolizzi, Joseph, Jo Ann Le Quang, Robert Taylor, and Robert Raffa. 2017. "The "Darknet": The New Street for Street Drugs." *Journal of Clinical Pharmacy and Therapeutics*, 42(6): 790–792.

Pohjonen, Matti. 2018. "Horizons of Hate: A Comparative Approach to Social Media Hate Speech." *Vox Pol*. https://eprints.soas.ac.uk/30568/1/HORIZONS_OF_HATE_A_COMPARATIVE_APPROACH.pdf.

Powell, Martine B., Sharon Casey, and Jon Rouse. 2021. "Online Child Sexual Offenders' Language Use in Real-time Chats." *Trends & Issues in Crime and Criminal Justice*, 643: 1–15.

Preuß, Svenja, Luna Pia Bley, Tabea Bayha, Vivien Dehne Alessa Jordan, Sophie Reimann, Roberto, Fina, Josephine Zahm, Hanna Siewerts, Dirk Labudde, and Michael Spranger. 2021. "Automatically Identifying Online Grooming Chats Using CNN-based Feature Extraction." *Proceedings of the 17th Conference on Natural Language Processing (KONVENS 2021)*, 137–146. https://aclanthology.org/2021.konvens-1.12.pdf.

Prisk, Dan. 2017. *The Hyperreality of the Alt Right: How Meme Magic Works to Create a Space for Far Right Politics*.

Peresin, Anita, and Alberto Cervone. 2015. "The Western Muhajirat of ISIS." *Studies in Conflict & Terrorism*, 38(7): 495–509.

Quayle, Ethel. 2020. "Prevention, Disruption and Deterrence of Online Child Sexual Exploitation and Abuse." *ERA Forum*, 21(3): 429–447.

Quayle, Ethel, and Emily Newman. 2016. "An Exploratory Study of Public Reports to Investigate Patterns and Themes of Requests for Sexual Images of Minors Online." *Crime Science*, 5(1): 1–12.

Quercia, Daniele, Jonathan Ellis, Licia Capra, and Jon Crowcroft. 2011. "In the Mood for Being Influential on Twitter." In *Privacy, Security, Risk and Trust (PASSAT) and 2011 IEEE Third International Conference on Social Computing (SocialCom)*, 307–314. Piscataway, NJ: IEEE. https://ieeexplore.ieee.org/stamp/stamp.jsp?tp=&arnumber=6113129.

Rai, Tage, and Alan Fiske. 2011. "Moral Psychology in Relationship Regulation: Moral Motives for Unity, Hierarchy, Equality, and Proportionality." *Psychological Review*, 118: 57–75.

Rai, Tage, and Alan Fiske. 2012. "Beyond Harm, Intention, and Dyads: Relationship Regulation, Virtuous Violence, and Metarelational Morality." *Psychological Inquiry*, 23: 189–193.

Rai, Tage, and Alan Fiske. 2016. "The Morality of Violence." In *A Very Bad Wizard: Morality behind the Curtain*, edited by Tamler Sommers, 253–271. New York: Routledge.

Rampton, Ben, and Louise Eley. 2018. "Goffman and the Everyday Interactional Grounding of Surveillance." *Working Papers in Urban Language & Literacies*, 246. https://www.academia.edu/37680030/WP246_Rampton_and_Eley_2018._Goffman_and_the_everyday_interactional_grounding_of_surveillance.

Rappoport, David. 2004. "The Four Waves of Modern Terrorism." In *Attacking Terrorism: Elements of a Grand Strategy*, edited by Audrey Cronin and James Ludes, 46–73. Washington, DC: Georgetown University Press.

Rasheed, Adil. 2015. *ISIS: Race to Armageddon*. New Delhi: Vij Books India Pvt Ltd.

Rashkin, Hannah, Eunsol Choi, Jin Yea Jang, Svitlana Volkova, and Yejin Choi. 2017. "Truth of Varying Shades: Analyzing Language in Fake News and Political Fact-checking." *Proceedings of the 2017 Conference on Empirical Methods in Natural Language Processing*, 2931–2937. https://aclanthology.org/D17-1317.pdf.

Razi, Afsaneh, Seunghyun Kim, Ashwaq Alsoubai, Gianluca Stringhini, Thamar Solorio, Munmun De Choudhury, and Pamela J. Wisniewski. 2021. "A Human-Centered Systematic Literature Review of the Computational Approaches for Online Sexual Risk Detection." *Proceedings of the ACM on Human-Computer Interaction*, 5: 1–38.

Recasens, Marta, Cristian Danescu-Niculescu-Mizil, and Dan Jurafsky. 2013. "Linguistic Models for Analyzing and Detecting Biased Language." *Proceedings of the 51st Annual Meeting of the Association for Computational Linguistics* (Volume 1: Long Papers). Association for Computational Linguistics, 1650–1659. https://aclanthology.org/P13-1162.pdf.

Reed, Alastair. 2018. "An Inconvenient Truth: Countering Terrorist Narratives: Fighting a Threat We Do Not Understand." *ICCT*. htpp://icct.nl/publications.

Reeve, Zoey. 2020. "Repeated and Wxtensive Exposure to Online Terrorist Content: Counter-terrorism Internet Referral Unit Perceived Stresses and Strategies." *Studies in Conflict and Terrorism*: 1–25. doi.org/10.1080/1057610X.2020.1792726.

Richards, A. 2015. "From Terrorism to 'Radicalization' to 'Extremism': Counterterrorism Imperative or Loss of Focus? *International Affairs*, 91(2): 371–380.

Rigotti, Edo. 2005. "Towards a Typology of Manipulative Processes." In *Manipulation and Ideologies in the Twentieth Century*, edited by Louis de Saussure and Peter Schulz, 61–83. Philadelphia: John Benjamins.

Romero, Daniel M., Brendan Meeder, and Jon Kleinberg. 2011. "Differences in the Mechanics of Information Diffusion across Topics: Idioms, Political Hashtags, and Complex Contagion on Twitter." *Proceedings of the 20th International Conference on World Wide Web*. 695–704. New York: ACM. https://dl.acm.org/doi/pdf/10.1145/1963405.1963503.

Rydgren, Jens. 2017. "Radical Right-Wing Parties in Europe: What's Populism Got to Do with It?" *Journal of Language and Politics*, 16(4): 485–496.

Said, Edward W. 1997. *Covering Islam: How the Media and the Experts Determine How We See the Rest of the World*. London: Vintage.

Said, Edward W. 2003. *Orientalism*. London: Penguin.

Sandvig, Christian. 2016. "Why I Am Suing the Government." *Social Media Collective Research Blog*. https://socialmediacollective.org/2016/07/01/why-i-am-suing-the-government/

Santibañez, Cristian. 2017. "Strategically Wrong: On the Relationship Between Generalized Deception and Persuasive Behaviour." *Journal of Pragmatics*, 114: 16–31.

Sarikaki, Katharine. 2010. "For Culture and Democracy: Political Claims for Cosmopolitan Public Service Media." In *Reinventing Public Service Communication*, edited by Petros Iosifidis, 88–100. New York: Springer.

Scannell, Paddy (Ed.). 1991. *Broadcast Talk*. London: Sage.

Scannell, Paddy. 2000. "For Anyone-as-Someone Structures." *Media, Culture & Society*, 22: 5–24.

Schneevogt, Daniela, Emily Chiang, and Tim Grant. 2018. "Do Perverted Justice Chat Logs Contain Examples of Overt Persuasion and Sexual Extortion? A Research Note Responding to Chiang and Grant (2017, 2018)." *Language and Law/Linguagem e Direito*, 5(1): 97–102.

Schultze, Quentin, and Randall Bytwerk. 2012. "Plausible Quotations and Reverse Credibility in Online Vernacular Communities." *ETC: A Review of General Semantics*, *69*(2): 216–234.

Scrivens, Ryan, and Maura Conway. 2020. "The Role of the Internet in Facilitating Violent Extremism and Terrorism: Suggestions for Progressing Research." In *The Palgrave Handbook of International Cybercrime and Cyberdeviance*, edited by Thomas Holt and Adam Bossler, 1417–1435. London: Palgrave Macmillan.

Scrivens, Ryan, Garth Davies, and Richard Frank. 2018. "Searching for Signs of Extremism on the Web: An Introduction to Sentiment-Based Identification of Radical Authors." *Behavioral Sciences of Terrorism and Political Aggression*, *10*(1): 39–59.

Seto, Michael C. 2019. "The Motivation-facilitation Model of Sexual Offending."*Sexual Abuse*, *31*(1): 3–24.

Seymour-Smith, Sarah, and Juliane Kloess. 2021. "A Discursive Analysis of Compliance, Resistance and Escalation to Threats in Sexually Exploitative Interactions between Offenders and Male Children." *British Journal of Social Psychology* *60*(3): 988–1011.

Silverstein, Michael. 1976. "Shifters, Linguistic Categories and Cultural Description." In *Meaning in Anthropology*, edited by Keith Basso and Henry Selby, 11–55. Alburqueque: University of New Mexico Press.

Silverstein, Michael. 2003. "Indexical Order and the Dialectics of Sociolinguistic Life." *Language and Communication*, *23*: 193–229.

Sims, Christopher. 2012. "Occidentalism at War: Al-Qaida's Resistance Rhetoric." *Altre Modernità: Saggi*, *8*(11): 206–220.

Sohn, Jeong Woong, and Kim Jin Ki. 2020. "Factors That Influence Purchase Intentions in Social Commerce." *Technology in Society*, *63*. https://doi.org/10.1016/j.techsoc.2020.101365.

Sorell, Tom. 2016. "Online Grooming and Preventative Justice." *Criminal Law and Philosophy*, *4*: 705–724.

Sorlin, Sandrine. 2017. "The Pragmatics of Manipulation. Exploiting Im/politeness Theories."*Journal of Pragmatics*, *121*: 132–146.

Soska, Kyle, and Nicolas Christin. 2015. "Measuring the Longitudinal Evolution of the Online Anonymous Marketplace Ecosystem." *24th USENIX Security Symposium* (15): 33–48.

Spencer-Oatey, Helen (Ed.). 2000. *Culturally Speaking: Managing Rapport Through Talk Across Cultures*. London: Continuum.

Spencer-Oatey, Helen. 2008. *Culturally Speaking: Culture, Communication and Politeness*. London: Continuum.

Sperber, Dan, Fabrice Clément, Christophe Heintz, Olivier Mascaro, Hugo Mercier, Gloria Origgi, and Deidre Wilson. 2010. "Epistemic Vigilance." *Mind & Language*, *25*(4): 359–393.

Spier, Troy. 2018. "Extremist Propaganda and Qur'anic Scripture: A 'Radical' Corpus-based Study of the Dabiq." *Discourse & Society*, *29*: 553–567.

Spagnoletti, Paolo, Federica Ceci, and Bendik Bygstad. 2021. "Online Black Markets: An Investigation of a Digital Infrastructure in the Dark Net." *Information Systems Frontiers*, 1–16. doi:10.1007/x10796-021-10187-9.

Spilioti, Tereza, and Caroline Tagg. 2017. "The Ethics of Online Research Methods in Applied Linguistics: Challenges, Opportunities, and Directions in Ethical Decision-making." *Applied Linguistics Review*, *8*(2–3): 163–168.

Sprecher, Susan, Stanislav Treger, Joshua D. Wondra, Nicole Hilaire, and Kevin Wallpe. 2013. "Taking Turns: Reciprocal Self-Disclosure Promotes Liking in Initial Interactions." *Journal of Experimental Social Psychology*, 49(5): 860–866.

Stacey, Emily (Ed.). 2017. *Combating Internet-Enabled Terrorism: Emerging Research and Opportunities*. Hershey, PA: IGI Global.

Sumnall, Harry, Michael Evans-Brown, and Jim McVeigh. 2011. "Social, Policy, and Public Health Perspectives on New Psychoactive Substances."*Drug Testing and Analysis*, 3: 515–523.

Szabla, Malgorzata, and Jan Blommaert. 2018. "Does Context Really Collapse in Social Media Interaction?" *Applied Linguistics Review*, 11(2): 251–279.

Tagg, Caroline, and Philip Seargeant. 2016. "Facebook and the Discursive Construction of the Social Network." In *The Routledge Handbook of Language and Digital Communication*, edited by Alexandra Georgakopoulos and Tereza Spilioti, 339–353. London: Routledge.

Tagg, Caroline, Philip Seargeant, and Amy Aisha Brown. 2017. *Taking Offence on Social Media Conviviality and Communication on Facebook*. London: Palgrave.

Tan, Lavinia, and Randolph C. Grace. 2008. "Social Desirability and Sexual Offenders: A Review." *Sexual Abuse*, 20(1): 61–87.

Tardy, Charles, and Kathryn Dindia. 2006. "Self-Disclosure: Strategic Revelation of Information in Personal and Professional Relationships." In *The Handbook of Communication Skills*, edited by Owen Hargie, 229–266. London: Routledge.

Taylor, Charlotte, and Anna Marchi (Eds.). 2018. *Corpus Approaches to Discourse. A Critical Review*. London: Routledge.

Tedeschi, James , and Richard Felson. 1994. *Violence, Aggression, and Coercive Actions*. Washington, DC: American Psychological Association. https://doi.org/10.1037/10160-000.

Teo, Peter. 2000. "Racism in the News: A Critical Discourse Analysis of News Reporting in Two Australian Newspapers." *Discourse & Society*, 11(1): 20–60.

Tetzlaff, David. 2000. "Yo-ho-ho and a Server of Warez: Internet Software Piracy and the New Global Information Economy." In *The World Wide Web and Contemporary Cultural Theory*, edited by Andrew Herman and Thomas Swiss, 99–126. London: Routledge.

Thurlow, Crispin, and Kristine Mroczek. 2011. *Digital Discourse: Language in the New Media*. Oxford: Oxford University Press.

Tolson, Andrew (Ed.). 2001. *Television Talk Shows. Discourse, Performance, Spectacle*. London: Lawrence Erlbaum Associates.

Tracy, Karen. 2017. "Facework and (Im) politeness in Political Exchanges." In *The Palgrave Handbook of Linguistic (Im) politeness*, edited by Jonathan Culpeper, Michael Haugh, and Daniel Kadar, 739–758. London: Palgrave Macmillan.

Turkle, Sherry. 1995. *Life on the Screen: Identity in the Age of the Internet*. New York: Simon & Schuster.

Tzanetakis Meropi, Gerrit Kamphausen, Bernd Werse, and Roger van Laufenberg. 2016. "The Transparency Paradox: Building Trust, Resolving Disputes and Optimizing Logistics on Conventional and Online Drugs Markets."*International Journal of Drug Policy*, 35: 58–68.

United Kingdom Parliament Online Safety Bill. 2022. https://publications.parliament.uk/pa/bills/cbill/58-03/0004/220004.pdf.

United Nations Office on Drugs and Crime (UNODC). 2021. *World Drug Report 2021*. https://www.unodc.org/unodc/en/data-and-analysis/wdr2021.html.

Van der Gouwe, Daan, Tibor Brunt, Margriet van Laar, and Peggy van der Pol. 2017. "Purity, Adulteration and Price of Drugs Bought On-line Versus Off-line in the Netherlands." *Addiction*, 112(4): 640–648.

Van Dijk, Teun. 1998. *Ideology: A Multidisciplinary Approach*. London: Sage Publications.

Van Dijk, Teun. 1999. "Discourse and Racism." *Discourse & Society*, 10(2): 147–148.

Van Dijk, Teun. 2006. "Discourse and Manipulation." *Discourse & Society*, 17(3): 359–383.

Van Dijk, Teun. 2017. "How Global Media Manipulated the Impeachment of Brazilian President Dilma Roussef." *Discourse & Communication*, 11(2): 199–229.

Van Gijn-Grosvenor, Evianne, and Michael Lamb. 2021. "Online Groomer Typology Scheme." *Psychology, Crime & Law*, 27(10): 973–987.

Van Leeuwen, Teun. 2007. "Legitimation in Discourse and Communication." *Discourse & Communication*, 1(1): 91–112.

Van Leeuwen, Teun. 2008. *Discourse and Practice: New Tools for Critical Discourse Analysis*. Oxford: Oxford University Press.

Van Leeuwen, Theo, and Ruth Wodak. 1999. "Legitimizing Immigration Control: A Discourse-Historical Analysis." *Discourse Studies*, 1(1): 83–118.

Vishwanath, Arun. 2015. "Habitual Facebook Use and Its Impact on Getting Deceived on Social Media." *Journal of Computer-Mediated Communication*, 20(1): 83–98.

Von Behr, Ines, Ana Reding, Charlie Edwards, and Luke Gribbon. 2013. *Radicalization in the Digital Era: The Use of the Internet in 15 Cases of Terrorism and Extremism*. Santa Monica, CA: RAND Corporation.

Ybarra, Michele L., and Kimberly J. Mitchell. 2005. "Exposure to Internet Pornography Among Children and Adolescents: A National Survey." *Cyberpsychology & Behavior*, 8(5): 473–486.

Yus, Francisco. 2021. *Smartphone Communication: Interactions in the App Ecosystem*. London: Routledge.

Wang, Ye Diana, and Henry Emurian. 2005. "An Overview of Online Trust: Concepts, Elements, and Implications." *Computers in Human Behaviour*, 21(1): 105–125.

Watkin, Amy-Louise, and Sean Looney. 2019. "The Lions of Tomorrow: A News Values Analysis of Child Images in Jihadi Magazines." *Studies in Conflict & Terrorism*, 42(1–2): 120–140.

Watts, Richard. 2003. *Politeness*. Cambridge: Cambridge University Press.

Weaver, Simon. 2010. "Liquid Racism and the Danish Prophet Muhammad Cartoons." *Current Sociology*, 58(5): 675–692.

Weber, Julia, and Edwin Kruisbergen, 2019. "Criminal Markets: The Dark Web, Money Laundering and Counterstrategies: An Overview of the 10th Research Conference of Organized Crime." *Trends in Organized Crime*, 22(3): 346–356.

Webster, Stephen, Julia Davidson, Antonia Bifulco, Petter Gottschalk, Vincenzo Caretti, Thierry Pham, Julie Grove-Hills, Caroline Turley, Charlotte Tompkins, Stefano Ciulla, Vanessa Milazzo, Adriano Schimmenti, and Giuseppe Craparo. 2012. *European Online Grooming Project. Final Report*. Brussels: European Commission Safer Internet Plus Programme. http:// www.europeanonlinegroomingproject.com/wp-content/file-uploads/European-Online-Grooming-Project-Final-Report.pdf.

Weimann, Gabriel, and Ari Ben Am. 2020. "Digital Dog Whistles: The New Online Language of Extremism." *International Journal of Security Studies*, 2(1): article 4. https://digitalcommons.northgeorgia.edu/ijoss/vol2/iss1/4/

Wenger, Etienne. 1998. "Communities of Practice: Learning as a Social System." *Systems Thinker*, 9(5): 1–10. https://participativelearning.org/pluginfile.php/636/mod_resource/content/3/Learningasasocialsystem.pdf.

Wesch, Michael. 2009. "YouTube and You: Experiences of Self-Awareness in the Context-Collapse of the Recording Webcam." *Explorations in Media Ecology*, 8(2): 19–34.

White, Peter. 2020. "The Putative Reader in Mass Media Persuasion: Stance, Argumentation and Ideology." *Discourse & Communication*, 14(4): 404–423.

Whittaker, Joe. 2019. "How Content Removal Might Help Terrorists." *Lawfare Blog*. https://www.lawfareblog.com/how-content-removal-might-help-terrorists.

Whittaker, Joe, and Lilah Elsayed. 2019. "Linkages as a Lens: An Exploration of Strategic Communications in P/CVE." *Journal for Deradicalization*, 20: 1–46.

Whittle, Helen, Catherine, E. Hamilton-Giachritsis, and Anthony Beech. 2014. "'Under His Spell': Victims' Perspectives of Being Groomed Online." *Social Sciences*, 3(3): 404–426.

Williams, Rebecca, Ian A. Elliott, and Anthony Beech. 2013. "Identifying Sexual Grooming Themes Used by Internet Sex Offenders." *Deviant Behavior*, 34(2): 135–152.

Wittel, Andreas. 2001. "Toward a Network Sociality." *Theory, Culture & Society*, 18(6): 51–76.

Winters, Georgia M., Leah E. Kaylor, and Elizabeth L. Jeglic. 2017. "Sexual Offenders Contacting Children Online: An Examination of Transcripts of Sexual Grooming." *Journal of Sexual Aggression*, 23(1): 62–76.

Winsor, Leah. 2020. "The Language of Radicalization: Female Internet Recruitment to Participation in ISIS Activities." *Terrorism and Political Violence*, 32: 506–538.

Wodak, Ruth. 2006. "Blaming and Denying." In *Encyclopaedia of Language and Linguistics*, edited by Keith Brown, 59–64. Amsterdam: Elsevier.

Wodak, Ruth. 2915/2020. *The Politics of Fear: The Shameless Normalization of Far-Right Discourse*. London: Sage.

Wolf, James, and Waleed Muhanna. 2011. "Feedback Mechanisms, Judgment Bias, and Trust Formation in Online Auctions." *Decision Sciences*, 42(1): 43–68.

Wortley, Richard, Stephen Smallbone, Martine Powell, and Peter Cassematis. 2014. *Understanding and Managing the Occupational Health Impacts on Investigators of Internet Child Exploitation*. Southeast Queensland: Griffith University Press.

Zelin, Aaron. 2013. "The State of Global Jihad Online: A Qualitative, Quantitative and Cross-Lingual Analysis." New American Foundation. https://www.washingtoninstitute.org/policy-analysis/state-global-jihad-online.

Zelizer, Barbie. 2010. *About to Die: How News Images Move the Public*. Oxford: Oxford University Press.

Zhang, Grace. 2013. "The Impact of Touchy Topics on Vague Language Use." *Journal of Asian Pacific Communication*, 23(1): 87–118.

Zickmund, Susan. 2002. "Approaching the Radical Other: The Discursive Culture of Cyberhate." In *Virtual Culture: Identity and Communication in Cybersociety*, edited by Steven Jones, 185–206. London: SAGE.

INDEX

For the benefit of digital users, indexed terms that span two pages (e.g., 52–53) may, on occasion, appear on only one of those pages.

Tables and figures are indicated by *t* and *f* following the page number